D0161591

Business Scandals, Corruption, and Reform

Business Scandals, Corruption, and Reform

AN ENCYCLOPEDIA

VOLUME 2: M–Z

Gary Giroux

GREENWOOD

AN IMPRINT OF ABC-CLIO, LLC
Santa Barbara, California • Denver, Colorado • Oxford, England

Library of Congress Cataloging-in-Publication Data

Giroux, Gary A.
  Business scandals, corruption, and reform : an encyclopedia / Gary Giroux.
    p. cm.
  Includes bibliographical references and index.
  ISBN 978–1–4408–0067–2 (cloth : alk. paper) — ISBN 978–1–4408–0068–9 (ebook)
1. Corporations—Corrupt practices—United States. 2. Business enterprises—Corrupt practices—United States. 3. Commercial crimes—United States. 4. Fraud—United States. 5. Swindlers and swindling—United States. 6. Business enterprises—Corrupt practices—United States—Prevention. 7. Fraud—United States—Prevention. I. Title.
HV6769.G57   2013
364.16′80973—dc23   2012040055

ISBN: 978–1–4408–0067–2
EISBN: 978–1–4408–0068–9

17 16 15 14 13   1 2 3 4 5

This book is also available on the World Wide Web as an eBook.
Visit www.abc-clio.com for details.

Greenwood
An Imprint of ABC-CLIO, LLC

ABC-CLIO, LLC
130 Cremona Drive, P.O. Box 1911
Santa Barbara, California 93116-1911

This book is printed on acid-free paper ∞

Manufactured in the United States of America

Portions of this book are excerpted from:

Gary Giroux, "What Went Wrong? Accounting Fraud and Lessons From the Recent Scandals," *Social Research*, Volume 75, No. 4, Winter 2008. Used by permission.

Gary Giroux. *Detecting Earnings Management*. Hoboken: John Wiley & Sons, 2004. Reproduced with permission of John Wiley & Sons, Inc.

Gary Giroux. *Earnings Magic and the Unbalance Sheet: The Search for Financial Reality*. New York: John Wiley & Sons, 2006. Reproduced with permission of John Wiley & Sons, Inc.

Contents

M

Madoff, Bernard L.

Bernard Madoff ("Bernie," 1938–) was a New York broker, investment adviser, chairman of NASDAQ, and the perpetrator of history's biggest Ponzi scheme. Madoff pleaded guilty to fraud, theft, money laundering, and perjury in 2009; he was sentenced to 150 years in prison. Despite being a major Wall Street player, he was a crook.

Madoff was born April 29, 1938, in Queens, New York. After graduating from Hofstra University, he started Bernard L. Madoff Investment Securities in 1960. With little capital, he traded over-the-counter securities of second-tier companies. This was a somewhat corrupt market (called the "under-the-counter market" for its poor reputation) where brokers often overcharged customers and securities could

Bernard Madoff (right) arrives at federal court for his hearing in New York on January 14, 2009. (AP/Wide World Photos)

take weeks to trade. Bernie became a wholesaler, specializing in efficiency and trading quickly to brokers. Madoff, one of the first traders to automate, developed a screen-based computer trading system. With this system, trading with Madoff proved relatively fast and inexpensive.

Madoff was active in the National Associated of Securities Dealers (NASD) and served as chairman in 1990. Madoff had a large market share and presumably made millions annually. His sons, Andy and Mark, ran the trading floor on the 19th floor of the Lipstick Building in midtown Manhattan, with the computer system housed on the 18th floor. This was a legitimate and successful business in a regulated industry.

The 17th floor housed Bernie's investment business, with a staff of about 20. This operation stayed independent of 19th-floor traders. Bernie became a Wall Street star, a NASDAQ leader, and a pillar of the community. This 17th-floor operation apparently was a hedge fund, possibly started in the 1970s. Family and friends were the first investors and the investor list grew over the years. Bernie formed relationships with other investment groups serving as "feeder funds," sending client money to Madoff for spectacular returns.

Madoff never made his investment strategy quite clear (common for hedge funds), but he claimed to use sophisticated techniques like "convertible arbitrage." High-yield (also called junk) bonds convertible into common stock presumably were used; simultaneously, the shares would be shorted—that was the claim. An alternative story was "split-strike conversion," a timing strategy of large stocks using both stocks and options. With proper hedging, money could be made whether the market went up or down, and Madoff paid consistent double-digit returns. Putting a name to some apparently sophisticated scheme satisfied investors and even gullible regulators.

Madoff likely used his legitimate investments firm to launder his Ponzi-scheme money. Madoff stated at his hearing that investor cash went straight to a Chase bank account, while investment activity was forged, with the 17th-floor traders moving money around to look like real activity. When investors asked for cash, this came from the same Chase bank account.

There were signs of trouble from time to time. Avellino & Bienes, one of Madoff's feeder funds, was accused of unregistered operation in 1992. The Securities and Exchange Commission (SEC) shut down the firm, forced it to pay back the money, and charged a $350,000 penalty. Madoff paid off Avellino & Bienes and was never investigated. Another SEC investigation started in 2006 on Madoff and feeder fund Fairfield Greenwich, based at least in part on the complaint of whistle-blower Harry Markopolos. The SEC did not look hard enough to find any evidence of fraud and closed the case. Other complaints surfaced and additional investigations were conducted, but no fraud was found.

The end came because of the bad economy, not diligent regulators piecing together an intricate fraud scheme. The size of Madoff's Ponzi scheme is estimated at $65 billion, but no exact figure is known. It is likely that investors kicked in about $20 billion (Bandler and Varchaver 2009, 66) and the remainder represented the "accumulated return" investors were promised. With the market bust of 2008, investors began withdrawing money—they probably thought Madoff used the failing banks as counterparties. By December, Madoff's money ran out. According to Steve Fishman in *New York*, Madoff confessed his scam to his sons: " '[I'm] finished,' he said. 'It's all just one big lie . . .' Andy and Mark called the SEC. The SEC contacted the FBI, which showed up at Bernie's apartment on December 11." Madoff was arrested and that was when investors and the rest of the world discovered the fraud.

Madoff pled guilty to 11 felonies in 2009, including securities fraud, wire fraud, mail fraud, and money laundering. Madoff is now in jail serving 150 years, leaving his family and staff to settle the investigations and lawsuits. Other Madoff confederates also pled guilty.

See also Accounting Fraud; NASDAQ; Ponzi, Charles; Ponzi Scheme; Securities and Exchange Commission (SEC)

References

Fishman, Steve. "The Monster Mensch." *New York*, February 22, 2009. http://nymag.com/news/businessfinance/54703/.

Kansas, Dave. "Madoff Does Minneapolis." In *SCANDAL!: Amazing Tales of Scandals That Shocked the World and Shaped Modern Business*, 310–320. New York: Time Inc. Home Entertainment, 2009.

Making the Number

Making the number means meeting the quarterly earnings targets (usually stated as earnings per share, EPS) forecast by financial analysts. When actual preliminary earnings estimates are below consensus forecasts, corporate executive can decide to raise reported EPS by manipulating the accounting numbers. Financial reality then becomes less important than "making the number."

Net income and EPS are the primary measures of financial performance and profitability. Berenson (2003) describes EPS as *The Number*, with the primary executives' goal of meeting the consensus analysts' forecast each quarter.

Institutional Brokers Estimates System (I/B/E/S) and Zacks Investment Research started publishing consensus forecasts in the 1970s. The forecasts became the standard benchmark to measure "earnings surprise," the difference between the consensus forecast and actual EPS. Executive compensation often was based, at least in part, on consistently meeting or beating the forecast. Unfortunately, the overemphasis of the meet-or-beat mentality is the short-term focus of performance rather than long-term trends. This mind-set became pervasive in the 1990s and resulted in a number of corporate failures including Enron in 2001 and WorldCom in 2002.

See also Earnings Forecasts; Earnings Manipulation; Financial Accounting Standards Board (FASB); Net Income and Other Bottom-Line Measures; Securities and Exchange Commission (SEC)

References

Berenson, Alex. *The Number: How the Drive for Quarterly Earnings Corrupted Wall Street and Corporate American.* New York: Random House, 2003.

Davidson, Sidney, and G. Anderson. "The Development of Accounting and Auditing Standards." *Journal of Accountancy*, May 1987, 110–27.

Giroux, Gary. *Earnings Magic and the Unbalance Sheet: The Search for Financial Reality.* New York: Wiley, 2006.

Manhattan Company

The Manhattan Bank (now part of J. P. Morgan Chase) started out as a water company, and thanks to the guile of Aaron Burr created a viable bank in competition with Alexander Hamilton's Bank of New York. The Manhattan Corporation, established by Democratic Party interests in 1799, showed the political rivalry in banking competition at the time.

Especially in the nineteenth century, providing clean water (and eliminating wastewater) proved to be one the most important functions of a city. Over centuries, polluted water meant diseases and periodic plagues. The commercial advantages of cities were contrasted by lower longevity rates in cities cause by diseases. Yellow fever hit New York City in both 1793 and 1798. The city's Common Council proposed a public works system, but Burr suggested a private company to supply water, saving the city the high costs and expected higher taxes. Even political rival Hamilton promoted the company. With city approval, Burr steered the new charter through the New York legislature. The key provision of the charter allowed the company to raise $2 million and use surplus capital for any purpose (stated as any "monied transactions not inconsistent with the constitution and laws of the state").

Water, of course, did not much interest Burr. The company did use an old well and build a small reservoir, but that was all. Burr did not solve the city's water problem, but he did have plenty of money to invest in the Bank of the Manhattan Company. At the time, Hamilton's Federalists controlled the Bank of New York and would not allow a Democratic competitor to get a charter. Burr had conned his rival, and his new bank became a success and the chief competitor to Hamilton's bank. Tammany Hall would soon control the Democratic political machine of New York City, in part based on Burr's illicit methods used to bring out the vote in the 1800 political election. The water solution had to wait until the city completed the Croton Aqueduct in 1842.

See also Burr, Aaron; Commercial Banking before the Federal Reserve; Hamilton, Alexander; State Banks, Early

References

Chernow, Ron. *Alexander Hamilton*. New York: Penguin Press, 2004.

Glaeser, Edward. *Triumph of the City: How Our Greatest Invention Makes Us Richer, Smarter, Greener, Healthier, and Happier*. New York: Penguin Press, 2011.

Margin Calls

When investors buy securities on credit (margin), the broker insists on a margin account representing some level of collateral (or equity position). When stock prices drop, the broker issues margin calls, requiring the investors to raise their equity position back up to the necessary minimum. If the added collateral is not forthcoming, the broker sells the shares to avoid losing money. The results are client losses plus a larger price drop in the market if the margin selling is widespread.

The United States' first financial scandal erupted because of margin calls. Former Treasury official William Duer speculated in bank stocks on credit in 1792 relying on insider information to make illicit gains, but causing a stock market bubble. When stock prices dropped, his creditors issued margin calls that he could not meet. The market collapsed and Duer was sent off to debtors' prison. The country was three years old. Credit has been essential to every asset bubble (and collapse) since then, and margin calls played a significant part.

Another unfortunate example was William Durant, one of the great entrepreneurs and speculators in the early twentieth century but a poor executive. He took over Buick early in the century and created General Motors (GM). Durant lost control in a 1910 recession, then founded Chevrolet with Du Pont's financial backing. Chevy bought a majority of GM stock and Durant resumed control. He bought more GM shares on margin. In the 1920 recession, the price of GM tumbled with an assist of Du Pont backed by J. P. Morgan. Margin calls on GM stock ended Durant's control and Du Pont took over, saving GM.

The Roaring Twenties introduced radio and a boom in other industries, especially automobiles and the electrification of homes and factories. The stock market rebounded after a recession in 1920, partly because new individual investors bought exciting new growth stocks on margin, paying as little as 10 percent. Brokers pushed stocks, investment trusts, and foreign bonds, all available on margin. Massive margin trading fueled speculation and the boom, but also contributed to big drops. Using dividends to pay for the interest on margin loans was one rationale; however, the loans could be at 8 to 10 percent or more and dividends yields dropped as stock prices climbed. Brokers made a profit on both commissions and interest. In the good times, margin buying increased the capital gains: borrowing 90 percent of the purchase price meant 10 times the profit. Brokers' loans hit some

$6 billion at the start of 1929. With a relatively small market drop, margin calls from brokers meant investors had to contribute more cash or the stock would be sold. Margin calls and resulting sales drove prices lower and investors, large and small, to ruin.

October 1929 saw the Dow dropping to 306, triggering margin calls from many brokers, insisting that speculators buying on margin put up more capital or the stock sold. Many sell orders and related stop-loss orders (which sell the stock when a stock drops to a specific price) traded Thursday, October 24, known as Black Thursday. Massive sell orders in the morning led to panic. Almost 13 million shares traded, a new record by far. The back rooms could not handle the volume, and the stock ticker fell behind by hours, increasing the panic as prices continued down. Uncertainty and new margin calls just sent the market lower. Stocks continued to decline through 1932, dropping almost 90 percent of their 1929 values.

The securities acts of the 1930s mandated "full and fair disclosure" of financial data, containing all information relevant to a "prudent" investor. Antifraud and liability sections increased the legal risks to accountants, now accountable to the public as well as firms audited. The initial legislation banned limited margin trading and short selling, and eliminated floor traders that bought and sold exclusively for their own accounts. Rather than pass these measures, legislation required the Securities and Exchange Commission (SEC) to study each of these issues. Ultimately, many of the perceived abuses were never eliminated. Margins continued to be allowed and Federal Reserve Regulation T allowed margins up to 50 percent; the New York Stock Exchange and other organizations made additional minimum rules, and individual brokers could have additional "house requirements." Other investment types also could be bought on margin, such as derivatives. Hedge funds such as Long-Term Capital Management (LTCM) relied on substantial margins to make big derivative bets. LTCM failed in 1998, requiring a Federal Reserve bailout. Hedge fund speculation using margins have continued and periodically have made leverage crises worse.

See also Altman's Z-Score; Credit Risk; Debt and Leverage; Long-Term Capital Management; New York Stock Exchange; Panics and Depressions; Securities and Exchange Commission (SEC)

References

Geisst, Charles. *Collateral Damaged: The Marketing of Consumer Debt to America*. New York: Bloomberg Press, 2009.

Giroux, Gary. *Financial Analysis: A User Approach*. New York: Wiley, 2003.

Market Manipulation

Stock and other markets have been manipulated roughly since they were created by the seventeenth-century Dutch. Without effective regulation, early speculators developed a multitude of schemes that proved effective or disastrous, such as tulip mania, the South Sea Bubble, or the failure of William Duer and the Panic of 1792. Several of the well-known robber barons of the nineteenth century were market manipulators, including Jacob Little, Daniel Drew, James Fisk, and Jay Gould. The Roaring Twenties proved equally corrupt as stocks were openly rigged, stock pyramiding created utility and railroad empires with little equity, and speculators bought large amounts of stock on margin. That era of manipulation collapsed with the Great Depression. The post–World War II period brought hostile takeovers, massive insider trading, and manipulation of the junk bond market. Late twentieth-century speculation led to the tech bubble and crash early in the twenty-first century. The major manipulation in the twenty-first century involved derivatives and debt securitization, especially of mortgages. The result was the subprime meltdown of 2008.

Contemporaries considered Daniel Drew (1797–1879), Jay Gould (1836–92), and James ("Jubilee Jim") Fisk (1834–72) the premier stock market manipulators in the nineteenth century. Drew started as a cattle drover and steamship operator before founding a Wall Street brokerage and bank in 1844. Drew was reputed to develop "watering the stock," originally by sending cattle to the water trough just before being weighed at market. He soon applied similar procedures to manipulate stock. Drew was a master of the bear raid, driving down prices by starting rumors, pretending to buy, and bribing journalists to pan the stock. He would then buy at the much lower prices. Drew became a mentor to both Gould and Fisk. Gould started speculating on Wall Street in the 1850s, specializing in railroads in part by raiding the companies (e.g., buying large quantities of stock after driving down prices— learning the practices from Drew) and pilfering the companies from the inside. Fisk made a fortune smuggling contraband Southern cotton during the Civil War, as well as being a war profiteer. Fisk later said, "You can sell anything to the government at almost any price you've got the guts to ask" (McCollough 1981, 60).

By the mid-1850s, another financial boom was underway, promoted in part by the 1849 California gold rush. Hundreds of railroad stocks traded in New York plus about a thousand bank and insurance stocks; however, most did not trade on the New York Stock Exchange (NYSE), which stayed away from "speculative issues." Robert Schuyler (a grandson of Revolutionary War hero General Philip Schuyler) was president of the Harlem and the New Haven Railroads. Irregularities were discovered in the railroads' accounts in 1854. Schuyler had illegally printed and sold some 20,000 shares of New Haven stock. Schuyler escaped to Canada with the ill-gotten gains. This was the first large-scale stock fraud in the United States, making Schuyler the most prominent crook of the era.

During the summer and fall seasons over the nineteenth century, cash left New York banks to pay for harvested western grains and other agricultural products. The farmers used the cash to pay down their loans and buy new seeds and equipment. As a result of this seasonal pattern, panics at this time usually occurred in the summer and fall. In 1857, farm prices fell as European products returned to market. That summer railroad stocks plummeted related to the financial insolvency of the Michigan Central Railroad. The Ohio Life Insurance and Trust Company failed in August after massive fraud was discovered. The result was the Panic of 1857. Wall Street brokers failed in mass. The major New York banks suspended gold payments, and European financial centers had similar problems. The failure of about half the members of the NYSE meant seats became available, and new NYSE members included Daniel Drew, Cornelius Vanderbilt, and Henry Clews, a cofounder of Livermore, Clews and Co.

Throughout the nineteenth century, speculation on margin led to panics and depressions as market manipulators took on too much risk, and failures led to market collapses. The Panic of 1873 was caused by the collapse of Jay Cooke's Philadelphia investment bank as the company was overextended financing the Northern Pacific Railroad. The Panic of 1893 was caused by the failure of the Philadelphia and Reading Railroad and the National Cordage Company, which produced panic selling by investors and calling of loans by banks, with overleveraged railroads particularly hard hit. The result was the failure of 150 railroads, resulting in over a quarter of rail track operated under receivership, plus bankruptcies of some 500 banks and over 15,000 businesses. The Panic of 1907, which followed an unsuccessful attempt to corner United Copper, led to significant banking and business reform, including the creation of the Federal Reserve System and the Federal Trade Commission.

The 1920s was a period of innovation including radio, automobiles, and the electrification of homes and factories. Speculation and the stock market boomed, aided by massive credit and widespread manipulation. Investment bank used "preferred list" sales of new securities at discount prices before the public issues. Stock pools existed, syndicates established by investment bankers, brokers, and others to manipulate stock price. At least 100 stocks were openly rigged before the Great Depression.

The NYSE became largest securities markct in the world in the 1920s, but still a private club operated to benefit members. The members controlled the market and had virtually total access to all market information. They included floor traders (trading only for their own accounts, without paying commissions) and specialists in specific stocks (making a market, but without limits on how they could profit from the stock or providing inside information to others). Members could conspire with each other, leading to stock pools, which could drive prices up or down for their own profit. Wash sales (selling among themselves to produce price patterns), bear raids, and short selling were profitable manipulations, with outsiders taking the losses.

The Great Depression led to large speculation losses, Wall Street failures, economic collapse, and a public with no interest in speculation. New Deal programs of the President Franklin Roosevelt administration brought financial regulation, including the Securities Acts of 1933 and 1934 and the creation of the Securities and Exchange Commission (SEC) to regulate securities markets and establish accounting disclosure rules. The post–World War II period brought a strong economy and eventually an increasing interest in the stock market. Manipulators returned to speculate, make fortunes, and con new investors.

Conglomerate mergers (acquiring nonrelated companies) became a common practice beginning in the 1950s, using accounting manipulation to show financial success and attract investors. Many would collapse in scandal and bankruptcy. Hostile takeovers became a major strategy in the 1960s as raiders developed strategies to take over companies with specific characteristics (e.g., poor performance, declining stock price, low leverage). Junk bond manipulator Michael Milken facilitated leveraged buyouts in the 1980s, further enriching himself through inside information from arbitrageur Ivan Boesky and others. Both would end up in jail for insider trading.

Derivatives trading became an important banking business after Fischer Black and Myron Scholes developed options pricing models in 1973. Derivatives could be valued, and trading actively to move risk exploded. Speculative scandals involving derivatives happened with some regularity, culminating in the collapse of hedge fund Long-Term Capital Management in 1998. Despite the obvious problems in the market, the derivatives market was further deregulated in defiance of common sense.

Twenty-first-century manipulation started with speculation on tech stocks, resulting in the collapse of NASDAQ, several corporate scandals including Enron and WorldCom, and a recession. Low short-term interest rates, continued financial deregulation, political encouragement of housing for subprime customers, a rapacious financial system securitizing substandard mortgages, and predatory mortgage practices led to the housing bubble, the collapse of housing prices, and then the collapse of the financial system with the subprime meltdown of 2008.

Over the decades, markets and regulations changed, but market manipulation continued in altered forms. The net results—bubbles, scandals, and financial collapse—remained and, if anything, became more severe. The subprime meltdown is the most severe worldwide financial crisis in history. The only potential remedy seems to be effective regulation, which has proved difficult to achieve and maintain.

See also Corporations; Drew, Daniel; Fisk, James ("Jubilee Jim"); Gould, Jason ("Jay"); New York Stock Exchange; Panics and Depressions; Railroads, Nineteenth Century; Securities and Exchange Commission (SEC); Subprime Meltdown

References

Giroux, Gary. *Earnings Magic and the Unbalance Sheet: The Search for Financial Reality.* Hoboken, NJ: Wiley, 2006.

Josephson, Matthew. *The Robber Barons.* New York: Harcourt, 1962.

Lewis, Michael. *Panic: The Story of Modern Financial Insanity.* New York: Norton, 2009.

McCullough, David. *Mornings on Horseback.* New York: Simon & Schuster, 1981.

Stewart, James. *Den of Thieves.* New York: Simon & Schuster, 1991.

Mark-to-Market Accounting

Mark-to-market is used for valuing financial instruments where a well-developed market exists (such as the stock market) with specific closing prices disclosed. This is a form of fair-value accounting (using market prices or other measures of current value at the balance sheet date) to recorded asset and liability values and recognized gains and losses on changes in fair value for the period. The use of fair value works well on valuing a portfolio of stocks trading on an exchange such as the New York Stock Exchange. Companies can, for example, own investment portfolios or have pension plans with a large stock component.

The essential logic for mark-to-market on a financial contract, say to value a long-term commitment, is that the actual contract price determines immediate profitability, while fulfilling the contract over time becomes mere bookkeeping. (Of course, it is only as the contract is fulfilled that actual cash is generated.) At the end of the fiscal year, financial instruments are revalued to the new market value for financial statement purposes. Consequently, earnings volatility increases as market values go up and down.

The problems of potential manipulation and fraud became apparent with the Enron scandal. Enron recorded long-term gas contracts with both suppliers and customers using mark-to-market, even when reliable market values on gas prices did not exist, say, 10 years out. Pricing became an exercise in "mark-to-model," using math models predicting values. Consequently, big gains could be recorded before any gas (or cash) changed hands simply by changing model assumptions. Because traders received bonuses based on the value of the trades, not on actual gas deliveries, optimistic model assumptions would be expected. The concept was to "front-load" profits (recognize them immediately). On a quarterly basis, if Enron's income was below expectations, recalculated contract values became even more manipulative. When gains were greater than expected, contract values were reduced to create big reserves (called cookie jar reserves) for potential future trading losses.

Central to accounting has been historical cost, recording most assets and liabilities at acquisition cost. This is usually a transactions price based on the market price at the acquisition date. It has much to offer, including reliability. It would be relevant even if the value of the dollar was stable and relative prices did not change over time. Unfortunately, inflation has been a significant problem in the post–World War II period. Paton and Littleton's *Corporate Accounting Standards* (1940) supported historical cost conceptually, and standard setters relied on it until inflation became a serious issue in the 1970s. Accounting income generally is realized revenue from transactions during the period less the corresponding historical cost using the matching principal. Potentially, those costs could be from past transactions quite different from current costs.

A key characteristic of the post–World War II period has been almost continuous inflation. The 2000 dollar was worth less than one-seventh of the 1950 dollar, as measured by the Consumer Price Index (CPI). The purchasing power of monetary assets (such as cash or accounts receivables) declines with inflation, while monetary liabilities (most liabilities; warranties are one of the few nonmonetary liabilities) essentially increase in value since they are paid back with "cheaper dollars." The costs of nonmonetary assets such as inventory and property, plant, and equipment usually rise with inflation.

Historical cost is transactions based and makes no adjustments for price changes. Expected realizable value adjusts for such factors as uncollectible accounts and renegotiated debt. Current costs and exit values consider the effects of specific price changes. Current costs focus on the cash equivalent amounts to replace existing assets or obligations. This information is considered particularly useful for valuing inventory and fixed assets. During the mid-1970s and early 1980s, the Securities and Exchange Commission (SEC) and Financial Accounting Standards Board (FASB) attempted to move financial reporting toward comprehensive inflation-adjusted information. The SEC in Accounting Series Release (ASR) No. 190 and the FASB in SFAS No. 33 required limited supplementary inflation-adjusted disclosures for large companies. The major disclosures were estimated inventory and fixed-asset current costs and constant-dollar restatements. Unfortunately, researchers could find no compelling evidence that investors actually used this information. This information is no longer required, due in part to lack of interest and relatively lower inflation rates.

A second regulatory approach is specific market pricing (and other measures of fair value). The rationale was: (1) little or no important information is provided in current costs of fixed assets (these the company will retain), but (2) investors need market values on other items. These include marketable securities, derivatives (such items as interest rate swaps and futures, which can be used to decrease risks or vastly increase risk), and other financial instruments.

Recent FASB pronouncements required market value or other fair-value measures for financial instruments. For example, derivatives, which are contracts "derived" from other financial instruments, are recorded at fair value (SFAS No. 123); pension assets use fair value, and liabilities are discounted using complex formulas (SFAS No. 87 and others); business combinations are limited to the purchase method, which records all acquisition assets and liabilities at fair value (SFAS No. 141); and stock options use fair-value calculations (SFAS No. 123).

Part of the profits from the housing bubble were from the mark-to-market gains. Unfortunately, market prices of financial assets collapsed during the subprime meltdown. Continued write-downs to fair value would have led to the failure of much of the financial system of the United States and contagion around the world. Instead of the Great Rescission, another depression was likely. In April 2009, the FASB issued a Final Staff Position (FSP FAS 157-4) providing guidance when asset prices are based on "disorderly sales" (such as forced liquidation), "not indicative of fair value." Guidance suggested using a "cash-flow derived value," effectively eliminating the need to mark down the distressed mortgages to market value. This new FASB rule proved effective in eliminating the stress caused by writing down the financial assets to market value. Banks were much less willing to sell the depressed financial assets at a big loss when they could keep it on their books at a higher value. This move away from mark-to-market reduced the financial losses to the banking system but left the toxic assets on the books of the banks.

See also Accounting Standards; Financial Accounting Standards Board (FASB); Great Depression; Pecora Commission; Sarbanes-Oxley Act of 2002; Securities and Exchange Commission (SEC)

References

Davidson, Sidney, and G. Anderson. "The Development of Accounting and Auditing Standards." *Journal of Accountancy*, May 1987, 110–27.

Financial Accounting Standards Board. *Discussion Memorandum: An Analysis of Issues Related to Conceptual Framework for Financial Accounting and Reporting: Elements of Financial Statements and Their Measurement.* Stamford, CT: FASB, 1976.

Giroux, Gary. *Dollars & Scholars, Scribes & Bribes: The Story of Accounting.* Houston, TX: Dame, 1996.

Giroux, Gary. *Financial Analysis: A User Approach.* New York: Wiley, 2003.

Giroux, Gary. "What Went Wrong? Accounting Fraud and Lessons From the Recent Scandals." *Social Research* 75, no. 4 (Winter 2008): 1205–38.

May Day (1975)

Deregulation of high fixed fees for buying and selling stocks was mandated by the Securities and Exchange Commission (SEC) on May 1, 1975. Because this was a major revenue source for investment banks, the business strategy for these banks was restructured to find additional revenue sources such as mergers and acquisitions, derivatives, and private equity investments.

Financial analysis used financial and other information to make recommendations and decisions about equity investments and other purposes. Investment banks provide considerable financial analysis service for both clients and their own investments. Prior to 1975, all brokerage firms used a fixed commission schedule based on number of shares and stock price. To generate business for their firms ("product differentiation"), they "bundled" other services including financial analysis research. The sales commissions were profitable enough to pay for sophisticated investor analysis. The government called this price fixing, and Congress banned fixed commission for trading stocks, ever since called "May Day" (the SEC put the ban into effect on May 1, 1975—183 years after the Buttonwood Agreement mandated fixed commissions). Commissions were now negotiated between buyers and sellers, dropping about half within three weeks, and retail brokerage was no longer the cash cow for investment banks. Eventually, discount brokers (providing cheap trades with little or no research) emerged, with Charles Schwab leading the way.

As Michael Lewis put it (1989, 62), "The dependable money machine broke down." With the advent of negotiable commissions, investment banks moved to more lucrative areas, and securities offerings competed with mergers and acquisitions as a major revenue source. Investment banks continually reinvented themselves after May Day, looking for additional lucrative revenue sources. Financial analysts shifted focus to aid stock deals, ending objective analysis on banking clients. Major analysts of the "tech bubble" era such as Henry Blodget and Jack Grubman were later prosecuted, fined, and banned from the industry. Investment banks agreed to reestablish the "Chinese Wall" between analysts and investment banking.

See also Blodget, Henry; Financial Analyst Scandal; Grubman, Jack; Investment Banking; Tech Bubble

References

Gasparino, Charles. *Blood on the Street: The Sensational Inside Story of How Wall Street Analysts Duped a Generations of Investors*. New York: Free Press, 2005.

Lewis, Michael. *Liar's Poker: Rising Through the Wreckage on Wall Street*. New York: Penguin Books, 1989.

Lewis, Michael. *Panic: The Story of Modern Financial Insanity*. New York: Norton, 2009.

Mahar, Maggie. *Bull: A History of the Boom and Bust, 1982–2003*. New York: Harper Business, 2004.

McKesson & Robbins Fraud

McKesson & Robbins (MR), a large pharmaceutical company during the 1930s, became the biggest Depression-era accounting scandal. It was discovered in 1938 that President Frank Coster (actually Philip Musica, previously convicted of fraud) embezzled over $18 million in cash by creating a fake division claiming over 20 percent of McKesson's assets. Audit firm Price Waterhouse failed to conduct a physical count of inventory or confirm receivables—now standard practices on all financial audits. The embarrassed accounting profession, for the first time, began setting auditing standards through the American Institute of Accountants (AIA, predecessor of the American Institute of CPAs), beginning with required inventory counts and confirming receivables.

The company started in 1833 as John McKesson's drugstore, joined by partner Daniel Robbins in 1840, manufacturing quinine and importing and distributing drugs from Germany. The company remained in the family until sold to Coster (Musica) for $1 million in 1927. When Philip was growing up, the Musica family ran a food import business, but he got into trouble for bribing customs officials and was sent to reform school. The next scam involved attempting to borrow money claiming to form an export hair business. Again caught, he spent three years in prison. Moving from petty crime, he became a "successful" bootlegger during Prohibition and changed his name to Frank Coster.

Early in the 1920s, Coster established Girard and Co. to make pharmaceuticals. One of the biggest "customers" was W.W. Smith, a dummy company actually run by his brother Arthur. Thanks largely to this fraudulent customer, Girard showed considerable fraudulent profits. Coster hired Price Waterhouse (PW, now Pricewater-houseCoopers), the premier accounting firm at the time, to audit the company. Coster provided all the documentation, and PW, seeing no need to physically court the inventory or verify receivables, gave Girard an unqualified (clean) opinion. With business success and a clean audit opinion, Coster easily borrowed from banks and sold stock.

With the reported growth and profit of Girard, Coster acquired MR in 1927, reorganizing it as McKesson and Robbins of Connecticut. PW continued as auditor. Coster expanded the company with a manufacturing plant in Bridgeport, Connecticut. During the 1930s, MR reportedly became the largest drug company in the United States, manufacturing over 200 drugs as well as being a major wholesale distributor; the company also produced and distributed wines and liquors.

National distribution did not exist for small drug companies across the United States, and in total this represented a billion-dollar business. Hundreds of wholesalers distributed drugs. Coster created a national distribution chain. Regional wholesalers joined the new company (now McKesson &Robbins of Maryland). It took considerable new debt to finance these acquisitions, financed through a large bond issue in 1929.

Sidney J. Weinberg, a director of McKesson & Robbins and a partner of Goldman Sachs & Company, bankers, was questioned by Assistant State Attorney General Ambrose V. McCall in New York on December 28, 1938, in the investigation into F. Donald Coster Mosica's manifold activities as president of the drug firm. Weinberg said he had no suspicion who Coster-Musica was but "accepted him as a successful businessman." (AP Photo/John Lindsay)

Coster proved to be a good businessman and grew MR even during the Depression. Unfortunately, he continued his fraud practices. Dummy companies, set up with confederates (including two of his brothers), continued pilfering the company. The American manufacturing part stayed legitimate. A separate bogus Canadian subsidiary existed for speculation and fraud. Paperwork showed manufacturing, inventories, receivables, and sales with cash flowing north and financial statements issued to bankers. With no real business, the Canadian subsidiary still claimed bogus profits of about $100,000 a year. Fake inventories and receivables made up about a quarter of MR total assets ($20 million relative to $87 million in total assets).

The only non-Musicas with access to the financial information were Controller John McGloon, a partner in deception, and PW, fooled throughout with fraudulent documents. MR treasurer Julian Thompson played no part in the conspiracy. He discovered the Canadian subsidiary to be a shell company and then investigated customer W.W. Smith. He checked with Dun and Bradstreet and discovered that the W.W. Smith report was forged; Thompson visited George Vernard at Smith (actually Musica brother Arthur), who would not show him the inventory. He confronted Coster with his findings.

Coster panicked and put the company into receivership in an attempt to extricate himself, which did not work. The Securities and Exchange Commission (SEC) started an investigation as did the New York attorney general, arresting Coster in December 1937. Fingerprints identified Coster as Musica. Musica killed himself before being indicted. Amazingly, Controller John McGloon became the only person who actually went to jail. The other Musica brothers and confederates pled guilty but served as government witnesses. MR survived through reorganization and emerged as a new company in 1941. McKesson still operates as a successful health care business with a market capitalization over $20 billion.

MR, the first conviction for filing false financial statements under the securities acts, became an extreme embarrassment to the accounting profession. Widespread fraud for a dozen years went undetected, even though the process involved only simply doctoring the books. At the time, audit procedures did not require inventory to be physically verified by the auditor or that customers' receivables be confirmed. That soon changed. A new accounting committee established auditing standards, and the SEC tightened audit reporting requirements. Companies were encouraged to have audit committees as part of the board of directors and improve internal controls.

See also Accounting Fraud; Accounting Standards; Auditing since SEC Regulations; Fraud; Great Depression; Securities and Exchange Commission (SEC)

References

Barr, Andrew, and Irving Galper. "McKesson & Robbins." *Journal of Accountancy*, May 1987, 159–61.

Dobson, John. "Crash." In *Bulls, Bears, Boom, and Bust: A Historical Encyclopedia of American Business Concepts*. Santa Barbara, CA: ABC-CLIO, 2006.

Galbraith, Kenneth. *The Great Crash 1929*. Boston: Houghton Mifflin, 1988.

Mellon, Andrew W.

Andrew Mellon (1855–1937) was an American industrialist and secretary of the Treasury from 1921 to 1932. Mellon was born into a banking family on March 24, 1855, in Pittsburg. After graduating from the University of Pittsburgh, Mellon joined the family business, cofounded T. Mellon and Sons Bank, invested in refining aluminum, which led to his control of Aluminum Company of America (ALCOA), and invested in interests in coal, iron, and other industries; the result was one of the great American fortunes, estimated to be worth between $300 and $400 million before the Great Depression.

Mellon was appointed Treasury secretary by Warren G. Harding in 1921 and remained on the job through the 12 years of Republican rule, including the Roaring Twenties, as well as the early part of the Great Depression. He emphasized the importance of business, including little interest in antitrust or most types of business regulation. Taxes and government spending fell and federal regulatory agencies stayed quiet. The top individual income tax rate dropped to 25 percent during most of this period (after rising to 73% during World War I). Under Mellon, the national debt from the war was cut in half.

Mellon favored a "leave the economy alone" approach when the Great Depression struck, famously stating, "Liquidate labor, liquidate stocks, liquidate the farmers, liquidate real estate . . . purge the rottenness out of the system." Unfortunately, the economy and financial system were so traumatized after a corrupt decade that the economy continued into an almost complete bank collapse and a severe economic crisis.

Mellon's income tax returns were investigated by the Roosevelt administration and he was indicted for tax evasion. He was eventually exonerated, but only after his death. He died on August 26, 1937, in Southampton, New York.

See also Commercial Banking after the Federal Reserve; Great Depression; New Deal; Roosevelt, Franklin Delano; Teapot Dome

References

Dobson, John. "Mellon, Andrew William." In *Bulls, Bears, Boom, and Bust: A Historical Encyclopedia of American Business Concepts*. Santa Barbara, CA: ABC-CLIO, 2006.

Zheng, Guoqlang. "Mellon, Andrew William." In *The American Economy: A Historical Encyclopedia*. Rev. ed. Edited by Cynthia Clark. Santa Barbara, CA: ABC-CLIO, 2011.

Mercantilism

Mercantilism (roughly 1500–1800) was a European economic/political perspective developed from merchant capitalism, designed to benefit the "mother country" and promote imperialism. Trade with Asia expanded and the discovery of the New World changed European wealth and power—especially the discovery of gold and silver by Spanish explorers. With the focus on precious metals and trade, nationalism and a strong navy became paramount. England (and other European powers) required a trade surplus to receive gold from a net balance of payments. A dominant naval power could hold colonies and control trade routes. Cheap imports of raw materials from the colonies would be used to produce finished goods in the home country, which could then be exported to colonies and other countries. Home-country merchants would dominate colonies and provide monopoly power over trade. For example, the British Navigation Acts beginning in the seventeenth century required trade goods to be shipped in English ships and all goods shipped initially to British ports.

Mercantilists favored free trade within a country, but opposed taxes and other restrictions on business activities. A strong central government was needed to standardize favorable regulations. A large population of low-cost labor also was a necessary component. A large contingent of regulators (including inspectors, judges, and enforcement officers) was required to monitor this system. Government chartering (early corporations) thrived under mercantilism, an organization structure ultimately transforming the economy. Eventually, vast regulations and monopolies stifled economic activity, and the mercantilist system was slowly replaced with a more competitive environment.

Great Britain did not allow banks or domestic minting of coins within the colonies. Related regulations prohibited Bank of England banknotes and British coins. Some colonies issued paper money, especially in times of war, and colonists made due with state paper and foreign coins in circulation. Colonial plantation owners and merchants relied on loans from English merchants. In turn, merchants gave credit to their own customers. Personal notes and bills of exchange served as nominal paper money. During the French and Indian War (1754–63) colonies issued (emitted) paper money and borrowed from local merchants using short-term notes (called Treasury notes in New England). After the war, rising local taxes paid off interest and retired both debt and paper currencies fairly rapidly (usually within a decade). At the start of the American Revolution, colonies had no direct experience with banking but expected to fund the war with paper money and loans.

The American colonies got out of the restrictive system by declaring independence and fighting a war for it, but most European colonies remained part of the mercantile system and gained freedom only in the twentieth century. Many aspects of mercantilism remained, especially the provision of raw material for the industrialized countries, and served as markets for finished goods.

See also Austrian School of Economics; Bank of England; Classical Economics; Morris, Robert; Paper Money; Smith, Adam; Washington, George

References

Dimand, Robert. "Mercantilism." In *The American Economy: A Historical Encyclopedia*. Rev. ed. Edited by Cynthia Clark. Santa Barbara, CA: ABC-CLIO, 2011.

Dobson, John. "Mercantilism." In *Bulls, Bears, Boom, and Bust: A Historical Encyclopedia of American Business Concepts*. Santa Barbara, CA: ABC-CLIO, 2006.

Oser, J. *The Evolution of Economic Thought*. New York: Harcourt, Brace & World, 1963.

Mergers

A merger is a combination of two companies into a single corporate entity and became common by the second half of the nineteenth century as major industrial firms attempted to eliminate "excessive competition" and create monopoly power. Standard Oil was among the first major industrial firms to consolidate an industry through acquisitions. Friendly incorporation laws, especially in New Jersey, facilitated the process. Industrials became big business in the United States largely through mergers.

The history of big business for the last century and a half includes considerable merger activity. The economy was booming during and after the Civil War. John D. Rockefeller gobbled up competing oil refiners, and eventually Standard Oil had a 90 percent market share. His stated purpose was to maintain reasonable prices by eliminating cutthroat competition and ensure consistent quality of kerosene and other oil products. Other saw him as a ruthless robber baron. By 1902 J. P. Morgan, the most powerful banker in United States, acquired Carnegie Steel and most of the rest of the industry to form United States Steel, the first billion-dollar corporation in the United States—formed by horizontal mergers on a vast scale. The financial reporting and auditing of United States Steel were excellent by the standards of the time, but involved "watering the stock" by overvaluing assets. The potential for misleading reporting has been a continual problem for business combinations.

Mergers can be used to reduce competition (horizontal mergers—those in the same industry, such as Standard Oil), expand activities into related areas (vertical mergers), or diversify (conglomerate mergers). Henry Ford introduced the moving assembly line and the cheap, standardized Model T a century ago. Ford used a vertical merger strategy to acquire related firms: parts dealers, ships and railroads for distribution, mines, and basic metal manufacturers. Ford owned most business components of auto manufacturing from mines to transportation to dealerships.

Mergers by large companies became more difficult with the Sherman Antitrust Act of 1890 and later antitrust legislation. Regulators often denied horizontal and vertical mergers because of diminished competition and monopoly potential. Conglomerate mergers, harder to attack on antitrust grounds, gave other entrepreneurs the potential for growth through acquisitions. Merger accounting manipulation created asset valuations and unexpected profits not generated through normal operations. Accounting standards did not focus on "financial reality" (this was the domain of economists, not accountants), and acquisitions allowed opportunities for manipulating the numbers.

Two theories of acquisition accounting developed and were standardized in the 1960s by the Accounting Principles Board (APB). The first was pooling of interests, which presumed the combining of "equal" companies using historical cost. The resulting company would record the assets and liabilities of the two companies based on existing book value without regard to current values. Depreciated property, plant, and equipment could have a relatively low book value and be a fraction of current (replacement) value. Patents and other intangible assets could stay unrecorded. Inventory could be manipulated down, for example, due to perceived obsolete inventory or expected bad debts. In total, the result created a low asset base and lower future operating expenses. The second theory, the purchase method, assumed that one company (the parent) acquired another (the subsidiary), and the accounting comes closer to economic reality. Using actual acquisition price (based on a cash or stock purchase) resulted in assets and liability restated to "fair value" (usually upward, sometimes by a lot), including the value of patents and other intangible assets. Of course, fair value is determined by "professional judgment." The difference between the acquisition price and restated fair value of net assets resulted in goodwill, basically a plug figure for the "premium paid," for this difference.

See also Accounting Standards; Acquisition Accounting; Cleverly Rigged Accounting Ploys (CRAP); Conglomerates; Hostile Takeovers; Standard Oil

References

Giroux, Gary. *Earnings Magic and the Unbalance Sheet: The Search for Financial Reality.* New York: Wiley, 2006.

Vincusi, W., John Vernon, and Joseph Harrington. *Economics of Regulations and Antitrust.* 2nd ed. Cambridge, MA: MIT Press, 1995.

Meriwether, John W.

John Meriwether (1947–) was a financial bank and hedge fund executive, innovator in fixed-income arbitrage, and central to the success and collapse of Long-Term Capital Management. Meriwether was born in Chicago on August 10, 1947. After graduating from Northwestern and then the University of Chicago with an MBA, Meriwether started as a bond trader for Salomon Brothers and founded Salomon's fixed income arbitrage group in the mid-1980s. A Treasury securities scandal at Salomon cost Meriwether his job in 1998, plus a $50,000 fine.

He cofounded the hedge fund Long-Term Capital Management (LTCM) in 1994 and took many of the Salomon traders with him, joined by Nobel Prize winners Myron Scholes and Robert Merton. Investors (with a minimum of $10 million) flocked to this high-powered team, and the hedge fund started with over $1 billion in equity. The initial results were breathtaking—40 percent returns in the first two years. By 1998, LTCM had an investment portfolio valued over $100 billion with derivatives having a notional (face) value in the trillions.

A major LTCM trading strategy speculated on emerging market bonds relative to short-term U.S. Treasuries, an arbitrage strategy based on high correlations between the two. Once the Asian currency markets collapsed beginning in mid-1997, the strategy failed and the securities did not converge in price. Russia defaulted on sovereign debt in 1998, and the strategy of buying Russian bonds and selling short

Treasuries also failed. LTCM traders kept buying Russian bonds as the value of the ruble collapsed. The flight to quality by most investors (buying U.S. Treasuries) meant virtually all these bets turned against LTCM.

The Federal Reserve, seeing the potential collapse of financial markets, organized a rescue package funded by a consortium of major banks. Ellis (2008, 604) called this "the largest-ever rescue effort by U.S. banks." After unwinding all the LTCM positions, the hedge fund was closed in 2000.

Within a year of the collapse of LTCM, Meriwether founded hedge fund JWM Partners, increasing funds under management from $250 million to $3 billion by 2007. The investment strategy was similar to that at LTCM, relying on arbitrage and high leverage. Unfortunately, the fund was battered by the subprime meltdown and closed in 2009. A new hedge fund, JM Advisors, opened in 2010.

See also Asian Debt Crisis; Brady Plan; Derivatives; Federal Reserve System; Hedge Funds: Long-Term Capital Management; Russian Kleptocracy and Default; Salomon Brothers

References

Lewis, Michael. *Liar's Poker: Rising Through the Wreckage on Wall Street.* New York: Norton, 1989.

Lowenstein, Roger. *When Genius Failed: The Rise and Fall of Long-Term Capital Management.* New York: Random House, 2000.

Partnoy, Frank. *FIASCO: Blood in the Water on Wall Street.* New York: Norton, 1997.

Partnoy, Frank. *Infectious Greed: How Deceit and Risk Corrupted the Financial Markets.* New York: Holt, 2003.

Merrill Lynch

Merrill Lynch (ML) became one of the "Big Five" investment banks of the late twentieth and early twenty-first-century history. Charles Merrill opened for business in New York City in 1914, soon joined by Edmund Lynch, focusing on creating a retail brokerage network. Thanks in part to mergers, it became one of the retail broker giants with operations in financial services, investment banking, and management. ML had a number of minor scandals in the twenty-first century, including improperly selling mutual funds and employee discrimination suits. After billion-dollar write-offs associated with mortgage holdings and near failure during the subprime meltdown, Bank of America bought the company in 2008.

Charles Merrill worked for a number of firms on Wall Street before setting up his own firm in 1914, when he merged with Edmund Lynch. By the 1920s, the company was successful, focusing on middle-class investors across the country. The firm also underwrote several stock issues, including Kresge, Western Auto, J.C. Penney, and Safeway Stores. Charles Merrill got out of the stock market before the crash of 1929 and advised his clients to depart also. During the Great Depression he sold his firm to E. A. Pierce, but both he and Lynch remained as limited partners. Merrill took over management in 1940. The new firm developed a huge network of branches and brokers to meet retail investment needs. The training of brokers was increased, and fixed salaries increased relative to commissions to ensure the brokers worked in the interests of the customers. When the market boomed after World War II, Merrill Lynch prospered and became the largest brokerage business on Wall Street.

In 1970, the New York Stock Exchange (NYSE) changed the rules and allowed members to go public. A number of "retail banks" went public in 1971–72, including Merrill Lynch, the biggest (others included Bache, Dean Witter, E.F. Hutton, and Paine Webber). Retail brokers went public in part to provide the needed capital to invest in the computer power then becoming available to process the large number of trades made for customers.

After "May Day" (May 1, 1975), the Securities and Exchange Commission (SEC) banned fixed commissions on securities trades. Commissions dropped in half almost immediately and continued down. ML and the rest of the retail brokerage industry lost their "cash cow" and had to look elsewhere for profitable business. New strategies increased risks to both bankers and clients. The investment bank of the post–May Day period focused on four financial innovations: high-yield debt (junk bonds), derivatives, securitization, and arbitrage trading. These all increased potential profits, but greatly increased risks and likely crashes. ML became a major securities underwriter and held asset management accounts valued at well over $1 trillion.

ML targeted state and local governments for complex derivative investments. These high-risk instruments seemed poor investments to conservative governments subject to regulatory constraints. Bonuses on high commissions proved too big an incentive to bond salespeople, and they effectively camouflaged the risks and high costs from the buyers. Government buyers—and ultimate losers—included San Jose, California, the state of West Virginia, Wisconsin Investment Board, San Diego and San Bernadino Counties, and the California Public Employees Retirement System, among others. The biggest loser was Orange County, which paid Merrill some $100 million in fees. County treasurer Robert Citron bought the complex securities from Merrill and lost the county some $1.7 billion, forcing the county into bankruptcy in 1994. Citron pleaded guilty to filing false and misleading financial statements and other felonies. Orange County sued ML, and the company paid $400 million to settle the case.

Turn-of-the-twenty-first-century Internet analyst Henry Blodget of Merrill Lynch became one of the stars analyzing the "New Economy." After fixed commissions of stock sales were banned, financial analysis shifted from objective research to customers to providing consistently positive analysis of client stock issues. A "Chinese Wall" supposedly existed separating stock deals and analysts, but firm research began blatantly supporting banking clients. Regulators showed little interest in the lack of research objectivity. Issuing initial public offerings (IPOs) became a major profit center for ML and other investment banks. The research strategy focused on serving as investment cheerleaders.

After the collapse of the tech bubble in 2000, the analysts' bias became obvious. Even as the tech sector collapsed, Blodget and the others continued with "buy" ratings. The SEC investigated the fraudulent IPOs, but ignored the conflicted analysts. Only after the tech collapse did the SEC, NASDAQ, and the New York Stock Exchange investigate and Congress hold hearings. New York attorney general Eliot Spitzer led an aggressive investigation. Blodget resigned (receiving an exit package from Merrill worth $12 million), was barred from the industry, and paid a fine of $2 million plus a $2 million disgorgement (a return of illegal or unethical profits). Spitzer and the banks involved reached a "global settlement" in 2002, with the banks paying combined fines of $1.4 billion while agreeing to stop the biased research. Various class action suits by investors led to more payouts.

During the twenty-first century, ML became a player in mortgage securitization, the lucrative high-risk securities that helped cause of subprime meltdown of 2008 and the Great Recession. Merrill Lynch executive Jeff Kronthal, head of fixed income, notified chief executive officer (CEO) Stanley O'Neal in 2006 that a large number of new mortgage holders did not make even a single payment associated with collateralized debt obligation (CDO) bundles. Given that underwriting standards had collapsed, Kronthal recommended that Merrill reduce its exposure to these instruments. This got Kronthal fired by O'Neal, and Merrill dramatically increased its exposure to CDOs in 2006–7. The result was a Merrill Lynch close to failure. O'Neal was ultimately fired, but received a gigantic exit package of $72 million.

Merrill Lynch started recording mortgage-related losses in 2007 and these quickly grew bigger. Merrill sold off various segments and turned to foreign investors to increase capital. Losses continued up as stock price dropped. As with Bear Stearns and Lehman Brothers, trading partners lost confidence and Merrill fell into the liquidity trap that ended the other two investment banks. Merrill fortunately found a willing buyer in Bank of America (B of A), receiving about $50 billion ($29 a share, a substantial premium over the market price). The deal was announced on September 14, 2008, just before the Lehman bankruptcy.

In mid-December, B of A wanted to back out of the deal because Merrill losses were much larger than expected—referring to them as the "deal from hell." According to Wessel (2009, 260), the Treasury Department pressured B of A with the threat of lawsuits and the likely firing of Lewis and the board of directors if the deal did not go through. Treasury provided additional capital and promised to limit potential losses from Merrill. The deal was finalized on January 1, 2009. The stock price of B of A fell 80 percent after September 2008 (and the stock price dropped below $4 a share in 2009).

Two minor scandals erupted. B of A disclosed that Merrill CEO John Thain paid out over $3 billion in bonuses just before the merger, but did not disclose this to B of A (Thain resigned shortly after that). B of A lobbied the Treasury for another $20 billion in capital because the Merrill losses were so much larger than anticipated, and shareholder lawsuits followed that announcement. ML is now the wealth management division of B of A, with some 15,000 financial advisers and over $2 trillion in client assets.

See also American Insurance Group; Bear Stearns; Goldman Sachs; Investment Banks; May Day (1975); Paulson, Hank; Securities and Exchange Commission (SEC); Structured Finance; Subprime Meltdown; Treasury Department

References

Gordon, John Steele. *The Great Game: The Emergence of Wall Street as a World Power, 1653–2000.* New York: Scribner, 1999.

Lowenstein, Roger. *The End of Wall Street.* New York: Penguin Press, 2010.

McLean, Bethany, and Joe Nocera. *All the Devils Are Here: The Hidden History of the Financial Crisis.* New York: Portfolio/Penguin, 2010.

Merrill, Charles, and E. A. Pierce. "Wall Street Goes to Main Street, 1940." In *Eyewitness to Wall Street.* Edited by David Colbert, 160–164. New York: Broadway Books, 2001.

Wessel, David. *In Fed We Trust: Ben Bernanke's War on the Great Panic.* New York: Crown Business, 2009.

Military-Industrial Complex

The military-industrial complex represents the reciprocal relationship between the military and industry, suggesting the overconsumption of war products to benefit the special interests involved. In his farewell address in 1961, President Dwight D. Eisenhower stated, "In the councils of government, we must guard against the acquisition of unwarranted influence, whether sought or unsought, by the military-industrial complex." The concept expanded to include all forms of reciprocal relationships between government and the private sector involving special interest influence and spending.

During most of his presidency, Eisenhower held down military costs, despite the opposition of the military, most of his cabinet and advisers, Congress, and big business. As supreme Allied commander and army chief of staff, he had the background to understand the legitimate needs of defense. The military wanted more weapons and more power, while the defense industry wanted lucrative weapons contracts. Both groups were experts at lobbying Congress, who wanted campaign contributions, jobs in defense contract plants, and backing to win reelection (and perhaps lucrative jobs after serving in government).

Military-business connections were hardly new and can be traced from the American Revolution. During the Civil War, businesses received profitable Union contracts for weapons, clothing, and supplies. In the First World War, the federal government eventually established the War Industries Board. The board had the power to purchase war materials and supplies, encourage industrial development, and finance government-owned production facilities. As usual, the government demobilized, resulting in a recession in 1920.

World War II saw a massive military buildup on a scale not seen in any previous war. After the war, economists predicted depression after an expected demobilization. President Harry Truman reduced federal expenditures including military spending. Fortunately, consumers used savings to spend lavishly on consumer goods and innovative programs such as the G.I. Bill (providing college funding and other benefits) helped avoid recession. The emerging Cold War resulted in large increases in military spending. An integrated Defense Department was created in 1947, after being recommended by the Hoover Commission. Within this structure, the army, the navy, and a newly independent air force competed for resources. The air force favored aircraft-delivered atomic weaponry, which became a budgetary jackpot. New aircraft and aerospace industries became increasingly dominant. In the post–World War II period, defense contractors often hired retired military, for both expertise and contacts in the military. With the exception of Boeing, which managed to serve both military and commercial customers, the major American aerospace corporations focused on expensive military products. Lockheed collected over $10 billion from 1961to 1967 on federal contracts, 90 percent of total sales. General Dynamics, McDonnell Douglas, North-American Rockwell, and Martin-Marietta all received the majority of their revenues from government contracts.

Business and political groups have blatant self-interests that can oppose the national interest. The processes that determine public policy are complex, dynamic, and subject to abuse. Part of the analysis of business corruption is the abuse of the political process.

See also Political Machines; Profiteering during the American Revolution

References

Dobson, John. "Military-Industrial Complex." In *Bulls, Bears, Boom, and Bust: A Historical Encyclopedia of American Business Concepts*. Santa Barbara, CA: ABC-CLIO, 2006.

Eisenhower, Dwight. Farewell Address. January 17, 1961. http://www.americanrhetoric .com/speeches/dwightdeisenhowerfarewell.html.

Perry, James. "Military-Industrial Complex (MIC)." In *The American Economy: A Historical Encyclopedia*. Rev. ed. Edited by Cynthia Clark. Santa Barbara, CA: ABC-CLIO, 2011.

Milken, Michael R.

Michael Milken ("Junk Bond King," 1946–) was an American financier who developed the high-yield/junk bond market in the 1970s to 1980s, only to see his empire crash and himself be imprisoned for securities fraud. After his release, he became noted for philanthropic activities, especially funding medical research. The high-yield market continued to be important after the fall of Milken.

Milken was born on July 4, 1946, in Encino California. After graduating from the University of California, Berkeley and Pennsylvania's Wharton School, he joined Drexel Firestone (later Drexel, Burnham and Lambert) as a bond researcher and trader. The investment banks at the time focused on investment-grade securities (those with Standard & Poor's ratings of BBB–AAA). Milken believed the high yields on non-investment-grade or junk bonds (those with Standard & Poor's ratings of BB and below) made them desirable because the yields more than made up for the added default risk. This he based on historic academic research showing that a diversified portfolio of junk bonds provided a high yield with little additional risk relative to higher-rated bonds. The problem was liquidity, the lack of a well-developed market.

In the mid-1970s, Milken established a bond-trading group for junk bonds at Drexel Burnham, setting it up in Beverly Hills, California. He found major investors in insurance companies and savings and loans (S&Ls) (the S&Ls became major buyers after being deregulated in the early 1980s). Drexel gave Milken near-autonomy, and his unit got 35 percent of the profit of the operation, most of which went directly to Milken.

With no competition at the start, Milken dominated junk bonds; as a market maker, he bought and sold them on demand and set the prices in an almost unregulated market. Milken kept the pricing information confidential to ensure that spreads remained high—buying at artificially low prices and selling at inflated prices. He established private partnerships to deal in client securities to further enrich himself, family, and friends, including arbitrage buying using direct insider information. Conveniently, trading on insider information is illegal only for stocks.

Milken's "monopoly profits" continued until competing banks entered the market. Milken proved to be particularly unethical when dominating this market and used his knowledge and influence to squeeze every dime of profit from side deals he could develop. Milken's lack of interest in playing by the ethical or legal rules eventually resulted in his downfall.

Milken expanded the market by issuing new securities, creating a primary junk bond market, starting with Texas International in the late 1970s. Milken sold a high-yield $30 million issue directly to his customers. Additional junk bond issues followed, creating a new market for profits. When companies financed by Milken's junk bonds came close to failure, he "restructured" the debt, increasing the amount of bonds outstanding and extending payments further into the future. In the short term, the junk default rate stayed low.

A major market was mergers and acquisitions, especially the leveraged buyout (LBO) financed by junk bonds. In 1981, Victor Posner acquired National Can in a hostile takeover, using an LBO with him owning 80 percent and management taking a 20 percent stake. When Posner's empire started collapsing, Milken arranged the sale of National Can to Nelson Peltz. Milken clients Boon Pickens went after Unocal, James Goldsmith after Crown Zellerbach, and William Farley after Northwest Industries.

In 1985 Kohlberg, Kravis and Roberts (KKR) made their first hostile takeover for Beatrice Foods. The takeover made KKR the principal private equity company of the era. KKR increasingly used Milken money to finance deals, including the acquisition of Storer Communications.

To boost his own profits Milken worked with arbitrageur Ivan Boesky, feeding him information and orders on what to buy and when. Boesky did the deals because Milken could not trade in his client's stock, then the two split the profits. In a typical repayment scheme, Milken sold bonds to Boesky, then Boesky would sell them back to Drexel at a higher price. As summarized by Stewart (1991, 219):

> Milken and Boesky were deeply intertwined in what was a sweeping criminal conspiracy. Taken together, the ventures were practically a catalogue of securities crimes, starting with insider trading, and including false public disclosures, tax fraud, and market manipulation, as well as a slew of more technical crimes. . . . The crimes were mere way stations toward outcomes, such as hostile takeovers, that were, on their face, perfectly legal.

By the late 1980s, many of Milken's junk bond-financed clients were on the verge of bankruptcy. Insurance company Integrated Resources, backed by $2 billion in Milken junk, declared bankruptcy in 1990, followed by retail giant Campeau Corporation (owner of Federated and Bloomingdale's). About a quarter of Milken's firms eventually failed. The boom in junk bonds was over. Most of the S&Ls involved in Milken's shady deals also failed and several S&L executives went to prisons.

Both Milken and Drexel Burnham were charged under the Racketeer Influenced and Corrupt Organizations Act (RICO), designed to fight organized crime. Guilty pleas and then the collapse of the junk bond market drove Drexel into bankruptcy. Charged with 98 counts of racketeering and securities fraud, Milken confessed to six felonies, including conspiracy with Boesky and securities fraud, and was sentenced to 10 years in jail. Total fines against Milken totaled over $1 billion. This was probably only a fraction of his accumulated wealth; *Forbes* estimated his net worth at $2 billion in 2010. After cooperating against former coconspirators and for good behavior, he spent less than two years in jail.

Milken founded the Milken Family Foundation in the 1980s, focusing on education and medical research (he recovered from prostate cancer). After his release from prison in 1993, Milken focused on his foundation and other philanthropic interests.

See also Boesky, Ivan; Bond Ratings; Insider Trading; Insider Trading Scandals of the 1980s; Junk Bond Market; Savings and Loan Deregulations and Failures

References

Dobson, John. "Savings and Loan Crisis." In *Bulls, Bears, Boom, and Bust: A Historical Encyclopedia of American Business Concepts*. Santa Barbara, CA: ABC-CLIO, 2006.

Giroux, Gary. *Financial Analysis: A User Approach*. New York: Wiley, 2003.

Stewart, James. *Den of Thieves*. New York: Simon & Schuster, 1991.

Minsky, Hyman

Minsky (1919–96) was a twentieth-century economist working at Washington University at St. Louis. He described the business cycle as a function of the supply of credit, based on investor confidence, describing the "financial instability hypothesis." The bursting of a credit bubble happens at the "Minsky Moment." He was born on September 23, 1919, in Chicago and received an MPA and PhD from Harvard in economics. He was an academic at Brown University, University of California at Berkeley, and Washington University.

Minsky described lending practices under three categories based on the quality of debt: hedge finance (safe), speculative finance (moderate), and Ponzi finance (risky). Minsky's model starts with standard banking practice where loans plus interest will be paid back as they come due from operating income. When lending becomes speculative, borrowers anticipate paying back interest from operating earnings but not return of principal. The borrowers have to refinance the principal when the loan matures. In a period of market euphoria, Ponzi finance loans will not generate enough cash to pay back either interest or principal. Ponzi finance will continue if asset values rise to cover finance payments. When asset prices fall, the system collapses as loan defaults expand and companies are forced into bankruptcy. Investor euphoria caused by rapidly rising asset prices (especially in real estate and stock) drive speculative and Ponzi finance. The point when asset prices collapse is the "Minsky moment" (see chapter 2 of Kindleberger and Aliber 2005).

Minsky's credit cycle can be explained in five cycles: displacement, boom, euphoria, profit taking, and panic. Displacement is the beginning of investor excitement, based perhaps on new technology (such as the Internet) or innovative finance. Speculative and Ponzi finance expands during periods of investor euphoria, because of the rapid rise in asset prices (usually either stock or real estate). Some smart traders take profits at the top of the market, and asset prices stall and then drop. When asset price bubbles burst (the "Minsky moment"), Ponzi finance collapses and speculative finance also is subject to failure. Confounding economists' attempt at a general theory, the reasons for booms resulting in euphoria differ with each cycle. Each case finds the banking system central or at least significant.

The Minsky model fits the recent subprime bubble and meltdown, but also explains the Great Depression and the nineteenth-century panics, despite significant differences in institutional framework, including the banking system and the level of technology. In its usefulness as an analytical tool for the nineteenth-century economy, the Minsky model illustrates both the strengths and weaknesses of such economic frameworks: the categories provide a means retrospectively to pull apart complex issues; however, the general nature of the propositions makes it problematic as a means of current analysis: one can see clearly enough that the Union Pacific began as a Ponzi (in Minsky nomenclature) that E. H. Harriman later transformed into a speculative scheme; Alfred Sloan clearly took William Durant's General Motors from Ponzi to speculative to hedge financing.

Minsky died on October 24, 1996, in Rhinebeck, New York.

See also Business Cycles; General Motors; Great Depression; Panic of 1819; Panic of 1837; Panic of 1857; Panic of 1873; Panic of 1893; Panic of 1907; Panics and Depressions; Union Pacific Railroad

References

Cassidy, John. "The Minsky Moment." *The New Yorker*, February 4, 2008. http://www.newyorker.com.

Kindleberger, Charles, and R. Alibe. *Manias, Panics, and Crashes: A History of Financial Crises*. 5th ed. Hoboken, NJ: Wiley, 2005.

Knoop, Todd. *Recessions and Depressions: Understanding Business Cycles*. 2nd ed. Santa Barbara, CA: Greenwood, 2010.

Reinhart, Carmen, and Kenneth Rogoff. *This Time Is Different: Eight Centuries of Financial Folly*. Princeton, NJ: Princeton University Press, 2009.

Roubini, Nouriel, and Stephen Mihm. *Crisis Economics: A Crash Course in the Future of Finance*. New York: Penguin Press, 2010.

Misery Index

After the term "stagflation" was introduced in the 1960s as a measure of low economic growth, high unemployment, and high inflation, economist Arthur Okun created the "misery index" by adding the unemployment rate to the inflation rate. This simple index measures the relative pain in economic activity. An index of, say, 5 percent suggests relatively low inflation and near-full employment; a double-digit misery index suggests some combination of higher inflation and/or unemployment.

The 1980s started with severe stagflation as measured by a misery index of 20.8 percent, an economic crisis not experienced before in the United States. Incumbent president Jimmy Carter lost in 1980, as Ronald Reagan started his "Reagan Revolution." However, the solution to the inflation problem remained in the hands of Federal Reserve chairman Paul Volcker. He cut the money supply and pushed interest rates into double digits, an economically painful but effective solution. Inflation rates came down, followed by unemployment. The misery index eventually fell below 10 percent in 1986.

Inflation rates remained low during the post–World War II period until the 1970s, with a consumer price index (CPI) below 2 percent until 1967. During the 1970s, the United States abandoned the gold exchange standard (that is, the U.S. dollar was no longer pegged to gold) and oil prices rose dramatically. The inflation rate based on CPI peaked at 13.55 percent in 1980. At the same time, recession drove the unemployment rate over 10 percent; the combination of both inflation and unemployment each in double digits made the period economically painful. After 1983, the inflation fell, followed by the unemployment, and the misery index was seldom mentioned.

Throughout the 1990 and well into the twenty-first century, neither inflation nor unemployment proved to be much of a problem. Unemployment became an issue with the Great Recession beginning in 2008, as unemployment rose from 4.6 percent in 2007 and hit double digits in 2009. The misery index moved back to double digits. In 2010, the misery index was 11.2 percent; although the inflation rate (CPI) was only 1.6 percent, the unemployment rate for the year averaged 9.6 percent.

See also Classical Economics; Federal Reserve System; Keynes, John Maynard; Stagflation; Volcker, Paul A., Jr.

References

Skidelsky, Robert. *Keynes: The Return of the Master; Why, Sixty Years after His Death, John Maynard Keynes Is the Most Important Economic Thinker for America.* New York: Public Affairs, 2009.

U.S. Census Bureau. *Statistical Abstract of the United States* (various years). http://www.census.gov.

Mississippi Bubble

The Mississippi bubble was a French financial scheme in the early eighteenth century triggering a speculative bubble and ending in collapse. The Mississippi Company was established in 1717 by Scottish economist John Law (1671–1729), controller general of France under Louis XV, to colonize and exploit the Mississippi River Basin and what became the Louisiana Territory.

After the War of the Spanish Succession in 1714, France was in financial chaos with a huge national debt and a weak tax system. John Law offered France his system of reform, and the regent for King Louis XV, Phillippe d'Orleans, appointed Law controller general of finances. Law made substantial reforms including replacing gold with paper currency, reviving overseas commerce, and creating a national bank. In 1716, Law was granted a license for the Banque Generale, which became the Banque Royale in 1718, with Law as director and the bank's notes guaranteed by the king. The bank had a monopoly on minting royal coinage and control over the money supply.

In 1717, Law was granted a charter for the Mississippi Company as a trading company to exploit the Mississippi River Basin, receiving a royal decree and a 25-year lease on the territory. The price set for the 200,000 shares was 500 livres, with 75 percent payable in government notes (then selling at a discount). The Mississippi Company acquired the royal tobacco monopoly and the various French companies involved in foreign trade. The Mississippi Company was merged into the Banque Royal, which exchanged part of the national debt into shares of the Mississippi Company (a technique copied by the South Sea Company). Unfortunately, much of the funding to finance trade in Mississippi remained in France to promote the government—including the opulent lifestyle of the regent.

A speculative bubble drove stock prices higher, Law continued to increase the supply of paper money, and inflation kicked in across France. Shares in the Mississippi Company rose to 10,000 livres in the course of 1719. The Mississippi Company issued a 40 percent dividend in 1720, driving the share price to 18,000 livres. Profits from Mississippi proved disappointing and the public lost confidence in paper money. At this point, speculators resolved to take their profits. The bubble burst and prices collapsed. As panic increased, citizens tried to redeem their bank notes for gold coin. The bank did not have the necessary specie and went bankrupt in October 1720.

Law was dismissed by the regent and forced to flee France, dying at the end of the decade in Venice, Italy. The company was taken over by the state, which raised taxes to pay off debt and ended most of the reforms instituted by Law.

See also Bubbles and Euphoria; Law, John; Panics and Depressions; South Sea Bubble; Tulip Mania

References

Balen, Malcolm. *The Secret History of the South Sea Bubble*. London: Fourth Estate, 2002.

Beckman, Robert. *Crashes: Why They Happen—What to Do*. Glasgow: Grafton Books, 1988.

Means, H. *Money and Power: The History of Business*. New York: Wiley, 2001.

Mitchell, Charles ("Sunshine Charlie")

Charles Mitchell ("Sunshine Charlie") (1877–1955) was chairman and president of National City (now Citigroup), the largest U.S. bank in the 1920s and the first to reach a billion dollars in deposits. Abuses and speculation at National City during the 1920s contributed to the Crash of 1929. Mitchell was indicted for tax evasion but not convicted.

Mitchell was born in Chelsea, Massachusetts, on October 6, 1877, where his father served as mayor from 1887 to 1988. He graduated from Amherst College and worked initially for Western Electric. Mitchell moved to New York City where he ran his own investment house. He became a vice president at National City in 1916, was elected president in 1921, and chairman in 1929. National City established National City Company as a securities business, one of the first commercial banks to move into securities investments. He was nicknamed "Sunshine Charlie" for his optimistic attitude and encouragement of investors to speculate throughout the 1920s. National City salesmen sold millions of dollars of speculative securities, with most of the money lost in the stock market crashes beginning in 1929. Mitchell remained chairman until 1933. Democratic senator Carter Glass (a former secretary of the Treasury) accused Mitchell of being "more than any 50 men responsible for this stock crash," accused of speculating in his own bank stock, illegal stock transactions, and tax evasion.

The bank's executives routinely borrowed millions of dollars from a "morale loan fund," which did not require repayment. Mitchell and other top executives received a base salary of $25,000 a year and split 20 percent of the annual profits as a bonus. In the late 1920s, this bonus totaled over $1 million a year for Mitchell (he received $3.6 million from 1927 to 1929—an exceptionally large salary for the time). Million-dollar salaries on Wall Street did not have to wait to the 1990s. The Pecora Commission demonstrated that the inflated compensation resulted from unsound banking and investment practices, like the profitable retailing of unstable South American bonds (most of which went bankrupt in the 1930s). Mitchell testified that he sold National City stock at a loss (to his wife) strictly for tax purposes. Mitchell resigned after his testimony and was later indicted by Assistant U.S. Attorney Thomas Dewey for tax evasion, but found not guilty. Mitchell did pay a million-dollar fine to the government in a civil suit. After his resignation from National City, Mitchell founded his own financial consulting firm. He died a wealthy man on December 14, 1955, in New York City.

See also Commercial Banking after the Federal Reserve; Crash of 1929; Great Depression; Morgan, John Pierpont; Pecora Commission

References

Dobson, John. "Crash." In *Bulls, Bears, Boom, and Bust: A Historical Encyclopedia of American Business Concepts*. Santa Barbara, CA: ABC-CLIO, 2006.

Galbraith, Kenneth. *The Great Crash 1929*. Boston: Houghton Mifflin, 1988.

Money Market Funds—Breaking the Buck 2008

A money market fund (MMF) is a mutual fund that invests in low-risk short-term debt securities and pays out the equivalent of short-term interest rates. Typical investments include Treasury bills, commercial paper, and corporate repurchase agreements. The MMF maintains its net asset value (NAV) at $1, with the yield changing over time with the interest it collects. If because of investment losses the value drops below $1, the MMF "broke the buck." Generally, if a MMF sustains losses, the mutual fund company would make up the losses to keep the NAV at $1.

A run on MMFs became part of the subprime meltdown in October 2008. Investors earn a small return, but with a safe principal. The only fear is "breaking the buck," losing principal value. Reserve Primary Fund, one of the oldest MMFs, broke the buck holding Lehman Brothers repurchase agreements. The day after Lehman declared bankruptcy and Reserve's Lehman holding became essentially worthless, the fund announced that the shares would trade at 97¢, not $1, creating within 24 hours a run on Reserve, with investors withdrawing almost $25 billion, and the fund ultimately liquidated. The run spread across the entire MMF category. The Federal Reserve stepped in, lending money to banks to buy commercial paper to support MMFs. It took some $150 billion in federal funds to stop the money market panic.

Once Reserve Primary Fund broke the buck, the financial players did not know what to believe. Bear Stearns and AIG were rescued in 2008, while Lehman was allowed to fail. Fannie May and Freddie Mac were put into conservatorship. The government had no coherent policy. Because they all had similar liquidity and solvency issues, the likely fate of MMFs and other financial institutions was unknown. Confidence in the system vanished and no cash changed hands for new debt. The Federal Reserve poured trillions of dollars into the market and confidence in the system was restored. Investors returned to MMFs and other securities markets, although interest rates since then collapsed almost to zero.

See also Federal Reserve System; Lehman Brothers; Paulson, Hank; Securities and Exchange Commission (SEC); Subprime Meltdown

References

Giroux, Gary. *Earnings Magic and the Unbalance Sheet: The Search for Financial Reality.* Hoboken, NJ: Wiley, 2006.

Lewis, Michael. *Panic: The Story of Modern Financial Insanity.* New York: Norton, 2009.

Sorkin, Andrew. *Too Big to Fail: The Inside Story of How Wall Street and Washington Fought to Save the Financial System from Crisis—and Themselves.* New York: Viking, 2009.

Wessel, David. *In Fed We Trust: Ben Bernanke's War on the Great Panic.* New York: Crown Business, 2009.

Money Trust

The "Money Trust" was the concept that major banks around Wall Street controlled the financial wealth and power to dominate American business. The Pujo Committee of 1913 provided evidence that the money trust, in fact, existed.

The money trust included J. P. Morgan as the most powerful but not the largest member plus National City Bank, First National Bank, Kuhn Loeb, plus Lee, Higginson and Kidder, Peabody of Boston. The Pujo Committee of 1913 (named for

House Committee on Banking and Currency chairman Arsène Pujo) determined that a cabal of bankers developed inordinate power over many industries and abused the public trust. Attorney Samuel Untermyer, committee counsel for the Pujo Hearings, defined the money trust as "an established identity and community of interest between a few leaders of finance, which has been created and is held together through stock-holding, interlocking directorates, and other forms of domination over banks, trust companies, railroads, public service and industrial corporations, and which has resulted in vast and growing concentration and control of money and credits in the hands of a few men."

J. P. Morgan was the dominant player primarily by consolidating industrial competitors into giant trusts or holding companies and perfected interlocking directorships with Morgan partners as directors to maintain control over these consolidations. By 1890, 300 trusts controlled 5,000 companies. Financial practices aided insiders, while relevant information to investors and other outsiders remained problematic and usually hidden. The outsiders by and large had to rely on limited stock exchange requirements and government regulations.

The Panic of 1907 was one of the glaring examples of money trust power and government fecklessness in financial markets. J. P. Morgan with the assistance of the other "members" saved several trust companies (at the time banks could not handle estates and related trust activity, which trust companies did) and a major brokerage house, bailed out New York City, and supported the New York Stock Exchange. Morgan served many of the functions of a central bank, and his actions averted catastrophe on Wall Street. Despite this intervention, the result of the panic was a depression.

As the success of the money trust increased, so did the journalistic and political attacks against Morgan and the other members. Congress did not want to see a repeat of events that left the federal government as a minor player. The Aldrich-Vreeland Act established the National Monetary Commission in 1908 to reform and regulate banking. Senator Nelson Aldrich chaired the commission.

The most famous congressional attack was the Pujo Committee hearings in 1913. The committee demonstrated the trust's immense power by proving that the banks combined the direct control of corporations using interlocking directorships with the banking role protecting the interests of bond and stockholders. As a direct result of these hearings, substantial reform legislation established the Federal Reserve System and the Federal Trade Commission, reducing the influence of the banks. However, they maintained considerable power until the market crash of 1929 and the Great Depression. Over the post–World War II period, banks regained much of their power, including the ability to increase leverage and risk and influence politicians and regulators.

See also Commercial Banking before the Federal Reserve; Commercial Banking after the Federal Reserve; Federal Reserve System; Great Depression; Investment Banking; Morgan, John Pierpont; Panic of 1907; Pujo Committee

References

Bruner, Robert, and Sean Carr. *The Panic of 1907: Lessons Learned from the Market's Perfect Storm*. Hoboken, NJ: Wiley, 2007.

Chernow, R. *The House of Morgan: An American Banking Dynasty and the Rise of Modern Finance*. New York: Atlantic Monthly Press, 1990.

Mitchell, L. *The Speculative Economy: How Finance Triumphed over Industry*. San Francisco: Berrett-Koehler, 2007.

Morris, Charles. *Money, Greed, and Risk: Why Financial Crises and Crashes Happen*. New York: Times Business, 1999.

Monopolies and Other Combinations

A corporation exercises monopoly power when it maintains control of an industry, used mainly to set prices and output levels. England granted monopoly power to various joint stock companies from the seventeenth century, such as the English East India Company and the Bank of England. Many of the American colonies were founded as joint stock companies with a royal charter. A number of American corporations dominated industries in the late nineteenth and early twentieth centuries, often with 80 to 90 percent of output. A number of these, including Standard Oil and American Tobacco, were broken up after antitrust prosecutions.

Emerging big industries in the late nineteenth century (e.g., oil and steel) faced overcapacity and, from their perspective, cutthroat competition. Too many sellers meant prices fell below production costs, especially during economic downturns. Marginal competitors could produce defective products, detrimental to the industry leaders maintaining high quality standards. Emerging leaders sought industry consolidations, either by (1) pooling agreements to regulate prices or limit relative sales levels, or (2) buying out or bankrupting competitors. Each approach had problems, both implementation and legal, especially when operating over large distances and across states. Albert Fink, vice president of the Louisville and Nashville Railroad, developed the first large-scale pool in 1875 (trying to survive the Panic of 1873), the Southern Railway and Steamship Association. The idea was to stabilize freight rates and allocate traffic over competing lines. Pools were viewed as illegal conspiracies of trade, not legally enforceable, and regularly were broken by rogues focusing on short-term advantage. With members cheating on pooling agreements and states suing to disband pools, other alternatives were needed.

In 1882, Standard Oil lawyer Samuel Dodd created the trust. John D. Rockefeller's Standard Oil was the dominant player in oil refining. The trust worked reasonably well for a time, attempting to overcome the legal problems of corporations attempting to operate across state lines. Under Dodd's scheme, stockholders exchanged their shares for trust certificates, and trustees became the directors of all the companies under the trust agreement—in this case, all the corporations under the Standard Oil umbrella. Ohio declared the trust illegal under

Ohio law, but the arrangement worked elsewhere and hundreds of companies combined in a multitude of trust agreements. The antitrust movement specifically targeted this type of agreement. When Standard Oil and others created trusts, many states passed tough antitrust legislation, with Massachusetts the most stringent.

The trust was inefficient to the companies on both regulatory and management grounds. A better answer was new state incorporation laws, led by New Jersey (dubbed "the traitor state" by opponents). Each state had unique incorporation provisions. New Jersey lowered the restrictions as much as possible and continued to change provisions even more favorably as companies lobbied for "improvements." According to Mitchell (2007, 31), "New Jersey presided over the degradation of corporate integrity from 1889 to 1913 ... It is how New Jersey changed the face of American corporate capitalism." Large consolidations—creating monopoly power became legal using the holding company.

In 1830, New Jersey chartered the Camden and Amboy Railroad, permanently exempted the railroad from taxes, and gave the Amboy veto power over other railroad charters. New Jersey's accommodations to corporations were based on fiscal problems, after acquiring huge debts from the Civil War. Other states, looking for additional revenue sources from franchise fees and taxes, liberalized incorporation and other corporate laws, including Delaware and West Virginia. New Jersey passed a corporate franchise tax in 1884, but taxes went unpaid by Amboy. Based on the success in Delaware and West Virginia, in 1889 New Jersey became the most accommodating, including a separate corporate agency (the Corporation Trust Company of New Jersey) to provide the details to make incorporation in New Jersey as simple as possible. By 1900, incorporation increased to about 2,000 and New Jersey paid off its massive debt. Over half of all industry-dominating trusts incorporated in New Jersey—some 170 out of 318 (53.5%) chartered as New Jersey corporations by 1904.

The holding company became the primary legal mechanism for monopoly power at the time. Similar to a trust, the holding company held the stock of the subsidiaries. The 1889 holding company act allowed New Jersey corporations to own stock and bonds in other New Jersey corporations. The 1893 act allowed the corporation to acquire the stock of companies incorporated outside of New Jersey, and the 1896 version allowed corporations to buy corporate shares using their own shares rather than cash. The 1899 law allowed the holding company to exist solely as a finance company strictly to own shares of other corporations. Standard Oil organized as a New Jersey holding company in 1899.

By the 1890s, J. P. Morgan and other investment bankers, seeking the enormous fees involved and financial power, attempted to consolidate all industries they could find. The initial driver was the trust, followed by the new incorporation laws of New Jersey (and other states). Financial statements were seldom issued, and reported earnings (in a period without accounting standards) were viewed skeptically even if disclosed. Investors paid attention to dividends paid, and a typical par value (stated value) of $100 could be maintained only if the appropriate dividend yield was maintained, perhaps 7 percent or $7 given a $100 par value. Critics viewed "overcapitalization" as a major problem. When an investment bank bought out a competitor in the industry to be consolidated, the seller expected a "buyer's premium," that is, cash or securities worth more than the book value of the company. When packaging the new monopoly-based combination, the prices actually paid for all acquisitions plus a substantial banker's commission and other fees would be built into the accounts of the new firm. This overcapitalization represented one definition of "watered stock."

The banker viewed overcapitalization as "monopoly returns" based on operation efficiencies (economies of scales) and monopoly pricing as competitors were gobbled up. Of course, investors expected dividends based on the new par value (assets would be written up to "fair value" and "goodwill" recorded to match the new par value). Thus, if $500,000 was the new par value (even though actual book value of the acquired companies might be $250,000), a 7 percent annual dividend rate would now be $35,000 instead of the $17,500 expected under the old book value. Dividends depend on cash either from earnings or paid out of equity. If the company did not maintain the expected dividend rate, down went the stock price.

The banker could issue the new stock in an initial public offering, expecting the new par value or higher. A study by the U.S. Industrial Commission early in the twentieth century discovered that the combined values of stocks and bonds totaled over $3 billion, but the net tangible assets were only $1.5 billion based on about 200 business combinations—100 percent overcapitalization, proof of massive fraud according to the critics. Today, corporate value is primarily determined by earnings power rather than book value, but this view was considered as corrupt at the time.

Muckraking journalists and injured parties including farmers and laborers lobbied for government regulation and reform. Because the most blatant monopoly practices were across states (interstate commerce), state regulations were not very effective against big business. The first effective federal regulation created the Interstate Commerce Commission to regulate railroads in 1887—it was decades later before really effective regulations passed, included rate setting and accounting requirements for the railroads.

Government then focused on antitrust agendas. The Sherman Antitrust Act of 1890 outlawed price conspiracies and monopolies, but achieved modest success in court cases and had relatively little impact on the overall monopoly movement. Substantial changes in regulation had to wait for the Woodrow Wilson administration, with the passage of the Clayton Act and the creation of both the Federal Trade Commission and Federal Reserve in 1914. Federal antitrust regulations remained and were periodically enforced with vigor, but big business was firmly established.

See also Corporations; Interstate Commerce Commission; Morgan, John Pierpont; Railroads, Nineteenth Century; Rockefeller, John Davison; Sherman Act; Standard Oil

References

Dobson, John. "Monopoly." In *Bulls, Bears, Boom, and Bust: A Historical Encyclopedia of American Business Concepts*. Santa Barbara, CA: ABC-CLIO, 2006.

Josephson, Matthew. *The Robber Barons*. New York: Harcourt, 1962.

Mitchell, Lawrence. *The Speculative Economy: How Finance Triumphed over Industry*. San Francisco: Berrett-Koehler, 2007.

Morgan, John Pierpont

John Pierpont Morgan (known as "Pierpont," 1837–1913) was born into the family banking business and set up a private bank in New York City in 1870. Morgan became an important railroad financier, a director of over 20 railroads, and a leader in the reorganization of failing businesses after the Panic of 1873. Reorganizations and combinations became a Morgan specialty ("Morganization"), and his bank created many of the largest commercial organizations of the time, including United States Steel in 1901. As the most powerful Wall Street banker, he was the nominal head of the "Money Trust" and subject to investigation by the congressional Pujo Committee in 1913.

Morgan got his start after his father, Junius Morgan, was hired by Baltimore merchant George Peabody. Peabody was a London merchant banker, specializing in dealing American state bonds and other U.S. securities. He hired Boston banker Junius Morgan and made him a junior partner in 1854. Morgan eventually took over control of Peabody. Junius's son, J. P. Morgan, was born on April 17, 1837, in Hartford, Connecticut. Morgan was educated in Europe and apprenticed on Wall Street, learning about the esoteric world of investment banking and the importance of accounting. He set up his own private bank in 1861, then partnered with important Philadelphia banker Anthony Drexel in 1871. The Morgan empire of father and son established partnerships in the financial capitals of London, New York, and Paris. The New York firm would become J. P. Morgan upon the death of Drexel in 1893.

During the Civil War, Morgan paid for a military stand-in when drafted,

American financier and banker John Pierpont Morgan was one of the richest men in the United States and a dominant figure in the U.S. economy during the late nineteenth and early twentieth centuries. Morgan led the consolidation movement of American business, culminating in the creation of United States Steel as the first billion dollar corporation. (Library of Congress)

then participated in a war-profiteering scam, financing a deal to resell rifles purchased from a New York armory and resold to John Fremont's army in Missouri. His later episodes of "saving" the financial world from disaster appear less unethical, but he made a profit on all of them.

Much of Morgan's early financial success and prestige came from financing and refinancing railroads, aided by Junius's banking connections with European investors. Early in his career, Morgan witnessed the raiding of the Erie and the Gould/ Fisk attempt at cornering the gold market in 1869. He fought Jay Gould over the small Albany and Susquehanna Railroad, which Gould tried to acquire as part of the Erie Railroad in 1870. Gould bought stock and had Judge George Barnard oust railroad founder Joseph Ramsey. Morgan got his own judge to oust the Erie forces and then merged the railroad with the Delaware and Hudson. Morgan became a member of the board of directors of the Albany and Susquehanna, his first directorship. Morgan consistently insisted on becoming a director (or having another Morgan partner on the board), the concept of "relationship banking" in order to protect the interests of the debt holders. Morgan partners eventually had board seats on more than 100 companies.

In 1879, Morgan assisted William Vanderbilt (son of Cornelius) in selling the majority of his shares in the New York Central in 1879, some 250,000 shares. Morgan's task was to sell the stock without the stock price collapsing. He sold a large block of 50,000 shares in Europe and other large blocks to major domestic buyers (surprisingly including Jay Gould). Morgan sold all the shares without the broad market finding out. His reward was a $3 million commission and a growing reputation as a railroad banker. This is the role of investment banking: aiding the customer and simultaneously enriching the bank.

The opportunities for railroad financing late in the nineteenth century mainly centered on reorganizing failing roads. Interest and dividend payments used up most cash; infrastructure maintenance and expansion had to be financed with borrowed money. Rate wars, rebates to large shippers, overbuilding using too much debt, and insider pilfering resulted in railroad failures and recurring panics. Morgan felt responsible for the securities he sold and attempted to maintain competent operations. Some railroads, notably the Pennsylvania, were renowned for professional management, while Morgan's railroads focused on conservative financing and operations.

The Panic of 1893 brought particular chaos to the markets, including the failure of hundreds of banks, thousands of commercial firms, and about a third of all railroads. About 60 percent of New York Stock Exchange issues were railroads. Morgan reorganized the Erie, Santa Fe, Northern Pacific, and New York Central. The railroads were downsized with easier credit terms and Morgan usually took control of the board. He also used voting trusts—stockholders traded their shares for trust certificates and a lien on the railroad's land and mineral holdings. By the end of the century, most railroads were consolidated into six giant systems using voting trusts.

In the latter part of the nineteenth century, manufacturing expanded, but faced antiquated state laws and considerable competition. Companies used pools and cartels to reduce competition with limited success. The trust pioneered at Standard Oil was the most successful combination technique. Later, liberal new incorporation laws in New Jersey became a better solution for owning corporations across states. Holding companies made it possible to own virtually entire industries. Morgan and other investment banks used these techniques to consolidate hundreds of companies into dozens of trusts and holding companies. Based on railroad experience, Morgan opposed competition and felt an obligation to his buyers. He sought competent management and financial disclosure in the form of annual reports. Based on his railroad experience, he focused on conservative operations and financing.

Morgan used multiple combination techniques to create industry giants. Morgan supplied the capital for Edison Electric Illuminating Company, and his mansion became the first private residence in New York with electricity, supplied by Edison in 1878, and his office the first on Wall Street. The consolidation of Edison Electric and competitor Thomson-Houston produced General Electric (GE) in 1892. The company failed during the Panic of 1893 and Morgan restructured GE. Other "Morganized" firms include American Telephone and Telegraph, International Harvester, Western Union, Westinghouse, and United States Steel. All were basically horizontal mergers, combining direct competitors. Generally, these industrial giants found that vertical integration both forward into distribution and sales and backward into suppliers were needed to compete successfully.

Morgan was nominal head of the Money Trust, which was the major force in creating some 300 trusts by 1890. Opposing the rising monopolies was the Sherman Antitrust Act of 1890, designed to eliminate monopolies and price conspiracies.

Morgan's name would become linked to Scotsman Andrew Carnegie, when Carnegie became the richest man when he sold out to Morgan. Carnegie immigrated to the United States as a boy and progressed up the business ladder, becoming a railroad executive in his early 20s. He made a small fortune as a speculator and investor, eventually focusing on iron and steel shortly after the Civil War. By the late 1880s, Carnegie Steel became the largest producer of coke, pig iron, and steel rails. Important Carnegie innovations included particularly efficient mass production of steel rails, as well as the use of vertical integration, from ore and coal mines to finished products.

The culmination of Morgan power was the formation of United States Steel in 1901. After consolidating much of Carnegie's competition, he famously bought out the 66-year-old Carnegie's empire for the princely sum of $492 million, certainly the biggest buyout until well into the twentieth century—making Carnegie the world's richest man with his $300 million share. With Carnegie Steel and over 200 other related companies, United States Steel controlled over 80 percent of steel capacity, and Morgan capitalized the firm for $1.4 billion—the first billion-dollar corporation and, by far, the largest company in the world (Rockefeller's Standard Oil became a distant second).

As both a major commercial and investment bank, J. P. Morgan & Co. had the power to serve some of the chief function of a central bank, in part because of the financial weakness of the federal government. Morgan bailed out part of the financial community during the Panic of 1893 and again during the Panic of 1907, limiting the damage to Wall Street. The United States was on the gold standard, and gold could quickly leave New York for Europe when panic occurred. Morgan's international banking connections could reverse this flow of gold.

The Treasury Department attempted to maintain $100 million in gold. The country ran a trade surplus, while the federal government had budget surpluses, keeping gold coming to the United States. The Panic of 1893 produced substantial business failures and falling markets. Foreign sales of U.S. securities dropped the Treasury supply of gold to $9 million. In desperation, President Grover Cleveland turned to Morgan. Morgan, with the help of other banks, responded by raising $100 million in gold from Europe using Treasury gold bonds, which sold quickly at a premium. The Treasury beefed up its reserves to $107.5 million, financial collapse was avoided, and Morgan pocketed a huge commission. A depression, however, was not avoided.

The Panic of 1907 was a more complex story, with a stock market crash, widespread speculation and manipulation, a failed corner (buying all available shares) and broker bankruptcy, bank runs, and the near insolvency of New York City. Morgan saved several trusts and a major brokerage house, bailed out New York City, and supported the New York Stock Exchange. The immediate cause was the Otto Heinze scheme to corner United Copper, which failed, and Heinze's brokerage went into bankruptcy; a general panic caused stock prices to collapse. The Knickerbocker Trust Company collapsed under a full bank run with customers lined up to withdraw their funds. The 70-year-old and semiretired Morgan sent a team to audit the books of Knickerbocker, determining the trust insolvent and allowed it to fail. The panic continued, and Morgan agreed to save the vulnerable Trust Company of America, famously stating "This is the place to stop the trouble." New problems crept up. Morgan had to work out a deal for United States Steel to buy Tennessee Coal, requiring the federal government to allow this merger. As New York City appeared insolvent and needing an emergency loan, Morgan contracted for a $30 million bond issue. Although collapse was averted, dozens of banks, trusts, and other corporations failed and a serious depression followed.

Morgan was praised on Wall Street, but Congress wanted a stronger federal government and a weaker Wall Street, preferably without the Money Trust. The National Monetary Commission was created in 1908 to reform and regulate banking. The commission led to the Pujo Hearings of 1913, which demonstrated the Money Trust's immense power by proving that the banks combined the direct control of corporations using interlocking directorships. As a direct result of these hearings, substantial reform legislation established the Federal Reserve System and the Federal Trade Commission.

Forced to testify during the Pujo Hearings, Morgan's performance was admired by the banking community, but shocked the public. He would not live to see the creation of the Federal Reserve. He died on March 31, 1913, in Rome.

See also Andrew Carnegie; J. P. Morgan Chase; Money Trust; Morgan Stanley; Panic of 1893; Panic of 1907; Pujo Hearings; Sherman Antitrust Act of 1890

References

Chernow, Ron. *The House of Morgan: An American Banking Dynasty and the Rise of Modern Finance*. New York: Atlantic Monthly Press, 1990.

Dobson, John. "Morgan, John Pierpont (J.P.)." In *Bulls, Bears, Boom, and Bust: A Historical Encyclopedia of American Business Concepts*. Santa Barbara, CA: ABC-CLIO, 2006.

Josephson, Matthew. *The Robber Barons*. New York: Harcourt, 1962.

Morgan Stanley

Morgan Stanley is a global financial services corporation with headquarters in New York City and a longtime "Big Five" investment bank. J. P. Morgan was the dominant banker around the turn of the twentieth century and nominal head of the "Money Trust." During the Great Depression, Congress passed the Glass-Steagall Act requiring the separation of commercial and investment banks. J. P. Morgan partners Henry Morgan and Harold Stanley separated from J. P. Morgan to form Morgan Stanley in 1935 and continued to serve the financial needs of major corporations.

Prior to World War II, Morgan Stanley was a major underwriter of United States Steel and railroad securities. In the post–World War II period, the bank managed securities issued for General Motors, IBM, and AT&T. Using innovative financial analysis computer models, Morgan Stanley established the field of professional financial analysis. The company established offices in London, Paris, and Tokyo, followed by Frankfurt, Hong Kong, Melbourne, Milan, Sydney, and Zurich.

Morgan Stanley was the first blue-chip investment bank to go into the hostile-takeover business. The bear market started in stocks about 1966, and rising inflation and interest made takeover targets seem relatively cheap by the early 1970s. Morgan Stanley's first takeover attempt involved International Nickel's (Inco) 1974 raid on Philadelphia battery maker Electric Storage Battery (ESB), maker of Ray-O-Vac and Duracell batteries, with an offer price of $27 a share. ESB resisted, assisted by Goldman Sachs, and found a white knight in United Aircraft (now United Technologies). United started a bidding war, with Inco winning the battle by increasing the bid to $41 a share. Unfortunately, ESB faced stiff competition in the battery business and soon was placed on the auction block. This was not a problem for the investment banks, which made big money on both transactions.

After Morgan Stanley, Merrill Lynch, Drexel Burnham, and First Boston jumped in to promote the aggressors. Over the decades of the 1970s and 1980s, hostile takeovers became bigger and more common and this became a major profit center for the banks. When Ronald Reagan became president in 1981, it was obvious that the government would seldom be interested in antitrust, and acquisitions expanded even more. The small mergers and acquisition (M&A) shops became major profit centers.

Morgan Stanley, a partnership since its original founding, went public in 1986, relatively early for a wholesale investment bank (Goldman Sachs by comparison did not go public until 1999). Because the bank was using "other people's money," it could take on more risks and increase the focus on short-term profitability to maximize executive compensation. In 1996, Morgan Stanley expanded its business by acquiring retail broker Dean Witter Reynolds from Sears. Underwriting included Apple, Netscape, Cisco, Compaq, and Google. In 2009, Morgan Stanley acquired Smith Barney.

The high-tech success in the 1990s meant investors wanted any company with Internet connections. A contributor to the tech frenzy was the small number of new Internet and other tech initial public offerings (IPOs). Well-known Internet analysts like Mary Meeker at Morgan Stanley recommended buy for almost all of them. Meeker and other analysts (especially Jack Grubman of Salomon Smith Barney and Henry Blodget of Merrill Lynch) became stars of the New Economy in the 1990s. Meeker, considered a leader of the tech craze, helped bring Netscape public in 1995 (Netscape jumped over 100% from its initial price on day one). The strategy focused on keeping the issuing companies happy, mainly by serving as cheerleaders to investors and the rest of the investment world. The banks also had other means to entice executives for their business. After the tech sector collapsed in 2000, the stars were suddenly among the worst stock pickers on Wall Street.

After the tech collapse early in the twenty-first century, the Securities and Exchange Commission (SEC), National Association of Securities Dealers (NASD), and New York Stock Exchange (NYSE) investigated and Congress held hearings. New York attorney general Eliot Spitzer and the banks involved reached a "global settlement" in 2002, with the banks paying combined fines of $1.4 billion while agreeing to reinstall the "Chinese Wall" and stop the conflicted research. Various class action suits by burned investors led to more payouts. In 2005, the NYSE fined Morgan Stanley $19 million for regulatory and other issues.

Morgan Stanley had early involvement in the mortgage market and invented the American Mortgage Investment Trust (AMIT) in 1992, generating substantial profit for Morgan and a derivative instrument complex enough that investors generally did not understand the underlying risk (see Partnoy 1997, 213–31, for a more thorough analysis). Principal could be separated (analogous to zero coupon bonds) from interest payments, paying a big rate. AMIT "trust units" generated sizable benefits, such as the ability to sell parts of the package at a substantial gain. The early profit turned into sizable long-term risk.

The total mortgage-related market approached $9 trillion by the end of 2008 (down slightly from the previous year). The mortgage and real estate markets collapsed, generating huge losses by investment banks. Morgan Stanley was an active player in subprime mortgages, but not the biggest. As of mid-2008, Morgan Stanley wrote down $13.1 billion, much less than the $38.3 billion of UBS or $24.1 billion of Merrill Lynch. Bear Stearns was forcibly bought out by J. P. Morgan, and Merrill Lynch by Bank of America, and Lehman Brothers declared bankruptcy in 2008.

The two remaining big investment banks, Goldman Sachs and Morgan Stanley, converted to bank holding companies, with access to the Federal Reserve's crisis cash. Mitsubishi's financial group invested some $9 billion in Morgan, while Goldman received $5 billion from Warren Buffett's Berkshire Hathaway. Congress established the Troubled Asset Relief Program (TARP) giving some $700 billion to Treasury. In October 2008, $25 billion went to each Citigroup and Bank of America; Morgan Stanley received $10 billion.

Morgan Stanley has three major business units. Institutional securities includes investment banking and related services for corporations and other large institutions, including new securities, mergers and acquisitions, restructuring, and so on. Global wealth management includes brokerage and investment advisory services. Asset management includes equity, fixed income, private equity, and alternative investments to institutions (including pensions, nonprofits, foundations, insurance companies and banks) and retail clients. In 2012, Morgan had total assets over $800 billion and a market value near $30 billion.

See also American Insurance Group (AIG); Bear Stearns; Goldman Sachs; Investment Banks; May Day (1975); Merrill Lynch; Morgan, John Pierpont; Paulson, Hank; Securities and Exchange Commission (SEC); Structured Finance; Subprime Meltdown

References

Chernow, Ron. *The House of Morgan: An American Banking Dynasty and the Rise of Modern Finance.* New York: Atlantic Monthly Press, 1990.

Gordon, John Steele. *The Great Game: The Emergence of Wall Street as a World Power, 1653–2000.* New York: Scribner, 1999.

Lowenstein, Roger. *The End of Wall Street.* New York: Penguin Press, 2010.

McLean, Bethany, and Joe Nocera. *All the Devils Are Here: The Hidden History of the Financial Crisis.* New York: Portfolio/Penguin, 2010.

Partnoy, Frank. *FIASCO: Blood in the Water on Wall Street.* New York: Norton, 1997

Morris, Robert

Robert Morris (1734–1806) was an American merchant and financier, and a signer of the Declaration of Independence, Articles of Confederation, and Constitution. He served as superintendent of finance during the turbulent times at the end of the American Revolution (1781–84) and established the Bank of North America (BNA), the first U.S. bank, in 1781. Morris was one of the original U.S. senators from Pennsylvania, serving from 1789 to 1795. Unfortunately, unwise speculation led to debtors' prison toward the end of the eighteenth century.

Morris was born in Liverpool, England, on January 20, 1734. He came to the United States in 1747 when his father became a tobacco agent in Maryland. Morris made a fortune as a Philadelphia merchant. During the Revolution, he loaned £10,000 to keep Washington's army in the field before the battles of Trenton and Princeton in 1776–77 and also funded privateers seizing cargoes from English ships. He served in the Continental Congress on several important committees.

Although he abstained from voting for independence, he signed the Declaration of Independence in August 1776.

In 1781, the Continental Congress was essentially broke and unable to pay war funding, when it appointed Morris the superintendent of finance. Morris proposed a national bank, which became the BNA, chartered by the Continental Congress in 1781 and opened in 1782. Morris's BNA functioned somewhat like a central bank. The bank accepted deposits, loaned money to merchants, and issued notes convertible into gold. Unlike continental currency, BNA notes traded at par (face) value. The bank loaned money to the government when needed. As superintendent of finance, Morris issued certificates rather than continental currency, eventually paying interest on these notes. He also issued "Morris notes" to finance government operations, guaranteed by him as both a banker and superintendent. In place of cash, he issued interest-bearing certificates to the soldiers and promised pensions to the officers. Unable to pass a federal tax to fund the war (Rhode Island voted against it), he resigned. The country under the Continental Congress staggered on in depression.

After Washington was elected president under the new constitution in 1788, he asked Morris to be secretary of the Treasury. Morris turned it down, suggesting Alexander Hamilton instead. Rather than Treasury secretary, he became a senator from Pennsylvania. Morris founded several companies (including canals and iron mills), but also was involved in several failed land speculations. He became the largest landowner in the United States, but could not pay his creditors, who forced him to debtors' prison in 1798. The Bankruptcy Act of 1800 was passed in part to get Morris out of jail, which happened in 1801.

See also Bank of North America; Bank of the United States, First; Commercial Banking before the Federal Reserve; Hamilton, Alexander; Land Speculators; Profiteering during the American Revolution

References

Dos Passos, John. "Robert Morris and the 'Art Magick' " *Great Stories of American Businessmen, from American Heritage.* New York: American Heritage, 1972.

Ferguson, E. James. *The American Revolution: A General History, 1763–1790.* Homewood, IL: Dorsey Press, 1971.

Vile, John. "Morris, Robert." In *The Constitutional Convention of 1787: A Comprehensive Encyclopedia of America's Founding.* Santa Barbara, CA: ABC-CLIO, 2005.

Mortgage-Backed Security (MBS)

A mortgage is a loan agreement with real property serving as collateral. A mortgaged-back security (MBS) is a securitized debt instrument backed by mortgages. These can be either residential real estate packages (RMBSs) or commercial real estate packages (CMBSs). The structured finance process of securitization uses the bundling of financial assets (including mortgages) to create asset pools to resell to credit investors. A bank can originate mortgages or buy mortgages from other banks or mortgage companies, which are pooled into the MBS. The bank generally turns to the bond-rating companies to get the MBS credit rated by risk slices, called tranches. The least risky tranches (least likely to default) will usually be rated AAA. The cash collected from debtors for interest and principal are paid to investors periodically. The use of MBSs became a major factor in the housing bubble and then the subprime meltdown of 2008.

The Department of Housing and Urban Development (HUD) developed the first MBSs in 1970 (these were sold by the Government National Mortgage Association, Ginnie Mae, a government-sponsored enterprise or GSE established in 1968 to promote home ownership). Banks began securitizing debt by the 1980s, and investment bank Salomon Brothers created the first private MBSs. Manipulative accounting treatment allowed savings and loans to sell mortgages, and Salomon as a real estate specialist took advantage of this to buy mortgages at favorable rates and securitize them at a substantial profit. Once MBSs received investment-grade ratings, global investors were easily found.

Bond-rating agencies Moody's, Standard & Poor's, and Fitch turned rating tranches of securitized debt into major profit centers. With only a few major banks issuing MBSs, accommodating the banks was necessary to retain this profitable business; otherwise the banks would move all the business to a competitor—an obvious conflict of interests existed. The ratings included substantial AAA rating even on subprime mortgages subject to predatory lending practices. Once housing prices started down in 2006, the rating agencies downgraded massive amounts of investment-rated MBSs and the MBS market collapsed.

Banks securitized transactions recorded as special-purpose entities (SPEs—that is, separate trusts or other legal entities and not recorded on the books of the banks). Citigroup had almost $2.2 trillion in SPEs. More than half were in MBSs and collateralized debt obligations (CDOs, $1.3 trillion), compared to total assets of $1.9 trillion and total equity of only $120 billion. Not only were these toxic assets to the banks, but they were hidden from view. It would take a multitrillions federal rescue to save the major banks from failure.

See also Bond Ratings on Structured Finance; Collateralized Debt Obligation (CDO); Credit Risk; Fannie Mae and Freddie Mac; Federal Reserve System; Investment Banks; Risk and Risk Management; Structured Finance; Subprime Meltdown

References

Allen, Larry. "Credit Ratings." In *The Encyclopedia of Money*. 2nd ed. Santa Barbara, CA: ABC-CLIO, 2009.

Coval, Joshua, Jakub Jurek, and Erik Stafford. "The Economics of Structured Finance." Harvard Business School Working Paper 09-060. 2008.

Jobst, Andreas. "A Primer on Structured Finance." *Journal of Derivatives and Hedge Funds* 13, no. 3 (2007): 199–213.

McLean, Bethany, and Joe Nocera. *All the Devils Are Here: The Hidden History of the Financial Crisis*. New York: Portfolio/Penguin, 2010.

Mozilo, Angelo R.

Angelo Mozilo (1938–) was cofounder, chairman, and chief executive officer (CEO) of Countrywide Financial, the largest mortgage finance company in the United States before the subprime mortgage collapse in 2008, originating 20 percent of all mortgages in the United States by 2006. The company avoided failure by being acquired by Bank of America (B of A) early in 2008 for $4 billion. Several states sued Countrywide for deceptive practices, and Mozilo faced charges of insider trading and securities fraud in mid-2009. Mozilo sold some $129 million in stock while Countrywide bought its own shares (propping up the stock price). The political part of the story, "friends of Angelo," were special mortgage rates to powerful politicians, including Senators Chris Dodd, Barbara Boxer, and Kent Conrad. Conde Nast *Portfolio* named Mozilo the second-worst CEO in American history.

Mozilo was born in New York City and graduated from Fordham University in 1960. He and David Loeb founded Countrywide in 1969. Loeb was president and chairman until 2000 (Loeb died in 2003), when Mozilo became CEO and chairman. Loeb was the strategic thinker, while Mozilo was the salesman. Loeb was more risk averse and conservative, while Mozilo focused on market share and becoming the biggest mortgage lender. When Mozilo took over, Countrywide became more aggressive. By 2004, Countrywide was in fact the largest mortgage lender, originating some 200,000 mortgages a month. Unfortunately, the company practiced typical predatory practices of the industry, including leading borrowers into high-cost products after claiming they would get "the best loan possible."

Subprime loans were particularly profitable, with high interest rates and various penalties for both prepayments and late payments. Over the years, less attention was paid to proper documentation and due diligence. Internal auditors found a large percentage of loans failing the company's quality control requirements. Because the mortgages that Countrywide originated were sold to Fannie, Freddie, or investment banks, they had little concern for delinquencies or defaults. Countrywide was charged lower fees by Fannie Mae, based on the substantial volume of mortgages sold to Fannie. Countrywide became the biggest seller of mortgages to Fannie, some 26 percent of loans in 2004.

Countrywide Financial led the way with automated loan approvals in 2004. Appropriate reviews and documentation for mortgages seemed to fall by the wayside. Countrywide also came up with the "103 percent loan," to fund the entire mortgage plus closing costs—the basic strategy being to underwrite mortgages quickly (including automating the process) and sell mortgage portfolios to banks. The majority of subprime loans had a loan-to-value ratio over 100 percent. About half the loans from 2004 were adjustable-rate mortgages with a low teaser rate but rising substantially in the future. Most of these were nonconforming mortgages, not meeting the standards of Fannie. Fortunately, investment banks bought these particularly toxic mortgages.

Countrywide expanded its lobbying activities under Mozilo, spending more than $1 million annually from 2003. The company also hired relatives of politicians and others and focused on people with political connections to sit on the board of directors. The VIP Program (Friends of Angelo sweetheart loans) started in 1998. In addition to politicians, the chairman of Fannie at the time, James Johnson, received six "sweetheart loans" totaling more than $10 million from Countrywide.

Like much of the financial community, Countrywide borrowed on the low-cost overnight market often using repurchase agreements. This became a problem as the housing market started collapsing in 2007. Mortgages in its portfolio fell in value and were increasingly difficult to resell. With rising anxiety around the entire mortgage market, continued borrowing in the overnight market became harder—in part because Countrywide's collateral became more difficult to value. The company was forced to draw down its multibillion lines of credit from banks and sell a stake in the company to B of A. B of A acquired Countrywide for $4 billion in January 2008—before the collapse of Bear Stearns. Countrywide had a market value of $24 billion the previous year. The deal closed in July 2008.

Countrywide became Bank of America Home Loans. Investigations by the Securities and Exchange Commission (SEC) and Justice Department became B of A's problem. The SEC charged Mozilo and other executives with insider trading and securities fraud. Mozilo settled, agreeing to pay $67.5 million in fines, most of which was covered by B of A and insurance.

See also American Insurance Group (AIG); Countrywide Financial; Credit Default Swaps; Fannie Mae and Freddie Mac; Federal Reserve System; Goldman Sachs; Lehman Brothers; Paulson, Hank; Structured Finance; Subprime Meltdown

References

Lowenstein, Roger. *The End of Wall Street*. New York: Penguin Press, 2010.

Morgenson, Gretchen and Joshua Rosner. *Reckless Endangerment: How Outsized Ambition, Greed, and Corruption Led to Economic Armageddon*. New York: Times Books, 2011.

Wessel, David. *In Fed We Trust: Ben Bernanke's War on the Great Panic*. New York: Crown Business, 2009.

Munn v. Illinois

Munn v. Illinois (1877) was a Supreme Court case establishing that states had the right to regulate business for the public good. Munn was a grain elevator operator with monopoly power to set outrageous prices among other corrupt practices.

Illinois passed legislation to regulate and set grain-warehousing prices, which Munn challenged in court. The Supreme Court, based on the "public interest" argument, upheld the state law, the start of relatively successful regulations of business by both state and federal governments.

The Illinois legislature responded to the National Grange movement, an association of farmers, in 1871 with legislation setting maximum rates that grain warehouses could charge for storing agricultural products. Munn and Scott was a Chicago grain warehouse found guilty of violating the law. Munn and Scott appealed, claiming the Illinois law was unconstitutional under the Fourteenth Amendment, by depriving them of property without due process. The Supreme Court favored the state of Illinois. Because grain storage elevators were available for public use, they could be regulated by the state. Later court decisions were less favorable and limited the state's power to regulate business.

See also Federal Trade Commission; Interstate Commerce Commission; Railroads, Nineteenth Century; Regulation of Business; Regulations and Regulatory Failures; Sherman Antitrust Act of 1890

References

Gordon, John Steele. *The Great Game: The Emergence of Wall Street as a World Power, 1653–2000.* New York: Scribner, 1999.

Mitchell, L. *The Speculation Economy: How Finance Triumphed over Industry.* San Francisco: Berrett-Koehler, 2007.

Viscusi, W., J. Vernon, and J. Harrington. *Economics of Regulation and Antitrust.* 2nd ed. Cambridge, MA: MIT Press, 1995.

Mutual Funds Scandals (2003)

Mutual funds are subject to limited Securities and Exchange Commission (SEC) regulations and oversight; historically, mutual funds have a clean regulatory record. However, that changed early in the twenty-first century, and investigations uncovered abusive practices favoring certain large clients, mainly associated with late trading and market timing.

Beginning in 2003, New York attorney general Eliot Spitzer, tipped off by a whistle-blower, investigated various abuses by mutual fund companies. Several mutual funds were accused mainly of late trading and market timing. Late trading takes advantage of the way mutual fund prices are set at the end of market trading at 4 p.m. Any orders received after 4 p.m. are executed following the next business day. Some mutual funds executed these late orders for "selected customers." The problem is that only these customers had complete information on the actual closing price, giving them an unfair advantage. To make the trades appear legal, they were booked as if the trades were received before market closing.

Market timing is an investment strategy that attempts to gain from short-term market fluctuations by moving in and out of market sectors quickly as prices change. These market traders were allowed to trade more often than allowed by the funds requirements. These trades increased the administrative cost of the mutual fund.

Following Spitzer, the SEC conducted a separate investigation and found the additional violation called "front-running," a type of insider trading. The mutual fund notified select customers, or in some cases employees, that the fund would be buying or selling specific stocks. Because mutual funds hold large positions, their block trading causes real price movements in most securities. The customer then bought or sold ahead of the mutual fund. With few exceptions, the culprits settled with Spitzer and the SEC by 2005, mainly paying relatively nominal fines, while not admitting guilt. In April 2003, every major investment bank (including Merrill Lynch, Citigroup, Lehman Brothers, Goldman Sachs, and Morgan Stanley) was fined a combined $1.4 billion by the SEC for defrauding investors—the biggest of the fraud cases.

See also Goldman Sachs; Lehman Brothers; Market Manipulation; Merrill Lynch; Morgan Stanley; Securities and Exchange Commission (SEC)

References

Giroux, Gary. *Earnings Magic and the Unbalance Sheet: The Search for Financial Reality.* Hoboken, NJ: Wiley, 2006.

Lewis, Michael. *Panic: The Story of Modern Financial Insanity.* New York: Norton, 2009.

N

NASDAQ

NASDAQ (National Association of Security Dealers Automated Quotations) is an American stock exchange, essentially replacing the over-the-counter (OTC) trading system. It is the largest electronic screen-based stock trading market in the United States, with the largest trading volume in the world. NASDAQ was created in 1971 by the National Association of Securities Dealers (NASD) and became the first electronic stock market. Basically, it replaced the OTC trading system. NASDAQ launched on February 8, 1971, with the composite index starting at 100. It currently trades almost 3,000 listed companies. Listed companies are registered with the Securities and Exchange Commission, have three or more market makers (serving as broker/dealers), and meet specific NASDAQ requirements for assets, capital, and other characteristics.

The NASDAQ 100 tracks 100 of the largest nonfinancial companies listed on the exchange. These include Amgen, Apple, Cisco, Dell, eBay, Google, Netflix, Starbucks, Whole Foods, and Yahoo. NASDAQ hit 1,000 in the summer of 1995 and continued up, 1999 being NASDAQ's stellar year, rising from 2,208 to 4,069. Starting at 2,810 in 1990, the Dow Jones Industrial Average (Dow) hit 5,000 by the end of 1995 and 10,000 by mid-March 1999. At the end of the millennium, the Dow stood at 11,497, near the peak of the tech bubble. However, the Dow represented mainly the large stogy stock of the "old economy." The hot tech market meant NASDAQ. The NASDAQ hit 5,000 in March of 2000 and reached its all time high of 5,049 on March 10, the peak of the tech bubble. After the peak, the NASDAQ composite quickly collapsed. By October 2002, the index dropped to 1,114, down almost 80 percent. Since then it recovered a bit more than half its 2000 high.

See also Blodget, Henry; Greenspan, Alan; Grubman, Jack; Madoff, Bernard L.; Mutual Funds Scandals (2003); New York Stock Exchange; Tech Bubble

References

Gasparino, Charles. *Blood on the Street: The Sensational Inside Story of How Wall Street Analysts Duped a Generations of Investors*. New York: Free Press, 2005.

Lewis, Michael. *Panic: The Story of Modern Financial Insanity*. New York: Norton, 2009.

Mahar, Maggie., *Bull: A History of the Boom and Bust, 1982–2003*. Harper Business, 2004.

NASDAQ. http://www.nasdaq.com.

National Bureau of Economic Research

The National Bureau of Economic Research (NBER) is best known for determining the periods of the business cycle. The NBER is a nonprofit economic research organization founded in 1920, with economist Wesley Mitchell as first staff economist. The main office is in Cambridge, Massachusetts.

The business cycle measures the ups and downs of economic activity, described in phases beginning with expansion, followed by crisis, recession, and recovery. The popular definition of a recession is two or more consecutive quarters of negative growth in gross domestic product (GDP). The maximum GDP before the decline is the peak of the business cycle; this is the start of a recession (or depression). The low point is the trough. The period from peak to trough is the length and time period of the recession.

The NBER definition of a recession is "a significant decline in economic activity spread across the economy, lasting more than a few months, normally visible in real GDP, real income, employment, industrial production, and wholesale-retail sales." The NBER has a contract with the Department of Commerce to determine business cycle dates (usually corresponding to peaks and troughs in real GDP).

According to the NBER website:

> Over the years the NBER's research agenda has encompassed a wide variety of issues that confront our society. Early research focused on the aggregate economy, examining in detail the business cycle and long-term economic growth. Simon Kuznets' pioneering work on national income accounting, Wesley Mitchell's influential study of the business cycle, and Milton Friedman's research on the demand for money and the determinants of consumer spending were among the early studies done at the NBER.

Around 20 members of the NBER over the years have been Nobel Prize winners, including Joseph Stiglitz, George Akerlof, Myron Scholes, Milton Friedman, Paul Krugman, Myron Scholes, Simon Kuznets, and Wassily Leontief.

In September 2010, the NBER announced that the Great Recession lasted from December 2007 to June 2009, becoming the longest since World War II, 18 months, with the largest drop in GDP, 4.1 percent. The bureau has analyzed business cycles starting with the 18-month recession beginning in December 1854, a total 33 cycles in 155 years (11 since World War II).

See also Business Cycles; Crash of 1929; Great Depression; Panic of 1819; Panic of 1837; Panic of 1857; Panic of 1873; Panic of 1893; Panic of 1907; Panics and Depressions

References

Kindleberger, Charles, and R. Alibe. *Manias, Panics, and Crashes: A History of Financial Crises*. 5th ed. Hoboken, NJ: Wiley, 2005.

Knoop, Todd. *Recessions and Depressions: Understanding Business Cycles*. 2nd ed. Santa Barbara, CA: Greenwood, 2010.

National Bureau of Economic Research. History of the NBER. http://www.nber.org.

Reinhart, Carmen, and Kenneth Rogoff. *This Time Is Different: Eight Centuries of Financial Folly*. Princeton, NJ: Princeton University Press, 2009.

Roubini, Nouriel, and Stephen Mihm. *Crisis Economics: A Crash Course in the Future of Finance*. New York: Penguin Press, 2010.

Net Income and Other Bottom-Line Measures

The "bottom line" is a calculation of revenues minus expenses (usually including gains and losses) used to measure the earnings performance of a company. Net income and earnings per share (EPS) are the primary bottom-line numbers, the most appropriate measures of earnings and most often used for quantitative analysis of profitability. Net income is a relatively complete measure of all business activity (close to what is called all-inclusive income), because it includes nonrecurring items in addition to normal operating income.

EPS is a performance measure presented in two formats on the income statement: (1) basic [(net income – preferred dividends) / weighted average number of common shares outstanding] and (2) diluted, which adjusts for the potential for additional shares associated with stock options, convertible securities and related factors. Berenson (2003) describes EPS as "The Number," with the primary executives' goal of meeting the consensus analysts' forecast each quarter.

Institutional Brokers Estimates System (I/B/E/S) and Zacks Investment Research started publishing consensus analyst forecasts in the 1970s. The consensus forecasts became the standard benchmark to measure "earnings surprise," the difference between the consensus forecast and actual EPS based on quarterly earnings. A downside of this information is the short-term focus rather than long-term trends, and that mind-set became pervasive in the 1990s. The most relevant number provided by analysts is future earnings. One-year and five-year EPS forecasts are extremely important. The problem is reliability. If the five-year forecast was consistently correct, developing investment portfolios would be easy.

Bottom-line measures are important, but analysts rely on different measures and alternative perspectives. Analysis normally begins with net income, with consideration of alternative definitions of earnings, including operating income, earnings before interest and taxes (EBIT), earnings before interest, taxes, depreciation, and amortization (EBITDA), income from continuing operations (usually after tax), net income adjusted for various things (such as dividends or eliminating certain nonrecurring or special charges), comprehensive income (CI), and any number of *pro forma* calculations of earnings (that is, not based on generally accepted accounting principles). Former Securities and Exchange Commission (SEC) chief

Table 15. Net Income and Other Bottom-Line Measures

Measure	Concern	Analysis
Operating margin (OM)	Declining or erratic OM, suggesting serious problems with basic operations.	Calculate OM percentage for several periods and compare to competitors.
EBIT and EBITDA	Large differences, suggesting big expenses associated with interest expense, taxes, depreciation, or amortization.	Calculate and evaluate component parts; compare across periods and to competitors.
Income from continuing operations versus net income	ICO substantially different from NI, because of nonrecurring items and related earnings manipulation potential.	Compare and calculate alternative return ratios.
Net income versus comprehensive income	Other comprehensive income items represent large losses, especially if these continue year after year.	Compare and calculate alternative return ratios; evaluate every other comprehensive income item.

accountant Lynn Turner developed the concept of EBBS—earnings before the bad stuff.

Each earnings measure provides different information. Corporations have flexibility, and differences by industry and other factors become important. The following table shows some standard bottom-line measures, areas of concern related to each, and common actions for addressing each. The most common operating measures are summarized in Table 15.

Definitions:

- **Operating margin** is sales less cost of sales (COS). COS has a direct relationship to sales, and this relationship normally is fairly constant. If margin is rising, it may signal increased efficiency (strategic outsourcing for example) and be a positive signal of future performance. Declining or erratic margin may indicate any number of operating or other problems.
- **Operating income** is sales minus operating expenses, which include cost of sales, selling, general, and administrative expenses (SG&A), research and development (R&D), and other items. Operating income differs by industry. Pharmaceuticals, for example, have low cost of sales, but high R&D and marketing costs. Retailers tend to have high cost of sales and zero or low R&D.
- **EBIT** (also called "operating earnings") is calculated as (income before tax + interest expense) and can be used as an indicator of a firm's ability to service its debt. EBITDA (also called "cash earnings") is EBIT + depreciation and amortization and can be used for an alternative analysis of cash flows. Depreciation and amortization are noncash expenses and major expense categories at many large corporations.
- **Income from continuing operations (ICO)** is a current-operations bottom line. ICO may be a better measure than net income, because it excludes nonrecurring items. ICO, EBIT, EBITDA, and operating margin are "above-the-line" measures, basically a focus on current operations. Net income is a "below-the-line"

earnings measure that includes nonrecurring items that are not part of ongoing operations. Nonrecurring items are erratic, should be rare, and presumably provide no information about the fundamental performance of a corporation. It follows from this argument that nonrecurring items should be analyzed separately.

- **Net income** is a relatively complete bottom-line measure, but does not include all gains and losses. A number of items, called other CI, are recorded directly to the balance sheet, known as "dirty surplus." CI includes all revenues, expenses, gains, and losses, consistent with an "all-inclusive" concept of earnings. That is, it is a measure of every revenue, expense, gain, and loss for the period.

See also Accounting Standards; Annual Report (10-K); Earnings Manipulation; Financial Accounting Standards Board (FASB); Financial Analyst Scandal; Securities and Exchange Commission (SEC)

References

Berenson, Alex. *The Number: How the Drive for Quarterly Earnings Corrupted Wall Street and Corporate America*. New York: Random House, 2003.

Davidson, Sidney, and George Anderson. "The Development of Accounting and Auditing Standards." *Journal of Accountancy*, May 1987, 110–27.

Giroux, Gary. *Earnings Magic and the Unbalance Sheet: The Search for Financial Reality*. New York: Wiley, 2006.

New Deal

The New Deal was the set of social and economic programs implemented by President Franklin D. Roosevelt (FDR), beginning in 1933 in response to the Great Depression. The focus was on the "3Rs of relief, recovery and reform": relief for the poor and unemployed, economic recovery, and reform of the financial system. Landmarks of the New Deal included increased federal regulations of the economy, new social programs, and greater power for labor unions.

In his acceptance speech for the 1932 Democratic nomination for president FDR promised his New Deal:

> Throughout the nation men and women, forgotten in the political philosophy of the Government, look to us here for guidance and for more equitable opportunity to share in the distribution of national wealth . . . I pledge myself to a new deal for the American people. This is more than a political campaign. It is a call to arms.

He defeated Herbert Hoover in a landslide and delivered. The FDR legend on getting out of the Depression is overstated, but the financial and social changes were dramatic and still part of the current political/economic landscape. On inauguration day, March 4, 1933, the country was in a financial crisis, with the banks of most states under "holiday" and the New York Stock Exchange (NYSE) closed. In his first inaugural address, FDR famously stated, "The only thing we have to fear . . . is fear itself . . . nameless, unreasoning, unjustified terror which paralyzes needed efforts to convert retreat into advance." The worst years of the Depression were 1932 and 1933; the economic woes of the later 1930s were primarily government created. Before 1940, with the war in Europe under way, the annual unemployment rate dropped below 10 percent only in 1937.

FDR is known for his first hundred days. During this time much of the "First New Deal" legislation passed, some 15 major bills, aimed to meet the needs of the various constituencies from banking and industry to farming. Fundamentally, Roosevelt wanted to stimulate recovery and then pass long-term reforms that would eliminate the possibility of future depressions. FDR used emergency programs like relief and work programs as governor of New York, but inherently conservative, he believed in a balanced budget. This limited the effectiveness of many of his underfunded progressive programs. (Despite balanced-budget efforts in some years, the federal government retained annual deficits every year of the FDR presidency.)

In March 1933, FDR took immediate action for the banking crisis. In his first inaugural address, he stated his impression of banking: "The money changers have fled from their high seats in the temple of our civilization. We may now restore that temple to the ancient truths." Roosevelt announced a national bank holiday—all banks were closed for a week and inspected by federal officials. Roosevelt did not nationalize the banks, the liberal position. Instead, FDR submitted an emergency banking act bill to Congress on March 9 (passed and signed into law the same day) to allow healthy banks to reopen under Treasury Department supervision with guarantees from the Resolution Finance Corporation (RFC) to loan banks money and invest in preferred stock. The RFC spent about a billion dollars in the next six months propping up banks, but about 4,000 banks (usually small local banks) failed. Within a month, FDR and Congress suspended the gold standard to stop the massive exodus of gold from New York, devaluing the dollar to 59¢; the Federal Reserve (Fed) no longer had a reason to prop up the dollar by keeping bond interest rates high.

FDR's first major relief program was the Federal Emergency Relief Administration (FERA), spending about $4 billion from mid-1933 to mid-1935, replaced by the Works Program Administration (WPA). Given the usual politics (e.g., the Senate favored small states while the House favored large states; each state wanted control within its borders), the challenge was to provide relief where it was most needed.

In 1935, Roosevelt attempted to eliminate the budget deficits. His economy bill, sent to Congress in March 1935, reduced government salaries and cut veterans' pensions, while maintaining the top tax rate of 63 percent. His budget director, Lewis Douglas, favored this approach and resigned the next year when New Deal programs meant increased spending. This "fiscal restraint," the traditional approach favored by many politicians and economists at the time, continued to be a priority as it had under Hoover.

Economist John Maynard Keynes championed enhanced government spending during a depression; because consumers and business did not spend, the government must stimulate the economy. In a 1933 letter to Roosevelt, Keynes stated:

> At the moment your sympathizers in England are nervous and sometime despondent. ... The average City man believes that you are engaged on a harebrained expedition in face of competent advice.

Keynes then focused on spending:

> The object of recovery is to increase the national output and put more men to work. Individuals must be induced to spend more ... or the business world must be induced ... to create additional current incomes ... or public authority must be called in aid to create additional current incomes through the expenditure of borrowed or printed money. ... Thus as the prime mover in the first stage of the technique of recovery I lay overwhelming emphasis on the increase of national purchasing power resulting from governmental expenditures which is financed by Loans and not by taxing present incomes. ... But preference should be given to those which can be made to mature quickly on a large scale, as for example the rehabilitation of the physical condition of the railroads.

On a 1934 visit to Washington, Keynes urged Roosevelt to promote spending.

Early New Deal efforts focused on stabilizing farm prices and reforming business and labor. The Agricultural Adjustment Act (AAA) was passed in May 1933, basically to raise farm prices by creating artificial food scarcity. The AAA paid farmers subsidies to restrict output of key products. Farm prices rose for the next three years, much to the frustration of consumers having to pay the higher prices; then the Supreme Court declared the program unconstitutional in 1936. A modified program to meet Court approval kept farm subsidies, and the federal government maintained farm policy subsidies ever since. Several other farm-related programs passed during the New Deal.

To reform business and labor, Roosevelt favored a cartel system of cooperation between business and labor to maintain or raise prices while simultaneously creating voluntary minimum wages and improved working conditions for labor. The National Industrial Recovery Act (NIRA) was passed in June 1933, creating the National Recovery Administration (NRA). The NRA negotiated "business codes" to set prices and wages by industry, plus a set of "fair practices." The initial response of the bill was a substantial increase in production before the program went into effect. Production fell off after that, but gradually increased until 1937. Business rightly assumed that the program would increase the cost of production.

The program could be modestly effective in some industries, but considerable cheating occurred and big businesses tended to set "fair practices" favoring themselves to the detriment of both small business and labor. The NRA had no enforcement mechanism, nor was it clear whether the program was a modest success or a fiasco. The NRA, a cartel violating long-held antitrust positions, was declared unconstitutional in 1935.

The NIRA also established the Public Works Administration (PWA), the first and largest public works program. Through 1935, the PWA spent over $3 billion on almost 35,000 projects. This popular agency proved to be one of the more fruitful areas of the attempted recovery. The Civilian Conservation Corps (CCC) provided some 3 million unskilled jobs for young men working in conservation and development of natural resources (including planting 3 billion trees and building some 800 parks). Late in 1933, the Civil Works Administration (CWA) created a low-skill temporary work program under Harry Hopkins. Much of the program included local make-work (a "boondoggle" according to Republicans), but it did put some 4 million people to work for the winter. FDR canceled the program in 1934 to cut the deficit.

The Glass-Steagall Act of 1933 dramatically reformed banking. The creation of the Federal Deposit Insurance Corporation (FDIC) insuring commercial bank deposits became a favorite with the public. (As Roubini and Mihm, 2010, 165, pointed out, "Between 1866 and 1933, Congress considered some 150 proposals for deposit insurance.") Roosevelt opposed the FDIC, because he thought it would unnecessarily prop up weak rural banks without benefiting sound banks. The major argument against deposit insurance is moral hazard; banks no longer have an obligation to protect depositors and can take on additional risks. From the bankers' perspective, the major provision of Glass-Steagall—a debacle to them—separated commercial banks from investment banks. The big banks, particularly the New York-Wall Street banks, had to decide whether to be commercial or investment banks, and many large institutions split. J. P. Morgan, for example, became a commercial bank, while its investment banking practice spun off as Morgan Stanley. Regulation Q allowed the Federal Reserve to set interest rates on bank deposits, which worked reasonably well until high inflation rates set in during the 1970s.

After the initial flurry of recovery programs, new agencies attempted to restructure much of the economy and provide long-term solutions. Many passed during the "Second New Deal" of 1934–36. Generally, these are the programs Roosevelt and his Brain Trust are remembered for. The Federal Housing Act (FHA) guaranteed low-interest loans for construction and repairs. The FHA chartered Federal National Mortgage Association (Fannie Mae) in 1938 to provide mortgage credit by purchasing FHA-insured mortgage loans. The Federal Communications Act established the Federal Communications Commission (FCC) to regulate of radio and other electronic media. The National Labor Relations Act created the National Labor Relations Board (NLRB), giving more power to unions.

The pension movement led to the Social Security Act of 1935, mandating old-age pensions plus unemployment insurance, disability, and other benefits. Social Security became the biggest of the New Deal programs. Tax collections started in

1937, but the first monthly retirement checks had to wait until 1940. FDR thought payroll taxes essential: "With those taxes in there, no damn politician can ever scrap my social security program" (quoted in Friedel 1990, 150).

With all this activity, the economy should have recovered, but it did not happen. Many of the programs were not particularly helpful, such as the NRA, and many had mixed results. For example, the farm programs drove up food prices, which did not benefit consumers. Other programs proved too small to be effective, including much of the public works relief effort. About the time public works employed substantial numbers providing a living wage to millions, Roosevelt cut them in an effort to economize. As the economy faltered, Roosevelt proposed increased taxes, including raising the corporate income tax from 13.75 percent to a graduated rate up to 16.75 percent plus higher personal and inheritance tax rates. The Revenue Act of 1935 imposed higher individual taxes, raising the top individual income tax rate from 63 percent to 79 percent. This did increase revenues somewhat and reduce the deficit, but helped decimate the economy. Also during the Depression years, states increased sales tax rates. Then the Social Security taxes kicked in beginning in 1937. Not to be outdone, the Federal Reserve tightened money in 1937–38, resulting in a government-created recession. By 1938, the unemployment rate increased to 12.5 percent. FDR can be given high marks for major social restructuring, but not for ending the Great Depression. That would take World War II.

See also Classical Economics; Crash of 1929; Roosevelt, Franklin Delano; Great Depression; Keynes, John Maynard; Pecora Commission; Reconstruction Finance Corporation (RFC); Securities and Exchange Commission (SEC); Wagner Act

References

Dobson, John. "Crash." In *Bulls, Bears, Boom, and Bust: A Historical Encyclopedia of American Business Concepts*. Santa Barbara, CA: ABC-CLIO, 2006.

Friedel, F. *Franklin D. Roosevelt: A Rendezvous with Destiny*. Boston: Little, Brown, 1990.

Galbraith, Kenneth. *The Great Crash 1929*. Boston: Houghton Mifflin, 1988.

Hafer, Rik. "Roosevelt, Franklin Delano." In *The Federal Reserve System: An Encyclopedia*. Santa Barbara, CA: ABC-CLIO, 2005.

Keynes, John. *An Open Letter to President Roosevelt*. 1933. http://Newdeal.feri.org/misc/keynes2.htm.

Roubini, Nouriel and Stephen Mihm. *Crisis Economics: A Crash Course in the Future of Finance*. New York: Penguin Press, 2010.

New York Stock Exchange

The New York Stock Exchange (NYSE) is the world's largest by market capitalization of listed companies. The NYSE was founded in 1792 by the Buttonwood Agreement as a private partnership. It would stay private until 2006. The

Trading floor of the New York Stock Exchange on Wall Street, New York City. (Library of Congress)

organization created a constitution in 1817 and was called the New York Stock and Exchange Board. In 2006, the NYSE merged with ArcaEX, creating a publicly-owned firm, then merged with Euronext. In 2011, Euronext merged with Deutsche Borse.

The Philadelphia Stock Exchange (PSE), established in 1790 as the Board of Brokers, met in the Merchants Coffee House trading government notes and bonds as well as bank stocks as they became available—beginning with Robert Morris's Bank of North America. The exchange developed markets in the first turnpikes and canals. After the War of 1812, the PSE remained the premier American exchange; the Second Bank of the United States was located in Philadelphia, and European investors flocked to the PSE. When Andrew Jackson eliminated the Second Bank of the United States in the mid-1830s, the preeminent status of PSE vanished. By then, the Erie Canal brought commerce to New York City, which soon emerged as a financial center.

Eighteenth-century New York City (Wall Street) brokers acted as middle men, dealing in trades from insurance to lotteries and securities. Securities trading initially focused on government bonds. As the number of government bond issues increased, more brokers specialized in securities, expanding into the stocks and bonds of chartered banks and insurance companies. As the number of securities traded increased, auctions were staged in coffeehouses. Some attended auctions merely to discover market prices and then proceeded outdoors to trade at lower commissions (curb brokers). Shortly after the speculative bubble and panic of 1792, two dozen brokers signed the Buttonwood (named for a sycamore tree in Manhattan) Agreement on May 17, 1792, the predecessor of the NYSE. These member brokers (calling themselves subscribers) continued meeting at coffee-houses and agreed to buy and sell at fixed commissions, a premium price over the curb brokers.

As business expanded in New York, brokers needed formal rules. The brokers sent William Lamb to study the PSE, and his report became the basis for a formal constitution in 1817. Seven firms with 28 members formed a Board of Brokers, renamed the New York Stock and Exchange Board (shortened to New York Stock Exchange in 1863) with a code of conduct. The code established a "call market," where the president read out the name of each security and the brokers then traded in that security. Business, conducted in a rented room at 40 Wall Street, took place twice daily, both morning and afternoon. Other rules established sales and delivery procedures. The exchange operated as a private market, not a public auction; non-exchange brokers lacked trading information, and government provided no oversight.

As the New York economy boomed in the early nineteenth century, thanks in part to the Erie Canal, a bull market developed. More brokers specialized in stocks and bonds. In 1827, the NYSE moved to its own quarters at the Merchants' Exchange. With the rise of specialization came the rise of inside information and significant advantages for those who knew how to manipulate the new arena. During the 1830s, rampant stock market speculation was fueled by state bank-issued paper money. The biggest day on the NYSE came on June 26, 1835, when over 7,800 shares were traded. At that time, some 80 commercial firms' securities were traded, including 70 banks and insurance companies and 10 railroads, canals, and gas companies. Late in his second term, President Andrew Jackson demanded gold for federal land sales to dampen land fever and withdrew funds from various banks to send cash to the states. Banks began to fail as a result of the Panic of 1837 ensuing, causing one of the longest depressions in American history.

By the mid-1850s, another boom cycle set in, prompted in part by the 1849 discovery of gold in California. Hundreds of railroad stocks traded in New York, plus over a thousand bank and insurance stocks. Not all of these were traded on the NYSE, which did not list "untested issues."

After the Panic of 1857, about half the members of the NYSE failed. Seats became available and new NYSE members included Cornelius Vanderbilt; Henry Clews, a cofounder of Livermore, Clews and Co., later a major seller of Union bonds during the Civil War; as well as Daniel Drew, a major market manipulator. The late nineteenth century would come to be called the "Gilded Age" with rampant manipulation and abuse and the creation of vast fortunes for successful market manipulators, including Jay Gould, who accumulated over $70 million in wealth.

The rise of monopolies of industrial firms and the powerful Wall Street "Money Trust" resulted in increased wealth and continued market manipulation. NYSE

abuses of the period included price manipulation of many companies, vast speculation including short selling on margin, and insider trading. After the Panic of 1907,
reform legislation passed in Congress. Attempts at securities regulations did not
pass until the1930s.

The NYSE became largest securities market in the world in the 1920s, but it was
still a private club operated to benefit the members. The members effectively controlled the market and had virtually total access to all market information. They
included floor traders (trading only for their own accounts, without paying commissions) and specialists in specific stocks making a market, but without limits on how
they could profit from the stock or providing inside information to others. Members
could conspire with each other, leading to stock pools, which could drive prices up
or down for their own profit. Wash sales (members selling among themselves to
produce price patterns), bear raids, and short selling could be immensely profitable,
with outsiders taking the losses.

The NYSE had 61 percent of all securities transactions in 1929 (rising to 76% in
1932). However, the NYSE made only feeble attempts to ensure financial disclosure for traded companies. Until 1910, the NYSE had an "unlisted department" of
firms that disclosed no financial information. Only after the 1929 crash did the
NYSE cooperate with the American Institute of Accountants (AIA) to consider
financial reporting reform. A committee of the AIA (now the American Institute
of Certified Public Accountants) started issuing accounting standards by the end
of the decade. In 1933, the NYSE required all listed companies to have annual
audits.

The great stock crash happened in 1929. The first big drop happened October 24,
Black Thursday. On October 29, Black Tuesday, the most devastating day on the
NYSE up to that time, the Dow Jones average (Dow) closed at 220. Prices continued down: from a peak of 386 the Dow fell to 41 in 1933. The market lost all cred-
ibility with the public. From 1929 to 1932, 11,000 banks failed, gross domestic
product declined 10 percent annually (a total of 46%), industrial production fell in
half, steel production dropped to 12 percent of capacity, and unemployment hit
25 percent. The Senate's Pecora Commission, investigating the causes of the
1929 crash, found no major wrongdoing by the NYSE, except lax enforcement.

Franklin Roosevelt (FDR) became president in March 1933. Roosevelt inherited
an immediate banking crisis. The NYSE closed beginning on inauguration day due
to the banking crisis, but when the market opened on March 15, the Dow went up
8 to 62. Market averages indicated a generally favorable reaction to FDR's leadership. The Dow reached 100 on July 3, 1933. The Dow peaked March 10, 1937, at
194 (up 153, 373% from its 1932 low), then headed down as a recession started
due to poor monetary and financial policy.

Richard Whitney, president of the NYSE from1930 to 1935, proclaimed the
magnificence of the exchange. He lived an ostentatious life, supported by borrowed
money. He also speculated on Wall Street and gambled. As an insider, speculation
worked modestly well. When the crash hit, he was effectively ruined. Whitney
remained a trustee of the NYSE Gratuity Fund, which made cash payments to the

estates of deceased members. Whitney, as broker to the fund, sold $225,000 worth of fund bonds. He embezzled the cash and continued to loot the fund for over $1 million. He did the same from the New York Yacht Club where he was treasurer. Whitney's total indebtedness was $27 million, and the story broke in 1938. Whitney's firm was suspended for insolvency, and the NYSE voted misconduct charges against him. District Attorney Thomas Dewey indicted Whitney for grand larceny. Whitney pleaded guilty and was sentenced to five to ten years at Sing Sing.

In the post–World War II period, the economy boomed, as did the NYSE. The Dow reached 208 in May 1946, but ended the decade at 199, all in spite of relatively good earnings during the second half of the 1940s. The public was not yet interested in returning to the stock market. This changed in the 1950s, as the economy boomed, inflation remained low, and investor confidence returned. The Dow topped the 1929 high by the end of 1954 (it took 25 years) and ended the decade over 670. The postwar boom in stock prices lasted until 1966. The bear market starting in 1966 ended about 1982. In a period of double-digit inflation, high-yielding Treasury and other bonds were just more attractive than stocks. As bond yields gradually came down (Treasuries fell from 13% in 1981 to less than 9% in 1986), stock and dividend yields looked more attractive. A new bull market started in the middle of 1982.

In 1970, the NYSE changed the rules and allowed members to go public. A number of "retail banks" went public in 1971–72, including Merrill Lynch, the biggest. Retail brokers went public in part to provide the needed capital to invest in the computer power then becoming available to process the large number of trades for their customers. Wholesale investment banks, including Goldman Sachs and Morgan Stanley went public later in the century. Once they were no longer partners investing their own money, investment banks became much bigger and took on more risk. The result would be recurring financial market instability.

The major catastrophe during the long bull market was the market crash of 1987. The Dow started 1987 at 1927, up 400 points (21%) from the previous year, hitting a high of 2,722 on August 25. On Monday, October 19, stock markets around the world dropped. U.S. trading began at the Chicago Mercantile Exchange (Merc), a half hour before the NYSE opened, the key indicator being the S&P 500 stock index futures. Within minutes, the S&P futures dropped 18 percent. When the NYSE opened, specialists were swamped with sell orders, delaying the opening of trades on individual stocks. Pension, mutual funds, and other institutional investors led the selling, mainly in block trades of hundreds of thousands of shares. The Dow dropped 508 points, almost 23 percent—the largest one-day drop ever. Experts blamed portfolio insurance, a derivative play designed to limit losses when stock prices fall.

Regulatory problems popped up against investment bankers, brokers, stock exchanges, and others involved in financial transactions. This included the 1998 case against NYSE floor brokers trading for their own profit. Floor brokers handled transactions for institutional traders and were not allowed to trade for their own accounts because of access to customer order-flow information. Nine brokers pled guilty and were sentenced to prison. In 1999, the SEC issued an enforcement action filed against the NYSE for failure to supervise the floor brokers adequately (Weiss 2003, 66–67).

The NYSE merged with Archipelago in 2005, making the NYSE a publicly traded company. The NYSE then sold one-year trading licenses, replacing the members. In 2007, the company merged with Euronext (based in Amsterdam), to form NYSE Euronext as "the first global stock exchange." In 2011, NYSE Euronext announced a merger with Deutsche Borse to form a new company 60 percent owned by Deutsche Borse and 40 percent by NYSE Euronext. However, the merger was denied by European antitrust authorities in 2012.

See also Accounting Standards; Bank of North America; Crash of 1929; Duer, William; Great Depression; Investment Banks; NASDAQ; Panic of 1837; Panic of 1873; Panic of 1907; Panics and Crashes; Stock Crash of 1987; Whitney, Richard

References

Gordon, John Steele. *The Great Game: The Emergence of Wall Street as a World Power, 1653–2000.* New York: Scribner, 1999.

Weiss, Gary. "Just a Minute Mr. Donaldson." *Business Week*, February 10, 2003, 66–67.

Northern Pacific War

The railroad war for the Pacific Northwest at the turn of the twentieth century involved two financier/railroad tycoon groups: E. H. Harriman and investment bank Kuhn, Loeb versus James Hill and J. P. Morgan. The "war" started with Hill's interest in the Chicago, Burlington, & Quincy (CB&O) to complete his northwest empire, opposed by Harriman. The Harriman and Kuhn, Loeb forces decided to buy out Hill's Northern Pacific and they came close to doing it, driving the stock price over $1,000. The two groups settled up, forming a joint holding company called Northern Securities incorporated in New Jersey. Theodore Roosevelt's Justice Department sued the combination under the Sherman Act as a monopoly and won, forcing the holding company to split up.

The Northern Pacific Railway Company (NP) was chartered by Congress on July 2, 1864. The purpose was to connect the Great Lakes with Puget Sound on the Pacific Ocean, opening up land for farms, ranching, lumber, and mining interests and linking the Pacific Northwest to the rest of the United States. Progress was slow until financier Jay Cooke developed an interest in 1870. Cooke borrowed to continue construction and became overextended. Cooke and Co. failed in 1873, the start of the Panic of 1873, and the Northern Pacific declared bankruptcy in 1875. Construction continued under Henry Villard, and the track was completed in 1883, operating near the Canadian border from the Great Lakes to the Pacific. The Panic of 1893 led to the failure of Villard and another bankruptcy for the railroad. The Northern Pacific became a J. P. Morgan project, one of many railroads reorganized in a process called "Morganization."

Morgan did not reorganize the failed Union Pacific (UP) after the 1893 panic. Instead, entrepreneur E. H. Harriman using Kuhn, Loeb took over the UP. In the meantime, James Hill, using Morgan money, consolidated the NP and Great Northern to dominate the northwest. The upcoming seven-month "war" of Harriman and Hill in 1901 turned on Hill's interest in the Chicago, Burlington, & Quincy (CB&O) to expand into Chicago, opposed by Harriman.

Harriman developed the audacious plan of controlling the NP rather than fighting for the CB&O and secretly started buying NP shares; Harriman almost had a majority before Morgan figured out what was going on. Morgan, in Europe, cabled his partners to buy 150,000 shares at any price. The price went over $200, then hit $1,000 a share. Short sellers (including Republican Party boss Mark Hanna), thinking they could make a killing, found themselves in a "short squeeze" as the financial titans cornered the market. The market crashed as stocks had to be sold to fund the NP shorts. NP shares dropped. Hill and Morgan kept control but the result was a panic. Morgan and Hill signed a truce with Harriman and offered the shares at $150 so speculators could cover their shorts and brokers avoided bankruptcy. The headline in the *New York Herald* was "Giants of Wall Street, in Fierce Battle for Mastery, Precipitate Crash That Brings Ruin to Horde of Pygmies." The new partners established Northern Securities, a holding company incorporating the NP, the Great Northern, and the Burlington, a megamerger over 17 states with 32,000 miles of track.

In 1903, the Justice Department under President Theodore Roosevelt created a separate Antitrust Division, under an assistant attorney general. Roosevelt's first big battle was the gigantic Northern Securities. The NP and Great Northern had been competitors and now had monopoly power, which they used. The government won a major victory when the Supreme Court ruled against the railroad in 1904 and the holding company was dissolved. Teddy remarked that the case "established the power of the Government to deal with all great corporations" (quoted in Morris 2001).

The three roads successfully merged in 1969 to form the Burlington Northern Railroad, later the BNSF Railway. The BNSF was acquired by Warren Buffett's Berkshire Hathaway in 2009.

See also Antitrust; Cooke, Jay; Morgan, John Pierpont; Railroads, Nineteenth Century; Roosevelt, Theodore; Sherman Antitrust Act of 1890; Transcontinental Railroad and the Credit Mobilier Scandal; Union Pacific Railroad

References

Josephson, M., *The Robber Barons*. New York: Harcourt, 1962.

Morris, Edmond. *Theodore Rex*. New York: Random House, 2001.

Vincusi, W. Kip, John Vernon, and Joseph Harrington. *Economics of Regulations and Antitrust*. 2nd ed. Cambridge, MA: MIT Press, 1995.

O

Off-Balance-Sheet Items

Off-balance-sheet items are assets and liabilities that belong to a company but are not recorded on the balance sheet. The most common off-balance-sheet items are operating leases and special-purpose entities (SPEs), both fundamental financing items that are widely used by corporations. The problem is they can be abused. The financial position of a company should be apparent from the balance sheet, but corporations can use operating leases and SPEs to hide liabilities and keep credit risks off the balance sheet. Major off-balance-sheet items are summarized in Table 16.

Leases usually are considered a financing arrangement, an alternative to buying fixed assets. The problem is the use of operating leases that are recorded as a rental contract and never show up on the balance sheet. The operating-leases issue is the clearest example of "rules-based" rather than "principles-based" accounting. The determination of an operating lease rather than a capital lease is based strictly on what are now called "bright-line" tests (the old term was "cookbook accounting"), such as the present value of minimum lease payments must be at least 90 percent of the fair value of the leased property. Thus, if the lease is set equal to 89 percent of the fair value, it is an operating lease—economic substance is irrelevant. Corporations seem to have mastered the technique.

The Securities and Exchange Commission (SEC) Report on off-balance-sheet arrangements (SEC 2005) found that 91 of the 100 largest firms used operating leases, compared to 39 percent using capital leases. The large companies had operating-lease commitments of $196 billion, and the estimate for all listed companies was $1.25 trillion.

Giroux (2006) reported that 19 of the Dow Jones Industrial Average 30 companies reported operating leases, averaging $4.8 billion ($71.4 billion in total). The value of McDonald's operating leases (according to footnote disclosures) was $12.87 billion or equivalent to 45.6 percent of total assets. Home Depot had 22.1 percent ($8.6 billion), while Wal-Mart had $10.3 billion. Retail companies and airlines are the industries where operating leases are particularly large, representing retail building and airplanes, respectively. Because these companies typically have considerable leverage recorded on the balance sheet, the additional obligations associated with these leases indicate higher credit risk.

Operating leases can represent long-term commitments that are in substance capital leases, but meet current accounting standards as operating leases. For example, McDonald's 2004 10-K reported that "at December 31, 2004, the Company was the lessee at 15,235 restaurant locations through ground leases (the Company

Table 16. Off-Balance-Sheet Items

Synthetic leases	An asset such as an office building is "sold" to the SPE and then leased back (sale-and-leaseback for accounting) to the originator. This is then treated as a capital lease for accounting purposes and as a loan for tax purposes. The company gets the tax benefits of interest and depreciation expense and the accounting benefits of off-balance-sheet treatment.
Securitize loans and mortgages	A bank "sells" outstanding loans or mortgages to the SPE; these receivables serve as collateral and the SPE repackages them and sells them as bonds or notes to investors. The bank remains as servicer and charges a fee to manage the original loans or mortgages, while the receivables are no longer on the books.
"Sell" receivables	A manufacturing firm making credit sales eliminates some percentage of the receivables by "selling" them to an SPE. The SPE uses the receivables as collateral to borrow the cash to fund the receivables, which is paid back to the company. The company now has cash and a lower receivables balance (suggesting that credit terms are more stringent than they really are).
Take-or-pay contracts	A take-or-pay contract requires the buyer to take some amount of product or pay a specific amount if refused. The contract can be used as collateral to fund a new manufacturing plant using an SPE.
Throughput arrangements	Similar to take-or-pay, used primarily by gas or oil pipelines and requiring a specific guaranty of acquisition. The throughput contract (similar to a forward contract) can be used as collateral to fund the construction of a pipeline using an SPE.
Asset construction projects	An SPE can be set up to finance future construction projects by using a forward contract on the project, which is then used as collateral by the SPE to fund the construction. The construction costs and corresponding debt are off the books of the builder. Upon completion, the company can then lease back the fixed assets as a synthetic lease for additional tax benefits.
In-substance defeasance	An existing debt agreement is placed in trust using an SPE against specific assets (e.g., government bonds with essentially equal terms); usually established to take advantage of lower interest rates than on existing debt.
Research and development costs	An SPE can be established to fund R&D, transferring the risk and avoid recognizing either the expense involved or liabilities used to fund the ongoing R&D.

leases the land and the Company or franchise owns the building) and through improved leases (the Company leases the land and buildings). Lease terms for most restaurants are generally for 20 years" (McDonald's 2004, 62). McDonald's reported no capital leases.

SPEs, which are separate legal entities created to keep liabilities off of the balance sheet, became particularly infamous with the financial collapse of Enron. In the third quarter 2001 10-Q, Enron had to consolidate three SPEs into the financial statements, while restating income (a net loss of $569 million) and equity (a net reduction of $1.2 billion). This forced Enron into bankruptcy. Much of Enron's long-term fraud used SPEs. Enron had thousands of SPEs, all off-balance-sheet and unreported before that quarterly report.

General Motors used SPEs to redevelop closed factories. AOL Time Warner, Microsoft, and many airlines used SPEs to create synthetic leases. Banks used them to consolidate and sell mortgages and other securitized debt to investors. Examples of SPE uses include the following:

Enron was the most egregious user of SPEs. Chief financial officer (CFO) Andrew Fastow and other executives skimmed off millions by acting as "independent third-party trustees" on various SPEs. Major banks followed Enron in various illicit uses of camouflaging debt in SPEs. Investment banks, especially in the 2005–8 period used SPEs to further boost leverage on top of 30-1 assets-to-debt on the balance sheet. Even after the 2008 subprime meltdown, banks continue to use SPEs to hold toxic assets and reduce reported leverage.

See also Debt and Leverage; Financial Accounting Standards Board (FASB); Securities and Exchange Commission (SEC); Special-Purpose Entities; Special-Purpose Entities at Enron; Subprime Meltdown

References

Giroux, Gary. *Earnings Magic and the Unbalance Sheet: The Search for Financial Reality.* New York: Wiley, 2006.

Giroux, Gary. "What Went Wrong? Accounting Fraud and Lessons from the Recent Scandals." *Social Research: An International Quarterly of the Social Sciences*, Winter 2008, 1205–38.

McDonald's Corporation. "Form 10-K." December 31, 2004. http://www.sec.gov/Archives/edgar/data/63908/000119312505042609/d10k1.pdf.

Securities and Exchange Commission. *Report and Recommendations Pursuant to Section 401(c) of the Sarbanes-Oxley Act of 2002 on Arrangement with Off-Balance Sheet Implications, Special Purpose Entities, and Transparency of Filings by Issuers.* Washington, DC: Securities and Exchange Commission, 2005.

Orange County Bankruptcy

Orange Country, California, home of Disneyland, declared bankruptcy on December 6, 1994, the biggest local government to file for bankruptcy up to that time, after massive losses of $1.7 billion in complex derivative investments. Merrill Lynch and other investment banks targeted state and local governments for complex derivative agreements. These high-risk instruments seemed poor investments to conservative governments subject to regulatory constraints. Bonuses on high commissions proved too big an incentive to bond salespeople and the banks camouflaged the risks and high costs from the buyers (after being sued, Merrill claimed it warned the Orange County treasurer repeatedly of the risks involved). Government buyers—and ultimate losers—included San Jose, California, the state of West Virginia, Wisconsin Investment Board, San Diego and San Bernadino Counties, and the California Public Employees Retirement System, among others. The biggest loser one was Orange County, which paid Merrill some $100 million in fees.

In addition to unsophisticated municipalities, insurance companies, mutual funds, and hedge funds made similar investments on short-term rates, at the time about 3 percent, while long-term rates were roughly 8 percent. The strategy was to borrow short term and invest long term. The economy was booming, and Federal Reserve (Fed) chairman Alan Greenspan raised the federal funds rate from 3 percent to 3.25 percent in February 1994, the first hike in five years, to fight inflation. The Fed continued to raise rates, up to 5.5 percent by year-end. Other short-term rates followed. Greenspan explained the strategy of a "soft landing" for the economy, but organizations that used complex derivatives speculating on maintaining low short-term rates experienced massive losses. The derivative instruments were high risk, and few financial experts predicted the brutal swings in the value of these instruments when short-term rates rose.

Democrat Robert Citron, longtime treasurer of Orange County, made big profits on derivative trades using more and more leverage (borrowing up to $13 billion to add to Orange County's $7 billion investment pool). The strategy was to borrow short term using repurchase agreements and invest in longer-term high yield securities. The complex, high-risk derivatives paid off as long as short-term interest rates stayed low. Included in Orange County's portfolio were "inverse floater structured notes," with very high interest rates, less some floating rate such as LIBOR (London interbank interest rate). So the structure might be 12 percent interest less the LIBOR rate. A "trigger note" paid a short-term high rate of interest as long as interest rates stayed below a specific cutoff. If interest rates rose above that trigger, the note extended in maturity at what became a low rate of interest, when interest rates were rising (Partnoy 1997, chapter 8).

One interesting episode was the last reelection of Citron, in 1994. His opponent was certified public accountant (CPA) John Moorlach, warning about the high risks of Citron's investment strategy and questioning Citron about investment specifics. He predicted a loss over $1 billion (which proved too conservative). Citron was reelected; apparently, voters were as little concerned about risks as Citron.

When interest rates rose in 1994, Orange County's investments collapsed, losing some $1.7 billion. Unable to roll over its debt, the government declared bankrupt. Citron bought the complex securities mainly from Merrill Lynch (plus smaller investments from Morgan Stanley), probably with little understanding about their risks. Citron pled guilty to filing false and misleading financial statements and other felonies. He received probation. Orange County sued Merrill, and the company ultimately paid $400 million to settle the case.

See also Black-Scholes Model; Black Swans; Derivatives; Gibson Greetings Derivatives Losses; Leeson, Nicholas W.; Greenspan, Alan; Procter & Gamble Derivatives Losses

References

Partnoy, Frank. *FIASCO: Blood in the Water on Wall Street*. New York: Norton, 1997.

Partnoy, Frank. *Infectious Greed: How Deceit and Risk Corrupted the Financial Markets*. New York: Holt, 2003.

P

Panic of 1819

The Panic of 1819 was the first major nineteenth-century panic, caused by speculation in land, secondarily in securities, during a period of inflation creating an asset bubble. When the Second Bank of the United States withdrew some $4 million in gold from the market, bank credit dried up, speculators failed in droves, and a depression lasting four years followed—the first major financial panic in the United States, although several minor panics occurred after the constitutional government was formed in 1788.

Problems began with the War of 1812, which caused substantial inflation. Most banks suspended specie payments (that is, refused to pay out gold for paper money). With no discipline associated with immediate repayment in gold, paper money and inflation exploded. When the war ended in 1815, a robust economy returned and American trade with Europe increased. Much of this economic success was fueled by the sale of goods to European countries recovering from war. However, U.S. banks did not return to the gold standard partially because the gold and silver supply decreased. Consequently, banks continued to print more paper money, resulting in further inflation and speculation in stocks and real estate.

The Second Bank of the United States was chartered in 1816. Unlike the First Bank of the United States, it was run by incompetent, corrupt officials; they accepted promissory notes for stock, acquired bank stock using false names to avoid legal ownership limitations, made loans to cronies without proper collateral, and allowed overdrawn accounts. The bank did not provide the monetary discipline expected of a central bank. Langdon Cheves became president of the Second Bank in 1819 and resumed specie payments for banks, that is, returned to a gold standard.

Also in 1819, a $4 million payment in gold was needed to pay back loans originally made for the Louisiana Purchase by the Treasury in 1803. The Second Bank of the United States called in state bank notes, demanding payment in gold. State banks called in their own loans, which causing a ripple effect and reduced the money supply. Simultaneously, European manufacturing dumped surplus products on U.S. markets. Interest rates rose, credit became hard to get, and speculators failed in mass. The result was a panic, causing a drop in land prices, widespread bank failures, business bankruptcies, and rising unemployment.

The federal government did almost nothing, including the Second Bank of the United States. President James Monroe passed the Land Act of 1820 (reducing public land prices to $1.25 an acre and the minimum land purchase from 160 to 80 acres) and the Relief Act of 1821 (extending credit for land already purchased and allowing land purchasers to return land they could not pay for). These laws had little effect on the resulting depression, which lasted until 1823. Many politicians and business people blamed the Second Bank of the United States including Andrew Jackson, who would later go to war against the bank.

See also Bank of the United States, Second Great Depression; Jackson, Andrew; Panic of 1837; Panic of 1857; Panic of 1873; Panic of 1893; Panic of 1907; Panics and Depressions

References

Clark, Cynthia. "Panic of 1819." In *The American Economy: A Historical Encyclopedia.* Rev. ed. Edited by Cynthia Clark. (Santa Barbara, CA: Greenwood, 2011).

Kindleberger, Charles, and R. Aliber. *Manias, Panics, and Crashes: A History of Financial Crises.* 5th ed. Hoboken, NJ: Wiley, 2005.

Knoop, Todd. *Recessions and Depressions: Understanding Business Cycles.* 2nd ed. Santa Barbara, CA: Greenwood, 2010.

Reinhart, Carmen, and Kenneth Rogoff. *This Time Is Different: Eight Centuries of Financial Folly.* Princeton, NJ: Princeton University Press, 2009.

Roubini, Nouriel, and Stephen Mihm. *Crisis Economics: A Crash Course in the Future of Finance.* New York: Penguin Press, 2010.

Panic of 1837

The Panic of 1837 involved banks, real estate, speculation, and easy money. President Andrew Jackson refused to renew the charter of the Second Bank of the United States; the federal government refused to accept paper currency for purchase of public lands—only gold and silver were acceptable (based on the Specie Circular of 1836). An economic crisis started earlier in England with the collapse of the textile industry and cotton speculation. Sluggish foreign trade and declining cotton prices made the depression, which lasted until 1843, longer and deeper.

The Land Act of 1820 reduced public land prices to $1.25 an acre. Land speculation, a continuing problem in the early United States, resulted in an asset bubble in the 1830s. Promoters bought large tracks of land to divide up and sell to small farms on credit. Land prices increased accordingly, causing another asset bubble. Annual sales, which averaged about $1.3 million annual in the 1820s, rose throughout the 1930s to $24.9 million by 1836.

The speculation was driven by easy credit, made available by the increasing number of state banks; by this time, "wildcat banking" (aggressive banks with little if any state regulation) became a common term. Nominal (not adjusted for inflation) bank capital rose from $61 million in 1830 to $251 million in 1836. Each bank issued its own banknotes, increasing the money supply and available cheap credit. Bank loans rose to $457 million in 1836, with circulating paper currency over $140 million.

Andrew Jackson lost considerable cash in banks and remained hostile to the banking industry. When Jackson came to the presidency, the Second Bank of the United States (Second Bank) operated somewhat like a central bank, including acting as the federal depository and fiscal agent. Second Bank president Nicolas Biddle served from 1822 until resigning in 1839, not long before the bank closed permanently in 1841. Congress passed the Second Bank's charter extension, but the bill was vetoed by Jackson.

Senator Daniel Webster served as Second Bank's legal counsel and a director of its Boston branch. Webster was a chief proponent of its rechartering, in large part because of cash incentives. In a letter to Biddle, Webster wrote: "I believe my retainer has not been renewed or refreshed as usual. If it be wished that my relation to the Bank should be continued, it may be well to send me the usual retainer" (quoted in Johnson and Kwak 2010, 21).

Jackson removed federal funds from Second Bank to his own preferred banks, which proceeded to print lots of paper money (Second Bank was much more conservative). This additional money increased the speculation of the period. Ironically, Jackson favored "hard money," despite destroying the bank best equipped to maintain it. The Specie Circular of 1836, which required gold and silver to buy public land, set off the Panic of 1837. Without the Second Bank, no central bank existed to limit the damage (conservative New England banks served this role regionally). The panic hit when Martin Van Buren was president, and he took most of the blame. Recovery started after Congress passed an additional tariff on foreign goods in 1842.

See also Bank of the United States, Second; Biddle, Nicholas; Jackson, Andrew; Minsky, Hyman; Panic of 1819; Panic of 1857; Panics and Depressions

References

Johnson, Simon, and James Kwak. *13 Bankers: The Wall Street Takeover and the Next Financial Meltdown*. New York: Pantheon Books, 2010.

Kindleberger, Charles, and R. Aliber. *Manias, Panics, and Crashes: A History of Financial Crises*. 5th ed. Hoboken, NJ: Wiley, 2005.

McWilliams, James. "Panic of 1837." In *The American Economy: A Historical Encyclopedia*. Rev. ed. Edited by Cynthia Clark. Santa Barbara, CA: Greenwood, 2011.

Reinhart, Carmen, and Kenneth Rogoff. *This Time Is Different: Eight Centuries of Financial Folly*. Princeton, NJ: Princeton University Press, 2009.

Panic of 1857

The discovery of gold in California in 1849 (also, Australia in 1851) started an economic boom in the 1850s. Gold steaming into New York and beyond increased the money supply, making more credit available in the United States and Europe. The

Close-up of a section of "The banks on a bust," a political cartoon about the Panic of 1857 that appeared in *Frank Leslie's Illustrated Newspaper* on September 12, 1857. It depicts the Ohio Life & Trust bank building with head and legs, seated on the ground with bottles labeled "Bear" and "Bull." Other banks with heads and legs are about to topple over. (Library of Congress)

result was expanding bank lending, inflated asset prices, and increased speculation. Land promoters increased real estate availability. Railroads played a big role, as easy credit led to massive construction projects by both strong and relatively weak lines, fueling railroad securities prices. The Crimean War (1853–56) and bad European harvests caused a boom in American agricultural exports and increased prices. This drove rural land speculation, railroad construction, and increased bank lending. With the end of the Crimean War and better European harvests, grain prices collapsed, resulting in a recession in the United States, which started in 1856.

The bankruptcy of the New York office of the Ohio Life Insurance and Trust Company was the trigger for the panic. British investors withdrew substantial sums from U.S. banks. The news traveled fast because of the telegraph, the new high-tech industry of its day. Investors sold securities, while depositors withdrew bank funds— banks and brokers failed en masse during the crisis. In addition, railroads (having borrowed heavily and subject to massive manipulation and pilfering by insiders) failed by the hundreds. Much of the land speculation revolved around new and prospective railroad routes, and the railroad failures meant collapsing land prices.

Tariff rates on imported goods were reduced up to 80 percent; this benefited the South but provided no major help to the rest of the country. The depression was short, but recovery was shallow—employment did not rise to normal levels until the Civil War.

See also Bubbles and Euphoria; Great Depression; Minsky, Hyman; Panic of 1837; Panic of 1873; Panic of 1893; Panic of 1907; Panics and Depressions; Railroads, Nineteenth Century; Robber Barons

References

Kindleberger, Charles, and R. Alibe. *Manias, Panics, and Crashes: A History of Financial Crises*. 5th ed. Hoboken, NJ: Wiley, 2005.

Knoop, Todd. *Recessions and Depressions: Understanding Business Cycles*. 2nd ed. Santa Barbara, CA: Greenwood, 2010.

Reinhart, Carmen, and Kenneth Rogoff. *This Time Is Different: Eight Centuries of Financial Folly*. Princeton, NJ: Princeton University Press, 2009.

Roubini, Nouriel, and Stephen Mihm. *Crisis Economics: A Crash Course in the Future of Finance*. New York: Penguin Press, 2010.

Panic of 1873

Railroads were a central cause of the 1873 panic. The transcontinental railroad was completed in 1869, followed by plans for additional cross-country routes both north and south. At the time, money was cheap and railroads overbuilt on leverage. Civil War financing hero Jay Cooke focused on the Northern Pacific Railroad; the panic began with the Northern Pacific failure, which led to the collapse of Cooke's Philadelphia investment bank, Jay Cooke and Sons. After Cooke's failure, the New York Stock Exchange closed for 10 days. Other overextended railroads and banks joined Cooke in bankruptcy. The resulting depression was a long one, lasting to 1879.

The global financial collapse actually started in Germany and Austria. The Franco-Prussian War ended in 1871 with reparation payments to the victorious Germans by the French. This caused German and Austrian speculation and euphoria in railroads, land, and securities. The Vienna Stock Exchange crashed in May of 1873. Jay Cooke relied on German investors to support his bank and railroad empire. Without this credit, Cooke collapsed.

The Coinage Act of 1873 again put the United States on the gold standard after trying bimetallism, limiting coinage to gold and ending the demand for silver. Silver prices declined resulting in a western silver-mining collapse. The major result was the decline in the supply of money, resulting in deflation, which particularly hurt railroads and farmers, as well as other debtors (that is, they would have to pay back their debts in more expensive dollars).

On September 19, 1873 (a day that became known as Black Friday), the New York Stock Exchange announced that the important investment banking firm of Jay Cooke & Company had collapsed after investing too heavily in railroad securities. This newspaper illustration depicts the closing of the Stock Exchange's doors to its customers on Saturday, September 20. The financial depression caused by the Panic of 1873 was one of the worst in American history. (Library of Congress)

Railroads focusing on long-term success would use conservative financing including relatively low leverage; the Pennsylvania, the New York Central, and others operated in this way, retiring debt when it came due and paying dividends. However, speculation was a common railroad practice, resulting in overbuilding using massive credit. By 1873, 35,000 miles of railroad track had been constructed since the end of the Civil War, making railroads the biggest nonfarm industry and largest employer. With the crisis, some 89 railroads went bankrupt, about a quarter of the industry.

Jay Cooke, a banker and railroad reorganizer, established Jay Cooke and Company in Philadelphia in 1861 as a private bank. He soon sold some $3 million in war loans for Pennsylvania. Fresh off his success financing the Union cause, Cooke became fascinated with the Northern Pacific Railroad, chartered in 1864, which was struggling mainly due to poor financing. Cooke had control by 1869 and took over construction. The financial collapse in Germany eliminated his major foreign funding source. The railroad was soon overdrawn; its bonds sold at deep discounts and employees were paid in vouchers by late 1872. No market existed for new Northern Pacific bonds. Jay Cooke closed its doors on September 18, 1873, leaving the Northern Pacific bankrupt and incomplete.

The failure of Jay Cooke triggered the panic. Banks called in their loans, depositors demanded cash, and speculators sold stocks and bonds. The New York Stock Exchange closed for 10 days. Money and credit dried up and hundreds of banks and brokers failed, followed by some 18,000 businesses. Another deep depression followed, during which the first widespread doubts about the inevitable benefits of unfettered capitalism took root in the United States. Soon after, political pressures put American state and federal governments on the road to regulation and reform, which has continued ever since.

See also Cooke, Jay; Great Depression; Minsky, Hyman; Panic of 1837; Panic of 1857; Panic of 1893; Panic of 1907; Panics and Depressions; Railroads, Nineteenth Century

References

Kindleberger, Charles, and R. Alibe. *Manias, Panics, and Crashes: A History of Financial Crises*. 5th ed. Hoboken, NJ: Wiley, 2005.

Knoop, Todd. *Recessions and Depressions: Understanding Business Cycles*. 2nd ed. Santa Barbara, CA: Greenwood, 2010.

Reinhart, Carmen, and Kenneth Rogoff. *This Time Is Different: Eight Centuries of Financial Folly*. Princeton, NJ: Princeton University Press, 2009.

Roubini, Nouriel, and Stephen Mihm. *Crisis Economics: A Crash Course in the Future of Finance*. New York: Penguin Press, 2010.

McWilliams, James. "Panic of 1873." In *The American Economy: A Historical Encyclopedia*. Rev. ed. Edited by Cynthia Clark. Santa Barbara, CA: ABC-CLIO, 2011.

Panic of 1893

The Panic of 1893 caused one of the worst American depressions on record. The specific cause of the panic was the failure of the Philadelphia and Reading Railroad and the National Cordage Company, which produced crazed selling by investors and calling of loans by banks, with overleveraged railroads particularly hard hit. The 150 railroad failures included the Baltimore & Ohio, Erie, Union Pacific, and Northern Pacific, resulting in over a quarter of rail track operated under receivership. Some 500 banks and over 15,000 businesses declared bankruptcy. Economic recovery started in 1896, but high unemployment and hard times remained through most of the decade.

The 1880s, generally a booming decade, witnessed the overbuilding by railroads using debt, which doubled the mileage of track from 1880 to 1890, as well as a huge rise in western silver mines. Rail overcapacity set the stage for the economic collapse, which was started by several events. London's Barings Bank almost failed over Latin America investing, which caused a panic in Britain. The Sherman Silver Purchase Act of 1890 increased the amount of silver bought by the Treasury for coinage. This resulted in the depletion of the federal gold supply as people exchanged silver certificates for gold (the act was repealed in 1893). The decrease in gold reduced the money supply and caused panic in the mining industry. The Barings collapse caused a European panic, which further reduced U.S. gold reserves as Europeans claimed American gold by selling U.S. investments. The McKinley Tariff of 1890 increased tariff duties almost 50 percent, disrupting international trade, which hurt farmers, who had to spend more on equipment, while selling fewer agricultural products abroad at lower prices.

The euphoria leading to speculation and overbuilding burst over the problems in Europe and falling American gold supply. The Philadelphia and Reading Railroad failed in February 23, 1893. The National Cordage Co., a rope manufacturer, failed after attempting to corner the market for imported hemp. Investors and speculators sold stock and bought gold. The run on gold led to a stock market crash on May 5, 1893, Wall Street's worst day until the 1929 crash. Economic recovery did not start until 1897, partly because of new gold strikes increasing the supply of money.

Labor strife was a major story over this period and particularly during the depression following the panic, with some 20 percent of laborers losing their jobs and the unemployment rate staying in double digits until 1899. When the economy was booming, firms resisted increasing employee salaries although inflation was typically a problem, disappointing labor. During business depressions, business usually dropped wages to maintain dividends. Severe strikes, such as the Pullman Strike of July 1894, erupted, often put down violently by the owners with the help of local police and federal troops.

See also Commercial Banks before the Federal Reserve; Gold Standard; Great Depression; J. P. Morgan; Panic of 1837; Panic of 1857; Panic of 1873; Panic of 1907; Panics and Depressions; Pullman Strike of 1894

References

Dobson, John. "Panic of 1893." In *Bulls, Bears, and Busts: A Historical Encyclopedia of American Business Concepts*. Santa Barbara, CA: ABC-CLIO, 2006.

Kindleberger, Charles, and R. Alibe. *Manias, Panics, and Crashes: A History of Financial Crises*. 5th ed. Hoboken, NJ: Wiley, 2005.

Knoop, Todd. *Recessions and Depressions: Understanding Business Cycles*. 2nd ed. Santa Barbara, CA: Greenwood, 2010.

Siry, Stephen. "Panic of 1893." In *The American Economy: A Historical Encyclopedia*. Rev. ed. Edited by Cynthia Clark. Santa Barbara, CA: ABC-CLIO, 2011.

Panic of 1907

The Panic of 1907 involved a stock market crash, tight money, speculation and manipulation, failed speculation, broker bankruptcy, bank runs, and the near insolvency of New York City. Speculation, high interest rates, and a volatile stock market preceded the panic. J. P. Morgan saved several trust companies (which specialized in estates and related trust activity, which banks could not handle at the time), plus related activities including rescuing New York City from collapse and propping up the New York Stock Exchange. The panic led to significant banking and business reform, including the creation of the Federal Reserve System and the Federal Trade Commission.

The immediate cause of the panic was speculator Otto Heinze's attempt to corner (buy all available stock) United Copper. When this scheme failed, Heinze's brokerage also failed, causing chaos in stock prices. At the time, trust companies made margin loans to stock speculators; when in trouble, the trusts called in these loans.

After the margin calls, the markets panicked further. This drove Europeans to sell and withdraw gold from New York City. The Knickerbocker Trust Company was overleveraged and collapsed when a bank run against the Knickerbocker occurred in October 1907. J. P. Morgan audited the books of Knickerbocker; and the trust company was allowed to fail when the auditors determined the trust insolvent.

As the panic continued, Morgan agreed to save the larger Trust Company of America, exclaiming, "This is the place to stop the trouble." Morgan got Treasury Secretary George Cortelyou to deposit federal funds into the New York banks to provide liquidity (John D. Rockefeller also contributed $10 million) and persuaded other banks and trust companies to provide loans. The support eventually worked with the help of the New York Clearing House, which issued $100 million in loan certificates to allow banks to settle accounts while still retaining the cash needed to prevent bank runs.

New problems crept up. First, Tennessee Coal, Iron and Railroad Company approached bankruptcy; however, the New York Stock Exchange's largest brokerage firm, Moore & Schley, borrowed heavily using Tennessee Coal as collateral. To avoid the collapse of Moore & Schley, Morgan worked out a deal for United States Steel to buy Tennessee Coal, requiring President Theodore Roosevelt to allow this merger (that is, the federal government would not sue U.S. Steel under the Sherman Antitrust Act). Roosevelt relented just before the market opened and that crisis averted. New York City needed an emergency loan to avoid bankruptcy; Morgan contracted for a $30 million bond issue from the City. Despite all the action engineered by Morgan, dozens of banks, trusts, and other corporations failed and a serious depression followed.

Without a central bank it was up to Morgan to avert catastrophe on Wall Street. Congress did not want to see a repeat of these events that left the federal government as a minor player. The Aldrich-Vreeland Act established the National Monetary Commission in 1908 to reform and regulate banking. Senator Nelson Aldrich chaired the Commission. The Commission and Congressional Hearings—the Pujo Hearings being the most famous—led to the creation of the Federal Reserve as a central bank in 1914; this was viewed either as the necessary institution to protect the banking system or a bailout mechanism for big banks financed by taxpayers. Other reforms at the time included the Clayton Act and the creation of the Federal Trade Commission. Forced to testify during the Pujo Hearings, Morgan's performance was admired by the banking community, while shocking a public unaware of the great power of New York's giant banks.

See also Commercial Banking before the Federal Reserve; Federal Reserve System; Money Trust; Morgan, John Pierpont; Panic of 1837; Panic of 1857; Panic of 1873; Panic of 1893; Panics and Depressions; Pujo Hearings; Roosevelt, Theodore

References

Bruner, Robert, and Sean Carr. *The Panic of 1907: Lessons Learned from the Market's Perfect Storm.* Hoboken, NJ: Wiley, 2007.

Jones, Russell. "Panic of 1907." In *The American Economy: A Historical Encyclopedia.* Rev. ed. Edited by Cynthia Clark. Santa Barbara, CA: ABC-CLIO, 2011.

Kindleberger, Charles, and R. Alibe. *Manias, Panics, and Crashes: A History of Financial Crises.* 5th ed. Hoboken, NJ: Wiley, 2005.

Knoop, Todd. *Recessions and Depressions: Understanding Business Cycles.* 2nd ed. Santa Barbara, CA: Greenwood, 2010.

Panics and Depressions

A panic is a severe economic disturbance such as a run on banks resulting in bank failures, usually caused by excess speculation. A typical result of a panic has been a depression, a long-term downturn in economic activity more severe than a recession (perhaps a decline in gross domestic product greater than 10%).

Panics and the resulting depression became common and recurring since the Industrial Revolution, starting in mid-eighteenth-century Britain. Panics occurred in the United States like clockwork every decade or so, with major depressions occurring roughly once every 20 years. Each had unique features and causes, but with similar economic circumstances. The United States literally started in depression during and after the Revolution, with recovery associated with the new constitutional government under George Washington in 1789. It did not take long for the first panic—1792, caused mainly by speculation in bank stocks. Fortunately depression was averted, thanks in part to the quick action of Treasury Secretary Alexander Hamilton. Big panics followed by depression came in 1819, 1837, 1857, 1873, 1893, and 1907 (plus many recessions in between). After the 1930s Great Depression, busts have been relatively minor, with more federal action and less severe effects.

The business cycle measures the ups and downs of economic activity, described in phases beginning with expansion, followed by crisis, recession, and recovery. The popular definition of a recession is two or more consecutive quarters of negative growth in gross domestic product (GDP). However, it is the National Bureau of Economic Research (NBER) that determines the business cycle. The NBER is an American economic think tank, founded in 1920 by economist Wesley Mitchell among others. The definition of a recession according to the NBER is: "a significant decline in economic activity spread across the economy, lasting more than a few months, normally visible in real GDP, real income, employment, industrial production, and wholesale-retail sales." The NBER determined that the Great Recession started in December 2007 (the peak) and ended June 2009 (the trough).

Various economic theories of the business cycle include John Maynard Keynes's general theory focusing on aggregate demand, Milton Friedman's contracting money supply, Joseph Schumpeter's long-wave theory focusing on technical innovation and creative destruction, or Hyman Minsky's model based on supply of credit. Minsky divided lending into three groups by relative quality: hedge finance (safe), speculative finance (moderate), and Ponzi finance (risky). Lending becomes increasingly speculative, and in Ponzi lending borrowers are unable to generate the cash to pay back either interest or principal. When asset prices fall, the system collapses as loan defaults expand and companies are forced into bankruptcy. The point when asset prices collapse is the "Minsky moment."

Roubini and Mihm (2010, 4) summarize the relationship of panics to capitalism:

> Crises—unsustainable booms followed by calamitous busts—have always been with us, and with us they will always remain. Though they arguably predate the rise of capitalism, they have a particular relationship to it. Indeed, in many important ways, crises are hardwired into the capitalist genome. The very things that give capitalism its vitality—its powers of innovation and its tolerance for risk—can also set the stage for asset and credit bubbles and eventually catastrophic meltdowns whose ill effects reverberate long afterward.

The term "panic" generally has not been used much in the post–World War II period, replaced by the concept of recessions, periods of declining economic activity. Although there have been a dozen recessions since World War II, only the "subprime meltdown" of 2008 had characteristics of a panic.

See also Bubbles and Euphoria; Business Cycle; Great Depression; Minsky, Hyman; Panic of 1819; Panic of 1837; Panic of 1857; Panic of 1873; Panic of 1893; Panic of 1907

References

Kindleberger, Charles, and R. Alibe. *Manias, Panics, and Crashes: A History of Financial Crises*. 5th ed. Hoboken, NJ: Wiley, 2005.

Knoop, Todd. *Recessions and Depressions: Understanding Business Cycles*. 2nd ed. Santa Barbara, CA: Greenwood, 2010.

National Bureau of Economic Research. "U.S. Business Cycle Expansions and Contractions." http://www.nber.org/cycles.html.

Reinhart, Carmen, and Kenneth Rogoff. *This Time Is Different: Eight Centuries of Financial Folly*. Princeton, NJ: Princeton University Press, 2009.

Roubini, Nouriel, and Stephen Mihm. *Crisis Economics: A Crash Course in the Future of Finance*. New York: Penguin Press, 2010.

Paper Money

Paper money was first used in seventh-century China to replace bulk shipments of coins. A similar idea started in medieval Europe, with bank notes (*nota di banco*) in fourteenth-century Italian city-states. A banknote is a promissory note issued by a bank and used as a negotiable instrument. The Bank of England was established in 1694 and has issued banknotes since then. The original ones were handwritten, then partially printed beginning in 1725, then fully printed from 1855. American colonies had early experience with paper currencies. Massachusetts Bay Colony issued paper money in the 1690s, and all the American colonies used notes of some kind during the eighteenth century, usually in times of war (Britain expected the colonies to retire the notes when the crisis was over and banned paper money in 1764). Printer Benjamin Franklin printed the money for several states.

Particularly famous was Continental currency, issued by the Continental Congress to fund the American Revolution. In theory, the currency would be repaid in Spanish-milled dollars, and dollars became the monetary standard rather than the pound. The decimal system (100¢ equals a dollar) was created by Robert Morris as superintendent of finance and approved by Congress. Franklin printed several of the Continental currency issues. Since most of the war funding came from paper money, the Continental rapidly depreciated and became near worthless ("not worth a Continental"). The British military made matters worse by counterfeiting the Continentals. The first American bank was the Bank of North America established in Philadelphia in 1783. It issued its own banknotes, backed by gold, which made it much more valuable than Continental currency.

The Constitution of 1788 gave the federal government the right "to coin money, regulate the value thereof, and of foreign coin, and fix the standard of weights and measures." The federal government under Treasury Secretary Alexander Hamilton assumed the debt of the states and agreed to pay all federal and state obligations, including Continental currency at face value. Under Hamilton, the First Bank of the United States in 1791 was chartered basically as a central bank. The Treasury was not given the right to issue paper currency, but the Bank of the United States could and did.

Few state banks were chartered in the late eighteenth century, but the number mushroomed in the nineteenth century. By 1805, there were 75 banks and 208 by 1813. Each bank issued its own notes and arranged for engraving those notes. Printed in convenient denominations (smaller denominations were more common in rural areas), the banks would issue them as loans (customers could also deposit the money and write checks, a procedure more common in urban areas). States required specie conversion—note holders could present them at the issuing bank and demand the face value in gold and silver coins. Reputable banks usually backed their notes by holding 20 percent or more in reserves in available specie. Initially, most states left the amount of reserves up to the bank, but later regulations usually required specific percentages.

Just after mid-eighteenth century, 1,000 state banks operated, each issuing its own unique banknotes, a banking system nightmare but a bonanza for engravers and printers, as well as counterfeiters. In theory, all these could have served as money, but in practice they often fell short because their value depended upon their acceptability. When presented for payment to merchants and other banks, notes rarely got accepted at face value. Instead, they suffered a discount based on such criteria as bank reputation (usually lower discounts for urban banks), distance away from the issuing bank, and so on. Some notes kept circulating after the issuing bank had failed, rendering them worthless. In this murky arena, note brokers set up shop in major cities, specializing in "correct" discount rates, and bank reference manuals called banknote reporters started listing the various paper in circulation and proper discounts. Fraud and counterfeiting boomed, adding to the hazard and confusion.

At the start of the Civil War, the Union had little cash. The 1862 Legal Tender Act authorized the Treasury to print $150 million in Treasury notes (called greenbacks because of their color), eventually raised to $450 million. The Union did not outlaw banknotes issued by state banks, but the National Bank Act of 1863 put a tax on these notes. The government believed that banknote companies were overcharging for printed greenbacks, and Treasury Secretary Chase moved the operation in-house (that is, printed by the newly established Bureau of Engraving and Printing). National banks were created by the National Banking Act of 1864, which reduced the financial chaos of the state-chartered banks. The country went off the gold standard until the war was over. The greenback depreciated and most silver coins disappeared from circulation. Fractional paper currency (5¢ to 50¢ in value) were issued and even postage stamps were used for change. In 1879, the government made the greenback redeemable to gold at face value.

After the Panic of 1907 and the Pujo Commission found considerable abuse by Wall Street's "Money Trust," the Federal Reserve System (Fed) was created by the Federal Reserve Act of 1913 as the long-missing central bank. The act gave the Fed the authority to issue Federal Reserve notes as legal tender, initially backed by gold (until 1933; foreign holders could exchange the notes for gold until 1971); some issues also were backed by silver. The notes are now backed only by the "full faith and credit of the U.S. government." Currently, over $1 trillion of Fed notes are outstanding.

See also Counterfeiting; Federal Reserve System; Hamilton, Alexander; Morris, Robert; State Banks, Early

References

Allen, Larry. "Counterfeit Money." In *The Encyclopedia of Money*. 2nd ed. Santa Barbara, CA: ABC-CLIO, 2009.

Goodwin, Jason. *Greenback: The Almighty Dollar and the Invention of America*. New York: Holt, 2003.

Perkins, E. *American Public Finance and Financial Services, 1700–1815*. Columbus: Ohio State University Press, 1994.

Patents and Invention Fraud

A patent is a form of licensing to grant exclusive intellectual property rights for a limited period in exchange for the public disclosure of an invention. Great American patents were issued (and subject to litigation and patent infringement)

for Eli Whitney's cotton gin, Samuel Morse's telegraph, Cyrus McCormick's reaper, Alexander Graham Bell's telephone, and many more. Equally important to the patent rights have been the patent infringements, both legal and illegal attempts to get around patent protections, and cases of outright fraud.

The earliest known patent statute was drafted by the city state of Venice, Italy, in 1474, largely to protect the city's guilds. Venice's Council was given the authority to grant monopoly rights to "novel and ingenious" devices for 10 years. England's Statute of Monopolies of 1624 declared that patents could be granted for "projects of new invention," later requiring a written description. American colonies granted patent protection, beginning with a process for making salt in Massachusetts in 1641.

The Constitution, completed in 1787, included the concept of copyrights and patents in Article 1, Section 8 ("enumeration of powers"): "to promote the Progress of Science and useful Arts, by securing for limited Times to Authors and Inventors the exclusive Right to their respective Writings and Discoveries." Congress passed the Patent Act in 1790, creating the Patent Board made up of Secretary of State Thomas Jefferson, Attorney General Edmund Randolph, and Secretary of War Henry Knox and granting a patent with monopoly protection for 14 years. The board met once a month at the State Department to review patent applications. The first patent, issued in July 1790, related to potash production.

Congress passed the second patent act in 1793, which basically "registered" any patent application with little or no regard for its originality and abolished the Patent Board. The job of registering patents went to State Department clerks. The most famous early patent issued under the revised law went to Eli Whitney for the cotton gin in 1793. The cotton gin was a boon to the South, and cotton became the staple southern product and promoted the need for continued slavery. Whitney wanted to gin the cotton himself in Georgia rather than selling gins, but priced his services too high. Others quickly produced illicit cotton gins, and Whitney spent the next 15 plus years defending his patent rights in Georgian courts with little satisfaction. In his frustration, Whitney stated, "I might as well go to Hell in search of Happiness as apply to a Georgia Court for Justice" (quoted in Gibby 2012, 42). To avoid bankruptcy, Whitney and partners licensed the cotton gin in several other states for a modest fee rather than fight infringement cases throughout the South. He eventually gave up and moved north to focus on manufacturing firearms using interchangeable parts. Whitney's problems proved typical. As stated by Gibby (2012, 49), "For every 800 patents issued in the early nineteenth century, 100 found their way to courts."

A major revision to the patent law was passed in 1836, and Henry Ellsworth became the first patent commissioner. Under the new law, miniature models were again required and patents examined for novelty. Under the new patent law, new patents representing the generation of innovation increased dramatically, from 5,000 in the 10-year period 1837–46 to over 130,000 from 1867 to 1876. Under Ellsworth, a number of particularly important patents were soon issued: the telegraph to Samuel Morse, vulcanized rubber to Charles Goodyear, the reaper to

Cyrus McCormick, and the revolver to Samuel Colt. All would become successful and all would have to fend off other manufacturing infringing on products, and others claiming to have actually invented their products or produced products unique enough to not infringe on these patents.

McCormick invented his reaper around the same time Obed Hussey invented his own model; the two fought it out in court. McCormick continued to fight patent infringers in court until his patent expired in 1848; then the focus shifted to improving the reaper and filing for new patents. Colt fought off any number of munitions companies. Although Colt received small orders from the army, his company failed in 1841. He eventually succeeded, after his revolvers proved successful in the Mexican War. His patent expired before the Civil War and he died in 1862, but his wife became the richest widow in the United States by the end of the Civil War. Morse's telegraph needed considerable infrastructure and it was not until 1844 that he received funding from Congress for a demonstration line from Washington, DC, to Baltimore. Goodyear spent some time in debtor's prison, after attempting to beat back infringers (his primary nemesis was Horace Day). He eventually established a market for rubber. In England, Thomas Hancock stole the Goodyear idea and got the vulcanized-rubber patent for England.

Many of the famous attorneys of the time were hired to defend patents. Charles Goodyear used Daniel Webster (then secretary of state) in the "Great India Rubber Case." Cyrus McCormick retained William Seward and Edwin Stanton (later, President Lincoln's secretary of state and war, respectively) and, for a time, Abraham Lincoln. Samuel Morse faced Salmon Chase (later Lincoln's secretary of the Treasury and chief justice of the Supreme Court) defending patent infringer Henry O'Reilly in the Great Telegraph case, claiming the telegraph had been invented before Morse. The Supreme Court ruled in favor of Morse and O'Reilly's company was soon bankrupt.

Attorney Elias Howe created the first large-scale "blocking patent." Howe developed a model of the first commercial sewing machine, which was patented in 1846. Howe's machine did not work effectively and he had no interest in actually manufacturing sewing machines. Dozens of inventors improved the technology, including Isaac Singer, making it commercially feasible. Singer received a patent on his improvements in 1851 and, through effective marketing, became a major manufacturer. Unfortunately for Singer, Howe had a "blocking patent," meaning he must be adequately compensated. Howe sued Singer (and many others) for patent infringement and received preliminary injunctions against the accused infringers in 1852. Most manufacturers soon were paying Howe a royalty of $25 per machine. Singer fought on, using fraud to convince a jury that the sewing machine was invented before Howe. Singer lost and paid Howe $15,000 plus a $25 per machine royalty. By 1867, over 900 sewing machine patents had been granted, resulting in mammoth lawsuits. Eventually, attorney Orlando Potter created a patent pool, with all the manufacturers paying a license fee plus additional royalties. The royalties were paid out to Howe and other "core" patent holders. Inventors, like Howe, receiving patents on products they had no interest in producing became known as "patent trolls."

The most famous patent troll was patent attorney George Selden who received a patent for a "gasoline road locomotive" in 1879. Using the available ideas, he hired a patent draftsman to prepare the necessary drawings. This became a blocking patent on all the American mechanics developing automobiles—Olds, Buick, Ford, and many more. He sued them all for patent infringement and they all signed up for a license with a 1.25 percent royalty on sales price. Henry Ford was the sole holdout; Ford would eventually win his case in 1911, years after introducing the Model T. He demonstrated that his cars used an Otto engine, not the Brayton-type covered by Selden's patent.

Alexander Graham Bell filed his telephone patent in 1876, the same day Elisha Gray also filed a telephone patent. Bell's interest was sending multiple signals down the same telegraph wire. Gray's patent was for an "instrument for transmitting and receiving vocal sounds telegraphically" (quoted in Gibby 2012, 174). Bell's application added a handwritten paragraph in the margin using similar language to Gray. Some experts feel that Gray had the better case, but Bell wan granted the patent rather than Gray. A special investigation was conducted in Congress in 1885 and Western Union sued Bell, but Bell's patent survived and his American Telephone and Telegraph (AT&T) dominated the industry for a century.

During much of the twentieth century, a large percentage of patents were filed and received by large corporations having substantial research and development budgets: AT&T's Bell Labs, IBM, Du Pont, and so on. IBM, for example, currently files some 10,000 patent applications a year. This was in part because of court cases that made receiving patents much more difficult, such as the "flash of genius" requirement introduced in a 1941 Supreme Court case (repealed by Congress in 1952). Scientists and inventors were more likely to be effective working for large companies rather than fighting the system individually.

Patents in the twenty-first century are difficult and expensive to get. The patent office is swamped with applications and often takes years before the analysis starts. Because of current laws and court cases, patent clerks are more likely to reject applications, and patent attorneys spend considerable effort and time (costing the inventor thousands of dollars) to reach an accommodation and receive a patent. Patent attorneys continue to file "paper patents" to achieve "blocking patents." In addition, lawsuits are prevalent, and settling even a frivolous case may be much less costly than fighting in court. Big corporations often file continuation applications to get broader claims using the additional patents. In summary, patents are an important part of innovation, but the current system needs improvement.

See also Constitution, U.S.; Ford, Henry; Fraud; Industrialization in the United States, Early; Regulation of Business

References

Collier, Christopher, and James Collier. *Decision in Philadelphia: The Constitutional Convention of 1787.* New York: Ballantine Books, 1986.

Gibby, Darin. *Why Has America Stopped Inventing?* New York: Morgan James, 2012.

Paulson, Hank

Henry M. Paulson Jr. ("Hank," 1946–) was chairman and chief executive officer (CEO) of Goldman Sachs and secretary of the Treasury from 2006 to 2009. Along with Ben Bernanke, chairman of the Federal Reserve (Fed), and Tim Geithner, president of the New York Federal Reserve, Paulson engineered the bailout of the financial sector during the subprime crisis of 2008. Paulson was born in Palm Beach, Florida, on March 28, 1946, and received a master of business administration (MBA) from Harvard Business School.

Paulson joined Goldman Sachs in 1974, becoming a partner in 1982, and succeeding Jon Corzine as \CEO in 1998. Under Paulson, Goldman went public in 1999—the last of the major investment banks to do so, creating substantial wealth for executives and former partners. Incentives as a public company were to increase risks to improve profits and executive compensation. President George W. Bush selected Paulson as Treasury secretary in mid-2006. Paulson was interested in a number of issues including improving United States-Chinese relationships, but was unprepared for the housing crisis.

Like most experts, Paulson was aware of the subprime problems and rising housing prices, but did not view it as a potential catastrophe—until it happened. Investment bank Bear Stearns proved the first major casualty of the subprime meltdown. The end came in mid-March 2008, when Moody's downgraded Bear debt. With lenders balking at extending short-term loans, and massive mortgage losses on the books, the company became effectively insolvent. Bear turned to the government for help. The key players for the government were Paulson, Bernanke, and Geithner at the New York Fed (where the Fed's monetary actions are actually carried out). J. P. Morgan Chase considered an acquisition of Bear until it discovered considerable "toxic assets" on Bear's books and backed out until the government agreed to "buy" $30 billion of these assets. Bernanke and the Fed used some accounting manipulation to establish a special-purpose entity called Maiden Lane LLC to buy the bad assets. Most experts criticized the role of the Fed. Former Fed chair Paul Volcker stated that the Fed went to "the very edge of its lawful and implied powers, transcending certain long embedded central banking principles and practices."

In July 2008, Paulson asked Congress for reforms of the government-sponsored enterprises (GSEs) and authority to pump money to Fannie Mae and Freddie Mac, which they granted in July 2008, a "bazooka" for financial support from Treasury as Paulson (2010) put it. As holders and guarantors of trillions of dollars of mortgages, Fannie and Freddie were failing. Consultants from Morgan Stanley suggested three alternatives about the GSE (Lowenstein 2010, 160): "(1) let the GSEs raise money on their own, which would essentially preserve the status quo; (2) 'conservatorship,' under which the twins would operate under federal stewardship; and (3) 'receivership,' close to a controlled liquidation." With foreign countries owning much of the debt, especially China and Japan, federal action was needed. (Paulson was particularly interested in maintaining close relationships with China.)

After continued Fannie/Freddie floundering, the Fed and Treasury got new GSE regulator Federal Housing Finance Agency (FHFA) to put the companies into "conservatorship" on September 7, 2008. Fannie CEO Daniel Mudd and other GSE executives considered this a hostile takeover and fought it without success. The CEOs were fired and Treasury promised $100 billion of cash. Treasury acquired $1 billion in preferred stock in each company convertible to a 79.9 percent ownership of common stock.

Lehman announced a third-quarter loss of almost $4 billion on September 10, 2008; credit lines were halted and Lehman was failing. The government needed a plan to save Lehman. According to Wessel (2009, 17), the options were: a "liquidation consortium" to buy the various Lehman assets, including the commercial real estate; a "white knight" to buy Lehman; or bankruptcy. Simultaneously, Merrill Lynch and American Insurance Group (AIG) were in need of government action. Bank of America, a potential Lehman buyer, agreed to acquire Merrill Lynch. The British bank Barclays was the only potential buyer of Lehman, but they did not want the toxic assets estimated at $50 billion nor Lehman's large commercial-property portfolio. Treasury and the Fed twisted the arms of the major banks to acquire the toxic assets and Barclays agreed to a deal. However, Barclays' British regulator Financial Services Authority (FSA) rejected the deal. Lehman was not bailed out and became the largest bankruptcy in American history on September 15, 2008.

Financial chaos reigned as credit markets froze up—lending essentially stopped in all commercial markets. The Fed and Treasury stepped in to restore financial markets. AIG was a big counterparty to many Lehman derivatives and other financial products plus insured massive amounts of mortgage-backed securities (MBSs) and other securitized debt around the world. The immense losses from Lehman and others meant AIG was insolvent. Bernanke and the Fed had no jurisdiction, AIG being an insurance company. It did not matter; AIG's collapse had to be avoided. The Fed loaned AIG $85 billion (as a credit facility, essentially a line of credit) at 8.5 percent above LIBOR (London interbank offered rate), plus the government got warrants that would give the taxpayers a 79.9 percent equity share in the business. AIG returned for more cash and by March 2009 had a total of more than $180 billion in federal aid.

Paulson and Bernanke requested congressional authorization to establish the Troubled Asset Relief Program (TARP). In his memoir *On the Brink* (2010), Paulson describes the process of getting legislative approval for a variety of actions, such as TARP, in some detail. He states: "No matter what the problem, large or small, there is no such thing as a quick solution when you deal with Congress. Frankly, you cannot get important and difficult change unless there's a crisis, and that makes heading off a crisis quite challenging" (Paulson 2010, 55). With 2008 a presidential election year, congressional action was particularly tough since both parties wanted a political advantage.

Paulson wanted TARP funding to buy toxic assets from the banks; the alternative plan (which Bernanke preferred) was to inject funds directly into the banks (similar to the Reconstruction Finance Corporation during the Great Depression), requesting $700 billion. The TARP bill was signed into law October 3, 2008. The TARP money could be used by Treasury to provide fresh capital, which the Fed could not do. By the end of the month, Treasury allocated $25 billion of TARP funding each to Citigroup and Bank of America, with lesser amounts to the less-troubled big banks (a total of $125 billion). Additional funds were distributed to many banks as well as nonbank financials such as American Express and AIG, plus auto giants General Motors and Chrysler.

In late October 2008, the Fed established a number of "Funding Facilities" to provide liquidity to keep financial markets functioning, including commercial paper and asset-backed-securities. Between open-market operations (the Fed funds rate dropped to 1% at the end of October) pumping hundreds of billions of cash into the economy and these various programs, the government prevented the collapse of the credit markets. By the December meeting, the Fed increased its total lending to $2.3 trillion (from $940 billion before the Lehman bankruptcy) (Wessel 2009, 251).

Time named Paulson as a runner-up for person of the year for 2008. Ironically, the magazine later labeled him as one of the "25 People to Blame for the Financial Crisis." He was replaced as Treasury secretary by Tim Geithner in 2009 when Barack Obama became president. In 2011, Paulson was named a senior fellow of the Harris School of Public Policy at the University of Chicago.

See also Bernanke, Ben S.; Fannie Mae and Freddie Mac; Federal Reserve System; Great Depression; Greenspan, Alan; Regulation of Business; Securities and Exchange Commission (SEC); Subprime Meltdown; Troubled Asset Relief Program (TARP)

References

Allen, Larry. "Federal Reserve System." In *The Encyclopedia of Money*. 2nd ed. Santa Barbara, CA: ABC-CLIO, 2009.

Lowenstein, Roger. *The End of Wall Street*. New York: Penguin Press, 2010.

Paulson, Henry. *On the Brink: Inside the Race to Stop the Collapse of the Global Financial System*. New York: Business Plus, 2010.

Sorkin, Andrew. *Too Big to Fail: The Inside Story of How Wall Street and Washington Fought to Save the Financial System from Crisis—and Themselves*. New York: Viking, 2009.

Wessel, David. *In Fed We Trust: Ben Bernanke's War on the Great Panic*. New York: Crown Business, 2009.

Paulson, John

John Paulson (1955–) was an investment banker and president of hedge fund Paulson & Co., famous for "the greatest trade ever," a giant bet against subprime loans in the mid-2000s—making him a billionaire and his company one of the largest hedge funds in the world. Paulson was born on December 14, 1955, in Queens, New York. After graduating from New York University and Harvard Business School, he started with a consulting firm, eventually becoming a merger and acquisition expert at Bear Stearns. He founded his own hedge fund in 1994, specializing in risk arbitrage (such as buying shares of companies expected to be acquired and shorting the acquirer), but also investing in high-yield securities, bankrupt firms, and so on.

After the tech collapse early in the twenty-first century, Paulson bought the debt of Enron, WorldCom, and other failed companies for pennies on the dollar. Simultaneously, the Federal Reserve lowered short-term interest rates to 1 percent, making short-term borrowing lucrative to financial firms. Mortgage rates fell, making housing more affordable. Government incentives and financial innovation such as mortgage-backed securities encouraged mortgage origination as fast as possible, with few incentives for due diligence. As mortgages expanded, so did housing costs. The Case-Schiller Index showed that housing prices doubled by 2005, way beyond historical norms—a classic housing bubble.

When the Fed increased interest rates beginning in 2004, Paulson looked for ways to short the mortgage companies. He asked employee Paolo Pellegrini: "Is there a bubble we can short?" (quoted in Zuckerman 2009, 7). Pellegrini suggested credit default swaps (CDSs, a derivative resembling insurance that pays off if the debt defaults). CDSs were available on companies and Paulson bought some, beginning with insurance company MBIA and finance companies Countrywide and Washington Financial.

CDSs were not available on securitized debt, but investment banks were willing to create a new product promising a high return for big buyers. Deutsche Bank bond trader Greg Lippman created the first mortgage-backed securities (MBSs) CDS in 2005, just in time for the housing bubble. His primary purpose was to use the CDSs to create "synthetic mortgages" to securitize because demand was insatiable. Not only generating commissions on new securities, additional sales were made from buyers and sellers of the CDSs—all generating substantial commissions. Paulson became a big buyer beginning in summer 2005, paying roughly a 1 percent annual premium for CDSs on BBB-rated subprime securities. Paulson was one of a few willing buyers (for CDSs they did not own), while the giant insurance company American Insurance Group (AIG), pension plans, and assorted others became sellers. The sellers were liable for huge payouts, but usually viewed the trade as "free money," collecting premiums with virtually no chance of defaults. The ABX index was created in July of 2006 to track the prices on subprime MBSs, the first price index for this market.

As stated by Zuckerman (2009, 120): "To Paulson, CDS contracts on risky mortgage bonds were an investment with minimal downside and almost unlimited potential, a dream trade with a likely 'asymmetrical outcome.'" There was a problem, however. As long as housing prices increased, mortgage borrowers could refinance to make payments. Mortgage default rates were lowest in those states like California where housing prices were the highest, but had the highest home price increases. Paulson would not collect on his bet until housing prices dropped (or at least stopped going up). Home prices stopped going up in 2006.

Another problem surfaced. Investment banks packaged less-than-stellar-performing MBSs into collateralized debt obligations (CDOs, essentially a portfolio of tranches of other debt instruments). Banks could package these debt slices into new securities and sell off most of them because of relatively high interest rates and investment-grade bond ratings. Consequently, the prices on MBS tranches were not falling, even as housing prices fell and mortgage defaults rose. Simultaneously, real estate financing experts viewed Paulson and others using similar trades as misguided or worse. Their reasoning was that housing prices never went down on a nationwide basis (at least since the Great Depression), MBSs was appropriately diversified, and the sophisticated computer models indicated little risk relative to the housing market.

Unlike other crises that could happen in minutes, the subprime crash developed over years. As early as 2004, several experts identified the housing bubble. Hedge funds and other traders started betting against the bubble (shorting home builders and mortgage companies, then CDSs when they became available). The rise in housing prices stopped in 2006 and real problems finally surfaced in 2007. Amazingly, major banks including Merrill Lynch, Morgan Stanley, and Deutsche Bank were still buying mortgage banks and other subprime lending companies in 2007. Despite the chaos, optimism was hard to suppress; the Dow Jones Industrial Average continued up, reaching its high in October 2007, 14,164.

As housing prices declined, mortgage defaults increased. Defaults were especially prevalent on recent mortgages, which were subject to virulent predatory practices and shoddy documentation. When mortgagees failed to make even the first payment, the mortgages were returned to the mortgage companies and these started failing in 2007. By summer of 2007, Standard & Poor's and Moody's started lowering ratings on structured finance securities to junk status. As the crisis worsened, many financial organizations were not showing losses or writing down bad mortgages (the companies are audited annually; there were major questions on the accounting during the first three quarters of many of these companies). Losses started showing up after the end of the fiscal year end when audits were finalized. Major banks were writing off billions in CDOs and taking other losses.

The ABX index of subprime loans started dropping in 2007 (it eventually fell to 2¢ in 2008). At that point, Paulson started making money as the value of his CDSs increased. Most of the CDS bets were done over-the-counter, did not trade frequently, and were difficult to price. The bank underwriters were reluctant to raise the prices on these (and thus admit that the value of their own structured finance holdings was dropping) or even provide market prices (in part because they were hard to value). In the spring of 2007, CDO prices started falling. In July, Bear Stearns hedge funds collapsed and the mortgage market was in its death throes. As the CDO market collapsed, more bankers were desperate for the CDSs owned by Paulson and other bears, driving up prices. As the value of CDSs increased, Paulson selectively sold part of his portfolio to lock in gigantic profits (also because of the potential for counterparty defaults).

Paulson's hedge fund had a gain for 2007 of about $15 billion. Paulson's personal share was almost $4 billion. As Zuckerman (2009, 254) stated it, "It was the largest one-year payout in the history of the financial markets"—the biggest trade ever. In 2008, chaos erupted in the investment banks including the bankruptcy of Lehman Brothers and almost the total collapse of the financial world. Chaos was not the word for Paulson & Co., which made another $5 billion in profit for 2008.

Paulson's success made him a financial superstar. Unfortunately, that meant he joined other big players testifying before Congress. He was also involved in the Securities and Exchange Commission's (SEC) civil fraud case against Goldman Sachs on CDO Abacus 2007-AC1. Paulson & Co. helped determine which securities to place in the CDO in order to bet against it (Paulson & Co. were not charged); Goldman sold the securities to various investors without informing them of the Paulson involvement. Goldman settled the case, paying $550 million to the SEC.

In 2012, Paulson was on *Forbes*'s list of wealthiest billionaires at number 61, worth $12.5 billion. Despite his newly acquired wealth, Paulson continued to run his hedge fund, although he lost money in 2010–11.

See also American Insurance Group (AIG); Bear Stearns; Credit Default Swaps; Derivatives; Goldman Sachs, Hedge Funds; Lehman Brothers; Subprime Loans

References

Lewis, Michael. *The Big Short: Inside the Doomsday Machine*. New York: Norton, 2010.

Weiss, Gary. "The Man Who Made Too Much." *Portfolio*. January 7, 2009. http://www.portfolio.

Zuckerman, Gregory. *The Greatest Trade Ever: The Behind-the-Scenes Story of How John Paulson Defied Wall Street and Made Financial History*. New York: Crown Business, 2009.

Pecora Commission

The Pecora Commission (1932–34) was a Senate investigation of the causes of the Crash of 1929, named for the last chief counsel, Ferdinand Pecora. After the crash, the economy went into depression and thousands of banks failed. Pecora uncovered many unscrupulous financial practices that shocked the nation and led to several reform bills that included the creation of the Securities and Exchange Commission (SEC).

President Hoover thought Wall Street and speculators in particular caused the crash. "Hoover now shared the average American's view of Wall Street as a giant casino rigged by professionals" (Chernow 1990, 351). The administration asked the Senate Banking and Currency Committee to investigate short selling, which it did in 1932. New York Stock Exchange (NYSE) president Richard Whitney, the first witness, called Hoover's charges ridiculous—proclaiming that the NYSE could do no wrong. Big manipulators, including Bernard "Sell 'Em Ben" Smith and Harry Sinclair (of Teapot Dome fame), testified about their own blatant manipulations, but felt no remorse. Others were out of the country when called, while

J. Pierpont Morgan Jr. (standing, center) is joined by the Van Sweringen brothers at the Senate Banking Committee inquiry into J. P. Morgan and Company in New York City, June 5, 1933. The Van Sweringens appear before the Senate to tell of their relationships, their interests, and the Morgan firm. Standing from left are, Oris Paxton Van Sweringen; Morgan; and Mantis James Van Sweringen. Seated from left are, Sen. Townsend of Delaware; Sen. Goldsborough of Maryland; Sen. Duncan Fletcher of Florida, new chairman of the committee; and Ferdinand Pecora, committee counsel. (AP Photo)

many claimed amnesia. The hearings dragged on, with the press ridiculing the Senate more than the bankers. The most prominent revelation before Pecora took over was the testimony on the failure and fraud of match king Ivar Kreuger.

Ferdinand Pecora became the fourth committee counsel in January 1933, a former assistant district attorney from New York. The Democrats now controlled Congress and the presidency after the 1932 election. President-elect Franklin D. Roosevelt would not be sworn in until March, but that did not stop the Democratically controlled Senate in session. The hearings were named for Pecora, and his findings shocked and angered the public. As summarized by Chernow (1990, 355):

With Pecora as counsel, the hearings acquired a new, irresistible momentum. They would afford a secret history of the crash, a sobering postmortem of the twenties that would blacken the name of bankers for a generation. From now on, they would be called banksters.

The hearings lasted through mid-1934, generating 10,000 pages of testimony. Pecora was named a commissioner of the new SEC after the hearings ended. According to the Committee on Banking and Currency (June 6, 1934), the hearings cost $250,000, but the IRS recovered some $2 million from tax fraud fines based on committee testimony.

Pecora Commission findings included many of the same issues as the 1913 Pujo Hearings in addition to new revelations. The investment trusts (with Goldman Sachs Trading Corporation the biggest) charged outrageous fees, providing little disclosure, lost massive amounts of money, and many went bankrupt. Leveraged trusts (buying most stocks on credit) and pyramiding leveraged trust (using borrowed money to buy other leveraged trusts) were other high-risk investments sold by Wall Street that failed in the Great Crash. Investment banks sold millions of dollars of high-risk South American and other foreign bonds for substantial fees, knowing of their likely defaults (which, beginning with Bolivia in 1931, most of them did). This demonstrated the potential unethical relationship between commercial and investment banking. Rather than take loan losses, the commercial banks transferred the high-risk loans to the investment bank operation to be repackaged as government bonds. Substantial commissions and banking fees replaced loan losses. The separation of commercial and investment banking with the Glass-Steagall Act became one of the first regulatory achievements by Congress after Pecora.

Pecora findings on pyramiding schemes of Samuel Insull (and others) in utilities and the Van Swearingen brothers in railroads outraged the public. J. P. Morgan developed complex tax-avoidance schemes. Morgan "preferred lists" distributed new issues of stocks to influential politicians and prized customers at favorable rates before they went public (a practice that is still legal, now called "spinning"). Rampant insider trading and pool-manipulated stock prices plagued dozens of major corporations. The president of Chase National shorted his own stock in 1929, using money borrowed from Chase. Bribed journalists planted favorable stories to boost stock prices (or to pan companies to lower prices).

Charles Mitchell, chairman and president of National City, ran the largest U.S. bank in the 1920s. National City executives borrowed millions of dollars from a "morale loan fund," repayment not required. Mitchell received bonuses over $1 million a year from 1927 to 1929. Mitchell sold National City stock at a loss for tax purposes. Mitchell resigned after his testimony, and later the Internal Revenue Service indicted him for tax evasion. Pecora demonstrated that the inflated compensation resulted, in part, from unsound banking and investment practices.

Pecora got a Senate resolution to enable him to investigate private banks—beginning with J. P. Morgan. Federal investigators went over the Morgan books for some six weeks. Chairman J. P. (Jack) Morgan's opening statement emphasized character:

> The private banker is a member of a profession which has been practiced since the middle ages. In the process of time there has grown up a code of professional ethics and customs, on the observance of which depend his reputation, his force and his usefulness to the community.

Morgan and Company avoided illegal acts, but the disclosures proved embarrassing. The partners paid no income tax in 1931 and 1932, because of stock losses. Morgan made loans to executives of competing banks. Morgan executives served as directors of 89 corporations, established stock pyramiding holding companies, used complex option warrants for compensation, and had preferred lists.

The Pecora Commission concentrated on the big institutional players, rather than where the most basic fraud and abuse were. NYSE firms followed listing requirements and generally furnished financial statements, and most were audited. Bucket shops and other marginal players sold fraudulent securities, estimated at $1 billion sold annually. In 1932 the attorney general had over 1,500 injunctions against individuals and firms and 146 criminal prosecutions. More than 30 stock exchanges sold "unlisted" securities, where no registration information existed. On the New York Curb Exchange (later the American Stock Exchange), the second-largest exchange, more than 80 percent of the companies traded were unlisted. These were subject to no regulation, resulting in huge commissions and high prices, and considerable potential for fraud and manipulation.

See also Crash of 1929; Glass-Steagall Act; Goldman Sachs Trading Corporation; Holding Company Pyramiding; Insull, Samuel; Investment Trusts; Kreuger, Ivar; Mitchell, Charles ("Sunshine Charlie"); Pujo Hearings; Roosevelt, Franklin Delano; Securities and Exchange Commission (SEC); Whitney, Richard

References

Chernow, Ron. *The House of Morgan: An American Banking Dynasty and the Rise of Modern Finance*. New York: Atlantic Monthly Press, 1990.

Chernow, Ron. "Where Is Our Ferdinand Pecora?" *New York Times*, January 5, 2009. http://www.nytimes.com.

Dobson, John. "Crash." In *Bulls, Bears, Boom, and Bust: A Historical Encyclopedia of American Business Concepts*. Santa Barbara, CA: ABC-CLIO, 2006.

Galbraith, Kenneth. *The Great Crash 1929*. Boston: Houghton Mifflin, 1988.

Pecora Commission testimony in *Records of the Commission on Banking and Currency, 1913–1946, 5.5*. National Archives. http://www.archives.gov/legislative/guide/senate/chapter-05.html#1913.

Penn Central Bankruptcy (1970)

Railroad bankruptcies increased in the post–World War II period. The biggest railroad of the time, Penn Central (PC), declared bankruptcy in 1970. Corporate bankruptcy following fraud brought lawsuits against the investment bankers, auditors, and other players, partly because of their "deep pockets." Penn Central proved particularly fascinating because of the distinguished history of the major railroads and partially because at the time of bankruptcy, the company had immense assets (being the largest bankruptcy in history up to that time).

The Pennsylvania Railroad and New York Central Railroad each operated since the mid-nineteenth century. The "Pennsy," founded in 1846, initially connected Harrisburg and Pittsburg. The New York Central, a merger of several New York railroads in 1853, mainly followed routes around the Erie Canal. The Mohawk and Hudson, the first of the railroads making up the New York Central, chartered in 1826, connected Schenectady to Albany. Railroad acquisition continued. Cornelius Vanderbilt took control of the New York Central in 1867. The Pennsy had the distinction of a railroad run by competent professional management by the mid-nineteenth century, making a number of management and accounting innovations.

The Pennsy remained the largest railroad in the nation during most of the twentieth century. Having acquired hundreds of railroads over its long existence, it controlled 10,000 miles of track. The railroad continuously paid out dividend over 100 years—the longest on record; it did not record a twentieth-century net loss until 1947. Limited revenue growth potential, rising costs, and overleverage led to its ultimate downfall, a fate common in the railroad industry, made worse by overregulation and mediocre management. The Pennsylvania started buying assets in the 1960, including Madison Square Garden, the Waldorf-Astoria, and Six Flags Amusement Park. The Pennsy essentially became a conglomerate, using acquisition accounting gimmicks to record profits. The stock price went up for a while, as did interest payments. Ultimately, the high cost of leverage led to bankruptcy.

Cornelius Vanderbilt gained control of the New York Central in 1867 and expanded routes and infrastructure to build a railroad empire. The railroad grew and prospered until well into the twentieth century. Robert Young's proxy fight put him in charge of the failing railroad in the 1950s. The financial position deteriorated in a similar fashion to the Pennsy as costs rose and revenues declined.

The Pennsylvania (Penn) and New York Central (NYC) merged in February 1968 to form Penn Central Transportation (PC), an ill-conceived merger of two large but poorly run railroads. The giant PC, with a combined $1.2 billion in debt, lasted only until June 1970. The ineptness of the new board and executive team, made up of a combination of former Penn and NYC executives and board members, proved a major problem. The president (from Penn) and chairman (from NYC) did not like each other and fought until Chairman Perlman quit. This merger of two mediocre companies with conflicting cultures increased the chaos. The accounting and other systems did not integrate, resulting in lost rolling stock and massive delays. The executives gave themselves lavish salaries and perquisites, while practicing insider trading and other self-dealing. Substantial dividend payments continued, again benefiting the insiders to the detriment of the long-run liquidity of the railroad.

PC's chief financial officer, David Bevan, lied to the board, investment banks, and auditors, as well as to the Interstate Commerce Commission (ICC), claiming the financial position was okay. This was believable because of the large nonrailroad asset base (including the largest real estate ownership in the nation), available for sale or collateral. Merger losses remained hidden and earnings were inflated. Bevan profited from insider trading in PC stock. The National Credit Office (the commercial paper rating subsidiary of Dunn and Bradstreet) continued to give PC a prime rating after conferring with PC and the company's banker Goldman Sachs, which specialized in commercial paper. Continuous commercial-paper sales provided the cash PC needed to stay in business.

The reorganization required after the merger required a large mortgage bond issue (secured by PC's real estate holdings) and $100 million or more in commercial paper. Commercial-paper interest rates were substantially lower than bank loans and long-term bonds. Goldman Sachs stopped issuing commercial paper for PC, the liquidity necessary to keep the PC operating.

Bankruptcy came in June 1970. Bankers, regulators, and analysts could not believe the railroad could fail given the company's asset holdings. The financial problems included large losses and the immense short-term debt PC relied on and could not roll over—the amount of Penn's commercial paper actually exceed total revenue by over $40 million. Penn defaulted on $87 million in commercial paper, and investors sued or settled with dealer Goldman Sachs—the largest commercial-paper dealer at the time. Goldman avoided its own failure by dragging out the litigation and ultimately settling up for much less than face value on much of the debt. The SEC censured Goldman for not informing commercial-paper customers about the poor financial position of the railroad. Auditor Peat Marwick (now KPMG) issued clean audit opinions and was charged with filing false financial statements.

All the key players were lazy or incompetent or committed fraud. To the outsiders, the inside players seemed complicit and stupid. This called into question the effectiveness of railroad regulator ICC, as well as other governmental offices. The federal government belatedly cleaned up the mess, forming Conrail in 1976, which included five other bankrupt railroads in addition to PC.

See also Acquisition Accounting; Corporations; Erie Railroad; Goldman Sachs; Interstate Commerce Commission; Railroads, Nineteenth Century; Securities and Exchange Commission (SEC); Vanderbilt, Cornelius ("Commodore")

References

Cohan, William. *Money and Power: How Goldman Sachs Came to Rule the World.* New York: Doubleday, 2011.

Van Sickle, Eugene. "Railroads." In *The American Economy: A Historical Encyclopedia.* Rev. ed. Edited by Cynthia Clark. Santa Barbara, CA: ABC-CLIO, 2006.

Pension Basics

A pension plan is a long-term commitment providing retirement benefits to employees. Pension plans can be either defined-contribution plans or defined-benefit plans. Under a defined-contribution plan (such as a 401 (k)) the employee (generally with employer matching) contributes a specific sum of money periodically, usually a percentage of salary. The retirement potential is the total amount available at retirement. The employer does not guarantee a specific retirement income. A defined-benefit plan requires the organization to pay a cash benefit (usually monthly), such as 2 percent of final salary for each year of service with the company. An employee with an expected final salary of $100,000 a year at retirement and 25 years of service would receive $50,000 a year from the retirement plan (2% × 25 × $100,000). The major issue of defined-benefit plans is the long-term liabilities and commitments—made more complicated by the requirement of a variety of assumptions and forecasts to determine the commitments.

Defined-contribution plans are simple and leave no outstanding liabilities, and most relatively new companies use them exclusively (Apple, Google and so one). The 401 (k) plans became available only in the 1980s. Older companies often have long-established defined-benefit plans (in part because these early plans used pay-as-you go, which did not require recorded future commitments as liabilities). Perhaps these companies were "paternalistic," looking out for the long-term interests of employees by guaranteeing their pensions (the companies take the risks, not the employees). On the other hand, given the vast number of assumptions and calculations, pensions have considerable manipulation potential.

Probably half of all American workers are covered by pension plans, with an increasing proportion using (or switching) to 401 (k) plans. American Express first offered pensions in 1875. By 1929, almost 400 plans were in effect in the United States and Canada. The early plans were pay-as-you-go, with expenses recognized only for cash payment to retirees. The costs of pensions have increased as life expectancies have gone up. For a number of reasons, a large percentage of corporate defined-benefit plans are underfunded.

In additional to contractual provisions, corporations are subject to Internal Revenue Service (IRS) rules and the Employee Retirement Income Security Act of 1974 (ERISA or Pension Reform Act) and the Pension Protection Act of 2006 regulations. Accounting standard setters changed pension accounting often: Accounting Research Bulletin (ARB) No. 36 (1948), ARB No. 47 (1956), Accounting Principles Board (APB) Opinion No. 8 (1966), State of Financial Accounting Standards (SFAS) No. 35 and 36 (1980), SFAS No. 87 (1985), and SFAS 158 (1996). Additional accounting regulations exist for government organizations.

Over time, accounting standards generally required more realistic assumptions and being closer to economic reality. As pension plans get bigger and more expensive and regulation increases, accounting rules get more complex. A fundamental issue is calculating pension costs that must be allocated to the current period and whether long-term liabilities must be recognized on the balance sheet (that is, for underfunded plans). Since pensions are voluntary, employers have the option to drop pension plans or cut back benefits.

Prior to SFAS No. 87, pension liabilities were not recorded. Under SFAS No. 87, the company records the pension assets less pension liabilities. A net liability means the pension in underfunded. During the 1990s, most defined-benefit pension plans were overfunded—largely because of the booming stock market. The plan assets of a defined-benefit plan represent the fair value of the investment portfolio. The projected benefit obligation (PBO) is the estimated liability (the present value of amounts the employer expects to pay retired employees based on employee service to date and expected future salary at retirement, as adjusted by various actuarial assumptions including average retirement age, mortality rates after retirement, and number of employers staying to retirement). The funded status of the pension plan is the fair value of plan assets less the PBO—the net asset (for overfunding) or liability (underfunding)—recorded on the balance sheet.

Pension accounting under SFAS No. 87 understated actual pension liabilities (amounts were "smoothed" over a decade or so); consequently, the amount recorded on the balance sheet was typically much less than funded status. For the 30 companies making up the Dow Jones Industrial Average (Dow 30), the average net asset position was overfunding of $4.6 billion, while funded status averaged a negative $1.8 billion (Giroux 2006, 112). Deficient accounting rules plus the tech bubble resulted in overfunded pension plans.

After the market crash in the early twenty-first century, more companies became underfunded. Many companies cut benefits to lower net pension expense. Simultaneously, companies often moved unfunded supplementary executive pensions into the overall pension, increasingly the underfunding recorded on the income statement. Several big bankruptcies of firms with major underfunding made it a political issue, since the Pension Benefit Guaranty Corporation, the federal agency responsible for making good on pension liabilities of bankrupt companies, also is underfunded.

Current accounting standards (based on SFAS No. 158, effective in 2006) require funded status to be reported on the balance sheet, moving to economic reality and larger reported underfunding of pensions. IBM reported their pension plans as underfunded by $7.9 billion for fiscal year 2010, compared to overfunding of $19.5 in 2004 (however, funded status in 2004 showed underfunding of $7.4 billion). Hewlett Packard went from a small pension surplus in 2004 to underfunding of $4.8 billion in 2010. Both are typical results based on the new standard. IBM cut pension benefits and used pension assets to fund employee lump-sum buyouts.

Pension accounting has extensive economic consequences. Pension plans are voluntary, so companies must continually decide to adopt, drop, or change pension plans. A great pension plan may keep employees loyal to the company, but at a substantial price if labor costs are a large share of production costs (and a larger cost as accounting requirements changed). If the pension costs are too great, the plan might be dropped, to the detriment of employees. Pension contracts may be changed, subject to labor contracts and federal regulations. The amounts calculated are based on various assumptions as well as specific decisions of management such as funding of prior service costs. Changes in pension pronouncements can have substantial direct economic consequences.

See also Accounting Standards; Financial Accounting Standards Board (FASB); Pension Underfunding and Manipulation; Retirement Benefits and Manipulation

References

Giroux, Gary. *Earnings Magic and the Unbalance Sheet: The Search for Financial Reality.* New York: Wiley, 2006.

Schultz, Ellen. *Retirement Heist: How Companies Plunder and Profit from the Nest Eggs of American Workers.* New York: Portfolio/Penguin, 2011.

Pension Underfunding and Manipulation

Defined-benefit pension plans are complex, involve long-term obligations, and are subject to substantial earnings management and possible abuse. Many large companies have large defined-benefit plans, although an increasing number are switching to defined-contribution plans. Giroux (2006, 112) evaluated the 30 companies making up the Dow Jones Industrial Average (Dow 30) for fiscal year 2004. Twenty-six (87%) of the Dow 30 had defined-benefit plans with total pension plan assets of $6.6 trillion, but were underfunded by a combined $47 billion. The underfunding averaged $1.8 billion a firm.

A 2005 Securities and Exchange Commission (SEC) report, *Arrangements with Off-Balance-Sheet Implications*, found that 81 percent of the large firms in their sample had defined-benefit plans, with a combined underfunding based on funded status of over $85 billion (but overfunded on the balance sheet by almost $90 billion based on accounting standards of the time). Extrapolating to the entire population of traded corporations, the SEC estimated that over $400 billion in real pension obligations was off-balance-sheet.

Each year the employer recognizes the net expense (pension cost), which includes the increase in the projected benefit obligation less the expected return on plan assets. The amount is an estimated average return percentage times the beginning balance of plan assets. It is always a positive, since it is a percentage based on average return—the actual return can be dramatically different from year to year. Companies have almost complete control of the assumption rates used, but have to disclose those rates. Based on a 2001 survey, the most common return on plan assets was between 9 and 10 percent. Return on plan asset rates for the Dow 30 were in the range of 7 to 9 percent for 2004. Blankley and Swanson (1995) found that firms do not change discount rates as often as should be done to use current market interest rates. This was particularly true when market rates were declining. By avoiding lowering discount rates, firms could report lower projected benefit obligation (PBO) and pension costs. Their findings showed substantial volatility in the actual rate of return experienced by firms. A major factor was how close the companies were near critical earnings thresholds (especially analysts' earnings forecast). IBM, for example, raised its expected return from 9.25 percent to 10 percent in 2000–2001, which increased IBM's pretax income almost 5 percent.

In *Retirement Heist* (2011), author Ellen Schultz describes a retirement crisis caused by the deceptive practices of corporate executives aided by consultants, bankers, and insurance companies. At the start of the twenty-first century, corporate pensions were overfunded (based on SFAS No. 87 accounting and large pension gains on stock investments in the 1990s) some $250 billion. Companies used over-funded pensions to downsize the workforce (using pension assets to pay severance benefits), move unfunded executive compensation benefits to the regular employee pension plans, include "excess pension assets" into sales of subsidiaries (with the "excess" increasing the price of the subs), and other manipulation techniques.

Bell Atlantic (which merged with GTE to form Verizon in 2000) used $3 billion in pension assets to finance the early retirement of 25,000 managers. DuPont pio-neered the use of pension assets to pay retiree health benefits in the 1990s, some $1.7 billion—later freezing pensions when the pension became underfunded (a deficit of $3.5 billion in 2004). During the 1990s, General Electric (GE) sold its aerospace unit to Martin Marietta (now Lockheed Martin), including pension assets overfunded by over $500 million. This "excess" was incorporated in the price paid by Martin Marietta (increasing the net gain recorded by GE) and, at the time, reduced GEs pension surplus. Thanks, in part, to several of these deals, GE's pen-sion went from a $24 billion surplus in 1999 to a $6 billion deficit in 2011.

Although pension plans were overfunded based on SFAS No. 87, corporations had incentives to reduce pension expenses to increase earnings. Consequently, many overfunded plans still cut benefits or froze pension benefits. The urgency for cutting benefits increased as several events eliminated surpluses. First, the col-lapse of the tech bubble and stock market collapse led to stunning investment losses early in the century (and again in 2008 related to the housing crisis). SFAS 158 required valuing pension plans based on funded status, which immediately shifted many retirement plans from reported surplus to deficit. Finally, the various manipu-lation techniques in use reduced funding levels even further. IBM went from a $7 billion overfunded plan in 1999 to a $7.4 billion underfunded plan in 2010.

Internal Revenue Service (IRS) rules limit the amount employees can earn in pensions, which was often not considered enough for executives. Consequently, many companies provide unfunded supplemental pensions (SERPs for supplemen-tal executive retirement plans) only to executives—IRS rules do not allow a deduc-tion for funding these plans. Intel moved $200 million in deferred compensation to executives into the regular pension plan in 2005. GE, one of the few companies that actually report the SERPs separately, has $5.9 billion, 15 percent of the total pen-sion liability. With substantial pension underfunding created by various shenani-gans, large corporations cut pension benefits, converting to cheaper 401 (k) plans, or eliminating pensions all together. SERPs are another factor for pension under-funding and add to the pressure to reduce pension benefits for average employees. Cigna introduced "new retirement programs," which implied improved benefits, but actually decreased payouts (and pension expense). One strategy was called "creeping takeaways," reducing benefits gradually with little fanfare. IBM cut pen-sions several times during the 1990s. As stated by Schultz (2011, 57), "By the late 1990s, roughly four hundred large companies, most of which had well-funded or overfunded pension plans, had cut pension benefits, primarily by changing to a less generous cash-balance plan, which for many older workers was no different from freezing their pensions."

See also Accounting Standards; Earnings Manipulation; Financial Accounting Standards Board (FASB); Pension Basics; Retirement Benefits and Manipulation

References

Blankley, Alan, and Edward Swanson. "A Longitudinal Study of SFAF 87 Pension Rate Assumptions." *Accounting Horizons*, December 1995, 1–21.

Giroux, Gary. *Earnings Magic and the Unbalance Sheet: The Search for Financial Reality.* New York: Wiley, 2006.

Schultz, Ellen. *Retirement Heist: How Companies Plunder and Profit from the Nest Eggs of American Workers.* New York: Portfolio/Penguin, 2011.

Plunkitt, George Washington

George Washington Plunkitt (1842–1924) was a New York politician, state senator, and Tammany Hall functionary, best known for his concept of "honest graft." He became rich mainly through land purchases needed for public projects. Reporter William Riordon recorded Plunkitt's description of honest graft in a series of statements at the New York courthouse:

My party's in power in the city, and it's goin' to undertake a lot of public improvements. Well, I'm tipped off, say, that they're going to lay out a new park at a certain place. I see my opportunity and I take it. I go to that place and I buy up all the land I can in the neighborhood. Then the board of this or that makes its plan public, and there is a rush to get my land, which nobody cared particular for before. Ain't it perfectly honest to charge a good price and make a profit on my investment and foresight? Of course, it is. Well, that's honest graft. (Riordon, chap. 1)

Plunkitt worked his way up the Tammany hierarchy. He reportedly explained, "I had a cousin, a young man who didn't take any particular interest in politics. I went to him and said; 'Tommy, I'm goin' to be a politician, and I want to get a followin'; can I count on you?' He said: 'Sure, George.' That's how I started in business. I got a marketable commodity—one vote. ... Before long I had sixty men back of me, and formed the George Washington Plunkitt Association" (Riordon, chap. 2). He developed his political success as ward boss in the Fifteenth District, a working-class Irish district in New York City. By 1870 he was assemblyman, alderman, police magistrate, and county supervisor, drawing three salaries simultaneously.

Plunkitt distinguished between looters and politicians:

The difference between a looter and a practical politician is the difference between the Philadelphia Republican gang and Tammany Hall [with no mention of Tweed]. . . . Why, I remember, about fifteen or twenty years ago, a Republican superintendent of the Philadelphia almshouse stole the zinc roof off the buildin' and sold it for junk. . . . It ain't fair, therefore, to class Tammany men with the Philadelphia gang.

Understand, I ain't defendin' politicians of today who steal. The politician who steals is worse than a thief. He is a fool. With the grand opportunities all around for the man with a political pull, there's no excuse for stealin' a cent. (Riordon, chap. 7)

Plunkitt had a long political career in both New York City and Albany as state senator and became wealthy. His perspective probably represents typical long-term machine politics: patronage, election fraud, and honest graft, just not too greedy and no blatant criminal acts. He focused on the benefits of the political machine, mainly how close political bosses were to their constituents.

Plunkitt was defeated in the 1904 election for state senate, ending his political career. He turned to political reporter Reardon to publish his "lectures" on the philosophy of nineteenth-century machine politics. This proved to be the end of an era as the progressive movement of Theodore Roosevelt and others reduced the influence of Tammany Hall and other political machines. Plunkitt died on November 23, 1924, in New York City.

See also Bribery; Burr, Aaron; Fraud; Political Machines; Roosevelt, Theodore; Tammany Hall; Tweed, William M. ("Boss")

References

Allen, Oliver. *The Tiger: The Rise and Fall of Tammany Hall*. New York: Addison-Wesley, 1993.

Brands, H. W. *American Colossus: The Triumph of Capitalism, 1865–1900*. New York: Doubleday, 2010.

O'Donnell, Edward. "The Sage of Tammany Hall." *New York Times*, August 28, 2005. http://www.nytimes.com.

Riordon, William. *Plunkitt of Tammany Hall*. New York: St. Martin's Press, 1993. Originally published in 1905.

Political Machines

Political machines are organizations affiliated with a party, rewarding political power and centered on a "boss" or small group. Patronage—the spoils system—proved a driving force in the creation of early machines such as Tammany Hall, the Democratic New York City machine. Machines spread to cities and states throughout the nineteenth century and, despite substantial reform movements, many continued well into the twentieth century.

Democracy was common early in U.S. history. However, before the secret ballot was introduced in the mid-nineteenth century to allow anonymous voting, open voting was common. Typically, voters announced their votes to clerks recording the results. This allowed the machines (and other powers) to monitor the votes. Getting constituents to vote as a block and then reward them through patronage jobs and other benefits was key to the success of the machine.

Tammany Hall, the Democratic political machine of New York City, was the first, longest, and likely the most corrupt machine in the United States. It developed its political influence early in the nineteenth century and reached its pinnacle under Boss Tweed shortly after the Civil War. Political influence and corruption continued well into the twentieth century.

The Tammany Society was founded in 1789 as "a benevolent and charitable organization for the purpose of affording relief to the indigent and distressed member of said associated, their widows and orphans and others who may be proper objects of their charity" (Allen 1993, 19).

William Mooney, an upholsterer, was the first Grand Sachem. Under Mooney, Tammany became Democratic and increasingly political. Aaron Burr spent considerable time in New York City, especially during the 1800 election making a presidential run. Burr proved to be a genius for political organization. He allied with Tammany members, who learned Burr's techniques for corrupt mastery of machine politics. Lying to newspaper reporters was a Burr specialty, using partisan newspapers and bribing reporters. On election day, Burr's cronies got out the vote for their members and ruthlessly denied the votes for opponents.

Corruption by Tammany members expanded. William Mooney (the original Grand Sachem) paid himself much more than the allotted $1,500 a year and absconded with goods (his "trifles for Mrs. Mooney" defense became the standard excuse for political pilfering). John Ferguson, mayor of New York in 1815, handed out patronage jobs wholesale to Tammany cronies. Patronage became the primary means for maintaining Tammany power. Tammany cronies met immigrants at the dock, finding them living quarters and jobs, and demanding their future votes. Voter fraud increased, including voting by underage males and herding new immigrants—not yet citizens and often not understanding English—to the polls. With voting done in the open, party workers ensured that new adherents voted the party line.

Tammany-controlled banks distributed thousands of shares of stock to Tammany elites. Burr ally Samuel Swartwout got appointed by President Andrew Jackson as collector of the Port of New York, the most lucrative tariff generator in the country. Swartwout had shady real estate holdings in New Jersey and Texas. He joined Burr's attempted coup out west, manipulated bank stocks, and attempted to corner Harlem Railroad stock. Swartwout fled the country when an investigation exposed the embezzlement of $1.2 million of customs funds. His successor as collector,

Tammany boss Jesse Hoyt, defaulted to Wall Street brokers, apparently caught before embezzling vast sums.

The master of political corruption was William (Boss) Tweed; he and his ring stole perhaps $200 million; he used pilfering tactics on an immense scale. His crimes proved too vast to avoid prosecution. Arrested and convicted in 1871, he died in jail in 1878. With the downfall of Boss Tweed, the entire ring was expelled from Tammany Hall. "Honest John Kelly" ("Honest" only by comparison to Tweed) became the new Grand Sachem and attempted to rescue Tammany from impotence. Structural changes improved discipline and Tammany's public image. The level of graft declined but corruption returned with rising political clout—based on elections success.

Among the most interesting players in this new era was George Washington Plunkitt, who worked up the Tammany ladder to become a successful politician in both New York City and as state senator in Albany. His later memoir described long-term machine politics success: patronage, election fraud, and honest graft, limited in scope with no blatant criminal acts.

Power and corruption increased when Richard Croker became Grand Sachem after the death of Kelly in 1886; he ruled Tammany for the rest of the century. Kickbacks and bribery returned, but were modest when compared to Tweed. Croker's real estate business used insider information and city-controlled property. He also took large security holdings from companies wanting to do business in the city. The police department was blatantly set up for plunder and allied with Tammany.

New Republican mayor William Strong started a reform movement in the 1890s, including a merit system introduced for city workers and reorganizing the Police Department. Theodore Roosevelt became a police commissioner, crusading against corruption and abuse. Corruption in the Police Department was particularly onerous under Police Chief Thomas Byrnes. Organized crime gangs had regular beats; Wall Street and other financial areas paid for additional protection. Each precinct was controlled by a captain receiving systematic bribes. Honest merchants paid protection money while illegal businesses paid considerably more. Police jobs had to be bought; the going rate for a captain apparently was $10,000, down to $300 for a patrolman. An investigation committee estimated the annual take at $15 million. Chief Byrnes soon retired and Roosevelt was able to institute a number of reforms.

At that time New York City consisted of Manhattan and the Bronx. Thomas Platt was the Republican boss of New York State around the turn of the twentieth century, known as "the Easy Boss" because of his courteous manner. He created the five districts of Manhattan, the Bronx, Brooklyn, Queens, and Staten Island into the metropolis New York City in 1898. The point was to increase his political power base and enhance his patronage potential. Tammany's relative influence declined. Election reform requiring voter sign-in and secret ballots made election fraud more difficult. Croker and Tammany managed to returned to power, but the corruption potential proved more limited.

Tammany maintained considerable influence during the early twentieth century. New York City mayor Jimmy ("Beau James") Walker, elected in 1926 and reelected in 1929, was the most colorful. The tough times with the Depression resulted in investigations of corruption that forced him to testify before the Seabury Commission. He resigned shortly thereafter and headed for Europe until the danger of criminal prosecution passed. Tammany never regained its former political power (although corruption continued, partly through organized crime) after Walker resigned in 1932. Longtime governor of New York and presidential candidate Al Smith had Tammany connections, but was never accused of corruption. Political machines across the nation followed in Tammany's footsteps.

Future president Martin Van Buren (1837–41) began as a lawyer from Kinderhook (he practiced law in New York City for a short time and joined Tammany during that period) and became a state senator and leader of the Democratic Party. Becoming U.S. senator in 1821, he maintained control of Democrats in New York using political surrogates while in Washington—the "Albany Regency." The "Regency Code" used patronage as the primary technique to keep the faithful in line. Van Buren's increasing power in Washington made both state and federal jobs available. Winning was everything to maintain control. Van Buren, backed by Tammany tactics, helped get Andrew Jackson elected president in 1828. Loyal Democrats got the patronage jobs (this was a first at the federal level); contracts to merchants and other businesses in New York City went to loyal Tammany members, based on connections and contributions. Lobbying city hall and Albany for franchise monopolies with cash in hand became required practice, covering everything from gas lighting to ice delivery.

The worst federal political abuses occurred during and after the Civil War. Simon Cameron was senator and the political boss of Pennsylvania; Lincoln named him secretary of war, one of many of his Republican rivals for president appointed to his cabinet. Corruption in the War Department was rampant under Cameron, criminal misconduct with the Union engaged in a war for its very survival. Soldiers grappled with tainted food, rifles and ammunition that did not fire, and so on. He was so corrupt that Congressman Thaddeus Stevens (chairman of the House Ways and Means Committee) told Lincoln that Cameron would steal anything but "a red hot stove." Cameron demanded a retraction and Stevens declared: "I believe I told you he would not steal a red hot stove. I will now take that back." Within a year, Lincoln sent Cameron to Russia as ambassador. Cameron defined "an honest politician" as "one who, when he is bought, will stay bought."

During the post–Civil War period, Roscoe Conkling was the New York Republican machine boss competing with Tammany Hall. During the administration of U. S. Grant, political patronage and corruption was especially rampant. While serving in the New York Assembly, Theodore Roosevelt referred to machine politicians from both parties as the "black horse cavalry." As a political reformer, Roosevelt was often stymied by the machines.

Roosevelt became president of the New York City Police Commission in 1895 and sought to reform a police department reputed to be the most corrupt in the United States. Police Chief Thomas Byrnes cooperated with gangs as long as they stayed away from the financial district, for which he was appropriately rewarded by the Wall Street robber barons. Thirty-five captains each controlled a precinct, with a regular system of payoffs to the authorities. A captaincy apparently could be had for $10,000, while securing a patrolman's job cost $300. The police department was closely connected to the political machines. Roosevelt, well aware of the corruption, created new disciplinary rules and regular inspections, and even walked the beats at night to make sure the officers were on duty. Roosevelt soon forced Byrnes's "retirement," followed by several other high-level departures, then mass resignation by corrupt officers afraid of criminal investigations. After that, Roosevelt focused on discipline and efficiency. As summarized by Morris (1979, 523), "Crimes were down, arrests up, corruption clearly on the wane." As demonstrated by Roosevelt, reform movements could be successful.

Ohio Republican Mark Hanna was William McKinley's manager in his 1896 presidential run and Republican Party chairman, effectively the United States' first nationwide political boss. He is particularly noted for saying, "There are two things that are important in politics. The first is money and I can't remember what the second one is" (quoted in Urofsky 2005, 4). When McKinley picked Ohio senator John Sherman as his secretary of state, Hanna was elected Ohio senator. Hanna concentrated substantial power and moved the Republicans in a more conservative direction. When Vice President Theodore Roosevelt became president upon McKinley's assassination, Hanna exclaimed, "Now that damned cowboy is president!" Hanna retarded Roosevelt's progressive legislation until his death in 1904.

Why is Chicago synonymous with corruption? The United States' number two city was a late starter in machine politics compared to New York City, but made up the corruption gap in the second half of the nineteenth century. The Great Chicago Fire of 1871 is the usual start date given to the developing machine. Ward politicians got their hold pointing their fingers to rivals as the cause of the fire. The leaders tightened their grip with the usual patronage and "vote early and often" campaigns. Michael McDonald created the first Chicago machine, followed by the Kelly-Nash machine. Organized crime became a big and growing influence especially during Prohibition. Menes (2006) focused on the 15 largest U.S. cities from 1850 to 1980. Chicago was unique in that corrupt administrations actually increased after 1930 (while corruption fell, often substantially, in the other cities)—to an astounding 92 percent.

The Chicago machine returned during the mayoral reign of Richard Daley, starting in 1955. The big events were the "Summerdale Scandal" of 1960 associated with police corruption and the riots during the 1968 Democratic convention. Son Richard M. Daley also became mayor. Former Illinois governor Rod Blagojevich was impeached in 2008 and sent to jail; his predecessor George Ryan was convicted of racketeering and other charges and sentence to six-and-a-half years in jail. Various governors, aldermen, and a mayor have been accused, indicted, and convicted of various crimes.

The other particularly infamous political boss was Tom Pendergast and his Kansas City machine. During the Great Depression, Pendergast dominated the

Jackson County Democratic Party and orchestrated fraudulent elections that routinely included beatings and shootouts. The Pendergast machine bribed police forces during Prohibition to allow alcohol and gambling. His companies regularly received government contracts, and legend has it that political opponents are buried under his Ready-Mixed Concrete. His most illustrious appointment was Harry S. Truman, named a county judge and later senator. Federal investigations resulted in Pendergast's conviction for income tax evasion.

See also Burr, Aaron; Fraud; Jackson, Andrew; Plunkitt, George Washington; Roosevelt, Theodore; Tammany Hall; Tweed, William ("Boss"); Van Buren, Martin

References

Allen, Oliver. *The Tiger: The Rise and Fall of Tammany Hall.* New York: Addison-Wesley, 1993.

Brands, H. W. *American Colossus: The Triumph of Capitalism, 1865–1900.* New York: Doubleday, 2010.

Menes, Rebecca. "Limiting the Reach of the Grabbing Hand: Graft and Growth in American Cities, 1880–1930." In *Corruption and Reform: Lessons from America's Economic History.* Edited by Edward Glaeser and Claudia Goldin, 63–94. Washington, DC: National Bureau of Economic Research, 2006.

Morris, Edmund. *The Rise of Theodore Roosevelt.* New York: Random House, 1979.

Urofsky, Melvin. *Money and Free Speech: Campaign Finance Reform and the Courts.* Lawrence: University Press of Kansas, 2005.

Pollution Externalities

In economics an externality is a transaction spillover, because costs/benefits are not transmitted by prices; instead third parties are usually affected. A common form of negative externality is pollution. Pollution is the introduction of contaminants into the environment that cause harm to the ecosystem—the interaction between living organisms and the environment.

The rise of business and the industrial economy required the use of coal, timber, iron ore, and other products creating contaminants and causing other environmental damage. Sanitation, safety, potentially harmful products, pollution, and environmental destruction became increasing concerns. As stated by Howard Zinn (2003, 663), "The 'market' did not care about the environment or the arts." Nineteenth-century big business destroyed the environment on a prodigious scale. As a naturalist, Theodore Roosevelt believed in protecting nature and called for government protection as part of his conservation plans, including what he called the "monopoly of natural resources" by the government. New legislation included the National Reclamation Act of 1902 and the Antiquities Act of 1906, which allowed the president to declare national monuments on public lands.

Pollution takes many forms: air, water, waste, light, soil contamination, littering, and so on—caused by multiple sources. Historically, the perpetrators bore no costs even when the damage was toxic and extreme. This is generally still true except for specific regulations that are enforced. Potential solutions are many, including recycling, mitigation, and control through technology (such as scrubbers, collection systems, treatment, creating markets for "pollution rights," or prohibition). All these methods have been used, with mixed results.

"Killer regulations" can increase costs, but solve major problems. Pollution controls are extremely expensive (and affected firms claim they are no longer competitive), but improve the environment. Food regulations at the start of the twentieth century increased costs, but saved countless lives from contaminated products. Corporate Average Fuel Economy (CAFE) standards increased production costs of automobiles (and when first required, put American manufacturers at a major disadvantage to foreign companies with smaller cars), but dramatically improved fuel economy. The Clean Air Act of 1990 created an emissions trading system for sulfur dioxide (the cause of acid rain), where the buying and selling of allowances became the accepted practice of utilities.

Regulations proved relatively effective if not necessarily efficient over the long run in most areas. The national parks are a success. Pollution controls were expensive to implement and sometimes unproductive and wasteful (plus unrepentant polluters often moved high-polluting operations overseas), but over time proved useful. Arguments going forward primarily involve the level of additional pollution controls needed, with the primary concern the matter of cost versus benefits (usually individual costs relative to social benefits). Regulations about food and drug safety, inspections and audits, and accuracy in advertising generally have been viewed as successful, despite episodes of inept and lax enforcement. Of course, types and levels of regulations are political issues, subject to political ideology.

See also Antitrust; Environmental Movement; Environmental Regulations; Food and Drug Regulations; Social (Corporate) Responsibility

References

Barton, David. *Business and Its Environment*. 4th ed. Upper Saddle River, NJ: Prentice Hall, 2003.

Diamond, Jared. *Collapse: How Societies Choose to Fail or Succeed*. New York: Viking, Penguin Group, 2006.

Morris, Edmond. *Theodore Rex*. New York: Random House, 2001.

Zinn, Howard. *A People's History of the United States*. New York: Harper Perennial Modern Classics, 2003.

Ponzi, Charles

Charles Ponzi (1882–1949) used a classic Ponzi scheme and gave it his name. He promised investors a 50 percent return in 45 days or a 100 percent return in 90 days, based on using postal reply coupons to generate the gargantuan return. He was born

Ex-convict Charles Ponzi, surrounded by Boston police and immigration officers, waves goodbye as he is deported to Italy in 1934. (Library of Congress)

in Lugo, Italy, on March 3, 1882, and became a small-time crook in Italy, immigrated to the United States, detoured to Canada to be jailed for fraud, and returned to the United States for his big scam. His scheme is the classic; hence his name describes a type of scam probably dating to the ancient world. The "to-good-to-be-true" Ponzi schemes are still around, most recently the cases of Bernie Madoff and Allen Stanford.

Ponzi discovered international reply coupons (IRCs), issued by the Universal Postal Union (UPU). The UPU established rules for mail exchanges across countries, including postal rates. IRCs, begun in 1906, could be exchanged for a postage stamp to a foreign country. A person can send an overseas letter and prepay the postage for a reply. IRCs could be purchased at different prices in different countries, partly because of fluctuating currency values, especially as several European economies were collapsing. Thus, if IRCs could be purchased in bulk in one country, they could be sold in another at a profit. That became the story he told potential "investors." He set up Securities Exchange Company in Boston early in 1920 and advertised in the local newspapers to pay 50 percent interest in 45 days or 100 percent interest in 90 days. Some of the local papers, such as the *Boston Post*, initially praised his scheme, generating ever more investors.

The problem was the IRC scheme did not work on a large scale. An IRC could be cashed in the United States for postage worth a nickel—a stamp, not cash, and it would take millions of IRCs to make the profits claimed. Zuckoff (2005, 95), for example, claimed 66 coupons bought in Rome for $1 would be worth $3.30 in Boston. Thus 66 million coupons would be needed to net $2.3 million in profits. The other problem Ponzi did not solve was how to convert the stamps into cash. Since he in fact did not invest in IRCs, the cash accumulated and he started spending it lavishly on a mansion, servants, and investments in other companies (possibly to generate the cash to actually pay off investors).

Ponzi had to deal with other crooks. Employee (and former cellmate in Montreal) Louis Cassullo stole from Ponzi and also forged Ponzi notes to sell to investors. Another employee sold his story to the *Boston Post*, claiming Ponzi was a crook. A Ponzi imitator, The Old Colony Foreign Exchange Company, moved in, hustling business away from Ponzi. The owner of a pawn shop, supplying Ponzi some of his first cash, sued Ponzi for millions, claiming that half the profits were his. Ponzi ultimately paid him off, just to end the lawsuit. Speculators bought Ponzi notes at a discount; pickpockets worked the line as bank runs had investors trying to invest and later to get their money back.

Ponzi major problem was attracting too much attention. The *Boston Post* investigated, followed by the Boston district attorney, state attorney general, U.S. district attorney, and state bank examiner. Postal authorities passed new regulations, outlawing the use of IRCs for speculation. The *Boston Post* discovered that the average annual sales for IRCs were $75,000 a year, while current-year sales were even smaller. Ponzi's investment funds were not buying any IRCs. Then the *Post* dug into his background and found his jail record in Montreal. The Boston district attorney discovered that investors paid Ponzi some $10 million and he issued notes for $14 million—all this in only eight months during 1920. The Securities and Exchange Company had no assets and only $200,000 ever recorded on the books. When arrested, Ponzi had little money left after the bank examiner froze his accounts and shut down the bank he bought and controlled.

Ponzi pleaded guilty to larceny and mail fraud. While on bail, Ponzi actually started another scam: developing a subdivision near Jacksonville during the Florida real estate bubble, 23 lots to the acre; fortunately for potential buyers, he was not free long enough to make that scam work. He went to prison for five years. Upon release, Ponzi was immediately deported. He ended up in Rio de Janeiro, and died in a Rio charity hospital on January 18, 1949. Ponzi investors eventually collected 37½ cents on the dollar by 1930.

See also Fraud; Madoff, Bernard S.; Ponzi Scheme; Securities and Exchange Commission (SEC)

Reference

Zuckoff, Mitchell. *Ponzi's Scheme: The True Story of a Financial Legend*. New York: Random House Trade Paperbacks, 2006.

Ponzi Scheme

A Ponzi scheme is a fraudulent investment scam promising substantial returns for investors, but paying early investors from the cash of later investors rather than actual earnings. With no real earnings, the scam must collapse at some point. The scheme is named for Charles Ponzi (1882–1949) who developed his own version in 1920. Major Ponzi scammers caught in the twentieth century include Bernard Madoff and Allen Stanford.

In his original scheme, Ponzi discovered international reply coupons (IRCs), issued by the Universal Postal Union (UPU). The idea is to send a person overseas a letter and prepay the postage for a reply. Ponzi figured out the possibility that the IRCs could be purchased in bulk in one country and sold in another at a profit. That became the story line. He set up Securities Exchange Company early in 1920 and started an advertising campaign in Boston to pay 50 percent interest in 45 days and 100 percent in 90 days, when banks typically paid an annual 5 percent rate. People were initially skeptical and money came in slowly. Then he paid the early investors the fantastic 50 percent return and the money started coming in fast, over $1 million a week.

The problem was the IRC scheme did not work. An IRC could be cashed in the United States for postage worth a nickel—a stamp, not cash, and it would take millions of IRCs to make the profits claimed. *The Boston Post* investigated, followed by the Boston district attorney, the state attorney general, U.S. district attorney, and the state bank examiner. The Boston district attorney discovered investors paid Ponzi some $10 million and he issued notes for $14 million—all this in only eight months during 1920. When arrested, Ponzi had little money left after the bank examiner froze his accounts and shut down the bank he bought and controlled. Ponzi pleaded guilty to larceny and mail fraud.

Ponzi's scam demonstrates the classic Ponzi scheme. First, it offered investors an unbelievable return based on a scenario that, on reflection, would not work. It then became a pyramiding scheme. Early investors were paid the promised return, which attracted new investors, who were in turn paid in a snowballing scheme suggesting a real investment opportunity. The scheme mushroomed until it collapsed. In this case, investigative journalists and government regulators proved to be Ponzi's downfall, fortunately for future unsophisticated investors, within a few months. A better-thought-out plan could go on for years, which has happened repeatedly.

Bernard Madoff was New York broker, investment adviser, chairman of NASDAQ, and the perpetrator of history's biggest Ponzi scheme. Madoff pleaded guilty to fraud, theft, money laundering, and perjury in 2009; he was sentenced to 150 years in prison. Madoff started an investment business, apparently a hedge fund started in the 1970s. Madoff has never made his investment strategy quite clear (common for hedge funds), but he claimed to use sophisticated techniques like "convertible arbitrage." High-yield bonds convertible into common stock were used and simultaneously shorted—that was the claim. An alternative story was "split-strike conversion," a timing strategy of large stocks using both stocks and options. With the market collapse in 2008, investors began withdrawing money and Madoff's money ran out by December. According to Steve Fishman (*New York*, 2009, http://nymag.com), Madoff confessed his scam to his sons. They called the Securities and Exchange Commission (SEC). The SEC contacted the Federal Bureau of Investigation (FBI), who arrested Madoff. Madoff pled guilty to 11 felonies in 2009, including securities fraud, wire fraud, mail fraud, and money laundering. Madoff is serving a 150-year sentence.

Allen Stanford (1950–) was chairman of Stanford Financial Group and responsible for a massive Ponzi scheme involving $8 billion in certificates of deposit. Stanford had a joint venture with his father, which he moved to the Caribbean after his father's retirement. He was rumored to be involved in bribery, money laundering, and political manipulation. He was charged with bribery and violating securities laws by the SEC, FBI, and other regulatory groups. He was convicted in 2012 and sentenced to 110 years in jail.

See also Fraud; Madoff, Bernard L.; NASDAQ; Ponzi, Charles; Securities and Exchange Commission (SEC)

References

Fishman, Steve. "The Monster Mensch." *New York*, February 22, 2009. http://nymag.com.

Kansas, Dave. "Madoff Does Minneapolis." In *SCANDAL!: Amazing Tales of Scandals That Shocked the World and Shaped Modern Business*, 310–320. New York: Time Inc. Home Entertainment, 2009.

Zuckoff, Mitchell. *Ponzi's Scheme: The True Story of a Financial Legend*. New York: Random House Trade Paperbacks, 2006.

Portfolio Insurance

Portfolio insurance (PI) is a derivative hedge to limits losses on stock portfolios, rather than really insurance. Selling S&P 500 index futures short became a common hedge against a stock portfolio fall. If stocks went down, then the losses were covered by the futures trade, although selling futures limited gains to be made on a rising stock portfolio. PI was invented by Hayne Leland and Mark Rubinstein, a pair of West Coast finance professors. Their company, Leland O'Brien Rubinstein, started selling the strategy in 1981. More and more institutions picked it up, and by the fall of 1987, with the stock market increasingly volatile, PI was a common product for hedging. Unfortunately, with so many investors using the same product, PI actually made a declining market worse as illustrated in the stock crash of 1987.

PI is called dynamic hedging because it requires continuous changes in the hedge as conditions change. The market dropped a lot on Friday the 16th. That meant considerable futures selling calculated over the weekend according to the PI models, to be implemented at the start of trading on Monday. The problem became liquidity, with just too many sellers having the same strategy clamoring for identical trades. As summarized by Bookstaber (2007, 18–19):

> Portfolio insurance firms sold nearly half a billion dollars of S&P futures, amounting to about 30% of the public volume. The futures prices dropped precipitously and the stock market had not even opened. About 15 minutes into the futures market decline, we started to see activity from an unexpected quarter, cash-futures arbitrageurs. Their attempts to capitalize on the apparent chasm between the cash and futures prices would be the red flag that triggered the stampede in the NYSE.

The arbitrageurs made matters worse; their sell trades were based on the Friday closing prices not a worldwide panic. The play was to sell short, assuming the sell order would be at the Friday close (the hedge play to simultaneously buy the futures long at the lower prices). Since many stocks were late to open and prices collapsed, the arbitrageurs lost big and made the collapse even worse. As prices kept dropping, the PI paradigm called for more selling. According to Bookstaber, PI programs sold over a billion dollars in futures that afternoon. The S&P 500 futures performed even worse than stocks, down 29 percent for the day.

Portfolio insurance is archaic. With modern technology, program trading is routine to quickly get investors out of down positions.

See also Derivatives; Great Depression; Greenspan, Alan; Panics and Depressions; Stock Crash of 1987

References

Bookstaber, Richard. *A Demon of Our Own Design: Markets, Hedge Funds, and the Perils of Financial Innovation*. Hoboken, NJ: Wiley, 2007.

Lewis, Michael. *Panic: The Story of Modern Financial Insanity*. New York: Norton, 2009.

McMurray, Scott, and Robert Rose, "The Crash of '87: Chicago's 'Shadow Markets' Led Free Fall in a Plunge That Began Right at Opening." In *Panic: The Story of Modern Financial Insanity*. Edited by Michael Lewis, 20–24. New York: Norton, 2009.

Preferred List (on Initial Public Offerings [IPOs])

Investment banks used "preferred list" sales of new securities at discount prices before the public issues, a practice common since the nineteenth century. J. P. Morgan "preferred lists" distributed new issues of stocks to influential politicians and prized customers at favorable rates before they went public. The use of preferred lists became particularly common in the 1920s and was described as one of the banking outrages of the decade by the Pecora Commission investigating the cause of the Crash of 1929. Unlike insider trading, pool-manipulated stocks, and other practices outraging the public, preferred-list sales were not banned by the securities legislation of the 1930s.

Investment banking practices remained relatively tame from the 1930s to the 1970s. Starting in the 1970s aggressive practices returned, including hostile takeovers, junk bonds, and expanded derivatives markets, increasing the role and power of the investment banks. In the 1990s, Internet and other high-tech startups were gobbled up by investors when IPOs came on the market. Preferred lists—now called "spinning"—became a major part of the market. James Surowiecki (2002) described major deals of the time. In 1997, Salomon Brothers offered WorldCom chief executive officer (CEO) Bernie Ebbers 200,000 shares of the Quest IPO. Within three days, Quest was up 27 percent and Ebbers started selling. According to Surowiecki (2002, 2), "Solomon helped Ebbers earn eleven million dollars flipping IPO shares". As a quid pro quo, WorldCom paid Salomon $140 million in underwriting fees for its own equity and debt issues from 1997 to 2001—in 2002 WorldCom became the largest bankruptcy in American history up to that time and Ebbers was sent to prison.

Part of the problem is the investment banker incentive to underprice IPOs to favored clients—money that could be used by the innovative startups. As stated by William Galvin, Massachusetts secretary of state, "The problem with IPO spinning is that it's bribery" (Surowiecki 2002, 2). Although the practice was well known by the early twenty-first century, the Sarbanes-Oxley Act of 2002, the financial reform legislation in response to the Enron and WorldCom frauds and bankruptcies, did not outlaw preferred list/spinning.

Politicians also get "preferred list" treatment. Peter Schweizer (2011, 40–46) described how former Speaker of the House Nancy Pelosi got in the IPO of Visa stock in 2008. Congressional legislation at the time was in the works (Credit Card Fair Fee Act) that threatened the profitability of Visa, creating an obvious conflict of interest. The legislation conveniently did not make it through the House, and the stock price of Visa went up substantially. Pelosi also received stock in IPOs from a number of other companies including Netscape in 1995 and oil man T. Boone Pickens's Clean Energy Fuels in 2010. Other politicians mentioned by Schweizer as recipients included Senators Robert Torricelli, Jeff Bingaman, and Barbara Boxer.

See also Morgan, John Pierpont; Pecora Commission; Sarbanes-Oxley Act of 2002; Securities and Exchange Commission (SEC); WorldCom

References

Chernow, Ron. *The House of Morgan: An American Banking Dynasty and the Rise of Modern Finance*. New York: Atlantic Monthly Press, 1990.

Schweizer, Peter. *Throw Them All Out: How Politicians and Their Friends Get Rich Off Insider Stock Tips, Land Deals, and Cronyism That Would Send the Rest of Us to Prison*. New York: Houghton Mifflin Harcourt, 2011.

Surowiecki, James. "The Bribe Effect." *The New Yorker*, October 7, 2002. http://www.newyorker.com.

Price Fixing

Price fixing is a conspiracy between buyers or sellers on the same side of a market to coordinate prices, volume, and/or market share. Early regulations against price fixing and monopoly go back to British common law during the Middle Ages, which were adopted by the American colonies. The U.S. Constitution established federal responsibilities (e.g., commerce with foreign nations, coinage of money, levying taxes) and left the regulations of corporations primarily up to the states. Many industrialists in the nineteenth century formed cartels to fix prices, from railroads to oil and steel, although these were generally unenforceable in state courts. Consequently, the cartels were often ineffectual when a member of the conspiracy violated the agreement.

The Sherman Act of 1890 was the first federal attempt to regulate price fixing and monopoly practices of big business. The act outlawed price-setting conspiracies, with mixed results in court. Long term, the government won several high-level cases. Section 1 of the Sherman Act focused on the actions of cartels and similar price fixing conspiracies: "Every contract, combination in the form of trust or otherwise, or conspiracy, in restraint of trade . . . is hereby declared to be illegal." In the Addyston Pipe Case, six pipe manufacturers divided sales territory and fixed prices, basically a cartel. The Supreme Court ruled price fixing a restraint of interstate trade and illegal in 1899, followed by many successful prosecutions of price conspiracy cases. Section 2 of the Sherman Act deals with monopoly cases: "Every person who shall monopolize . . . any part of the trade or commerce . . . shall be deemed guilty of a misdemeanor."

Despite the Sherman Act, manufacturers of heavy electrical equipment conspired to fix prices for decades. General Electric (GE) and Westinghouse were the major companies in the conspiracy, which also involved many smaller manufacturers. During the 1940s, GE was charged in over a dozen antitrust cases, but getting caught did not involve large penalties. Despite the claims by lawyers and top executives to stop illegal practices, many executives did not consider collusion and other illegal behavior as unethical—these activities continued. As one ethically challenged GE manager exclaimed, "Sure, collusion was illegal, but it wasn't unethical" (Smith 2009, 107). Competing companies were willing to offer deep discounts to win new business. Conspiracy to fix prices and market share solved the dilemma, with GE and Westinghouse getting the bulk of the business as the largest manufacturers. Regular meetings determined who got the contract and at what price. As with virtually all illegal acts, incentives drove behavior. Executive career success at GE depended on performance.

The Senate began hearings on the conspiracy in 1959, and the Department of Justice launched a Sherman Act investigation. Evidence led to grand juries and indictments. Forty companies and 18 executives were charged with conspiracy. Most of the companies cooperated with the Justice Department and provided additional evidence. All the conspirators pled guilty to most of the charges. Seven executives were given jail sentences, the first time convicted white-collar executives actually went to jail.

Prior to 1975, all brokerage firms used a fixed commission schedule based on number of shares and stock price. To generate business they "bundled" other services including financial analysis research. The commissions were profitable enough to pay for sophisticated investor analysis. The government called this price fixing, and Congress banned fixed commission for trading stocks, ever since called "May Day" (the Securities and Exchange Commission put the ban into effect on May 1,

1975). Commissions were now negotiated between buyers and sellers and dropped in half within three weeks.

GE and other defense contractors got caught in a number of bribery and mispricing cases in the 1980s and 1990s. The Pentagon Defense Contract Management Agency established a special investigation office in 1990 because these charges were so widespread. Twenty-two indictments were filed against GE, and the government recovered over $200 million. Over the years, GE faced dozens of cases and settlements totaling about $1 billion. Other related cased include the Wedtech Scandal of the 1980s, for bribing government officials for defense contracts, and the Cunningham Scandal of 2005. Defense contractors bribed Congressman Duke Cunningham and other officials for federal contracts. Cunningham was convicted and received an eight-year jail sentence.

In January 2007, German global conglomerate Siemens was fined €396 million by the European Commission for price fixing in European Union electricity markets through a cartel involving 11 companies. The commission found evidence of price fixing, rigged bids, and shared markets by the cartel members.

See also Clayton Act; General Electric and Westinghouse Heavy Equipment Scandal; Morgan, John Pierpont.; Rockefeller, John Davison; Sherman Antitrust Act of 1890; Trust Movement

References

Giacalone, Joseph. "Antitrust Policy in the United States." In *Encyclopedia of the Age of the Industrial Revolution, 1700–1920*. Edited by Christine Rider. Santa Barbara, CA: Greenwood, 2007.

Smith, Richard. "The Incredible Electrical Conspiracy. In *SCANDAL!: Amazing Tales of Scandals That Shocked the World and Shaped Modern Business*, 104–119. New York: Time Inc. Home Entertainment, 2009.

Vincusi, W. Kip, John Vernon, and Joseph Harrington. *Economics of Regulations and Antitrust*. 2nd ed. Cambridge, MA: MIT Press, 1995.

Procter & Gamble Derivatives Losses

Procter & Gamble (P&G) announced losses of $100 million trading derivatives in the spring of 1994, one of hundreds of companies caught in the derivatives crisis of 1994. William Procter and James Gamble, both immigrants, became partners making soap and candles in 1837. New products were developed (e.g., Ivory Soap in the 1880s, Crisco in 1911) and demand increased. Acquisitions led to other brands, including Folgers Coffee, Pepto-Bismol, and Gillette razors. P&G now has 20 billion-dollar brands. It is part of the Dow Jones Industrial Average and the S&P 500. In 2011, P&G was fined by the European Commission for a price-fixing cartel with Unilever.

In the early 1990s, many companies gambled on the level of interest rates, using complex derivatives, and generated large fees to the investment banks. At the time, P&G had over $2 billion in derivative trades, mainly to hedge against currency and interest rate changes. Their auditor required P&G to reclassify the derivatives as speculative rather than hedges and disclose the loss. P&G blamed derivatives giant Bankers Trust (BT) for selling them speculative derivative instruments when they were in the market to hedge and sued. During the early 1990s, BT became the most profitable bank in the United States. Levinson stated (1994, 1): "P&G is a heavy user of derivatives. According to its lawsuit, Bankers Trust promised that a $200 million adjustable-rate derivative could be converted to a low fixed rate, but then refused to let it lock in the promised rate. Because it couldn't fix the rate, P&G claims, it lost $102 million when the rates rose."

BT's apparent focus was on generating fees on complex deals, without regard to customer interests. BT's reputation declined and it was acquired by Deutsche Bank in 1998. P&G executives were interested in hedging, while P&G treasurer Raymond Mains was willing to incur high risk to increase income, probably with little understanding of the risks. This was only a blip for P&G, which is one of the largest companies in the world with a market capitalization of over $200 billion in 2012.

See also Derivatives; Gibson Greetings Derivatives Losses; Investment Banks; Long-Term Capital Management; Orange County Bankruptcy

References

Levinson, Marc. "Exiled on Wall Street; Bankers Trust: A Bum Rap for Derivatives?" *Newsweek*, November 14, 1994. http://www.newsweek.com.

Partnoy, Frank. *FIASCO: Blood in the Water on Wall Street*. New York: Norton, 1997.

Partnoy, Frank. *Infectious Greed: How Deceit and Risk Corrupted the Financial Markets*. New York: Holt, 2003.

Professional Ethics

Professional ethics are standards of behavior expected from those with special knowledge and skills. Attorneys, accountants, medical professionals, and others are licensed or certified by government entities to provide special skills and are required to follow codes of conduct and professional behavior. Other groups such as boards of directors commonly have ethical standards required by the organizations they represent or other groups.

The Securities and Exchange Commission (SEC) requires codes of ethics for various professions involved in securities markets and financial reporting, including securities advisers, investment companies, and accountants. The SEC requires audits to be conducted by certified public accountants (CPAs) subject to professional ethics and licensed by states. Scandals caused by market failures result in accusations that others are to blame, partly because of violating professional ethics. After Enron failed in 2001, the senior executives at Enron all resigned and testified before Congress (most took the Fifth). The company's bankruptcy represented a financial failure. Chairman and chief executive officer (CEO) Kenneth Lay claimed that all accounting issues were accepted by auditor Arthur Andersen. Many of the special-purpose entities that now seem deceptive were developed by Andersen as part of their consulting operation.

According to Lay, Enron was an audit failure caused by auditor ethics violations rather than the violation of corporate board or management ethical lapses. Lay was convicted of criminal activity, but he was partially right—the ethical standards at Andersen had fallen. Andersen took shortcuts (or worse) to satisfy Enron, and in the end shredded valuable evidence, which resulted in the conviction and failure of Andersen.

Recent federal legislation attempts to strengthen professional ethics requirements. The Sarbanes-Oxley Act of 2002 strengthens the requirement for corporate governance and established the Public Company Accounting Oversight Board (PCAOB) as an independent board to regulate the audits of public companies. The Dodd-Frank (Financial Reform) Bill passed in 2010 in response to the financial crisis of 2008 included increased consumer protections through the Consumer Finance Protection Agency and requires stockholders to vote on executive pay packages.

See also Accounting Fraud; Arthur Andersen; Corporate Governance; Dodd-Frank (Financial Reform) Bill; Earnings Manipulation; Enron; Ethics; Fraud; Lay, Kenneth L.; Public Company Accounting Oversight Board (PCAOB); Sarbanes-Oxley Act of 2002

References

Byrne, John. "Restoring Trust in Corporate America: Business Must Lead the Way to Real Reform." *Business* Week, June 24, 2002.

Giroux, Gary. *Detecting Earnings Management*. Hoboken, NJ: Wiley, 2004.

Goldin, Thomas, Steven Skalak, and Mona Clayton. *A Guide to Forensic Accounting Investigation*. Hoboken, NJ: Wiley, 2006.

Previts, Gary, and Barbara Merino. *A History of Accountancy in the United States*. Columbus: Ohio State University Press, 1998.

Schilit, Howard. *Financial Shenanigans: How to Detect Accounting Gimmicks & Fraud in Financial Reports*. New York: McGraw-Hill, 2002.

Profiteering during the American Revolution

With only a third of the population being "patriots" during the American Revolution (1775–83), many colonists worked at profiting from the war. Quartermasters used commissary agents to buy war supplies, typically merchants paid on commission trading on their own accounts. Success meant getting functioning goods of reasonable quality on time for the least amount of cash. Sellers followed the tenets of capitalism, seeking inflated profits, selling inferior goods including spoiled food, preferring gold to paper, and playing one side off against another. The British typically paid in gold, making many merchants loyalists. During the 1777–78 winter at Valley Forge, for example, soldiers nearly starved although vast quantities of agricultural goods existed nearby, with farmers and merchants unwilling to sell for Continental paper currency.

Corruption existed throughout the quartermaster chain of command. Thomas Mifflin, a Philadelphia merchant, acted as the first quartermaster general. He used commissary agents of varying competence and honesty to buy necessary supplies—often merchants paid on commission—who traded on their own accounts in addition to serving in official government capacities. Conflicts of interest were obvious, but these were typical business patterns of the time and supplies got delivered. Mifflin may have been part of the problem and was later accused of embezzlement and resigned. According to Chernow (2011, 318), "Washington had already developed doubts about Mifflin, whom he thought had exploited his job as quartermaster general for person profit." He later served as governor of Pennsylvania, demonstrating that corruption accusations were not detrimental to a political career. Nathanael Greene became quartermaster general in 1778, but the typical profiteering problems continued.

The Continental Congress funded the Revolution primarily with paper money. Inflation surged as the war continued, partly because of the war's disruption of both foreign trade and domestic commerce (including large purchases of supplies by the British), but mainly because of the depreciating paper currencies. The Continental Congress had issued millions in paper before independence was declared and the printing presses kept rolling. As the value of paper money declined, the presses spit out currency in greater quantities, some $226 million by 1779. Continental currency essentially collapsed by then, worth some 2½¢ on the dollar, as declining colonial prospects for victory made redemption seem increasingly unlikely.

Speculation, basically an investment in uncertainty, became a major issue. Speculators, especially in the postwar period, were accused of causing the country's inflation and economic collapse, unfairly enriching themselves at the expense of poor soldiers selling Continental currencies and notes at a pittance to survive. The ultimate speculators, the merchants and bankers, were usually well connected and privy to inside information on the potential for repayment by the various states and national government.

The British used counterfeiting as a war policy designed to sabotage the war effort. British counterfeiters easily faked the Continental money and ran advertisements in New York newspapers offering bogus paper at bargain prices. Loyalists and profiteers distributed the fake cash (at a substantial profit). A few of these distributors (called "shovers") got caught. Nevertheless, a vast amount of counterfeit money circulated, further depressing the value of paper currency. Even some local charlatans such as Henry Dawkins (an engraver) and Isaac Ketcham (Dawkins's accomplice) got into domestic counterfeiting. When caught, Ketcham accused others of counterfeiting, including members of Washington's personal guard.

Privateers, well-armed merchants, roamed the seas looking for booty, capturing some 2,000 ships and selling cargoes in American ports. Merchant and banker Robert Morris funded several privateer ships. During the Revolution, privateers probably outnumbered the American navy by at least 10 to 1.

See also Bank of the United States, First; Constitution, U.S.; Continental Currency and American Revolution Financing; Hamilton, Alexander; Morris, Robert; Washington, George

References

Chernow, Ron. *Washington: A Life*. New York: Penguin Press, 2010.

Perkins, Edwin. *American Public Finance and Financial Services, 1700–1815*. Columbus: Ohio State University Press, 1994.

Proxy Statement

Corporations issue proxy statements annually before the annual stockholders' meeting (but after the annual financial report, 10-K, has been filed with the Securities and Exchange Commission [SEC]). Proxy statements concern issues to be voted on by the stockholders and are useful to evaluate corporate governance. Stockholders vote on directors, and considerable information is given on each director or prospective director. Proxy statements also include information on board committees, which must include audit committees and compensation committees. Important information is presented on the audit, including auditor, audit cost, and nonaudit fees. Executive compensation is presented in some detail, which is particularly important to understand management performance incentives. As more disclosures on corporate governance are required, the proxy statement becomes increasingly important to evaluate the both governance and the earnings management environment.

Specific disclosures required in a proxy statement are useful for financial analysts and other financial users. Biographical and other information are presented for the board member up for election (usually every year), including compensation and participation on board committees. Each board committee is identified, including their responsibilities, board members, number of meetings, and so on. Boards must have an audit committee and executive compensation committee. The audit committee is critical to ensure that procedures to pick the external auditor are understood as important, audit and nonaudit fees are appropriate, and the audit committee meets periodically with the auditor to review results. The role of the compensation committee is important because this identifies the incentive structure of the chief executive officer (CEO) and other senior executives. Poorly designed compensation structures can lead to incentives focusing on short-term profits over long-term performance and other considerations.

Executive compensation is detailed for the top six executives. Compensation has four basic components: base salary, bonuses (usually tied to current earnings), stock options or restricted stock, and various perquisites. In 2012, the top 10 CEOs had total compensation of $43 million or greater, led by McKesson CEO John Hammergren at $131 million.

See also Accounting Standards; Annual Report (10-K); Corporate Governance; Financial Accounting Standards Board (FASB); Revenue Recognition and Manipulation; Securities and Exchange Commission (SEC); Stock Options Scandals

References

Giroux, Gary. *Earnings Magic and the Unbalance Sheet: The Search for Financial Reality.* New York: Wiley, 2006.

Giroux, Gary. *Financial Analysis: A User Approach.* New York: Wiley, 2003.

Securities and Exchange Commission. Executive Compensation. http://www.sec.gov/answers/execomp.htm.

Public Company Accounting Oversight Board (PCAOB)

The Public Company Accounting Oversight Board (PCAOB) is a nonprofit organization created by the Sarbanes Oxley Act of 2002 (SOX) to oversee the auditing of public companies—those trading on American stock exchanges. Shortly after the failures of Enron and WorldCom, Congress passed SOX, which increased audit requirements of public companies and gave the PCAOB broad powers to regulate the audit process. Both public companies and auditors must register with the PCAOB. The PCAOB replaced a committee of the American Institute of Public Accountants (AICPA), the auditor's trade organization, as the regulator of financial audits.

Despite a slow start—the Securities and Exchange Commission (SEC) under former chairman Harvey Pitts had difficulty picking the five-member board—the initial board was chaired by former president and chief executive officer (CEO) of the Federal Reserve Bank of New York William McDonough. Former general counsel of the SEC James Doty has been chairman since 2011. Each board member of the PCAOB is selected by the SEC to serve a five-year term, with the possibility of reappointment for a second term.

The PCAOB establishes auditing standards and regulates audit of public firms through registration, inspections of audits and quality control, and investigations and disciplinary actions for violations of laws and professional standards. As of 2011, the PCAOB issued 15 audit standards and adopted several preexisting rules as "interim standards." In addition the PCAOB adopted a number of ethics and independence rules, quality control standards, and staff audit practice alerts (as "guidance" for new circumstances).

The reports of the initial inspections of the Big Four (Deloitte and Touche, Ernst & Young, KPMG, and PricewaterhouseCoopers) were completed in 2004. The PCAOB inspects audit firms that issue 100 or more audit reports annually and all other auditors at least once every three years. The reports are available on the PCAOB website (http://www.pcaob.org), including quality control criticisms (portions of which are kept confidential). As part of its enforcement process, the PCAOB issues Settled Disciplinary Orders based on disciplinary proceedings. Over 35 proceedings have been settled, including Big Four auditor Deloitte and Touche in 2007.

PCAOB funding is based on SOX Section 109, which states that the PCAOB's budget will be funded by the "issuers." Annually, the PCAOB completes its budget (which must be approved by the SEC), and "accounting support fees" are set based on the market value of publicly traded companies (over $25 million in market value). The 2011 total budget outlays for the PCAOB were $204.4 million (up from $103.3 million in 2004), and accounting support fees (those charged to public companies) were $202.3 million.

See also Accounting Fraud; Auditing since SEC Regulation; Sarbanes Oxley Act of 2002; Securities and Exchange Commission (SEC)

References

About the PCAOB. n.d. http://www.pcaobus.org.

Giroux, Gary. *Detecting Earnings Magic*. Hoboken, NJ: Wiley, 2004.

Pujo Hearings

After the poor response of the federal government in the Panic of 1907, congress called for hearings on Wall Street power and the "Money Trust," resulting in the House Banking and Currency Committee hearings of 1912–13, named after subcommittee chairman Democrat Arsène Pujo from Louisiana. The hearings were led by committee counsel Samuel Untermyer. The findings resulted in the creation of the Federal Reserve System, Federal Trade Commission (FTC), and Clayton Antitrust Act.

The Pujo Committee accused six major banks (J. P. Morgan, First National, National City, Kuhn, Loeb, Kidder Peabody, and Lee, Higginson) of leading the Money Trust, working as a cabal to control the nation's money and credit. Other banks mentions by Pujo included National Bank of Commerce, Chase National Bank, Guaranty Trust Company, Bankers Trust Company, Illinois Trust and Savings, Continental and Commercial National Bank of Chicago—a total of 18 banks reputed to be associated with the Money Trust. The companies cooperated rather than competed with each other for new securities issues; a lead bank negotiated a deal with the issuing company and formed a syndicate using the other members to underwrite the issue. The partners at Morgan, First National, and National City served on each other's boards (forming interlocking directorships) and owned large blocks of stock in the other banks. The partners at the various banks became directors at hundreds of corporations, which tied the companies to their banks for future credit needs. The bankers claimed these as necessary moves to protect the interests of bond holders, also their customers.

As defined by the Pujo committee, the Money Trust was:

> An established and well-defined identity and community of interest between a few leaders of finance which has been created and is held together through stock holdings, interlocking directorates, and other forms of domination over banks, trust companies, railroads, public service and industrial corporations, and which resulted in a vast and growing concentration of control of money and credit in the hands of a few men. (Pujo Committee Report 1913, 130)

The committee discovered such New York Stock Exchange (NYSE) abuses as price manipulation, speculation, and lending for short sales. The revelations led to reform legislation. In 1914, the Clayton Act prohibited interlocking boards of competing companies, the Federal Reserve Act established the Federal Reserve System as the central bank, and the Federal Trade Commission Act created the FTC, whose mission is consumer protection and elimination of "anticompetitive" business practices. However, the major securities regulations were the ineffective state Blue Sky Laws (which were unable to regulate interstate commerce). Attempts at securities regulations (such as the Owen bill of 1914) did not pass until the New Deal.

Untermyer was an early supporter of Woodrow Wilson for president and continued as a major Washington player after the Pujo Committee disbanded. He helped draft the Wilson-era legislation that included the Federal Reserve Act, Federal Trade Commission Act, and the Clayton Act.

See also Clayton Act; Commercial Banking before the Federal Reserve; Federal Reserve System; Federal Trade Commission (FTC); Morgan, John Pierpont; Panic of 1907

References

Dobson, John. "Pujo Committee (Money Trust)." In *Bulls, Bears, Boom, and Bust: A Historical Encyclopedia of American Business Concepts*. Santa Barbara, CA: ABC-CLIO, 2006.

Josephson, Matthew. *The Robber Barons*. New York: Harcourt, 1962.

Mitchell, Lawrence. *The Speculation Economy: How Finance Triumphed over Industry*. San Francisco: Berrett-Koehler, 2007.

Pujo Committee Report 1913. *Money Trust Investigation: Investigation of Financial and Monetary Conditions in the United States under House Resolutions Nos. 429 and 504*. http://fraser.stlouisfed.org.

Pullman Strike (1894)

This labor debacle began as a wildcat strike by workers against the Pullman Palace Car Company and spread to railroads across the east under the American Railway Union (ARU) of Eugene Debs. The ARU called for a boycott of any trains with Pullman cars, and some 125,000 workers on 29 railroads went on strike. The railroads hired strikebreakers, marshals paid by the railroads, state militia, and federal troops. Railroad lawyers obtained injunctions against the union leaders for supporting the strike, arresting Debs and other union officials. The intervention of 12,000 federal troops resulted in additional violence. The combination of federal firepower and enforcing injunction broke the strike, tactics that would continue for decades and limit union power.

In 1881 George Pullman built Pullman, Illinois, as a company town, renting homes to laborers and requiring employees to use company stores and other services, while charging relatively high rents and rates for services. After the Panic of 1893 and the resulting depression, Pullman laid off about half his employees and cut the wages of the rest; however, he did not reduce the rents he was charging. Pullman workers began to join the ARU. A grievance committee of workers asked for relief from Pullman, but was rejected and members of the grievance committee were fired. The local union called a strike, followed by a lockout and firing of the workers. When Pullman rejected arbitration, the ARU called for a general boycott; railroad workers were not to handle any Pullman cars. Debs ordered the workers to avoid wrecking property or causing violence.

The General Managers' Association of railroad executives ordered that workers removing Pullman cars would be fired, which was normally followed by the entire crew walking off the job. By July 1894, the strike included almost all Midwest railroads. No matter the plight of the workers, several papers took the side of the railroads. The *New York World* stated that it was "war against the government and against society" (quoted in Dubofsky and Dulles 2004, 160). Attorney General Richard Olney, a friend of the railroads, focused on delivering the mail as the federal interest. He had 3,400 men sworn in as special deputies (but paid by the railroads) to protect the trains. Strikers and deputies clashed and riots broke out. Federal troops were sent to Chicago. More trains were shut down, additional property was damaged, railroad stores were looted, and violence continued. The *New York Times* blamed Debs and called him "a lawbreaker at large, and enemy of the human race" (Dubofsky and Dulles 2004, 163).

Olney obtained an injunction prohibited anyone from interfering with the operations of the mails. Debs offered to call off the strike, which was rejected by the owners. Instead, Debs and other ARU leaders were arrested. The workers gradually gave up and returned to work. Debs was charged with engaging in a conspiracy in restraint of trade under the Sherman Act and jailed for six months. Debs was radicalized in jail and became a socialist, believing that labor would never be treated fairly under capitalism.

The Pullman Strike was the first use of the injunction of striking workers under the Sherman Act of 1890. The vast resources of giant industries, police, and federal troops, and the use of the courts enforcing the Sherman Act became the tools to keep labor in check for decades. In addition to radical movements such as socialism, Marxism, and anarchy, the populist movement became increasingly important beginning in the 1890s.

See also American Federation of Labor/Congress of Industrial Organizations (AFL-CIO); Haymarket Affair; Homestead Strike (1892); Labor Movement, U.S.; Railroads, Nineteenth Century; Sherman Antitrust Act of 1890; Triangle Shirtwaist Fire (1911); Wagner Act

References

Atkins, Albert. "Labor." In *The American Economy: A Historical Encyclopedia*. Rev. ed. Edited by Cynthia Clark. Santa Barbara, CA: ABC-CLIO, 2011.

Dubofsky, Melvyn, and Foster Dulles. *Labor in America: A History*. 7th ed. Wheeling, IL: Harlan Davidson, 2004.

Livesay, Harold. *Samuel Gompers and Organized Labor in America*. Boston: Little, Brown, 1978.

R

Raiding the Erie Railroad, 1868

Cornelius Vanderbilt went after the Erie Railroad to complete his New York railroad empire. He had to fight three of the toughest and most unscrupulous robber barons on Wall Street: Daniel Drew, Jay Gould, and Jim Fisk. In a major fight involving thousands of shares and millions of dollars, Vanderbilt would lose—one of the few times in his life. The story involves an attempted corner, using judges to subvert justice, and bribing legislators for favorable legislation.

The Erie Railroad was chartered in 1832 to run from the Hudson River north of New York City to Lake Erie. Construction began in 1836 but was not completed until 1851, substantially over budget. Speculator Daniel Drew served as an Erie director beginning in 1851 and later treasurer; much of his wealth came from manipulating of Erie securities. The Erie fell into bankruptcy in 1859 and reemerged as the Civil War was starting in 1861. In 1866, Drew made a successful bear raid on the Erie using convertible bonds to cover stock sold short.

Soon after Drew's bear raid, steamboat and railroad tycoon Cornelius Vanderbilt went after the Erie to complete his New York railroad empire. Before the annual stockholders' meeting, Vanderbilt acquired enough stock and proxy votes to have majority control, and his buying continued. Drew, still treasurer, immediately became his enemy and planned his counterstrategy.

Recently signed New York state legislation, paid for with Drew's cash, allowed railroads to exchange its shares for other railroads under lease. Drew leased the worthless Buffalo, Bradford, and Pittsburgh to the Erie for $9 million. The Erie sold convertible bonds, of which $5 million went to Drew's broker, who swiftly converted to 50,000 shares of stock. Drew sold the new stock to the firms of Jay Gould and "Jubilee Jim" Fisk (who also served as Erie directors), and they became his partners in crime.

The Commodore bought the new stock, apparently unaware these were brand-new securities. Once alerted, Vanderbilt's forces got accommodating judge George Barnard (elected periodically rather than appointed for life, New York judges needed patronage to win office and retain it, thus almost all of them were party affiliated) to issue a restraining order on these activities. Drew had his own judge compel the Erie to convert the bonds. Judge Barnard (member of the Tammany Ring) then issued contempt proceedings against the Erie directors. Drew and his cronies caught wind of the arrest warrants and fled across the Hudson to New Jersey with all the loot, including some $7 million in cash. Drew, Gould, Fisk, and the other directors, now called the Erie Ring, moved the Erie headquarters to Jersey City. Neither they nor the Commodore were done manipulating.

In this 1870 Currier & Ives print, Cornelius Vanderbilt and James Fisk race for control of New York's rails. Throughout 1868 and 1869, the two men fought for control of the Erie Railroad. Here, Vanderbilt straddles his two railroads, the Hudson River and the New York Central, admonishing his competitor, "Now then Jim—No jockeying you know!" The dwarflike Fisk, sitting astride the Erie Railroad, replies, "Let em rip Commodore—But don't stop to water or you'll be beat." (Library of Congress)

The Erie Ring, using cash in hand, convinced the New Jersey legislature to charter the Erie as a New Jersey railroad as insurance if their luck ran out in New York. Meanwhile, the Erie Ring had their Albany forces convince the legislature to introduce a bill legalizing the stock issue and forbidding consolidation of the Erie with Vanderbilt's New York Central. The Commodore's forces and big purse bought enough legislators to defeat the bill. Jay Gould arrived in New York City, but was promptly arrested based on the contempt warrant; making bail, he arrived in Albany with cases of cash. A new bill, looking like the one just defeated, soon surfaced in the Senate. Gould proved to have a bigger wallet than Vanderbilt on this round and the bill passed.

The next stage was the New York House version with the representatives expecting substantial loot. But the Commodore had enough and sent this note: "Drew. I'm sick of the whole damned business. Come and see me. Van Derbilt" (Josephson 1934, 133). They settled up. The Commodore sold his stock back to the Erie Ring for around $5 million, a million or two short of what he paid for it, and stayed away from the Erie from then on. The Erie Ring won.

Gould soon became the new president of the Erie and Fisk vice president, driving Drew out from Erie management. They made Tammany's accommodating Boss Tweed a director. Shortly thereafter, Gould issued $10 million in convertible bonds and proceeded to loot the railroad until finally ousted in 1874, leaving the railroad ruined and bankrupt the following year.

See also Drew, Daniel; Fisk, James ("Jubilee Jim"); Gould, Jason ("Jay"); Erie Railroad; Railroads, Nineteenth Century; Robber Barons; Vanderbilt, Cornelius ("Commodore")

References

Adams, Charles, and Henry Adams. *Chapters of Erie and Other Essays*. Boston: James A. Osgood, 1871.

Brands, H. W. *American Colossus: The Triumph of Capitalism, 1865–1900*. New York: Doubleday, 2010.

Josephson, Matthew. *The Robber Barons*. New York: Harcourt, 1962.

Railroads, Nineteenth Century

Railroads became an important mode of transportation developed during the Industrial Revolution to move people and cargo over land. The English created the first railroad system to haul coal from mines, beginning in the seventeenth century. The locomotive, superseding horses and mules, was basically a steam engine turned on its side, placed on a wagon, and connected to the wagon's wheels. Railroads became a commercial transportation success for hauling goods and people over land by the early nineteenth century and in the United States by the late 1820s.

A railroad corporation needed a huge capital base for track, locomotives, and cars, requiring funding by passive investors. Railroad promoters needed both political backing (needing state chartering and potential public funding) and external capital. Promoters could be visionaries wanting progress for the United States; a larger number wanted to promote commercial interests (especially merchants and land speculators), a few wanted empires based on monopoly power (Commodore Vanderbilt was on early proponent), and many focused only on short-term looting. Promoters often acquired large tracks of land, some given as outright government land grants. Construction involved difficult work, initially done almost exclusively by hand by people with little or no experience. Civil engineering eventually became an important profession, first taught at West Point, then expanded to other universities. Construction fraud was widespread, usually benefiting promoters using their own "construction companies." Cities could be encouraged to give land and cash to ensure the rail lines ran through their towns. Railroad securities could be manipulated by promoters and other speculators.

The Baltimore and Ohio Railroad Company (B&O) was chartered by Maryland in 1827, the first successful commercial American railroad. Baltimore merchants founded the B&O to expand markets from Baltimore to the Potomac and then on to the Ohio River, some 300 miles. This would open up the West to Baltimore merchants attempting to compete with New York's Erie Canal. The line to the Ohio was expected to be completed in 10 years at a cost of $5 million. The B&O did reach the Ohio, but it took 25 years and cost $15 million. The B&O almost went bankrupt before completing the line to Wheeling (on the Ohio River) in 1853.

By contrast, the Erie Railroad chartered in 1832, initially ran from Piermont, on the Hudson River north of New York City, to Dunkirk, on Lake Erie, near New York City, to near Buffalo, Lake Erie, and the Great Lakes. For a short time, the Erie was the longest railroad in the world. Funding for the Erie called for both common stock and bonds to fund the high construction costs, with many of the bonds convertible into stock (and some convertible in either direction). For a variety of reasons, with looting by directors and managers a major factor, the Erie rarely made a profit. Convertible securities were often used by speculators to make a quick profit. The raid for the Erie in 1868 became one of the best documented corrupt events of the century, in part using convertibles. Erie infrastructure now exists only in pieces absorbed by other lines.

The federal government subsidized railroads during much of their early history, to both promote economic development and link different areas of the country. Federal land grants to railroads were particularly generous, some 131 million acres from 1850 to 1880. Loans were provided in many cases based on the track mileage completed.

Railroad track in the United States at 3,000 miles in 1840, increasing to 30,000 miles by 1860, connecting the large cities and ports in the northeast United States and elsewhere. After the Civil War, railroad networks stretched across the country. The building of the first transcontinental railroad was a major achievement. Federal legislation authorized and helped fund railroad bonds and land grants. Construction started in California (Central Pacific heading east) and Nebraska (Union Pacific heading west) before the Civil War was over. The two railroads were the biggest corporations of the time. Also significant was Credit Mobilier, the most infamous American scandal of the nineteenth century. The underlying corruption was similar to other railroads, as were the substantial bribes to politicians. The difference was the large scale and congressional hearings documenting the corrupt government officials.

Railroads developed top-down management structures, what Livesay (1975, 29) called "modern bureaucratic management structures [created] because they had no choice. Their size and complexity precluded the use of traditional methods of finance and management." The largest manufacturers hired hundreds of workers, while big railroads hired thousands. Only the military had experience moving people and materials, and railroads used a military line-and-staff organization structure. The long-term key was maximum traffic flow at minimum cost. These systems were generally in place by the end of the Civil War.

In 1865, the Pennsylvania Railroad ("Pennsy") with 3,500 miles of track and 30,000 employees was the largest private business in the world. The Pennsy developed the first professional management system, managed by engineers rather than financiers or speculators. Engineer J. Edgar Thomson became president in 1852. He, assisted by Vice President (and later president) Thomas Scott, transformed the administration into a line-and-staff structure and improved the accounting and financial system. As summarized by Chandler (1977, 109): "To meet the needs of managing the first modern business enterprise, managers of large American railroads during the 1950s and 1860s invented nearly all of the basic techniques of modern accounting." The Pennsy used 144 sets of records related to financial, capital, and cost accounting. They used the operating ratio (operating revenues to operating expenses) as a standard way to measure performance by volume. Later, Albert Fink of the Louisville & Nashville developed the ton mile as the basic measure of unit cost. These techniques became standard when uniform accounting methods were adopted by a convention of state railroad commissioners in 1879; the Interstate Commerce Commission adopted uniform railroad accounting in 1887. Following the Pennsy, managers began to make lifetime careers in railroad operations.

After skilled businesspeople developed the ability to run railroads professionally, railroads became the first industry to consolidate, especially in the 1880s and 1890s. Competition meant volatile pricing and potential rate wars, often with relatively inefficient operations. Professionals saw the need to improve efficiency in size. Rather than loading and unloading passengers and goods every few hundred miles, consolidated routes could continue almost nonstop across country. Standardization of track, signaling, accounting, and labor practices also brought cost savings. Reduced competition meant higher rates could be charged, although large shippers such as Standard Oil could demand favorable rates. Investors saw the potential for greater dividends and rising stock prices; speculators saw the chance to bet on prospective mergers and, those with large funds, to control railroad empires.

The initial consolidation of small struggling railroads formed Cornelius Vanderbilt's New York Central. After his victory in the Erie wars, Jay Gould acquired and leased various railroads related to the Erie mainly for short-term gain. His acquisitions spurred Thomson and Scott of the Pennsylvania to expand their own lines westward to remain competitive. The Pennsy also invested in steel and mining companies, as well as rail-related companies such as Pullman Palace Car Company. The B&O also expanded west. Gould was not successful with the Erie expansion, but tried again in 1880 with the Union Pacific, only to sell out in 1882 and attempt to create a major western railroad by acquiring multiple small lines. In addition to professional managers and speculators, investment bankers including J. P. Morgan and Kuhn Loeb consolidated railroads during this period. Monopoly power increased economies of scale and various operating efficiency, but also brought the potential for exorbitant freight rates.

The railroads were overextended because of consolidation and massive building, creating huge debt payments. Despite obvious corruption, investors, including many overseas buyers, bought up available railroad stocks and bonds. The Panic of 1893 drove 150 railroads into bankruptcy, including the B&O, Erie, and Union Pacific. This became a buying opportunity to the banks, and Morgan, for example, created Northern Securities as a holding company controlling the Northern Pacific, Great Northern, and other railroads over 17 states.

The Interstate Commerce Commission (ICC) was passed in 1887 to monitor the railroad industry, in part to ensure that rates were "reasonable and just." The simultaneous continuation of both cutthroat competition and monopoly pricing (on different routes) continued well beyond the initial passage of the ICC. The Sherman Antitrust Act was passed in 1890 to preclude monopolies and price conspiracies. One of the successful prosecutions was Morgan's holding company, Northern Securities in 1901.

See also Corporations; Erie Railroad; Gould, Jason ("Jay"); Interstate Commerce Commission; Morgan, John Pierpont; Sherman Antitrust Act of 1890; Vanderbilt, Cornelius ("Commodore")

References

Chandler, Alfred. *The Visible Hand: The Managerial Revolution in American Business.* Cambridge, Massachusetts: The Belknap Press, 1977.

Dobson, John. "Railroads." In *Bulls, Bears, Boom, and Bust: A Historical Encyclopedia of American Business Concepts.* Santa Barbara, CA: ABC-CLIO, 2006.

Josephson, Matthew. *The Robber Barons.* New York: Harcourt, 1962.

Livesay, Harold. *Andrew Carnegie and the Rise of Big Business.* New York: Longman, 1975.

Van Sickle, Eugene. "Railroads." In *The American Economy: A Historical Encyclopedia.* Rev. ed. Edited by Cynthia Clark. Santa Barbara, CA: ABC-CLIO, 2006.

Reconstruction Finance Corporation (RFC)

The Reconstruction Finance Corporation (RFC) was a federal agency established by President Herbert Hoover in 1932, primarily to provide short-term loans to banks during the Great Depression. The Emergency Relief and Construction Act of 1932, the final Hoover-period attempt, provided public works programs and created the RFC to aid states for relief programs, plus loans to banks and other financial institutions as well as invest in bank stock. The useful role of the RFC expanded under President Franklin Roosevelt. The RFC continued under Roosevelt primarily as a federal lending agency, with expanded responsibilities during World War II, until it closed in 1953.

At the end of the 1920s, there were 25,000, mostly small, American banks, and most of these were not affiliated with the Federal Reserve (which provides liquidity to member banks). The RFC was created in January 1932 specifically to provide the needed loans to banks. Initial capital of $500 million came from the Treasury Department plus the right to borrow additional funds. Over its life, the RFC borrowed $51.3 billion from the Treasury and $3.1 billion from the public. In addition to bank support, the RFC was also authorized to loan to railroads, thrifts, life insurance companies, and other organizations. Charles Dawes was named its first president. An unexpected problem was the full-transparency requirement of the law. Banks seeking funding could see an immediate bank run and other companies could lose the confidence of customers and suppliers.

Roosevelt kept and reorganized the RFC and appointed Texas banker Jesse Jones as head. Beginning in Detroit, a nationwide bank panic started before Roosevelt took office in March 1933. On March 9, 1933, the Emergency Banking Act gave the RFC authority to purchase bank preferred stock and other securities. From 1933 to 1935, the RFC purchased over $1 billion in preferred stock and bonds from 6,000 banks.

RFC loaned $2.5 billion to agriculture, in part through the Commodity Credit Corporation (which now operates in the Department of Agriculture). New Deal legislation allowed the RFC to make loans to business and buy and sell mortgages (and later provided the initial funded to establish the Federal National Mortgage Association, Fannie Mae). RFC provided funding to the Export-Import Bank to expand foreign trade.

Preparing for World War II, eight RFC subsidiaries were established to assist the war effort. For example, the Rubber Development Corporation developed synthetic rubber after Japan took over Asian rubber plantations. Over $20 billion in loans were made through the wartime subsidiaries. After the war, RFC efforts started winding down. Shortly after Dwight D. Eisenhower was inaugurated as president in 1953, legislation passed to terminate the RFC and all activities stopped by 1957 (a number of RFC programs were transferred to other federal agencies, including the Small Business Administration, Export-Import Bank, and Fannie Mae).

See also Banking after the Federal Reserve; Crash of 1929; Fannie Mae and Freddie Mac; Great Depression; New Deal; Resolution Finance Corporation; Roosevelt, Franklin Delano

References

Batkiewicz, James. *Reconstruction Finance Corporation*. 2010. http://eh.net/encyclopedia.

Dobson, John. "Reconstruction Finance Corporation." In *Bulls, Bears, Boom, and Bust: A Historical Encyclopedia of American Business Concepts*. Santa Barbara, CA: ABC-CLIO, 2006.

Friedel, F. *Franklin D. Roosevelt: A Rendezvous with Destiny*. Boston: Little, Brown, 1990.

Galbraith, Kenneth. *The Great Crash 1929*. Boston: Houghton Mifflin, 1988.

Redlining

Sociologist John McKnight first used the term "redlining" in the 1960s to describe the practice of banks to draw "red lines" on maps to mark areas where the banks would not make loans—such as black neighborhoods in inner cities. The term was later expanded to apply to discrimination in general.

One of the public policy problems of home ownership until the 1960s was the "whites-only" attitude even by federal agencies. Minorities also were separated from whites geographically, a practice called "redlining." Eugene Robinson

(2010) referred to this as a form of "commercial segregation" used in the North, while the South maintained "legal segregation." Minorities, often viewed as uncreditworthy, were declined loans or approved for mortgages at higher interest rates, with little regard for income or credit history.

Redlining got a big boost from the federal government's New Deal legislation. The National Housing Act of 1934, which established the Federal Housing Administration (FHA), and other legislation, made it difficult for inner-city families to obtain mortgages—"Type D" neighborhood were literally outlined in red (desirable "Type A" neighborhoods were outlined in blue) and considered risky for mortgages—often black neighborhoods. Lenders had to make decisions based on FHA standards to receive FHA insurance and FHA manuals instructed bankers to avoid neighborhoods with "inharmonious racial groups." This led to further deterioration of these areas. A few banks, such as ShoreBank in Chicago, fought racist lending practices.

Civil Rights legislation beginning in the 1960s included efforts for a more inclusive home ownership policy, including the Fair Housing Act of 1968 outlawing redlining and other forms of discrimination. The Community Reinvestment Act (CRA) of 1977 required banks to reduce discriminatory lending practices. During the Clinton administration, a National Homeownership Strategy policy increased home ownership to minority groups. HUD strategy focused on helping people move out of public housing into their own homes, requiring private lenders to increase subprime lending. The Bush administration carried out a similar program, encouraging Fannie Mae and Freddie Mac to expand holdings of subprime mortgages.

Some banks practiced "reverse redlining" to target poor, especially minority, communities to market expensive subprime loans (often called "ghetto loans"), typically using predatory practices.

See also Banking after the Federal Reserve; Debt and Leverage; Fannie Mae and Freddie Mac; Mortgage-Backed Security (MBS); Regulation of Business; Subprime Meltdown

References

Hafer, Rik. "Redlining." In *The Federal Reserve System: An Encyclopedia*. Santa Barbara, CA: ABC-CLIO, 2005.

Robinson, Eugene. *Disintegration: The Splintering of Black America*. New York: Doubleday, 2010.

Regulation of Business

Regulations are the rules for controlling social and human behavior. Business regulations go back to the dawn of civilization, and precedents for American business regulations came mainly from Britain, which stressed property rights and rule of law. British common law, for example, had regulations against price fixing and monopoly practices. The U.S. Constitution established federal responsibilities (including commerce with foreign nations, coinage of money, and levying taxes) and initially left most regulation of business up to the states. Problems arose because of conflicting rules across states and the inability of states to deal with expanding business in interstate commerce. Much of financial history centers on the dynamic patchwork of state and federal attempts at appropriate regulations, plus judicial review. Businesses, in the meantime, sought regulatory responses in their own self-interest—not the public interest. Politicians and regulators also had their own interests, once again, not necessarily the public interest.

Regulations related to economic factors (direct and indirect) existed throughout American history and went through periods of stiff and lax enforcement for a variety of reasons. Greater enforcement of British-imposed regulations on taxes and trade after decades of lax enforcement led to the American Revolution. Economic peaks were more common during lax-enforcement periods, in part because the regulators did not want to disrupt prosperity—and usually encouraged by politicians on the dole from key participants. Regulatory budgets and enforcement increased after collapse (part of the "solution"), with key players tenaciously fighting the new rules. New regulations after the subprime collapse were slow to develop, although Congress eventually passed the Dodd-Frank bill in 2010.

The nineteenth century offers a number of examples of the difficulty of business regulations, especially when industries want total freedom. Daniel Yergin (2011, 279) notes that "in the nineteenth century, steamboats regularly blew up, but Congress waited 40 years until a long series of accidents led to safety regulations." In the late nineteenth century, the Locomotive Acts (also called Red Flag Laws) promoted by railroads, required automobiles to speed limits of two miles an hour in cities and four miles an hour in the country and to be led by a pedestrian waving a red flag or carry a lantern. (Similar laws were passed by some American states.) As a result, the auto industry developed in Germany and the United States (especially around Detroit, without hindering regulations), but not in England—until the Red Flag Laws were eventually repealed.

Nineteenth-century financial regulation developed an unusual banking system with limited federal oversight. Each state had unique rules, from conservative bank requirements to wildcat banking with little capital or reserves, large issues of paper money, counterfeiting, and many bank failures. Commercial banks were partially nationalized during the Civil War, and federal controls increased ever since. The United States existed without a central bank until the creation of the Federal Reserve System in 1913.

Transportation first with canals and then railroads created large businesses and, eventually, a nationwide distribution system. State and then federal regulations followed real and perceived abuses. Industrial firms started as small, relatively local affairs and increased in size due to improved distribution channels, economies of scale, and ruthless entrepreneurs creating business empires. Bankers helped consolidate business into monopolies industry by industry. Competence and professional management, incompetence and corruption—both brought success to some and failure to others. The most corrupt and ruthless could be the winners. State regulations proved modestly effective at best against big business operating in interstate commerce, requiring a federal response to the most pressing issues; these included public/consumer/employee safeguards, limits on monopoly power, and outright law breaking. Monopoly power meant controlling both prices and product to consumers, eliminating competitors, and possibly stifling innovation. The effectiveness of government to promote efficient commerce, while simultaneously imposing limitations on predatory practices of big businesses (plus a whole host of other types of market failures) is difficult to measure and subject to alternative judgments.

The federal government first regulatory attempt was the Interstate Commerce Commission Act of 1887. Railroads were the largest and most important industry following the Civil War, and bubbles and busts related to railroad building on credit and securities manipulation contributed to major panics in the second half of the nineteenth century. Railroads were accused of major abuse by customers, especially farmers who established granger movements to protect their own interests.

The act created the Interstate Commerce Commission (ICC) as a federal agency that attempted to control railroad practices and rates, especially the elimination of predatory pricing. The Interstate Commerce Commission Act banned railroad rebates, required the publication of rates, and prohibited both pooling agreements and "unjust and unreasonable rates." A Supreme Court case ruled that the ICC could not fix rates. Finally, in 1906, the Hepburn Act specifically gave the ICC the right to set maximum rates. Compliance was never 100 percent and rebates continued for decades. Typical of federal agencies, the ICC was underfunded and had only limited enforcement powers. Over time, the ICC became more interested in protecting the railroad industry rather than the public (a practice called capture theory).

The Sherman Antitrust Act of 1890 attempted to limit monopoly power and price conspiracies. The Justice Department created an Antitrust Division and various later federal agencies investigated business practices, particularly the U.S. Industrial Commission and U.S. Bureau of Corporations. These new agencies took a broad perspective on business abuse and regulation. Before World War I, new legislation created the Federal Reserve and the Federal Trade Commission, plus the Clayton Act increased antitrust powers. The government responses limited some of the worst abuses of growing business power, although regulatory success proved mixed.

The U.S. Industrial Commission was created in 1898 to "investigate questions pertaining to . . . manufacturing . . . and to report to Congress and to suggest such legislation as it may deem best upon the subject." The commission held hearings and the final report showed the ineffectiveness of state regulations. The Theodore Roosevelt administration created the Department of Commerce and Labor in 1903. Within it, the Bureau of Corporations issued several industry studies before combining with the Federal Trade Commission in 1914. The studies of Standard Oil and the "beef trust" were followed by successful anti-rust prosecutions. The bureau stated its major concerns: "Under present industrial conditions, secrecy and dishonesty in promotion, overcapitalization, unfair discrimination by means of transportation and other rebates, unfair and predatory competition, secrecy of corporate administration, and misleading or dishonest financial statements are generally recognized as the principal evils." Many bills were introduced in Congress to regulate business, but none were successful. However, considerable information was gathered and used for later legislation.

After the Panic of 1907 and the Pujo Hearings, the demand for regulations increased; and under the Woodrow Wilson presidency, Congress created the Federal Reserve System and Federal Trade Commission, and passed the Clayton Antitrust Act, all in 1913–14. These new laws expanded to role of the federal government into banking and monetary policy, antitrust and related business regulations, and additional consumer protections. After a period of lax enforcement in the 1920s, the New Deal of President Franklin D. Roosevelt passed many stringent regulations on banking and business.

The 1960s and 1970s saw new regulations in safety and environment (including the creation of the Environmental Protection Agency), followed by deregulation under the Reagan Revolution in the 1980s. Deregulation brought debacles in the thrift industry in the 1980s and a lax business environment in the 1990s. The collapse of the tech bubble in 2000 and the business scandals that followed led to the Sarbanes-Oxley Act of 2002, which greatly increased business regulations. Lax enforcement in the financial sector led to the subprime meltdown in 2008, followed by the Dodd-Frank reform bill of 2010. The expectation is that periods of lax enforcement and deregulation will be followed by new business scandals and then additional regulations.

See also Antitrust; Banking after the Federal Reserve; Banking before the Federal Reserve; Capture Theory; Clayton Act; Deregulation; Federal Reserve System; Federal Trade Commission (FTC); Regulations and Regulatory Failures; Roosevelt, Franklin Delano; Roosevelt, Theodore; Securities and Exchange Commission (SEC); Sherman Antitrust Act of 1890

References

Josephson, Matthew. *The Robber Barons*. New York: Harcourt, 1962.

Mitchell, Lawrence. *The Speculation Economy: How Finance Triumphed over Industry*. San Francisco: Berrett-Koehler, 2007.

Viscusi, W., J. Vernon, and J. Harrington. *Economics of Regulation and Antitrust*. 2nd ed. Cambridge, MA: MIT Press, 1995.

Yergin, Daniel. *The Quest: Energy, Security, and the Remaking of the Modern World*. New York: Penguin Press, 2011.

Regulation and Regulatory Failures

Regulations are government laws and procedures for allocating responsibilities and constrain certain activities. Regulations are established for a reason, mostly following evidence of abuse or market failure. Consider speed limits. Rationales for speed limits include safety and promoting fuel economy. If the speed limit is 55, a large percentage of drivers will be averaging 56–60 and a few substantially above that. In those towns with a reputation for enforcement, expect most of them to slow down. In areas where the police seldom visit, expect many to floor it. Many people are breaking the law and few if any can go through life without violating some rule or regulation. Additional factors may also come into play. A smuggling merchant or privateer may be a hero at home, but jailed (or worse) if caught by the other side. John D. Rockefeller, often called a robber baron for ruthlessly eliminating competition and negotiating secret railroad rebates, created the modern integrated oil giant and many of the concepts of the modern large corporation. Michael Milken, convicted and jailed as a crook, created the junk bond market, which continues to be important today; some consider him a hero and a smaller group claims he did nothing wrong.

Regulations have proven relatively effective if not necessarily efficient over the long run in most areas. Food safety and inspection is a long-term success, but with periodic blemishes. Pollution controls were expensive to implement and sometimes unproductive and wasteful (plus unrepentant polluters could ignore regulations or move operations overseas), but over time proved useful. Arguments going forward primarily involve the level of additional pollution controls needed, the primary concern the matter of cost versus benefits (individual costs relative to social benefits). Regulations about food and drug safety, inspections and audits, and accuracy in advertising generally have been viewed favorably, despite episodes of inept and lax enforcement, overregulation, and outright corruption by regulators. The majority of the public views social programs such as Social Security favorably, although detractors exist, especially as future payments become increasingly problematic.

On the other hand, there have been many regulatory failures and regulations result in unintended consequences. Banks are necessarily heavily regulated. Banking in the United States started during the American Revolution and bank regulations became state affairs. Except for the Banks of the United States (First and Second), banking continued under state control until the Civil War when legislation made switching from a state to a national bank desirable. The Federal Reserve, created in 1914, proved rather incompetent during the Great Depression. The 1920s developed an especially corrupt financial sector, which helped bring down the economy. Fortunately, investment banks of the time were relatively small partnerships; otherwise they would no doubt have caused even greater damage. The New Deal introduced vast new regulations of business and particularly the securities and banking sectors, as well as the reorganization of the Federal Reserve. The banks took a long time to recover—and much longer to cause major havoc.

Until the 1980s, financial corruption and failures usually were local affairs. Poorly designed deregulations of thrifts led to vast corruption and the failure of much of that industry. Systemic risk problems (the chance the entire market will collapse) have been around ever since. Investment banks incorporated and greatly expanded their use of exotic and unusually risky new products as well as their own risk levels. Drexel Burnham failed because of the junk bond scandal of Michael Milken in 1990. Throughout the 1990s, derivative fiascoes happened one after another, culminating with the collapse of Long-Term Capital Management (LTCM). The financial sector participated as an accomplice to the corporate corruption and tech collapse early in the twenty-first century.

Banks relied on quantitative specialists to create new products and inflicted them on an unsuspecting world over the last three decades. The political powers believed in deregulation, encouraged by the lobbying efforts of the financial industry, presumably allowing greater innovation and efficiency. Federal Reserve (Fed) Chairman Alan Greenspan was a true believer in deregulation: markets were supposed to provide stability and self-regulation. Despite many episodes of banking bailouts by the Fed, Greenspan claimed deregulation worked. The subprime meltdown eliminated this perspective, even for Greenspan. As he stated in congressional testimony in 2008, "I found a flaw in the model that I perceived as the critical functioning structure that defines how the world works" (reported in Andrews 2008, 1).

What does this say about regulation and the role of the government? Despite the frustrations and added costs of stringent rules, they are necessary. In fact, regulations are everywhere. Local and state governments regulate all kinds of things, from construction to pets. Federal regulations can seem particularly onerous and have from the beginning—Jefferson's Democratic Republicans opposed "excessive federal power" from the start. The challenge is not to eliminate regulations, but to make them efficient and effective.

An open question is why business cannot create entirely free markets and make them work effectively. Corporations face considerable internal obstacles to abuse. Managers up the line consider the welfare of the corporation, generally frowning on corruption. The board of directors has the stewardship responsibility of stakeholders' interests. An annual financial audit is required by all exchange-listed companies. Bond raters analyze the debt issues. These are internal oversight requirements (granted—with considerable government mandates), but the responsibilities all take place before the federal regulators (particularly the Securities and Exchange Commission and Internal Revenue Service) do their jobs.

Academic research indicates internal oversight works reasonably well most of the time. Generally, this research focuses on violators (executive, governance, and audit failures) as exceptions, often because of specific weaknesses: weak corporate governance, overwhelming incentives to cheat (stock options and other forms of executive compensation lead the list), or periods of lax enforcement (these groups are not immune to euphoria). The internal regulators also get paid by the very executives they are supposed to regulate. The added corporate governance and audit requirements of the Sarbanes-Oxley Act of 2002 did not stop the subprime crisis of 2008. Executive compensation leads the list of incentives for abuse. To stop bad behavior, incentives have to be structured correctly. The overall track record of the private sector has not been that effective.

See also Antitrust; Clayton Act; Deregulation; Federal Reserve System; Federal Trade Commission (FTC); Regulation of Business; Securities and Exchange Commission (SEC); Sherman Antitrust Act of 1890

References

Andrews, Edward. "Greenspan Concedes Error on Regulation." *New York Times*, October 24, 2008. http://www.nytimes.com/2008/10/24/business/economy/24panel.html.

Josephson, Matthew. *The Robber Barons*. New York: Harcourt, 1962.

Mitchell, Lawrence. *The Speculation Economy: How Finance Triumphed over Industry*. San Francisco: Berrett-Koehler, 2007.

Viscusi, W., J. Vernon, and J. Harrington. *Economics of Regulation and Antitrust*. 2nded. Cambridge, MA: MIT Press, 1995.

Repo 105s

A Repo 105 is a repurchase agreement accounted for as a sale rather than a loan. After the financial statements are completed, the company reverses the transaction. On March 11, 2010, Lehman Brothers' Repo 105 scam was exposed by the bankruptcy court examiner. Lehman had failed in September 2008, the largest bankruptcy in American history. Note that several banks used Repo 105s.

A repurchase agreement (repo) is a short-term loan, exchanging cash for securities as collateral, and then reversing the transaction at the end of the term (the repurchase), often overnight. In a Repo 105, the value of the collateral represents 105 percent of the cash received. (Lehman also used Repo 108, requiring collateral of 108% of cash received, usually for equity securities.) Based on English law rather than American (and accepted by Lehman's international auditor PricewaterhouseCoopers and domestic auditor Ernst & Young), the repos were booked as a "sale" rather than a loan, allowing Lehman to show up to $50 billion of cash replacing securities without recognizing any liabilities. After the revelation by the bankruptcy court filing, the Securities and Exchange Commission (SEC) announced an investigation to determine if other companies used similar techniques. New York attorney general Andrew Cuomo filed charges against Ernst & Young, claiming "Lehman engaged in a 'massive accounting fraud' and that Ernst & Young aided the bank by approving an accounting treatment that produced a short-term reduction in the bank's debt—the so called Repo 105 transactions" (Reed 2010).

In 2011, the Financial Accounting Standards Board (FASB) amended accounting requirements for repurchase agreements, changing the criteria for assessing effective control on repurchasing or redeeming the assets serving as collateral.

See also Accounting Fraud; Debt and Leverage; Financial Accounting Standards Board (FASB); Fraud; Investment Banks; Lehman Brothers; Securities and Exchange Commission (SEC); Subprime Meltdown

References

De La Merced, Michael, and Julia Werdigier. "The Origins of Lehman's 'Repo 105.'" *New York Times*, March 10, 2010. http://dealbook.nytimes.com.

"FASB Amends 'Repo 105' Loophole." *The Accountant*, May 2011. http://www.vrl-financial-news.com.

Reed, Kevin. "E&Y Sued over Lehman's Audit." *Accounting Age*, December 21, 2010. http://www.accountingage.com.

Resolution Trust Corporation (RTC)

Congress created the Resolution Trust Corporation (RTC) in 1989 to clean up the savings and loan (S&L) mess, specifically to sell off the assets of failed thrifts after the S&L crisis of the 1980s. The Financial Institutions Reform, Recovery, and Enforcement Act of 1989 (FIRREA) established the RTC with the intent of liquidating the assets of S&Ls declared insolvent by the Office of Thrift Supervision. Estimates of the total costs to the government ranged to $500 billion and the final bill totaled over $100 billion.

The RTC managed a huge amount of defunct real estate and had the mission of selling off the assets of the failed thrifts. Mortgages not in default were sold. The hard part was disposing of assets no one wanted in the middle of a recession, included mortgages in default, partially built commercial properties, and various other real estate properties in overbuilt areas. Many of the properties ended up being auctioned off in billion-dollar blocks for a fraction of book value. The RTC disbanded in 1995 after liquidating $394 billion in assets of almost 750 S&Ls. In 1989, the Office of Management and Budget had estimated the cost at $257 billion. Other estimates approached half a trillion dollars. The final bill to taxpayers from the RTC totaled $87 billion, a fraction of earlier estimates (Greenspan 2007, 117). Other losses brought the total taxpayer-financed tab to $165 billion.

See also Bond Ratings; Fraud; Insider Trading; Insider Trading Scandals of the 1980s; Junk Bond Market; Keating, Charles H., Jr.; Lincoln Savings and Loan Association; Milken, Michael R.

References

Davison, Lew. *The Resolution Trust Corp. and Congress, 1989–1993*. Federal Deposit Insurance Corporation. 2006. http://www.fdic.com.

Greenspan, Alan. *The Age of Turbulence: Adventures in a New World*. New York: Penguin Press, 2007.

Stewart, James. *Den of Thieves*. New York: Simon & Schuster, 1991.

Retirement Benefits and Manipulation

Corporations can provide retirement benefits such as health insurance in addition to pension, called other postemployment benefits (OPEB). Historically, these costs were recognized on a pay-as-you-go basis—cash was paid out, but no liabilities were recognized on the corporation's public accounting statements. The accounting rules have changed to require recognition of liabilities, included in Statement of Financial Accounting Standards (SFAS) No. 106, issued in 1990, which required OPEB. The new rules also required disclosures, similar to the way pensions were disclosed. Additional requirements were added with SFAS No. 132 and SFAS No. 158. As health care costs rose, these financial obligations increased.

OPEB accounting and disclosure is similar to defined-benefits pensions. Corporations are required to disclose their net liability position (cumulative obligations less any OPEB investment assets). After SFAS No. 106 became effective in 1990, many companies established ceilings on how much they would pay for retirement health care (a spending cap) or dropped retirees from coverage, including Sears, Caterpillar, IBM, and Delta Airlines. IBM hit its spending ceiling in 2002 and spending in this category remained flat, with retirees paying for the increased costs. Sears both established a ceiling and cut retirees, reducing health care increases from 14 percent to 6 percent by 1999.

In some industries (military contractors or utilities), costs are reimbursed and increasing costs are funded by the customers. McDonnell Douglas (now part of Boeing) used "pump and dump" after losing a defense contract in 1991—conveniently after SFAS No. 106 was issued. The company assumed that health care inflation would be 15 percent a year, leading to a $1.5 billion after-tax charge-off. The following year McDonnell began to phase out all health care coverage for all nonunion retirees. During the phase-out period, health care costs were paid for from pension assets, resulting in substantial gains on the income statement (Schultz 2011, 67–69).

Another post-SFAS No. 106 example was Pacific Gas & Electric (PG&E), which reported a large liability in part based on high inflation assumptions for future health care and obtained rate increases of $181 million in 1993. After the rate increase, PG&E cut both health care benefits and its workforce. Using "creeping takeaways" (basically annual cuts), retiree-benefit expenses dropped 90 percent by 1999. The California Utility Commission eventually clawed back much of the manipulated gains (Schultz 2011, 71).

OPEB cost continued to be cut in the twenty-first century, but even with cuts, OPEB commitments are still underfunded. Of the 30 firms making up the Dow Jones Industrial Average (Dow 30), 26 had OPEB obligations in 2004 (Giroux 2006, 108–11). All but 2 reported a negative funded status (net liabilities) averaging $6.1 billion (total $146.6 billion). A Securities and Exchange Commission (SEC) report on off-balance-sheet items found that 74 of the largest 100 firms had OPEB plans in 2003 and estimated that about 15 percent of all traded corporations report OPEB plans. Estimated total underfunding for all traded firms of $337 billion ($538 billion for both pension and OPEB). The annual expense for OPEB in 2004 averaged $491 million for the Dow 26, a total of $12.7 billion.

Common tactics for cutting OPEB costs include tightening eligibility requirements by age and years of service, removing dependents from coverage, and increasing premiums, deductibles, and other costs. Part of OPEB earnings management is related to quarterly earnings targets. If the company is just 1¢ per share short of consensus analysts' forecasts, companies can lower expenses by increasing retiree premiums and reducing benefits. Caterpillar did just that in 2002, generating a $75 million gain. Whirlpool did it in 2003 to generate a $14.5 million gain to beat the consensus forecast of $1.31 by 4¢, then another cut in benefits in 2009 for an $89 million gain (Schultz 2011, 76–79). Retirement benefits continue to be a major issue after the 2008 meltdown, in both the public and private sectors. It is uncertain whether or not retirement commitments will be met in the future, forcing many employees to remain in the workforce longer or to accept a lower standard of living in retirement.

See also Accounting Standards; Earnings Manipulation; Financial Accounting Standards Board (FASB); Pension Basics; Pension Underfunding and Manipulation; Securities and Exchange Commission (SEC)

References

Giroux, Gary. *Earnings Magic and the Unbalance Sheet: The Search for Financial Reality.* New York: Wiley, 2006.

Schultz, Ellen. *Retirement Heist: How Companies Plunder and Profit from the Nest Eggs of American Workers*. New York: Portfolio/Penguin, 2011.

Revenue Fraud

Fraud is intentional deception for personal gain. Accounting fraud is the deliberate misstatement of financial information for benefit of managers and is closely related to earnings manipulation. Revenue fraud involves the recognition of revenue, either in a different period than when earned or nonexistent revenues.

Fictitious sales are outright fraud and a criminal act, and include some of the most infamous accounting scandals. Examples include Equity Funding and ZZZZ Best. Equity Funding was a massive computer fraud from the 1970s. Bogus insurance policies and related bogus data were entered into the computer system, suggesting a booming company. ZZZZ Best was in the insurance restoration business in the 1980s. However, most of the restoration projects recorded did not exist. Critical Path, an Internet company providing outsource services such as messaging, used a version of back-pocket deals of $4 million (fictitious sales recorded only if needed to meet earnings targets, to be later charged to bad-debts reserve), recorded a $7 million sale to a group of big shareholders as resellers (disallowed by auditor PWC), and recognized revenue before it met accounting criteria—i.e., the generally accepted accounting principles (GAAP). The Securities and Exchange Commission (SEC) and U.S. attorney charged several managers with fraudulent acts and insider trading.

Table 17. Revenue Fraud

Corporation	Year	Findings
AOL	1997	Reversed $7 million in revenue on long-term contract recognized immediately
Campbell Soup	2001	Shipping and handling costs reclassified from net sales to cost of sales
Centex	2001	Net revenues restated to include freight and delivery costs billed to customers
Clorox	2001	Coupon cost included in advertising expense (now deducted from sales)
CMS Energy	2002	Round-trip trades
ConAgra Foods	2001	Immediate recognition of deferred delivery sales, vendor rebates, and advance vendor rebates (also, related understated bad-debts reserve).
Concord Camera	2001	Immediate recognition on shipments to a customer, when payments were expected over an extended period; deferring revenue of $1.7 million resulting in a larger net loss
Dillard's	2001	Reclassified shipping and handling reimbursements to other income
Harrah's Entertainment	2001	Recognition of sales incentives and "free products and services" to be delivered in the future—now reported as contra-asset items rather than expenses
Hewlett-Packard	2001	Delay recognition from date of shipment to date of delivery, plus restatement of costs previously recorded to SG&A and now charged directly against revenue, based on SAB 101
Raytheon	2000	Bill and hold sales, ownership passed to buyer but before modifications made and delivery
TJX	2000	Immediate recognition of layaway sales, now deferred based on SAB 101
Xerox	2002	Immediate recognition associated with bundled leases, to be reallocated to equipment, service, supplies, and financing
Xilinx	1999	Immediate recognition for shipments to international distributors, now deferred until products are sold to end customer

Note: Adapted from Giroux (2004, 125–26).

The Treadway Commission report, which reviewed alleged fraud of 200 companies from 1987–97 based on SEC enforcement actions, found that over 50 percent of the frauds involved overstating revenues or recording revenues prematurely or fictitiously (SOCO 1999). A General Accounting Office (GAO) report on restatement of financial statements (GAO 2002) found that 38 percent of the 919 restatements investigated for the period 1997–2002 involved revenue recognition manipulation, the most important category by far. Many of these restatements were later identified as fraud based on SEC investigations and enforcement actions and various lawsuits. The most common reasons were earlier recognition than allowed by GAAP or recognizing questionable or fictitious revenue. The Government Accountability Office (GAO) updated the study in 2006, identifying restatements issued by 1,100 companies from mid-2002 to September 2005 (GAO 2006). Results were similar to the earlier study.

According to the GAO report, the most authoritative survey available, 72 S&P 500 companies restated earnings over the five-year period analyzed. Of these, 31 (43%) involved revenue recognition issues. (Note that several restatements included multiple violations.) Table 17 summarizes the nature of the revenue recognition issues for some of these restatement firms.

The violations ranged from minor to severe. More serious examples include many of the listed concerns, such as round-trip sales (CMS Energy), recognition of vendor rebates (ConAgra), revenue based on sales incentives (Harrah's Entertainment), and bill and hold sales (Raytheon). A key question is to what extent the existence of restatements signals an earnings manipulation environment.

SeaView Video Technology recognized revenue before items were shipped. According to a GAO report, the former chief executive officer (CEO) of SeaView "misstated the company's sales and revenue figures; improperly recognized revenues; misrepresented the nature and extent of the company's dealer network; falsely touted purported contracts and agreements with large retailers; misrepresented the company's ability to manufacture, or to have manufactured, its products; and misrepresented SeaView's likelihood of achieving certain publicly announced sales targets" (GAO 2002, 196).

Financial analysts are seldom able to demonstrate the existence of revenue fraud or manipulation, because relatively little is disclosed about the details or process of recognizing revenues. Instead, it is up to auditors (internal and external), the SEC, and other regulators to spot the fraud. Consequently, investors and other users of financial statements have to wait until the fraud is reported (or rely on weak signal of potential fraud such as rising receivables relative to sales).

See also Accounting Fraud; Accounting Standards; Conservative versus Aggressive Accounting; Financial Accounting Standards Board (FASB); Fraud; Revenue Recognition and Manipulation; Securities and Exchange Commission (SEC)

References

Committee of Sponsoring Organizations of the Treadway Commission (COSO). *Report of the National Commission on Fraudulent Financial Reporting*. New York: COSO, 1987.

General Accounting Office. *Financial Statement Restatements: Trends, Market Impacts, Regulatory Responses, and Remaining Challenges*. Washington, DC: GAO, October 2002.

Giroux, Gary. *Detecting Earnings Management*. Hoboken, NJ: Wiley, 2004.

Government Accountability Office. *Financial Statement Restatements: Update of Public Company Trends, Market Impacts, and Regulatory Enforcement Actions*. Washington, DC: GAO, July 2006.

Mulford, Charles, and Eugene Comiskey. *The Financial Numbers Game: Detecting Creative Accounting Practices*. New York: Wiley, 2002.

Revenue Recognition and Manipulation

According to the Financial Accounting Standards Board (FASB), revenue is recognized when (1) realized or realizable and (2) earned. Realizable means cash is received or the probability of receiving cash is very high. Revenue is earned when the earnings process is substantially complete. Generally, this will occur by the time the product is delivered or service rendered.

The Securities and Exchange Commission (SEC) improved revenue recognition criteria in 1999 with Staff Accounting Bulletin (SAB) 101, *Revenue Recognition in Financial Statements*. Prior to that, various recognition rules existed, usually by industry. The basic criteria are stated in the SAB: "The accounting literature on revenue recognition includes both broad conceptual discussions as well as certain industry-specific guidance. . . . The staff believes that revenue generally is realized or realizable and earned when all of the following criteria are met: persuasive evidence of an arrangement exists, delivery has occurred or services have been rendered, the seller's price to the buyer is fixed or determinable, and collectability is reasonably assured."

Executives have incentives (mainly based on compensation based on accounting numbers) to cheat, with early recognition of revenues a common approach used. This is called "aggressive revenue recognition," usually accompanied by increasing receivables. Revenue recognition is primarily a timing issue. Possible alternatives include recognition when sale is made, when product is shipped, when product is received and accepted by the customer, or when cash payment is received. The standard SAB criteria are delivery and passage of title to the buyer. Manipulation usually means recognition at an earlier point in the earnings cycle.

For a manufacturing company, key sales events include the initial sale, shipment to the customer, customer billing, receipt and approval of the product by the customer, and cash payment. Revenues from separate services and warranties are usually deferred until earned, usually with the passage of time. Although cash is received, revenue is not yet recognized because it has not yet been earned.

As with warranties and service contracts, prepaid items such as magazine subscriptions and insurance policies are deferred and revenue recognized over the prepaid period covered. Engineering and construction companies build major capital and infrastructure project over several years. Revenues can be recognized either under completed contracts (no revenue is recognized until the project is completed) or percentage of completion at the end of the accounting period (where revenue is recognized based on the estimated completion of the project). For example, Boeing uses both for aircraft construction. For commercial aircraft, revenues generally are recognized when deliveries are made (completed contracts). For government cost reimbursement contracts, revenue is recognized based on scheduled milestones (percentage of completion).

Timing is key in revenue recognition, whether specific revenue should be recognized this period or in the future. Important exceptions exist to sales-based revenue, including commodities with liquid markets where revenues can be recognized when production is complete and the use of percentage-of-completion method on long-term construction contracts. Software company MicroStrategy used a basic fraud strategy to ensure that earnings targets were made every quarter. MicroStrategy did not sign or date sales contracts; instead, these were dated only when management decided, after the fact, in which quarter to assign revenue to meet earnings targets.

Revenue manipulation is difficult to detect, given accounting creativity to meet earnings targets. Revenue recognition policies are described in the first footnote to the financial statements. The policy should be consistent with industry standards. Table 18 describes some specific concerns related to revenue recognition.

Table 18.   Revenue Recognition and Manipulation

Topic	Concern	Detection Strategy
Sales—trends	Changes in sales, especially unexpected increases, and related items such as receivables and inventory.	Review quarterly and annual changes, including information on specific segments.
Combined product and service sales	Revenues on long-term services recognized immediately as revenue rather than over the life of the service contract.	Review accounting policies and breakout of revenues for products and services (if available in note disclosure).
Recognizing revenues on service contracts before service is performed	Another form of aggressive recognition, more difficult to justify since SAB 101.	Review policy descriptions, notes and MD&A for evidence.
Leases recorded as sales	Long-term leases recorded immediately as revenue rather than recognized over the life of the lease.	Evaluate companies that use long-term leases to sell their products; consider accounting policies, specific notes, and unusual sale trends.
Sales-installment sales method	Long-term credit terms; immediate recognition as revenue and other problematic procedures	Usually industry specific (e.g., durable goods, land sales); evaluate sales methods and related notes.
	Aggressive policies for shipping and handling charges, insurance, and set-up	

(*continued*)

Table 18.   (Continued)

Topic	Concern	Detection Strategy
Shipping, handling, and other sales-related items	costs. Are these treated as revenue items and when should they be recorded?	Review policy descriptions and revenue footnotes; compare to how related costs are treated; compare to competitors.
Bill-and-hold sales	Product sold with the stipulation that delivery will occur in a later period; could represent blatant manipulation.	Difficult to evaluate based on annual reports; generally rely on media or SEC coverage.
Reporting out-of-period sales	Timing is everything, in this case essentially reporting sales from early the next fiscal year in the current period.	Difficult to evaluate based on annual reports; rely on external sources & media.
Channel stuffing	Deep discounts to wholesalers to encourage end-of-period sales, another blatant manipulation scheme.	Unless specifically stated in the notes or MD&A, can only be detected by auditors, regulators, etc.
Round-trip transaction	Transaction with related parties for the sole purpose of meeting sales and earnings targets.	Another method to inflate revenue; unlikely to be detectible; evaluate for fraud environment; review related-party notes.
Excessive sales incentives, such as deep discounts	Given for the sole purpose of boosting end-of-period sales to achieve sales targets.	Review accounting policies, MD&A, & notes, but difficult to detect.
Disclosure of affiliated and related-party sales	Do these, in fact, represent revenues or simply exchanges? Potential for transactions to boost sales, but without economic substance.	Review notes on related-party transactions and other disclosures that suggest suspect sales.
Prepaid revenue items	Is revenue recognized immediately for multiyear commitments?	Review policy descriptions, MD&A, and notes.
Long-term construction contracts	Percent-of-completion method allows considerable judgment on estimating revenue; aggressive (early) recognition.	Determine which method is used and, if percent-of-completion, review notes and quarterly and annual reporting trends.
Other front-end recognition of revenues	Any number of aggressive recognition strategies, before revenue is earned.	Review recognition policies and notes for evidence of front-ending.
Fraud, including fictitious sales	The most infamous cases of revenue abuse are fraud and other criminal acts.	Fraud is usually detected by the auditors, the SEC, or whistle-blowers; evaluate for fraud environment.
Back-pocket sales	Fictitious sales recorded only if needed to make earnings targets.	Detected only after the fact, usually as the result of a regulatory action or lawsuit.

Several manipulation techniques have gone by such names as bill-and-hold, channel stuffing, and reporting out-of-period sales. Bill-and-hold means a sales agreement has been reached, but goods will not be shipped in the current period. This was used by chief executive officer (CEO)Al Dunlap at Sunbeam to manipulate earnings targets in the mid-1990s. Channel stuffing is shipping products at deep discounts to get customers to accept these goods (a relatively common technique). Bristol-Myers Squibb boosted 2001 earnings using deep discounts to encourage wholesalers to buy more drugs. In the late 1990s, Lucent Technologies overestimated telecom equipment demand and simultaneously lost market share. Channel stuffing was the short-term answer, using deep discounts and easy credit. The company soon collapsed with the rest of the telecom industry. Out-of-period sales is recording sales in the current period, when the sales should be recognized later. Companies using these methods usually have to restate earnings and are subject to lawsuits charging fraud.

Seller financing has been used to inflate sales (a common technique of the telecommunications industry around the turn of the twenty-first century). Motorola lent $3 billion to untrustworthy customers to purchase wireless gear—$2 billion of which had to be written off. Cisco Systems gave a major customer 135 percent vendor financing. Another method is the round-trip transaction. The telecommunications industry used a version of this technique called capacity swaps, essentially swapping fiber optics capacity in different geographic areas under long-term contracts. WorldCom, Global Crossing, and others immediately recognized the "sale" as revenue and recorded the "purchase" as a capital expenditure. Various discounts, zero-interest loans, and other sales incentives are common in the auto industry.

A General Accounting Office (GAO) report on restatement of financial statements (GAO 2002) found that almost 4 out of 10 of the over 900 restatements investigated (1997–2002) were revenue recognition, many later identified as fraud. After the passage of the Sarbanes-Oxley Act in 2002, restatements increased but fewer involved revenue recognition (according to a later GAO report).

See also Accounting Fraud; Accounting Standards; Conservative versus Aggressive Accounting; Financial Accounting Standards Board (FASB); Fraud; Revenue Fraud; Securities and Exchange Commission (SEC)

References

Giroux, Gary. *Detecting Earnings Management.* Hoboken, NJ: Wiley, 2004.

Goldin, Thomas, Steven Skalak, and Mona Clayton. *A Guide to Forensic Accounting Investigation.* Hoboken, NJ: Wiley, 2006.

Mulford, Charles, and Eugene Comiskey. *The Financial Numbers Game: Detecting Creative Accounting Practices.* New York: Wiley, 2002.

Previts, Gary, and Barbara Merino. *A History of Accountancy in the United States.* Columbus: Ohio State University Press, 1998.

U.S. Securities and Exchange Commission. *Revenue Recognition in Financial Statements.* Staff Accounting Bulletin 101. 17 CFR Part 211. http://www.sec.gov/interps/account/sab101.htm.

Risk and Risk Management

Risk can be defined as exposure to loss and the potential that a certain action will lead to a loss (or other undesirable outcome). Corporate risks are associated with various financial and market uncertainties. Risk management attempts to reduce

Table 19. Risk and Risk Management

Commodity risk:	Changing prices of commodities such as agricultural goods, industrial metals, oil, and other energy products.
Interest rate risk:	Interest rate fluctuations, complicated by fixed versus variable rates and duration (maturity dates).
Market value risk:	Price fluctuations for items that trade on a market, including commodities, stocks, credit instruments, and currencies.
Foreign exchange risk:	Currency fluctuations against all other currencies, creating substantial risks for global corporations.
Event risk:	Uncertainties associated with any number of potential events, including fire, strikes, and hostile governments. Insurance can protect against some event risks.
Credit risk:	Probability of default on debt or corporate bankruptcy.
Counterparty risk:	Both parties on contracts assume the risk that the other party will default.

or control the multitude of risks associated with a complex corporation. Risks include the following (the complete list is essentially endless).

Corporations can use hedges to manage specific risks. Natural hedges include matching asset and liability interest rates or foreign currencies. Derivatives are the most common form of artificial hedges. Hedges can reduce many of the risks listed above; however, all financial risks cannot be eliminated simultaneously. A derivative is a financial contract *derived* from another contract, event, or transaction. Complex financial arrangements can be made by using derivatives, always for specific reasons. Derivatives categories include options, futures and forwards, swaps, and collars. Corporations are expected to reduce or manage various risks using derivatives.

Corporations can use speculating, as a specific strategy or attempting hedging incorrectly. Banks and hedge funds often specialize in derivatives. They are a major revenue source for large banks, which make markets and establish specialized derivative instruments and strategies to meet the perceived needs of customers. Banks also trade for their own accounts and can use derivatives as risk management tools or as revenue generators (often with built-in extreme risk). Warren Buffett called derivatives "weapons of mass destruction." Hedge funds can hedge or speculate on virtually anything where they believe they have an edge. Long-Term Capital Management (LTCM) was extremely successful until the markets went awry in 1998. It took a Federal Reserve-sponsored bailout to unload LTCM's positions. Table 19 describes major risks faced by corporations.

Hedging effectiveness measures hedging instruments' ability to offset specific corporate risks. Many derivatives can match the risk, such as direct currency or interest rate swaps or forward contracts on specific commodities being hedged for price changes. However, direct hedges are not always available and substitutes can be considered, such as commodity forwards on correlated (similar) products or index derivatives to hedge specific debt contracts. Given derivative debacles associated with the subprime meltdown, especially the use of credit default swaps, many analysts are skeptical of the ability of so-called experts to use complex derivatives and other risk-management techniques.

See also Accounting Standards; Altman's Z-score; Bond Ratings; Credit Risk; Derivatives; Financial Accounting Standards Board (FASB); Revenue Recognition and Manipulation; Securities and Exchange Commission (SEC)

References

Geist, Charles. *Collateral Damaged: The Marketing of Consumer Debt to America*. New York: Bloomberg Press, 2009.

Giroux, Gary. *Detecting Earnings Management*. New York: Wiley, 2004.

Giroux, Gary. *Earnings Magic and the Unbalance Sheet: The Search for Financial Reality*. New York: Wiley, 2006.

Rite Aid

Rite Aid, a retail drugstore with about 3,400 drugstores, was one of several companies with accounting scandals in the 1990s, especially during 1997–98. The company started in 1962 as Thrif D Discount Center and expanded through acquisitions, becoming Rite Aid in 1968.

Fraud manipulations included misstated cost of goods sold (COGS) (such as unearned vendor allowances recorded as a reduction in COGS), failure to write down slow-moving and obsolete inventory; failure to expense stock appreciation rights; capitalizing maintenance costs and repairs to property, plant, and equipment; misstating lease obligations; failure to expense cost of store closures; and failure to recognize compensation costs such as vacation pay and incentive compensation. In other words, Rite-Aid used any manipulation technique possible to generate expected earnings.

Rite Aid restated earnings in 1999 for fiscal years 1997–98. The Securities and Exchange Commission (SEC) required further restatements, and auditor KPMG resigned late in 1999. A class action lawsuit charged the company, directors, executives, and auditor KPMG with false and misleading financial statements, and the SEC began a formal investigation, which was settled in 2002, charging the company with financial fraud. Deloitte & Touche replaced KPMG, and Rite Aid subsequently restated earnings through 2000. The vice chairman served 6 years of a 10-year prison sentence and several other executives were fired.

Rite Aid recovered and is a Fortune 500 company with a $1 billion market capitalization and 4,700 stores.

See also Accounting Fraud; Auditing since SEC Regulation; Fraud; Great Depression; Revenue Fraud; Securities and Exchange Commission (SEC); Sunbeam; Waste Management

References

Davidson, Sidney, and G. Anderson. "The Development of Accounting and Auditing Standards." *Journal of Accountancy*, May 1987, 110–27.

Dobson, John. "Crash." In *Bulls, Bears, Boom, and Bust: A Historical Encyclopedia of American Business Concepts*. Santa Barbara, CA: ABC-CLIO, 2006.

Giroux, Gary. *Financial Analysis: A User Approach*. New York: Wiley, 2003.

Mulford, Charles, and Eugene Comisky. *The Financial Numbers Game: Detecting Creative Accounting Practices*. New York: Wiley, 2002.

Schilit, Howard. *Financial Shenanigans: How to Detect Accounting Gimmicks & Fraud in Financial Reports*. 2nd ed. New York: McGraw-Hill, 2002.

Roaring Twenties

The 1920s was the decade of lax Republican rule, beginning with Warren G. Harding as president in 1920 and a Republican-controlled Congress. Harding's "return to normalcy" brought back widespread corruption. Scandals plagued the hapless Harding, considered one of the worst presidents in history. Once the short recession that started the decade was over, a long economic boom started, with considerable innovation (radio, electricity, airlines, and automobiles), and the stock market roared. Unfortunately, the 1920s did not end well. The Great Depression, beginning with the Crash of 1929, proved long and painful.

Harding's presidency provided one of the greatest business-political scandals ever, Teapot Dome. Harding's attorney general, Harry Daugherty, was corrupt and established something of a police state for personal gain using the forerunner of the Federal Bureau of Investigation. Commerce Secretary Albert Fall was convicted of bribery for his part in the Teapot Dome scandal, the only cabinet secretary up to that time to serve prison time. This also was the decade of Charles Ponzi and his contribution to business jargon, the Ponzi scheme.

The 12-year rule of Republican presidents (1921–33) did little in antitrust or business regulation, while taxes and government spending fell. The top individual income tax rate dropped to 25 percent during most of this period (down from the 73% during rate of World War I). Treasury Secretary Andrew Mellon, a business tycoon, favored business and Wall Street.

During the decade, certain industries struggled. Commodity prices stayed low with dire consequences to agriculture and to a lesser extent oil and other industries. Rural banks were hard hit. Farm prices, which rose sharply during World War I, caused a banking boom and the number of banks rose to 30,000. Farmers bought land on credit as prices rose, only to see farm prices plummet in the 1920s. Farmers failed and bankers foreclosed. About 500 banks collapsed in 1921 and over 5,000 over the decade.

From 1920 to 1929, gross domestic product (GDP, not adjusted for inflation) rose a modest 19 percent, but only 4.2 percent per capita. The unemployment rate rose to double digits in 1921, then declined back to about the 5 percent rate. The rate dropped to 2.9 percent in 1926, but rose to 4.7 percent in 1928. The best economic numbers were in 1929, suggesting at the start of the year continued prosperity; many noted authorities (and politicians) stated that the boom would be permanent.

Certain industries became stock market favorites, including autos, radio, movies, airlines, and electric utilities. All had been around before the 1920s, but this was a decade of innovation and success in these industries. With a bull market in the second half of the decade, these high-tech stocks exploded.

American Marconi Wireless started in 1899, with radio technology first used on ships. The navy during World War I took over this small company, but returned the company to its original owners in 1920, which changed its name to Radio Corporation of America (RCA) under the direction of David Sarnoff. Sarnoff turned RCA into a radio network with some 19 stations, National Broadcasting Company (NBC). RCA revenues rose from only $4 million in 1921 to $182 million in 1929, as the number of radios sold went from 100,000 to 4.4 million over the same period. RCA formed Radio-Keith-Orpheum (RKO) in 1928, expanding into movies. Other small 1920s startups later became movie giants included Paramount, Columbia, Warner Brothers, and Loew's.

Thomas Edison created the lightbulb in 1879 and started the electric utility industry. Utilities expanded across the urban United States as technology improved and new household appliances ran on electricity. Utility holding companies became huge industrial empires in the 1920s, often using highly leveraged pyramiding schemes.

The aviation industry started with the Wright Brothers, but commercial applications required improved technology and safety. World War I demonstrated the applications of airplanes in war and commerce. Mail delivery became an early commercial use, assisted by government subsidies (Charles Lindbergh was a mail pilot). Pan American Airlines, created in 1927, became the major U.S. international airline by in the 1930s. Mail delivery contracts provided needed revenue, and the company flew successfully through Central and South America. A 1930 merger of some 80 small airlines created American Airways (now American Airlines). Other airlines founded about this time included Delta, Braniff, United, Trans World, Northwest, and Eastern; all achieved success, although some later crashed.

After the 1921 recession, the economy recovered and recorded growth over the rest of the decade. The Dow Jones Industrial Average (Dow) started the decade just over 104, bottomed out at 66 in August 1921 during the short recession that year, and did not stay above 100 until August of 1924. The Federal Reserve pushed interest rates lower in support of Britain returning to the gold standard in 1925. "Cheap money" encouraged the boom and allowed greater speculation using borrowed money. Brokers pushed stocks, investment trusts, and foreign bonds, all available on margin. After 1925, the boom was on and the market rose to 200 in December 1927. Stock euphoria created a bubble and the Dow hit 300 in January 1929, on increased volume. From the rare million-share day at the start of the decade,

5 million-share days became common by 1928. Brokers claimed that just too few shares were available.

Securities market regulation relied on modest state laws and stock exchange rules, with no federal interference. With few rules to break and state laws easy to circumvent, the 1920s financial culture was deceptive, with questionable deals, high leverage, and little concern for underlying risks. Insider trading was common and legal. Investment bank used "preferred lists" to sell new securities at discount prices to favored people (customers, politicians, celebrities) before new stock issues were available to the public. Stock pools existed, syndicates established by investment bankers, brokers, and others specifically to manipulate stock prices, and at least 100 stocks were openly rigged. Some companies issued unauthorized stock and forged stock certificates. The chairman of Chase Bank speculated in his own stock and sold short during the 1929 crash. The president of the New York Stock Exchange (NYSE) would later be jailed for embezzlement. The head of National Bank was arrested for income tax evasion. This was a period when salaries of these large bank presidents often topped a million dollars a year.

By the 1920s, the NYSE was the largest securities market in the world; however, it was basically a private club operated to benefit the members with virtually no federal oversight. The members controlled the market and had access to all market information. Member could conspire with each other and manipulate stock prices for their own profit. Other inside techniques used included wash sales (selling among themselves to produce price patterns), bear raids, and short selling.

The stock boom was fueled by speculation and margin trading, which increased volatility and the potential for large price drops. With margin trading, brokers made a profit on both commissions and interest. Brokers' loans increased to $6 billion by the start of 1929. With a relatively small market drop, margin calls from brokers meant investors had to cover the loss with more cash or the stock would be sold.

Financial information was "a private matter," allowing companies to manipulate, misrepresent, and conceal relevant performance data. The rationale for nondisclosure focused on providing secret information benefiting competitors. Financial analysts emphasized the balance sheet early in the century. The income statement typically was ignored, because it was open to misrepresentation. Consequently, dividends were the paramount consideration, representing real cash payments. Whether they came out of earnings or capital was anyone's guess.

At the start of the century, railroads dominated securities markets (60% of New York Stock Exchange firms) and were considered safe investments because they paid relatively consistent dividends. As industrial firms became more prominent (44% of NYSE firms by 1920), the income statement received more serious attention, with dividends based primarily on earnings results. Of course, dividends did not guaranty performance. Kreuger and Toll Co. did not disclose financial information. The accounts were fraudulent, and interest and dividend payments were made from the cash receipts of new securities issues. Kreuger and Toll collapsed in the 1930s.

Few safeguards existed, based on limited state regulations, the investment banker review, lawyer reviews, or stock exchange rules. Audits were voluntary, but conducted by most NYSE firms (although the corporations determined what "an audit" meant). State regulation proved ineffective given the interstate economy and legal loopholes. The prospectus, typically four pages or less in length and written by lawyers, protected the bankers from lawsuits, while advertising securities issues always presenting a positive image.

Big corporations and banks did not see the need for full financial disclosure. J. P. Morgan, an exception, demanded audited financial statements of clients and annual financial statements, unusual for the time. The New York Stock Exchange had 61 percent of all securities transactions in 1929 (rising to 76% in 1932). However, the NYSE made only feeble attempts to ensure disclosure. Until 1910 the NYSE had an "unlisted department" of firms that disclosed no financial information. The NYSE did not require audited financial reports until 1933.

See also Auditing from Medieval Period to SEC Regulation; Crash of 1929; Great Depression; Pecora Commission; Ponzi, Charles; Regulation of Business; Teapot Dome

References

Chernow, Ron. *The House of Morgan: An American Banking Dynasty and the Rise of Modern Finance*. New York: Atlantic Monthly Press, 1990.

Ellis, Charles. *The Partnership: The Making of Goldman Sachs*. New York: Penguin Press, 2008.

Galbraith, Kenneth. *The Great Crash 1929*. Boston: Houghton Mifflin, 1988.

Robber Barons

The term "robber baron" was applied to wealthy nineteenth-century American businessmen, beginning with John Jacob Astor, and by the 1890s applied to those using questionable practices to accumulate vast wealth. Theodore Roosevelt referred to them as the "wealthy criminal class." The term was originally applied to medieval German nobles charging tolls on the Rhine River. *New York Times* editor Henry Raymond used the term in the 1850s to describe Cornelius Vanderbilt's steamship empire. Matthew Josephson popularized the term with his book by the same name in the 1930s. More recent historians, on the other hand, such as Allan Nevins and Alfred Chandler, focused on the importance of such industrialists as John D. Rockefeller creating efficient industries out of chaos.

Muckraking journalists investigated big business with a vengeance (the father of crusading journalist Ida Tarbell, for example, was ruined by John D. Rockefeller), branding promoters and leaders of large combinations as "Robber Barons of the Gilded Age." Politicians, when not accepting large cash payments, lambasted the

Close-up from a political cartoon from *Puck* magazine, June 14, 1882, "Our robber barons," by Bernhard Gillam. The print depicts Jay Gould, labeled "R. Road Monopolist," William H. Vanderbilt, labeled "Corporations," Cyrus W. Field, labeled "Telegraph Monopoly," Russell Sage, labeled "Stock Jobbing," and George M. Robeson labeled "Congress," robbing a "Tax Payer" of his "Income." (Library of Congress)

industrialists and tried to regulate them as conspiracies and monopolies. The view is more favorable today thanks in part to business historians, but the tension between the concepts of tycoon versus crook continues.

The robber barons, viewed as the villains of the day, suffered from the perception of illegal acts of conspiracy and monopoly to the detriment of both consumers and potential competitors. Given a fairly primitive legal environment relative to interstate commerce, avoiding illegal acts proved somewhat more difficult as the industrial powers grew. Crusaders paid less attention to sanitation, safety, potentially harmful products, pollution, and environmental destruction. Labor issues, on the other hand, rose in importance. Managers viewed property rights as sacrosanct and cared little about the rights or needs of labor or the public. Maintaining interest and dividend payments remained essential, while protecting and caring for workers raised little concern.

A partial list of nineteenth-century robber barons includes:

- Astor, John Jacob (fur trade, real estate)
- Carnegie, Andrew (iron, steel)
- Drew, Daniel (finance, speculation)
- Fisk, James (speculation)

- Flagler, Henry (oil)
- Frick, Henry (steel)
- Gould, Jay (speculation, railroads)
- Morgan, J. P. (banking)
- Rockefeller, John D. (oil)
- Vanderbilt, Cornelius (steamboats, railroads)

John Jacob Astor (1763–1848) was the first American multimillionaire, creating a fortune in fur trading and real estate, plus money lending, shipping, and railroads. Astor traded furs with the Indians in upper New York State and Canada, establishing a fur shop in New York City. He established Astoria as a fur trading post in Oregon Territory in 1811 and extended trading in the west, becoming the largest trading company in the United States. In the 1830s, Astor focused on the promise of New York City as a great trading metropolis and bought large tracts of Manhattan real estate, usually renting the property to others for development. He accumulated a fortune valued at $20 million when he died on March 29, 1848—the United States' richest person at the time.

Andrew Carnegie (1835–1919) was a Scottish-American businessman, creating Carnegie Steel, and later became a major philanthropist. He acquired the training and financial resources to turn his steel company into the world's largest by transferring railroad management methods to manufacturing: "He made his own company so efficient that his competitors were forced to emulate him" (Livesay 1975, 29). Carnegie started investing and speculating in the 1850s. He typically knew next to nothing about the various businesses, but relied on his managerial background and hired experienced people. His focus was on cost data detailing labor and materials used per unit of output. Carnegie's entrance into iron and steel began in 1872, forming a company to manufacture Bessemer steel (the Bessemer process improved steel quality and allowed steel production in mass) and this soon became his sole interest. He built various steel plants, using modern equipment, a useful accounting system, and close control over productivity, becoming the low-cost producer. As one of the world's largest freight customers, Carnegie also received secret rebates from the railroads because of the large size of shipments.

His focus on low cost and using the newest high-tech equipment and procedures, resulting in Carnegie Steel being the largest producer of coke, pig iron, and steel rail by the late 1880s. To further his competitive advantage he built integrated steel complexes with a diversified product line and used vertical integration, buying operations from ore and coal mines to producing finished products. Like almost all industrialists, he considered labor as a cost of doing business and treated his employees poorly. This was, in part, another method to hold down production costs. A stain on his reputation was the brutal results of the Homestead Strike, one of the bloodiest in U.S. history.

J. P. Morgan famously bought out Carnegie's empire for $480 million, the biggest payoff until well into the twentieth century. Morgan stated, "Mr. Carnegie,

I want to congratulate you on being the richest man in the world" (Carnegie later claimed to have sold too cheap). With Carnegie Steel and over 200 other related companies, Morgan created United States Steel, which controlled over 80 percent of steel capacity. Morgan capitalized the firm for $1.4 billion—the first billion-dollar corporation. After selling Carnegie Steel to J. P. Morgan, Carnegie turned to philanthropy.

Jay Gould ("Mephistopheles of Wall Street," 1836–92) was possible the United States' most despised man at the time. Most of his fortune was built on pilfering railroads. Typically, he bought railroads cheaply (often manipulating the price down through false rumors and selling short), pulled out available cash, then merged and renamed them, doctored their books, and sold them at a profit. Early in his career, he speculated with Daniel Drew and James Fisk. The most infamous exploits were their defense in "the Raiding of the Erie Railroad" against Cornelius Vanderbilt and the attempted corner of gold in 1869. He later controlled the Union Pacific Railroad and Western Union. When he died in 1892, his estate was valued at $72 million.

John Pierpont Morgan (1837–1913) was born into the family banking business and set up a private bank in New York City in 1870. Much of Morgan's early financial success and prestige came from financing and refinancing railroads, aided by his father's banking connections with European investors. The opportunities for railroad financing late in the nineteenth century mainly centered on reorganizing failing roads. Rate wars, rebates to large shippers, and insider pilfering resulted in railroad failures and recurring panics. Morgan felt responsible for the securities he sold and attempted to maintain competent operations.

The Panic of 1893 brought particular chaos to the markets, including the failure of hundreds of banks, thousands of commercial firms, and about a third of all railroads. About 60 percent of New York Stock Exchange issues were railroads. Morgan's approach for reorganizing the failed railroads became "Morganization," and included the Erie, Santa Fe, Northern Pacific, and New York Central. By the end of the century, most railroads were consolidated into six giant systems using voting trusts. Morgan perfected the use of interlocking directorships to maintain monopoly power over most major industries. By 1890, 300 trusts controlled 5,000 companies. J. P. Morgan won particular renown for the formation of United States Steel in 1901, the largest company in the world.

Morgan had the power to serve some of the chief functions of a central bank, in part because of the financial weakness of the federal government. He bailed out part of the financial community during both the Panic of 1893 and the Panic of 1907, limiting the damage to Wall Street. Morgan was praised on Wall Street, but Congress wanted a stronger federal government and a weaker Wall Street, leading to the Pujo Hearings of 1913, which demonstrated the "Money Trust's" immense power by proving the banks combined the direct control of corporations using interlocking directorships with the banking role over commercial lending practices. As a direct result of these hearings, substantial reform legislation established the Federal Reserve System and the Federal Trade Commission.

John D. Rockefeller (1839–1937) was an American oil tycoon, founded Standard Oil Company, and dominated the oil industry from the 1870s well into the twentieth century. He was a successful entrepreneur and consolidated oil refining in the United States either by buying out or bankrupting competitors. He started as a trade merchant and later formed a commodity merchant business, which proved quite successful during the Civil War. Pennsylvania oil discoveries beginning in 1859 resulted in several oil refineries built in Cleveland. Rockefeller transitioned from merchandising to oil and bought his first refinery in 1863. Shipping was a major selling cost. Rockefeller's operations were big enough to move from barrels to tank cars and got lower shipping rates from railroads as his production capacity grew.

Rockefeller's promoted technical innovations that increased quality, provided more standardization, created new products, and reduced costs. After the Civil War there were too many oil wells and refineries, driving down prices ("ruinous competition" according to Rockefeller), while many companies produced inferior products. Rockefeller thought two choices existed, either cooperation across firms or consolidation. He dissolved his partnership in 1870 and created Standard Oil Company (SO) in Ohio, which controlled about 10 percent of total American refining capacity. SO bought out many competing refiners, primarily in Cleveland, beginning in 1872, becoming the largest refiner in the world. Bribing politicians became a necessary step to pursue illicit acts.

By 1877, SO controlled all major refining centers. Rockefeller claimed a fair price was offered, but complained about new entrants extorting money from SO. Lawsuits against SO and Rockefeller became commonplace. SO accumulated corporations across the country, although SO of Ohio was outlawed from owning out-of-state corporations. SO lawyer Samuel Dodd created the trust to solve the ownership-across-state-lines problem in 1880. Trust agreements assigned executives as trustees holding stock in companies outside the state. SO took advantage of New Jersey's new incorporation laws allowing holding shares in out-of-state companies. When New Jersey amended the incorporation laws, Standard became a holding company with Standard of New Jersey controlling stock of 40 affiliates in 1899. Lawsuits continued.

Rockefeller retired from active management by the mid-1890s, although he kept the title of president and the company was actually run by the vice president, John Archbold. President Theodore Roosevelt's attorney general sued SO in 1906 under the Sherman Act to dissolve the company. The Supreme Court in 1911 ruled against SO, which was broken up into 33 independent companies. Rockefeller's fortune grew and he turned to philanthropy.

Cornelius Vanderbilt ("Commodore," 1794–1877) was an American tycoon in steamships and railroads, the country's richest man when he died, worth $100 million. The Commodore made his fortune with steamboats, earning him the honorary title. Vanderbilt launched his first steamboat, the *Citizen*, in 1828, beginning his own career as a transportation entrepreneur. As he bought more steamships, Vanderbilt pioneered new routes.

Vanderbilt saw the railroads as the next great transportation technology. He acquired railroad shares in the 1840s, eventually buying the Harlem Railroad and the Hudson River Railroad and turning them from decrepit money-losing railroads to efficient, profitable lines. He would link up the short rail lines with his own steamboats. His primary plan was to systematically seize power of the transportation companies around New York City.

Vanderbilt bought the New York Central in 1867 and added it to his earlier acquisitions, creating a railroad empire across the state and the best route, "the Water Level Route," paralleling the Erie Canal and Hudson River. Vanderbilt would effectively have monopoly power over New York State with the acquisition of the Erie Railroad. Vanderbilt went after the Erie to complete his railroad empire, but failed as the conniving Daniel Drew, aided by Jay Gould and James Fisk, exchanged convertible bonds for stock to maintain control. The Commodore bought stock, unaware these were brand-new securities. Vanderbilt settled up with Drew, selling his stock back and losing at least a million dollars. Vanderbilt continued his railroad empire. When he died in 1877, he left most of his $100 million estate to his son William.

See also Astor, John Jacob; Drew, Daniel; Fisk, James ("Jubilee Jim"); Gold—the Corner of 1869; Gould, Jason ("Jay"); Morgan, John Pierpont; Raiding the Erie Railroad, 1868; Rockefeller, John Davison; Vanderbilt, Cornelius ("Commodore")

References

Adams, Charles, and Henry Adams. *Chapters of Erie and Other Essays*. Boston: James A. Osgood, 1871.

Brands, H. W. *American Colossus: The Triumph of Capitalism, 1865–1900*. New York: Doubleday, 2010.

Dobson, John. "Interstate Commerce Commission." In *Bulls, Bears, Boom, and Bust: A Historical Encyclopedia of American Business Concepts*. Santa Barbara, CA: ABC-CLIO, 2006.

Josephson, Matthew. *The Robber Barons*. New York: Harcourt, 1962.

Livesay, Harold. *Andrew Carnegie and the Rise of Big Business*. New York: Longman, 2000.

Morris, Edmund. *The Rise of Theodore Roosevelt*. New York: Random House, 1979.

Rockefeller, John Davison

John D. Rockefeller (1839–1937) was an American oil tycoon, founded Standard Oil Company, and dominated the oil industry from the 1870s well into the twentieth century. He was a successful entrepreneur and consolidated oil refining in the United States by either buying out or destroying competitors. He successfully overcame the legal limitations of operating across states, including the use of trust agreements and helped create the modern American corporation. Based on his ruthless elimination of competitors, negotiation of substantial railroad rebates, and monopoly practices, he was investigated by regulators and journalists and considered one of the worst of the robber barons in the late nineteenth century. After his effective retirement from Standard Oil, he became a philanthropist.

Rockefeller was born on July 8, 1839, in Richford, New York, to a traveling salesman specializing in patent medicines. Trained as a bookkeeper, Rockefeller became a successful entrepreneur beginning in Cleveland, Ohio. He started as an assistant bookkeeper to a trade merchant and later formed a commodity merchant business, which proved quite successful during the Civil War. Pennsylvania oil discoveries beginning in 1859 resulting in several oil refineries built in Cleveland. Rockefeller, sensing the potential for success, transitioned from merchandising to oil and bought his first refinery in 1863. At the time, 6 oil refinery centers existed in the United States and 20 refineries operated around Cleveland. Demand remained high during the Civil War, especially for kerosene used for lighting. Many other uses were discovered including various lubricants necessary for a growing industrial base in the United States.

Shipping was a major selling cost, both oil shipped to the refinery and from the refinery to customers. Rockefeller's operations were big enough to move from barrels to tank cars and got lower shipping rates from railroads as his production capacity grew. He made regular big shipments using his own tanker cars and shipped long distances. This greatly reduced railroads' costs, and much of the savings was passed to Rockefeller using secret rebates. Rebates were considered an outrage to small shippers at the time, although a common railroad practice. The rebates became illegal nationwide with the Interstate Commerce Act of 1887. In the meantime, an increasing amount of oil was shipped by pipelines.

Rockefeller's promoted technical innovations that increased quality, provided more standardization, created new products, and reduced costs. He converted the sulfuric acid residue to fertilizer and found markets for by-products such as benzene, paraffin, and petroleum jelly. Rockefeller also focused on ways to reduce fire danger by improved production and shipping methods. Gasoline was a problem; except for using it to run some machinery, this was a waste product often dumped into nearby streams.

After the Civil War there were too many oil wells and refineries, including 60 refineries in Cleveland alone in 1866. This level of competition drove down prices, while many companies produced inferior products. Kerosene prices remained low for years. Rockefeller saw potential failure because of "ruinous competition." Rockefeller though two choices existed, either cooperation across firms or consolidation. Standard Oil Company (SO) bought out many competing refiners, primarily in Cleveland, beginning in 1872. Once Rockefeller bought out major rival Clark, Payne and Company, SO became the largest refiner in the world.

He dissolved his partnership in 1870 and created SO in Ohio, with Rockefeller holding 27 percent of the outstanding shares. At the time, SO controlled about 10 percent of total American refining capacity. Ohio incorporation laws banned stock ownership in other states, but Rockefeller ignored the law and kept SO's out-of-state ownership confidential. Rockefeller played the railroads serving

Cleveland (Pennsylvania, Erie, and New York Central) against each other for bargain rates. Among the deal makers was Jay Gould, at the time a director of the Erie, with SO receiving a 75 percent rebate for shipments on the Erie. Rockefeller provided incentives, including agreeing to assume legal liability for fires and accidents and a pledge of a minimum number of carloads (60 at one time) a day—at the time he needed other refiners to meet this requirement, an early form of cooperation. This promoted the concept of an oil monopoly that would benefit railroads through lower costs and higher profits.

SO formed a cartel with the Pennsylvania Railroad in 1871, creating a shell company called South Improvement Company (SIC), seemingly solving competitive problems for both refiners and railroads. The Erie and New York Central Railroads joined this conspiracy, along with various refiners. The railroads increased freight rates and gave rebates to the SIC refiners. Each railroad got a set amount of traffic. After the creation of the SIC was discovered, the Pennsylvania legislature canceled the agreement and forced the SIC to shut down. After that, bribing politicians became a necessary step to pursue illicit acts. "A tremendous amount of money changed hands as businessmen and legislators trafficked in mutual manipulation" (Chernow 1998, 209).

The oil industry was hit hard by the Panic of 1873, but SO was well positioned because of economies of scale and lower production costs. More refiners sold out to SO. Rockefeller remained ruthless to those not selling out by dropping prices and making it difficult for them to either obtain crude or ship refined products. By 1877, SO controlled all major refining centers. Rockefeller claimed a fair price was offered, but complained about new entrants extorting money from SO. SO competitors, on the other hand, complained they were intimidated by threats and offered prices below actual value. However, these perspectives often followed lawsuits or interviews with journalists many years later.

Lawsuits against SO and Rockefeller became commonplace. Clarion County, Pennsylvania, indicted Rockefeller and other SO executives in 1879 on conspiracy to monopolize and manipulate prices. SO executives in Pennsylvania were arrested and had to post bond. Rockefeller lived in New York at the time and avoided arrest. SO settled many disputes with drillers and refiners over buyouts and rebates out of court, resulting in charges being dropped. In summary: "In spring 1879 Rockefeller began a thirty-year career as a fugitive from justice, learning to stay nimbly ahead of the law" (Chernow, 1998, 212).

SO accumulated corporations across the country, although SO of Ohio was prevented by law from owning out-of-state corporations. The growing empire was difficult to control, while simultaneously legal problems hindered operations. SO lawyer Samuel Dodd created the trust to solve the ownership-across-state-lines problem in 1880. Trust agreements assigned executives as trustees holding stock in companies outside the state. Legally, the trustees owned these companies and distributed dividends of the various subsidiaries to Standard shareholders as individuals. SO's major operations were incorporated in each state. The SO trust agreement, signed at the start of 1882, created a board of trustees, located in New York

City. The board received the stock of the SO companies. The stockholders (not the corporations) received trust certificates in place of shares, with about a third of the certificates owned by Rockefeller. The companies followed the trustees' orders and the system proved to be reasonably efficient.

Efficiency was a major goal and costs declined dramatically. While Rockefeller ran the company, retail prices fell substantially. His successors were much less willing to pass on cost savings. At the time, the potential for oil remained was unknown. Until 1885, no known producing fields existed outside of Pennsylvania; future demand was also unknown. Rockefeller never questioned the long-term supply or demand and continued to develop both. He proved to be right and became the richest man in the world.

SO took advantage of New Jersey's new incorporation laws allowing holding shares in out-of-state companies. SO of New Jersey became the center of the SO empire and acquired all the shares of the affiliates. The old executive trust committee was dissolved and the committee members became the senior executive of the affiliates, winning election as the directors. When New Jersey amended the incorporation laws, SO became a holding company with Standard of New Jersey controlling stock of 40 affiliates in 1899. Lawsuits continued.

Rockefeller retired from active management by the mid-1890s, although he kept the title of president, and the company was actually run by the vice president John Archbold. Journalists such as Henry Demarest Lloyd and Ida Tarbell went after both Rockefeller and SO. Both wrote popular books about Rockefeller and Standard. Tarbell viewed Rockefeller and other executives as competent but corrupt and quoted diatribes from almost anyone who disliked Rockefeller. Rockefeller's image was ruined, whether deserved or not.

Theodore Roosevelt's attorney general sued SO in 1906 under the Sherman Act to dissolve the company. SO lost the case in the federal circuit court and appealed to the Supreme Court. The Supreme Court in 1911 upheld the circuit court's ruling—SO would be broken up, creating 33 independent companies from the SO subsidiaries. The long-retired Rockefeller was on the golf course when he heard the news of the Supreme Court decision. He immediately turned to his playing partner and said, "Buy Standard Oil." This proved to be good advice. Rockefeller held over a quarter of the old shares and these were replaced by an equivalent amount in each of the new independent corporations. Unlike almost all other great monopolies, the old SO had been "undercapitalized." Most of the new companies traded on the New York Stock Exchange, and unlike the original SO, issued annual reports. Within a year, the prices of most of the new oil companies doubled or more, in part because of high dividends; stock prices continued up over the next decade. Rockefeller went from being rich to being the world's first billionaire.

Rockefeller turned to philanthropy, outdoing even Andrew Carnegie. In the 1880s, he created Spellman College for African American women and gave extensively to the University of Chicago. In 1901 he created the Rockefeller Institute for Medical Research (later Rockefeller University) and formed the Rockefeller Foundation in 1913. He died on May 23, 1937, at the age of 97. Several of his descendants entered politics including grandsons Nelson Rockefeller (New York governor and vice president) and Winthrop Rockefeller (governor of Arkansas), as well as great-grandson Jay Rockefeller (West Virginia senator).

See also Antitrust; Corporations; Gould, Jason ("Jay"); Railroads, Nineteenth Century; Regulation of Business; Robber Barons; Sherman Act; Standard Oil Company

References

Chernow, Ron. *Titan: The Life of John D. Rockefeller, Sr.* New York: Random House, 1998.

Dobson, John. "John Davison Rockefeller." In *Bulls, Bears, Booms, and Busts: A Historical Encyclopedia of American Business Concepts.* Santa Barbara, CA: ABC-CLIO, 2006.

Josephson, Matthew. *The Robber Barons.* New York: Harcourt, 1962.

Roosevelt, Franklin Delano

Franklin D. Roosevelt (FDR, 1882–1945) was assistant secretary of the navy during World War I, governor of New York, and 32nd president of the United States, serving longer than any other president and elected four times. He brought the country through the Great Depression and most of World War II and was responsible for New Deal legislation creating numerous federal agencies, including the Securities and Exchange Commission.

FDR was born on January 30, 1882, in Hyde Park, New York, into one of the oldest Dutch families in the United States. He went to Harvard when his cousin Theodore was president. Roosevelt began his political career as a New York State senator in 1911. He resigned in 1913 to become assistant secretary of the navy. FDR served as governor of New York from 1929 to 1932, the early years of the Great Depression, where he experimented with economic stimulus and job creation plans.

In the 1932 presidential race, FDR won in a landslide promising a New Deal. On inauguration day, March 4, 1933, he famously stated, "The only thing we have to fear . . . is fear itself . . . nameless, unreasoning, unjustified terror which paralyzes needed efforts to convert retreat into advance." Banks in most states and the New York Stock Exchange (NYSE) were closed. Also in his first inaugural address FDR stated, "The money changers have fled from their high seats in the temple of our civilization. We may now restore that temple to the ancient truths." FDR announced a national bank holiday—all banks were closed for a week and inspected by federal officials. He submitted an emergency banking bill to Congress to allow healthy banks to reopen under Treasury Department supervision with guarantees from the Reconstruction Finance Corporation (RFC) to loan banks money and invest in preferred stock. The RFC spent about a billion dollars over the next six months bailing out banks; however, 4,000 banks (usually small poorly capitalized local banks) still failed. Within a month, FDR and Congress suspended the gold standard to stop the massive exodus of gold from New York, devaluing the dollar to the old equivalent of 59¢. The Federal Reserve (Fed) no longer had a reason to prop up the dollar by keeping bond interest rates high and started a more productive monetary policy.

During FDR's first hundred days, 15 major bills of his "First New Deal" legislation passed, aimed to meet the needs of the various constituencies from banking and industry to farming. Roosevelt wanted to stimulate the economy and pass long-term reforms that would eliminate the possibility of future depressions. He had used emergency programs like relief and work programs as governor of New York; but inherently conservative as were most politicians and economists at that time, he believed in a balanced budget. This limited the effectiveness because many of his programs were underfunded.

The president's first major relief program was the Federal Emergency Relief Administration (FERA), spending about $4 billion from mid-1933 to mid-1935, replaced by the Works Program Administration (WPA). Early New Deal efforts focused on stabilizing farm prices as well as business and labor reforms. The Agricultural Adjustment Act (AAA), passed in May 1933, raised farm prices by creating artificial food scarcity. The AAA paid farmers subsidies to restrict output of key crops. The Supreme Court declared the program unconstitutional in 1936. A modified program to meet Court approval kept farm subsidies and the federal government maintained farm policy subsidies ever since. Several other farm-related programs passed during the New Deal.

The Glass-Steagall Act of 1933 introduced bank reform. The creation of the Federal Deposit Insurance Corporation (FDIC) insuring commercial bank deposits was a favorite with the public and continues in force. The major provision, claimed to be a debacle by the banking industry, separated commercial banks from investment banks. The big banks, particularly the New York-Wall Street banks, had to decide whether to be commercial or investment banks and many large institutions split. J. P. Morgan, for example, became a commercial bank, while its investment banking practice spun off as Morgan Stanley. Regulation Q allowed the Fed to set interest rates on bank deposits, which worked reasonably well until high inflation rates set in during the 1970s.

FDR favored a cartel system of cooperation between business and labor to raise prices while establishing voluntary minimum wages and improved working conditions for labor. The National Industrial Recovery Act (NIRA) passed in June 1933, creating the National Recovery Administration (NRA), which negotiated "business codes" to set prices and wages by industry, plus a set of "fair practices." The program increased the costs of production, and considerable cheating occurred because big businesses set "fair practices" favoring themselves rather than small businesses or labor. The NRA, a cartel violating long-held antitrust positions, was declared unconstitutional in 1935.

The NIRA also established the Public Works Administration (PWA), the first and largest public works program. Through 1935, the PWA spent over $3 billion on 35,000 projects. The Civilian Conservation Corps (CCC) provided 3 million young men unskilled jobs working in conservation and development of natural resources. Late in 1933, the Civil Works Administration (CWA) created a low-skill temporary work program under Harry Hopkins. Much of the program included local make-work (a "boondoggle" according to Republicans), but it did put some 4 million people to work for the winter. FDR canceled the program in 1934 to cut the deficit, putting those 4 million out of work. This was an example of introducing misplaced conservatism in an attempt to balance the budget.

Every year of the 1930s under FDR, Treasury ran a deficit (stated in millions), often greater than total revenue. With continuing deficits, real political pressure developed to raise taxes and cut spending. FDR's economy bill, sent to Congress in March 1935, reduced government salaries and cut veterans' pensions, while maintaining the top tax rate of 63 percent. This "fiscal restraint," the traditional approach favored by many politicians and economist at the time, continued to be a priority as it had under Hoover while limiting New Deal program effectiveness. It just did not work; the economy turned down and the deficits continued.

FDR shifted to major restructuring of the economy, creating new agencies to provide long-term economic solutions—the "Second New Deal" of 1934–36. The Federal Housing Act (FHA) guaranteed low-interest loans for construction and repairs. The FHA chartered Federal National Mortgage Association (Fannie Mae) in 1938 to provide mortgage credit by purchasing FHA-insured mortgage loans. The Federal Communications Act (FCC) established the regulation of radio and other electronic media. The National Labor Relations (Wagner) Act created the National Labor Relations Board (NLRB), giving more power to unions.

The pension movement led to the Social Security Act of 1935, mandating old-age pensions plus unemployment insurance and disability and other benefits. Social Security eventually became the biggest of the New Deal programs. Tax collections started in 1937, with the first monthly retirement checks starting in 1940. FDR thought payroll taxes essential: "With those taxes in there, no damn politician can ever scrap my social security program" (Friedel 1990, 150).

FDR's programs were a mixed success. For example, the farm programs drove up food prices, improving farm incomes but a detriment to consumers. Other programs proved too small to be effective, including much of the public works relief effort. About the time public works employed substantial numbers and provided a living wage to millions, Roosevelt cut them in an effort to economize. As the economy was recovering, Roosevelt proposed increased taxes, including raising corporate income taxes and higher personal and inheritance tax rates. The Revenue Act of 1935 raised the top individual income tax rate from 63 percent to 79 percent. Social Security taxes kicked in beginning in 1937. In addition to fiscal policy setbacks, the Fed tightened money in 1937–38, resulting in a recession within the Depression. By 1938, the unemployment rate increased to 12.5 percent. It took World War II to end the Great Depression.

FDR ran for an unprecedented third term in 1940 and defeated Republican Wendell Willkie. War had started in Europe with the Nazi invasion of Poland and FDR determined to make the United States the "Arsenal of Democracy," supporting Great Britain and the Soviet Union with military support using the Lend Lease Program. Japan attacked Pearl Harbor. FDR proclaimed, "Yesterday, December 7, 1941—a date which will live in infamy," and the United States was at war. World War II would be long and costly in both lives and military spending. By early 1945, allied forces were defeating both Germany and Japan. Roosevelt died on April 12, 1945, in Warm Springs, Georgia, shortly before Germany surrendered. Vice President Harry Truman assumed the presidency.

See also Crash of 1929; Fannie Mae and Freddie Mac; Great Depression; Labor Movement, U.S.; Pecora Commission; Reconstruction Finance Corporation (RFC); Roosevelt, Theodore; Treasury Department; Wagner Act

References

Dobson, John. "Crash." In *Bulls, Bears, Boom, and Bust: A Historical Encyclopedia of American Business Concepts*. Santa Barbara, CA: ABC-CLIO, 2006.

Friedel, F. *Franklin D. Roosevelt: A Rendezvous with Destiny*. Boston: Little, Brown, 1990.

Galbraith, Kenneth. *The Great Crash 1929*. Boston: Houghton Mifflin, 1988.

Hafer, Rik. "Roosevelt, Franklin Delano." In *The Federal Reserve System: An Encyclopedia*. Santa Barbara, CA: ABC-CLIO, 2005.

Roosevelt, Franklin. First Inaugural Address. March 4, 1933. http://www.bartleby.com/124/pres49.html.

Roosevelt, Theodore

Theodore Roosevelt ("Teddy," 1858–1919) was the 26th president of the United States, vice president, governor of New York, and colonel of the Rough Riders in the Spanish American War. Roosevelt was a leader of the progressive movement, instituting important regulations and conservation through the creation of national monuments and other means. He was born on October 27, 1858, in New York City into a prosperous Dutch family. Although sickly, he obtained an excellent education and built himself up physically. He became a self-taught naturalist, writer, cowboy, and politician.

After graduating from Harvard, Roosevelt started in politics in the New York State Assembly in 1881, at a time when patricians stayed away from politics. Typically, he started with considerable enthusiasm and work effort—although New York Republican politicians were controlled by Boss Roscoe Conkling and achieved riches through patronage, blackmail, and bribery. Despite being honest and independent of the Conkling machine, Roosevelt excelled through hard work while claiming that many of his competitors were "equally deficient in brains and virtue." He referred to machine politicians as the "black horse cavalry."

After his first wife died after childbirth, Roosevelt rebuilt his life by building a cattle ranch in the Dakotas. He returned to New York City politics, but was defeated for mayor in 1886. President Benjamin Harrison appointed him to the Civil Service Commission in 1889, where he served until 1895. The Civil Service Reform (Pendleton) Act of 1883 required many federal jobs based on merit rather than patronage. Despite the Pendleton Act, most federal jobs were still based on patronage and those covered by the act often were subject to abuse—fraud on civil service exams, for example. Roosevelt proved to be the most famous and hardest-working commissioner, calling for investigations of abuse of massive corruption in New York, Indianapolis, Baltimore, and Milwaukee, including dismissals and prosecution of corrupt officials.

Roosevelt became president of the New York City Police Commission in 1895 and sought to reform a police department reputed to be the most corrupt in the United States. Police Chief Thomas Byrnes cooperated with gangs as long as they stayed away from the financial district for which he was appropriately rewarded by the Wall Street robber barons. Thirty-five captains each controlled a precinct, with a regular system of payoffs to the authorities. A captaincy apparently could be had for $10,000, while securing a patrolman's job cost $300. The police department was closely connected to the political machines. Roosevelt, well aware of the corruption, created new disciplinary rules and regular inspections, and even walked the beats at night to make sure the officers were on duty. Roosevelt soon forced Byrnes's "retirement," followed by several other high-level departures, then mass resignation by corrupt officers afraid of criminal investigations. After that, Roosevelt focused on discipline and efficiency. As summarized by Morris (1979, 523), "Crimes were down, arrests up, corruption clearly on the wane." New York City's political leaders wanted him out of the city and lobbied for a Washington job for Roosevelt, which soon came. Unfortunately, within a few years, Tammany Hall was back in charge of the city and the police department returned to business-as-usual corruption under machine politics.

Roosevelt was appointed assistant secretary of the navy in 1897 and he helped prepare the navy for the Spanish-American War. When war was declared against Spain after the sinking of the *Maine* in Havana Harbor in 1898, he resigned from the navy and founded with Colonel Leonard Wood the First U.S. Volunteer Cavalry Regiment (called the Rough Riders by journalists). The regiment was sent to Cuba, Wood was promoted to brigadier general, and Roosevelt was promoted to colonel and given command of the regiment. The colonel and regiment gained fame for the charges of Kettle Hill and San Juan Heights on July 1, 1898. The war was soon won and Roosevelt returned home a hero.

The colonel ran for governor of New York in 1898 while facing a "tax scandal" (he had declared himself a Washington resident to avoid New York taxes). When thinking about withdrawing from the race, political boss Thomas Platt asked him, "Is the hero of San Juan Hill a Coward?" That did it; he ran and was elected governor of New York before the year was over. Once again, his focus was on eliminating corruption. Under his leadership, a new civil service law was passed in the state as were laws improving working conditions. The relationship between Boss Platt and Roosevelt was an uneasy one: "a combination of enmity and friendliness, clashes and compromise" (Morris 1979, 772).

Roosevelt attempted to eliminate corruption and machine politics. Prompted by New York insurance interests and other big business, Republican boss Thomas Platt lobbied President William McKinley to make Roosevelt his running mate. He was added to the ticket and elected vice president in 1900. Edmund Morris has recorded some telling remarks by major parties involved with Roosevelt's campaign (1979, 763–67, 773). An overjoyed Platt exclaimed, "We're all off the Washington to see Teddy take the veil" (to the powerless vice presidency). Roosevelt thus became a thorn in the side of McKinley aide and Ohio political boss Mark Hanna (Hanna was chairman of the Republican National Committee and senator from Ohio until his death in 1904). An exasperated Hanna stated, "Don't any of you realize that there's only one life between this madman and the Presidency?" Hanna later said, "The best we can do is pray fervently for the continued health of the President." Roosevelt's main claim to fame as vice president was his statement: "Speak softly and carry a big stick."

Tragedy soon struck. McKinley was shot on September 6, 1901, attending the Pan-American exposition in Buffalo. He died on September 14 and Roosevelt was sworn in as president the same day. Although he pledged to keep McKinley's policies, he moved from conservatism toward progressivism. This brought on the latest outburst from Hanna: "Now look—that damned cowboy is President of the United States!" (Morris 2001, 30).

Roosevelt was interested in the labor movement and considered it the major problem of the United States in the twentieth century. Labor unions were gaining and exercising power, and business responded with force. When the United Mine Workers went on strike in 1902, the president's fact-finding commission stopped the strike and got higher wages and reduced hours for the workers—the first time the federal government intervened in a strike to benefit workers.

The turn of the twentieth century was the era of the trust movement, as industries combined using acquisitions and trusts to create oligopoly or near-monopoly industries. Roosevelt was ambivalent about the trust movement. Markets typically functioned more smoothly under oligopolies and in some cases (kerosene for example) prices came down. However, the accumulated power had economic and political ramifications, including the potential for eliminating competitive markets while driving political actions favoring the trust to the detriment of the public. J. P. Morgan created dozens of trusts including United States Steel, General Electric, and Western Union and several consolidated railroads. Morgan's philosophy was: "I owe the public nothing." The bankers believed that Wall Street controlled the economy, not the White House or government in general.

The Sherman Antitrust Act of 1890 banned monopolies and price conspiracies, but antitrust suits under the Sherman Act were used sparingly in the 1890s. Roosevelt expanded antitrust cases to eliminate what he considered "bad trusts." In 1903, the Justice Department created a separate Antitrust Division under an assistant attorney general. Roosevelt's first big battle was Northern Securities, the railroad holding company of James Hill and J. P. Morgan. Morgan personally went to Washington to intervene, stating to the president, "If we have done anything wrong, send your man to my man and we can fix it up." Roosevelt would have none of it and the case proceeded. A government victory was won when the Supreme Court ruled against the railroad in 1904. Roosevelt remarked that the case "established the power of the Government to deal with all great corporations." More antitrust suits followed.

Upton Sinclair's 1906 novel, *The Jungle*, exposed Chicago's unsanitary meat-packing industry. Sinclair focused on the poor working conditions, but the public, outraged by the filthy products, called for government action to guarantee healthy meat. A surprise inspection orchestrated by Roosevelt resulted in the Neill-Reynolds Report, which corroborated Sinclair. The Meat Inspection Act passed in 1906 on the same day as the Food and Drug Act. The act established sanitary standards for meat processing and mandatory inspections of livestock before and after slaughter.

Big business destroyed the environment on a prodigious scale. As a naturalist, Roosevelt believed in protecting nature and called for government protection as part of his conservation plans, including what he called the "monopoly of natural resources" by the government. New legislation included the National Reclamation Act of 1902 and the Antiquities Act of 1906. The Antiquities Act protected Indian ruins but also allowed the president to declare national monuments of public lands. Roosevelt soon named dozens of sites national monuments including Grand Canyon (now a national park), national forests, federal bird refuges, and federal irrigation projects.

In 1907, Otto Heinze attempted to corner United Copper, resulting in the failure of his brokerage firm and the start of the Panic of 1907. J. P. Morgan personally intervened, starting with propping up the Trust Company of America. Morgan needed federal assistance, and Treasury Secretary George Cortelyou deposited federal money into New York banks to provide liquidity. To avoid the failure of large broker Moore & Schley, Morgan wanted United States Steel to acquire Tennessee Coal, Iron and Railroad Company, which was headed toward bankruptcy. This was accomplished only after Roosevelt reluctantly agreed to the merger, promising not to sue under the Sherman Act. New York City needed an emergency loan to avoid bankruptcy; Morgan served many of the functions of a central bank and his actions averted catastrophe on Wall Street. However, Congress and the president did not want to see a repeat of events that left the federal government as a minor player. The federal government passed major reform legislation but it would have to wait for the Woodrow Wilson administration.

Roosevelt won the Nobel Peace Prize for mediating the Russo-Japanese War and built up the navy, creating the Great White Fleet, which sailed around the world. The Panama Canal was built after he recognized Panama when it split from Colombia.

The president promised not to run again in 1908; instead, his hand-picked successor, William Howard Taft, was elected, promising to continue to Roosevelt policies. Roosevelt went on a year-long African safari, with stops in major European cities. Irate at Taft's more conservative policies as president, Roosevelt vowed to win the nomination for president in 1912. Rebuffed by the Republican machine, which renominated Taft, he ran under the Progressive (Bull Moose) ticket. While on the campaign trail, he was shot in the chest in an assassination attempt, but gave his 90-minute speech anyway. Both Roosevelt and Taft lost to Democrat Woodrow Wilson. Wilson would continue to pursue a progressive agenda somewhat similar to Roosevelt's, including creation of the Federal Reserve and Federal Trade Commission.

After the disappointing presidential election, Roosevelt headed on a Brazilian jungle expedition in 1913–14. While traveling down the Amazon, he suffered from a tropical fever and infection that nearly killed him. He never fully recovered and died at Oyster Bay, New York, of a heart attack on January 6, 1919. The message telegraphed to his family: "The old lion is dead."

See also Antitrust; Food and Drug Regulations; Morgan, John Pierpont; Northern Pacific War; Panic of 1907; Political Machines; Tammany Hall

References

Brinkley, Douglas. *The Wilderness Warrior: Theodore Roosevelt and the Crusade for America*. New York: HarperCollins, 2009.

Bruner, Robert, and Sean Carr. *The Panic of 1907: Lessons Learned from the Market's Perfect Storm*. Hoboken, NJ: Wiley, 2007.

Morris, Edmund. *The Rise of Theodore Roosevelt*. New York: Random House, 1979.

Morris, Edmond. *Theodore Rex*. New York: Random House, 2001.

Russian Kleptocracy and Default

As Russia emerged from the Soviet Union in the 1990s, Russian-style privatization led to "kleptocracy" due to rampant corruption and stealing of prime assets. State-owned businesses were turned over to prominent insiders with connections to the Communist power structures, prominently the "oligarchs" (the name implying rich, powerful, and corrupt). Many of these were businesspeople making fortunes on the black market during Soviet rule, especially during the 1980s period of Mikhail Gorbachev's perestroika. Russia's first president, Boris Yeltsin (from 1991 to 1999), relied on oligarchic political help to get elected. Capital flight during this period caused substantial economic unrest as much of the cash and other assets controlled by the oligarchs left the country.

The Asian currency crisis hit in July 1997, after overleveraging led to a stock and real estate bubble that crashed. Then the Russian crisis erupted, in a post-Soviet Russia experimenting with capitalism. This was a Russia with vast oil and gas reserves needed by Europe (plus thousands of nuclear weapons). In other words, Europe and the world wanted an economically and politically stable country.

The Russian government issued new bonds to pay off old Soviet-era bonds and interest payments. Declining oil prices, an overvalued ruble, and government deficits were ruining the economy. No useful reforms were forthcoming. Russian bureaucrats stole much of an International Monetary Fund (IMF) rescue package as Russian securities and currency markets collapsed in 1998. As the inflation rate moved toward 100 percent and government bond interest rates approached 200 percent, Russia defaulted on its ruble-based debt in August, unexpected because a government default based on the domestic currency is unusual; the government can always print more money.

Because Russia's economy is oil based, the country bounced back when oil prices rose beginning in 1999. But at the time of the worldwide financial crisis in 1998, there was potential for global financial collapse and depression. Part of that potential resulted from the collapse of Long-Term Capital Management, which had bet heavily (and incorrectly) on the Russian ruble. A Federal Reserve-sponsored bailout averted that disaster.

Under the presidency of Vladimir Putin (2000–2008, 2012–), many oligarchs were purged due to tax evasion and other illegal acts, although their fall from power was likely politically based. Putin's power rested on an increasingly totalitarian state. Oligarchs could succeed only if they were allied with Putin. Mikhail Khodorkovsky, president of oil giant YUKOS and Russia's richest man, was financially ruined and sent to prison for challenging Putin.

See also Asian Debt Crisis; Brady Plan; Derivatives; Hedge Funds; Long-Term Capital Management

References

Lewis, Michael. *Panic: The Story of Modern Financial Insanity*. New York: Norton, 2009.

Partnoy, Frank. *FIASCO: Blood in the Water on Wall Street*. New York: Norton, 1997.

Partnoy, Frank. *Infectious Greed: How Deceit and Risk Corrupted the Financial Markets*. New York: Holt, 2003.

S

Salomon Brothers

Salomon Brothers was a Wall Street investment bank founded by Arthur, Herbert, and Percy Salomon in 1910, becoming the largest issuer and trader of bonds in the United States. Solomon also created the first non-government-guaranteed mortgage-backed security, later focusing on trading activities. With the deregulation of savings and loans (S&Ls or thrifts) in the 1980s, mortgage trading at Salomon made huge profits—one of the subjects of Michael Lewis's *Liar's Poker*. Under managing partner John Gutfreund, Salomon went public in 1989. In 1991, Solomon was caught submitting false bids to the Treasury Department to purchase more bonds than allowed and was fined $290 million. Shortly after that scandal, Salomon was acquired by Travelers Group (now Citigroup).

When interest rates rose rapidly in the 1970s, thrifts were stuck with low-interest-rate long-term mortgages and a declining deposit base. Congress deregulated the industry, allowing them to expand into new areas of lending and accepting deposits. In addition, a new accounting rule in the early 1980s allowed S&Ls to amortize the losses over the life of the mortgages, allowing the thrifts to postpone recognizing the loss. Expanding into new products such as jumbo certificates of deposit, selling losing mortgages made sense, which happened by the billions. Salomon Brothers was the market maker at the time and had a virtual monopoly. That meant Salomon made a fortune by acquiring the mortgages at excessively low prices, and the thrifts booked bigger losses than necessary.

Journalist (and former Salomon salesman) Michael Lewis suggested that former Salomon chief executive officer (CEO) John Gutfreund was to blame for all investment bank problems because he took Salomon public. The remaining investment banks followed (the retail-based Merrill Lynch went public earlier). Investment banks were traditionally partnerships, meaning their own money was on the line; high risk and bad decisions would mean financial ruin for all the present and past partners. With a corporation, the executives (formerly partners) take in big compensation, while the stockholders take all the risks. More risk means greater profits and more compensation for the executives. When the high-risk schemes blow up, the executives move on (perhaps with substantial compensation despite the failures), and the stockholders are the big losers (as is the public if the bank fails and bailed out by the government). Leverage and risk skyrocketed to increase potential return; executive compensation went up—until collapse happened. Except for a few big losers, compensation stayed high. Lewis was surprised only that it took 20 years before investment banks blew up the financial world.

Salomon Brothers, the longtime leader in the Treasury market, served as a primary dealer. The Treasury system was an auction market where a select few primary dealers bid on Treasuries as they were issued. The Treasury Department had a 35 percent cap for any purchase of Treasuries issues, instituted because Salomon had routinely placed bids for far more than the amount of securities issued. Salomon trader Paul Mozer submitted false bids to increase the share for Salomon. The scandal erupted when Treasury discovered Mozer's fraud for the February 1991 five-year note. Mozer submitted a 35 percent bid in Salomon's name and two additional bids in the names of Salomon clients Quantum Fund and Mercury Asset Management, without their knowledge. After winning all the bids (about 90% of the total auction amount) Mozer wrote up a sell ticket back to Salomon for the acquisitions of the customers, but without the usual confirmations. It turned out that Mercury also entered the auction, which put Mercury above the 35 percent limit. The Treasury letter of admonishment busted the scam. Salomon handled the incident poorly and Mozer actually continued to make false bids.

When the story broke later that year, Mozer, Mozer's boss John Meriwether, and CEO John Gutfreund were fired. John Meriwether, a star at Salomon Brothers, founded Salomon's fixed-income arbitrage group in the mid-1980s. After being fired, he founded the hedge fund Long-Term Capital Management in 1994 and took many of Salomon's star performers with him. Salomon paid $290 million in fines and later was acquired by Travelers Group, now Citigroup. Mozer received a four-month sentence and was fined over $1 million. Government investigations uncovered frauds similar to Mozer's in other government bond markets such as federal home mortgages. "Cease and desist" orders and fines went out to several Wall Street firms.

See also Investment Banks; Long-Term Capital Management; Meriwether, John W.; Savings and Loan Deregulations and Failures; Treasury Department

References

Lewis, Michael. *Liar's Poker: Rising through the Wreckage on Wall Street.* New York: Penguin Books, 1989.

Wessel, David. "The Cartel, 1991." In *Eyewitness to Wall Street.* Edited by David Colbert, 281–284. New York: Broadway Books, 2001.

Sarbanes-Oxley Act of 2002

The Sarbanes-Oxley Act (SOX) was the most significant change to the regulation of financial markets and financial accounting since the original securities acts of 1933 and 1934. The new rules provide reform and major changes in corporate governance, auditing, responsibilities of the chief executive officer (CEO) and chief financial officer (CFO), and Securities and Exchange Commission (SEC) enforcement. SOX created a new auditing regulator, the Public Company Accounting Oversight Board (PCAOB). SOX regulations also required actions by the stock exchanges, SEC, and other regulatory bodies. The provisions of the act have been substantial enough that net costs, benefits, and unforeseen consequences are still debated.

The U.S. economy at the start of the twenty-first century went terribly wrong, with the bursting of the tech bubble, stock price crash, and a recession. Big companies including Enron and WorldCom failed and executives were indicted for fraud and other illegal acts. Congress held public hearings to express outrage and, eventually, regulate. The initial Enron hearing occurred soon after bankruptcy was declared at the end of 2001. The most important committee hearings in 2002 were the House Financial Services Committee, with the Subcommittee on Capital Markets focusing specifically on the Enron collapse, and the Senate Government Affairs Committee on the fall of Enron. Concurrent investigations were made by the SEC, Justice Department, and Labor Department (on improperly blocking employee selling of Enron stock). The House Financial Services Committee later held hearings on the massive fraud at WorldCom.

SOX was passed by both houses of Congress on July 25, shortly after WorldCom's bankruptcy, and the it was signed on July 30, 2002, by President George W. Bush as Public Law No. 107-204. SOX has 11 parts (called titles), and each title is divided into a number of sections. Generally, the most important topics are referred to by the title and/or section numbers. Thus the important section on internal-control requirements is Section 404, Management Assessment of Internal Controls, under Title 4, Enhanced Financial Disclosures. Many of the sections are direct regulatory responses to specific issues from Enron and other corporate scandals. The act is summarized in Table 20.

The key provisions include the requirements for improved corporate governance; substantial new audit requirements including the formation of the PCAOB and auditor independence rules; executive responsibility over financial reports and internal controls; and increased annual report and proxy statement disclosure requirements, including additional information on off-balance-sheet procedures in management discussion and analysis and non-GAAP (generally accepted accounting principles) disclosures.

Corporate governance is the structure in place to oversee the management of an organization and the first line of defense for avoiding, detecting. and eliminating financial abuse. A weak governance structure is more likely associated with misleading accounting information. The board of directors has two vital functions: (1) a broad overview on operating policy and strategic planning and (2) corporate oversight. It is up to the board of directors to ensure that the business strategy in place is viable and operations follow this strategy. The boards of Enron, WorldCom, and the other financial fiascos early in the twenty-first century all had irresponsible governance characteristics. SOX emphasized governance requirements because of this obvious relationship.

SOX shifted the responsibility for corporate governance to the oversight of the SEC and specific rules adopted by the stock exchanges. The New York Stock

Table 20. Sarbanes-Oxley Act of 2002

Title I—Public Company Accounting Oversight Board (PCAOB)	Creates the PCAOB as a nonprofit corporation to regulate the audit of public companies. The board registers public accountant firms, sets audit standards, and inspects the public accountant firms. The funding of the PCAOB is provided by annual support fees from the public companies. The SEC selects the five-member board and provides general oversight.
Title II—Auditor Independence	To attempt to improve auditor independence, several nonaudit services are prohibited, including bookkeeping, financial information services, appraisal and actuarial services, internal auditing, management and human resources, broker and investment advisory functions, and legal and other nonaudit expert services. The lead audit partner must be rotated every five years and the auditor must report to the audit committee.
Title III—Corporate Responsibility	This section promotes various aspects related to corporate governance and specific actions required of key players. The audit committee must be made up of independent board members and is responsible for the appointment, compensation, and oversight of the audit firm. The CEO and CFO are responsible for all aspects of the financial reports and certify that they contain no untrue statements. Insider trading is prohibited during pension blackout periods (an issue with Enron employees).
Title IV—Enhanced Financial Disclosures	This title requires the SEC to study issues and write regulations dealing with special-purpose entities and other off-balance-sheet transactions. It beefs up conflict-of-interest provisions of executives, including prohibiting personal loans and reporting insider trades. Perhaps the major section (404) requires management's report on assessment of internal controls.
Title V—Analyst Conflicts of Interest	The SEC is required to ensure that the national stock exchanges design rules addressing conflicts of interest by securities analysts (which has been done by the major exchanges).
Title VI—Commission Resources and Authority	The act specified the amount of funding to the SEC for fiscal year 2003. The overall funding of the SEC was increased substantially. There are various technical requirements for various groups.
Title VII—Studies and Reports	The General Accountability Office (GAO) is required to prepare reports on public accounting firms and investment banking. The SEC is required to report on credit rating agencies, security professional violators, and enforcement actions.
Title VIII—Corporate and Criminal Fraud Accountability	Describes specific crimes and penalties involved, including destruction of corporate audit records, falsifying records associated with federal investigations and bankruptcy, statute of limitations for securities fraud, federal sentencing guidelines, and other aspects of securities fraud. Also included are whistle-blower protections.
Title IX—White-Collar Crime Penalty Enhancements	Prescribes penalties for failure of corporate officers to certify financial reports and increases various potential criminal penalties for various offences.
Title X—Corporate Tax Returns	The federal income tax returns should be signed by the CEO of corporations.
Title XI—Corporate Fraud and Accountability	Called the Corporate Fraud Accountability Act of 2002, this includes penalties for tampering with records of an official proceeding, increases various criminal penalties, and authorizes the SEC to prohibit individuals for serving as officers or directors.

Exchange (NYSE) and NASDAQ rewrote the corporate governance standards for listed companies. New rules included the requirement that the majority of the board must be independent of the company, executive sessions would take place without the presence of management, and new rules for the audit, compensation, nominating, and governance committees were required. The members of all of these committees would be independent directors. The audit committee has the responsibility to hire, set compensation, replace, and provide oversight of the audit functions (both internal and external), based on SOX Section 301 and additional SEC requirements.

SOX mandated extensive changes in the audit process. These include the creation of the PCAOB to oversee the audits of public companies, audit committees rules, the banning of many nonaudit services by the auditor to improve perceived auditor independence, required rotation of audit partners, and additional audit-related requirements including the certification of internal controls by both the auditor and corporate executives.

Several of the requirements were considered controversial (especially banning nonaudit services and the expanded internal-control requirements) and not well supported by academic analysis. Former chairman of the SEC Arthur Levitt was particularly vocal on auditor independence and apparently influenced Congress. Research has found no evidence that nonaudit services influence auditor independence. It is more difficult to criticize internal-control requirements (the concept of adequate internal controls has been central to auditing for decades and also required by federal law). Most of the complaints so far have been related to the high costs, presumably compared to expected minimal benefits, and the overregulation of the auditors in the field. The high costs were particularly found in the early years of enforcement.

Section 302 of SOX requires that both the CEO and CFO certify that that each financial report (10-K and 10-Q) filed with the SEC include a report that "fairly presents, in all material respects, the financial condition and results of operations of the issuer." Section 906 of SOX indicates that failure to meet the criteria could result in a fine up to $1 million and 10 years in jail (up to $5 million and 20 years if they willfully provide false information). The CEOs at Enron, WorldCom, and other financial fiascos claimed ignorance of the accounting fraud. Given continuing fraud and few convictions, that provision does not seem particularly effective.

Financial disclosure was extensive before SOX. However, not everything was disclosed adequately or even disclosed at all (Enron's special-purpose entities [SPEs] were a glaring example). SOX requires more disclosures in specific areas where information was lacking in the past. The SEC now requires that off-balance-sheet arrangements (including SPEs) must be disclosed in management discussion and analysis (MD&A) including a table summarizing certain contractual obligations, critical accounting policies, and estimates.

Funding has been a key regulatory problem for federal agencies; rather than retire agencies, opponents just underfund them. Thus, over 70 years the SEC has been curtailed by budget cuts, more often under Republican administrations. During the 1990s, the role of the SEC was expanded and economic growth including new industries based on the new high-tech technologies, while SEC budgets remained tight. The SEC had to prioritize its responsibilities and focus on what it considered key areas. Much of the SEC effort in the later 1990s was on initial public offerings (IPOs), especially for Internet and other New Economy companies. In the meantime, relatively little effort was put into the annual financial evaluation of established companies—Enron, for example.

SOX and other federal legislation modified the funding for the SEC, Financial Accounting Standards Board (FASB), and PCAOB. SEC funding comes directly from Congress as an annual appropriation. Since SOX, funding levels were substantially increased and staff levels increased. PCAOB funding is based on SOX Section 109, which states that the PCAOB's budget will be funded by the "issuers." Annually, the board completes its budget (which must be approved by the SEC), and "accounting support fees" are set based on the market value of publicly traded companies (with over $25 million in capitalization). SOX Section 109 also funds the FASB using the same approach, that is, charging corporations for FASB operations. Prior to SOX, the FASB was funded largely by donations from audit and corporate groups, making independence an issue.

Major complaints exist in the corporate community that SOX did indeed go too far. Implementation costs were extensive, while perceived benefits not obvious. Complaints by the Chamber of Commerce and other corporate groups centered on the cost of implementing Section 404 requirements for internal control. Proponents of SOX made a few relevant points. First, internal-control review is a fundamental audit procedure; second, the Foreign Corrupt Practices Act from the late 1970s required by federal law that companies have internal controls, and that companies have had two or more years to comply with SOX. Under this view, internal-control implementation and certification should not be a significant issue. Opponents focus on the high costs and the nitpicking attitude of auditors. Another sticking point is the relatively higher cost burden placed on smaller companies (where internal controls often were weaker).

Despite the additional regulatory burden and implementation costs, SOX has been a relative success. The two key points are (1) the specific SOX mandates such as the creation of the PCAOB and specific audit committee requirements and (2) the requirements for action by the SEC and other groups such as new corporate governance rules of the major stock exchanges and the new SEC rules on financial disclosures. SOX improved corporate governance, enhanced responsibilities for the senior corporate executives, provided better funding for the SEC, and made substantial changes in auditing requirements. Although these did not have much effect on the subprime meltdown, fewer issues were observed from industrial companies.

See also Accounting Fraud; Accounting Standards; Annual Report (10-K); Corporate Governance; Enron; Fraud; Public Company Accounting Oversight Board (PCAOB); Securities and Exchange Commission (SEC); WorldCom

References

Giroux, Gary. *Detecting Earnings Management*. Hoboken, NJ: Wiley, 2004.

Sarbanes-Oxley Act of 2002. Public Law 107-204. July 30, 2002. http://www.sec.gov.

Savings and Loan Deregulations and Failures

Savings and loans (S&Ls, thrifts) are financial institutions specializing in taking in savings deposits to fund mortgages and other loans. The Philadelphia Savings Fund society established in 1816 was the first savings bank in the United States. S&Ls became popular after legislation during the Great Depression promoted them to provide long-term mortgages in roughly the current form. Deregulation of the industry in the 1980s led to reckless management by much of the industry and the S&L crisis in the mid-1980s. Roughly half the industry failed, costing American taxpayers over $100 billion. New legislation at the end of the 1980s decade changed the industry, including creating the Office of Thrift Supervision and the Resolution Trust Corporation to dispose of the assets of failed thrifts.

The S&L crisis of the 1980s demonstrated the unintended consequences of poor public policy, in this case the badly planned and implemented deregulation of an industry. As inflation and interest rates rose into the 1980s, the entire S&L industry verged on collapse. As Former Federal Reserve chairman Alan Greenspan put it (2007, 114), "As originally conceived, an S&L was a simple mortgage machine, not much different from the Bailey Building and Loan run by Jimmy Stewart in *It's a Wonderful Life*." Federal law essentially created the thrift industry in its current form with the Federal Home Loan Bank Act of 1932, which encouraged long-term amortized mortgages (that is, the principal would be paid off by the end of the loan term—with 30 years the most common period). The S&L took in short-term savings accounts paying a low, regulated interest rate, say 3 percent, then originated mortgages. The mortgages might pay 6 percent, but were long term with 30 year loans the most common. In a low inflation and interest environment, the industry remained successful if unspectacular. The rising interest rates of the 1970s ruined the relationship.

Investors withdrew their money from the S&LS to seek higher interest rates elsewhere. Not allowed to raise rates beyond the maximum (based on Regulation Q of the Federal Reserve [Fed]), the thrifts had to sell mortgages to raise the cash for the withdrawals. With higher interest rates, the mortgages sold at a substantial loss, devastating capital. The market value of S&L mortgage assets fell to $86 billion below book value by 1981. S&Ls lost over $11 billion before tax between 1981 and 1982. Without a regulatory fix, the industry of 3,000 firms (it had been 6,000 in 1960) headed toward failure.

Congress went to work to fix the problem. Rather than a direct bailout, the solution relied on accounting gimmicks and deregulation. The S&Ls wanted to get out of their low-paying mortgages and Congress devised the way. Tax and accounting changes camouflaged the losses. If the mortgage portfolio had a remaining average life of 20 years, only 5 percent of the loss would be recognized each year. Tax breaks allowed the thrifts to sell their mortgage portfolios. Losses could offset any taxes paid over the previous 10 years. New accounting rules allowed the S&Ls to amortize the losses over the period of the original mortgages. In other words, the thrifts could spread out the losses. Suddenly, selling mortgages at huge losses made sense, which happened by the billions. Salomon Brothers was the market maker (acting as both a buyer and seller of mortgages) and made a fortune.

The major catastrophe came from the wrongheaded Garn-St. Germain Act of 1982, a Reagan-era deregulation initiative: "An Act to revitalize the housing industry by strengthening the financial stability of home mortgage lending institutions and ensuring the availability of home mortgage loans." The deregulation allowed S&Ls to loan money for most purposes, including areas they knew nothing about. They could also invest in corporate bonds, and Michael Milken encouraged them to invest in his junk bonds. The caps on interest paid on deposits had been lifted in 1980 and S&Ls moved into jumbo certificate of deposit (allowed beginning in the mid-1970s). Structuring an S&L also changed. Rather than the previous requirement of a minimum of 400 investors, a single person could own an S&L; that single owner could be a real estate developer, a conflict of interest leading to severe corruption. New owners often had mafia connections. S&Ls still had federal deposit insurance, raised to $100,000, making taxpayers liable for thrift failures.

The industry grew in size in the 1980s, to 3,600 firms with $1.5 trillion in assets. The financial health of the industry improved through the mid-1980s, then collapsed. Deregulation of the S&Ls encouraged illicit practices and corrupt executives to engage in extensive speculation and fraud. Organized crime also exploited the thrift mess. The S&L federal regulator, Federal Home Loan Bank Board (FHLBB), started curbing risky thrift practices in 1985, limited the amount of investments in certain categories, and banned certain commercial real estate investments. FHLBB auditors found many violations, especially by big S&Ls. Ultimately, despite FHLBB regulations, the aggressive practices effectively destroyed the industry, resulting in thousands of failures and a massive government bailout.

Columbia Savings & Loan of Beverly Hills was one of the first S&Ls to move into junk bonds, starting in 1982, as assets jumped from less than $400 million in 1982 to $10 billion in 1986. Columbia CEO Tom Spiegel became the highest-paid thrift executive at $10 million a year. Columbia lost $1.4 billion in 1989–90, going bankrupt in 1991. Spiegel was acquitted on criminal charges and paid a small civil fine. Hundreds joined the high-yield bond market, mainly through Michael Milken. Milken overcharged them and often sold them the riskiest of the junk. Many would be in default before the end of the decade. The collapse of the junk bond market at the end of the decade made the S&L crisis worse.

The crooked S&L executive most remembered from the crisis is Charles Keating, owner and CEO of Lincoln Savings. Lincoln used much of its deposit base to invest in junk bonds. Lincoln relied on a massive accounting fraud to claim profitability, including swapping properties with other companies and recording these as sales. As a major contributor to political campaigns, Keating's access to politicians resulted in the "Keating Five" episode, trying to get the regulators to stop investigating him. The Resolution Trust Corporation (RTC), Congress, Internal Revenue Service (IRS), Federal Bureau of Investigation (FBI), Securities and Exchange Commission (SEC), and various state and local regulators investigated Keating and Lincoln Savings, accusing Keating of mismanagement and fraud. Keating pled guilty to fraud and was sentenced to 12 years in prison, serving 4 years. The bailout of the failed Lincoln cost taxpayers $2.6 billion.

Congress created the RTC to sell off the real estate assets and mortgages of failed S&Ls. Disposing of assets during a recession proved difficult, especially mortgages in default, partially built commercial properties, and real estate properties in overbuilt areas. Many of the properties ended up being sold at auction in billion-dollar blocks for a fraction of cost. The RTC disbanded in 1995 after liquidating almost 750 S&Ls. In 1989, the Office of Management and Budget had estimated the cost at $257 billion. Other estimates approached half a trillion dollars. The final bill to taxpayers from the RTC totaled $87 billion, a fraction of earlier estimates (Greenspan 2007, 117). Other losses brought the total taxpayer-financed cost to $165 billion.

See also Boesky, Ivan; Bond Ratings; Insider Trading; Insider Trading Scandals of the 1980s; Junk Bond Market; Keating, Charles H., Jr.; Milken, Michael R.; Resolution Trust Corporation; Securities and Exchange Commission (SEC)

References

Dobson, John. "Savings and Loan Crisis." In *Bulls, Bears, Boom, and Bust: A Historical Encyclopedia of American Business Concepts.* Santa Barbara, CA: ABC-CLIO, 2006.

Garn-St. Germain Act of 1982. http://www.fdic.gov/regulations/laws/rules/8000-4100 .html.

Giroux, Gary. *Financial Analysis: A User Approach.* New York: Wiley, 2003.

Greenspan, Alan. *The Age of Turbulence: Adventures in a New World.* New York: Penguin Press, 2007.

Stewart, James. *Den of Thieves.* New York: Simon & Schuster, 1991.

Scrushy, Richard M.

Richard Scrushy (1952–) was founder and chief executive officer (CEO) of health care company HealthSouth, charged with 85 counts in the HealthSouth accounting scandal but acquitted. He was later convicted of bribery and mail fraud. Scrushy was born in August 1952 in Selma, Alabama. After graduating from University of Alabama at Birmingham (UAB) in respiratory therapy, he taught at UAB and a community college, then took a position in respiratory therapy at Lifemark Corp., rising to chief operating officer. Scrushy founded HealthSouth in 1984 to build free-standing outpatient surgical clinics, going public in 1986. A buying binge turned this into a billion-dollar company by the mid-1990s, using manipulative merger accounting to improve profitability.

Scrushy became one of the best-paid CEOs in the nation and made over $100 million in 1997, thanks largely to cashing out stock options. He sold an additional $74 million in 2002 shortly before the company failed. Medicare accused HealthSouth of illegally adding costs to outpatient physical therapy and other programs and later changed its funding arrangements to avoid losses. HealthSouth profits dropped substantially and the company was plagued by additional accusations of fraud and various lawsuits. In mid-2002, HealthSouth restated earnings back to 1997—some $2.5 billion in total, equal to most of its total reported earnings. In September 2002, the Securities and Exchange Commission (SEC) began an investigation and charged the company, Scrushy, and other senior executives with accounting fraud. The stock, downgraded by S&P to CCC, suspended trading on the New York Stock Exchange (NYSE) following an SEC order. Scrushy and several other senior executives were fired, as was auditor Ernst & Young. An FBI investigation led to Justice Department charges of securities fraud, wire fraud, mail fraud, and money laundering.

Scrushy was the first CEO charged under the SOX provisions for knowingly filing false reports with the SEC. Ten HealthSouth executives pled guilty, including five former chief financial officers (CFOs), and testified against Scrushy. Despite seemingly overwhelming evidence, Scrushy was acquitted. He did settle with the SEC for $81 million. He was later convicted of bribery and other charges related to a state lottery campaign (unrelated to HealthSouth) and he was sentenced to almost seven years in jail. He is currently serving his time in Texas.

See also Accounting Fraud; Acquisition Accounting; Enron; Fraud; HealthSouth; Sarbanes Oxley Act of 2002; Securities and Exchange Commission (SEC)

References

Giroux, Gary. *Detecting Earnings Management.* New York: Wiley, 2004.

Helyar, John. "The Insatiable King Scrushy." In *SCANDAL!: Amazing Tales of Scandals That Shocked the World and Shaped Modern Business*, 267–279. New York: Time Inc. Home Entertainment, 2009.

Securities Acts of 1933 and 1934

After the Crash of 1929 and early in the Great Depression, the Pecora Commission discovered many blatant acts of abuse and substantial speculation in the securities markets (such as the New York Stock Exchange). The federal government assumed the responsibility for regulating financial markets with the Securities Act of 1933. The act was based on the British Companies Acts, earlier unsuccessful congressional legislation from the progressive era, and blue sky laws of various states (regulating the buying and selling of securities). The 1933 act kept securities regulation under the Federal Trade Commission. Lobbying by bankers and industry had only modest effect (the regulations were somewhat watered down from the initial proposals), because of the public outcry from the Pecora hearings and the general feeling that Wall Street was responsible for the Great Depression. As stated by Seligman (2003, 66), it was "the rare time when money talked and nobody listened." The 1934 bill attempted to improve securities regulation relative to the 1933 act. The creation of the Securities and Exchange Commission (SEC) specifically to regulate securities markets became the hallmark of the bill.

The Securities Act of 1933 (called the "truth in securities" law) required companies to prepare registration statements and provide financial information before securities were sold and prohibited fraud and misstatements before the sale of securities. In 1934, Congress attempted to pass a more radical bill (Fletcher-Rayburn bill) to strip powers away from the New York Stock Exchange (NYSE) and the other 30-plus exchanges. The NYSE and financial and business lobbies defeated the initial bill. The final bill, the Securities and Exchange Commission Act of 1934, a watered-down version of Fletcher-Rayburn, created the SEC. The Securities and Exchange Commission Act required the registration of stock exchanges, giving the SEC authority to approve stock exchange rules, and also required periodic reporting (mainly annual at the time) by public corporations to the SEC.

The securities acts mandated "full and fair disclosure" of financial data in registration statements, containing all information relevant to a "prudent" investor. Antifraud and liability sections increased the legal risks to accountants, now accountable to the public as well as firms audited. The initial legislation limited margin trading, short selling, and eliminated floor traders buying and selling exclusively for their own accounts. Rather than pass these measures, legislation required the SEC to study each of these issues. Ultimately, many of the perceived abuses were never eliminated.

Public corporations with over $5 million in assets and 500 stockholders were required to register with the SEC and file periodic reports before new securities could be issued to the public. The SEC issued Accounting Series Releases (SARs), Regulation S-X, and Staff Accounting Bulletins (SABs) on procedures for companies to issue prospectuses as well as annual reports (10-Ks) and, later, quarterly reports (10-Qs). Under current arrangements, SEC reporting requirements are in addition to private sector accounting standards (currently issued by the Financial Accounting Standards Board).

The utilities industry practices of the 1920s were among the most corrupt in the United States, with 53 utility holding companies (including Insull) going bankrupt in the 1930s. Congress passed the Public Utility Holding Company Act of 1935, effectively outlawing holding company structures (it allowed a holding company to control only a single utility system), giving the SEC the authority to restructure the business practices of the entire industry.

See also Accounting Standards; Annual Report (10-K); Auditing since SEC Regulation; Crash of 1929; Great Depression; Pecora Commission; Roosevelt, Franklin Delano; Securities and Exchange Commission (SEC)

References

Dobson, John. "Crash." In *Bulls, Bears, Boom, and Bust: A Historical Encyclopedia of American Business Concepts*. Santa Barbara, CA: ABC-CLIO, 2006.

Galbraith, Kenneth. *The Great Crash 1929*. Boston: Houghton Mifflin, 1988.

Securities Act of 1933. http://www.sec.gov/about/laws/sa33.pdf.

Securities and Exchange Commission Act of 1934. http://www.sec.gov/about/laws/sea34.pdf.

Securities and Exchange Commission (SEC)

The Securities and Exchange Commission (SEC) is a federal agency created in 1934 for the enforcement of federal securities laws and regulation of the securities industry, stock exchanges, and related markets. According to the agency's website, the mission of the SEC is: "to protect investors, maintain fair, orderly, and efficient markets, and facilitate capital formation."

When the stock market crashed in October 1929 and the Great Depression followed, people lost faith in both the stock market and the banking system. Franklin Roosevelt won the presidential election of 1932 promising a New Deal to end the Depression and restore confidence in basic capitalistic institutions. The federal government assumed the responsibilities for protecting investors within the investment markets, especially the stock market. The major legislation included the Securities Act of 1933 and the Securities and Exchange Act of 1934, with additional legislation passed over time. Under the 1933 act, securities regulations were to be under the Federal Trade Commission (FTC). This responsibility was transferred to a new agency, the SEC, with the 1934 act. The market and accounting structure established by the SEC is the basic regulatory framework existing now.

The SEC has five commissioners, each appointed to five-year terms. Joseph P. Kennedy (father of President John F. Kennedy) was the first chairman of the SEC. Public corporations must register with the SEC's Division of Corporation Finance. Newly offered securities require a registration statement; annual and quarterly filings (Forms 10-K and 10-Q for companies with over $10 million in assets and securities held by more than 500 owners) are required from all public companies, as well as proxy statements, merger and acquisition filings, and other documents. Registration statements and other information are available to the public shortly after filing on the EDGAR (electronic data-gathering analysis and retrieval) database. The Division of Enforcement investigates potential violations of securities laws. Common violations include insider trading, misrepresenting or omitting important securities information, manipulating stock price, and sales of securities without SEC registration.

During the early years, the SEC stayed active and well funded, with a staff of over 1,700 before World War II. Post–World War II budget cuts meant a less active and less effective agency. Examination and inspections typically were cut or perpetually late. As new administrations begin, regulatory agency budgets typically are cut or expanded (generally, Republican administrations have been the major cutters). The rationale for cutting is economy and "need for less regulation." The aggressiveness of the SEC, largely dependent on funding levels, has been a contributor to the relative climate of how much corporate aggressiveness and investor speculation is permissible. Given the SEC's broad mandate for regulation, SEC budget cuts meant less review of corporate financial reports and financial scandals more likely to follow. Periodic scandals erupted, most often during periods of lax enforcement—such as the collapse of the tech bubble early in the twenty-first century. The culprits were often caught during downturns, leading to investor rage, congressional hearings, more regulation, and increased SEC funding.

SEC requirements increased corporate disclosures, including the issuance of annual reports (10-K) within 60 days of the end of the fiscal quarter, quarterly reports (10-Q), annual proxy statements, and description of material events (8-K). The SEC makes these reports available to the public online through the EDGAR system.

An unusual number of scandals were discovered in the late 1990s and early twenty-first century. Accounting scandals from the 1990s included Sunbeam, Waste Management, Cendant, and Rite Aid. Substantial derivatives-related events also occurred, the most dramatic being the collapse of Long-Term Capital Management in 1998. The major scandals at the start of the new century were Enron and WorldCom, both accounting scandals leading to bankruptcy and highlighting the need for reform. Congressional hearings after the Enron scandal at the end of 2001 (a major long-term fraud case and the largest bankruptcy in the United States up to that time) led to potential legislation. The SEC did not do a thorough financial analysis of Enron, in part because of limited funding and the focus on new initial public offerings (IPOs), especially high-tech companies, and a somewhat relaxed attitude from a long period of economic prosperity. It was the fall (and discovery of large-scale fraud) of WorldCom in 2002, a company larger than Enron, that led to the massive reform bill, Sarbanes-Oxley Act of 2002 (SOX). The act required new corporate governance requirements, dramatically increased audit regulation, and increased SEC responsibilities.

Although SEC oversight increased after SOX, the agency was relatively passive about the financial sector and the developing subprime mortgage scandal, although the SEC had oversight responsibility of investment banks. The SEC also missed the Madoff Ponzi scheme (and other relatively minor failures). New regulatory requirements were included in the Dodd-Frank Financial Reform Bill of 2010, but few new requirements were given to the SEC. Although a number of investigations were made and charges filed against financial firms after the fall of Lehman Brothers and the credit crisis beginning in October 2008, the SEC has not recovered the earlier respect as a competent watchdog agency.

See also Accounting Fraud; Annual Report (10-K); Cendant; Crash of 1929; Enron; Great Depression; Long-Term Capital Management; Madoff, Bernard L.; Pecora Commission; Rite Aid; Sarbanes-Oxley Act of 2002; Securities Acts of 1933 and 1934; Sunbeam; Waste Management; WorldCom

References

Dobson, J. "Crash." In *Bulls, Bears, Boom, and Bust: A Historical Encyclopedia of American Business Concepts*. Santa Barbara, CA: ABC-CLIO, 2006.

Galbraith, Kenneth. *The Great Crash 1929*. Boston: Houghton Mifflin, 1988.

Giroux, Gary. *Detecting Earnings Management*. Hoboken, NJ: Wiley, 2004.

Securities Act of 1933. http://www.sec.gov/about/laws/sa33.pdf.

Securities Exchange Act of 1934. http://www.sec/gov/about/laws/sea34.pdf.

U.S. Securities and Exchange Commission. "The Investor's Advocate." http://www.sec.gov/about/whatwedo.shtml.

Sherman Antitrust Act of 1890

The Sherman Antitrust Act was the first federal law to attempt to regulate big business using antitrust provisions. The law specifically outlaws price-fixing conspiracies and monopoly practices. While hundreds of companies were combining to achieve monopoly power or conspiring to price prices or limit competition in other ways, only a few cases were prosecuted by the Department of Justice. The government won several big cases, and the Sherman Act and antitrust in general can be considered at least a modest success.

The "trust" was invention by Standard Oil and used by many industries to consolidate, including tobacco, beef, sugar, milk, and many more. Several states passed antitrust laws, often prompted by organized labor, the agricultural Granger movement, and other populists. These proved only modestly successful because of state limits on interstate commerce. Federal legislation was needed. During the 1888 election cycle, both parties campaigned on antitrust reform. Early in 1890 John Sherman, Republican chairman of the Senate Finance Committee, introduced a short bill, which quickly passed Congress. Sherman declared in Congress, "The purpose of this bill is to enable the courts of the United States to apply the same remedies against combinations which injuriously affect the interests of the United States, that have been applied in the several states to protect local interests."

The Sherman Act states, "Every contract, combination in the form of trust or otherwise, or conspiracy, in restraint of trade or commerce . . . is declared to be illegal." However, key terms were not defined, leaving the judiciary to make it work. The first three presidents with the Sherman Act's legal authority (Benjamin Harrison, Glover Cleveland, and William McKinley) were less than enthusiastic supporters and only 18 cases were filed. Antitrust has continued, with both periods of active and successful prosecutions and almost total inaction.

Price-fixing bans started under common law in medieval England. Section 1 of the act bans price-fixing conspiracies: "Every contract, combination in the form of trust or otherwise, or conspiracy, in restraint of trade . . . is hereby declared to be illegal." In the Addyston Pipe Case, six pipe manufacturers formed a cartel that divided sales territory and fixed prices. This agreement was ruled illegal by the Supreme Court in 1899. Several successful price conspiracy prosecutions followed. Section 2 dealt with monopoly: "Every person who shall monopolize . . . any part of the trade or commerce . . . shall be deemed guilty of a misdemeanor."

"Trust Buster" Theodore Roosevelt (president from 1901 to 1909) prosecuted more cases than his three predecessors. Roosevelt focuses on what he considered "bad trusts": "corporate misrepresentations of material facts, overcapitalization, unfair competition, monopoly pricing and unfair treatment of workers had to be stopped" (Mitchell 2007, 133). He and his two successors, Taft and Wilson, filed 230 antitrust cases. Roosevelt's Justice Department created a separate Antitrust Division in 1903. Northern Securities was Roosevelt's first big case, a railroad holding company created by J. P. Morgan; the Supreme Court ruled against the railroad in 1904. Roosevelt remarked that the case "established the power of the Government to deal with all great corporations." The "abuse theory" assumed that the monopolist used abusive business practices and that became the standard rationale to sue.

Later antitrust cases dissolved Standard Oil and American Tobacco, both decided by the Supreme Court in 1911. As giant companies, they were among the original 12 members of the 1896 Dow Jones Industrial Average. James Duke combined many small companies to form American Tobacco in 1890. The Supreme Court ruled the company in restraint of trade and monopolized the tobacco business in interstate commerce; American Tobacco was broken up into four still large companies: American Tobacco, R. J. Reynolds, Liggett & Myers, and Lorillard.

During the "Roaring Twenties" of Republican administrations, little enforcement was done and vigorous enforcement did not resume until the 1940s. Prior to 1940, Aluminum Company of America (Alcoa) had a near monopoly on aluminum production based on patent protection and barriers to entry. In 1938, the Justice Department sued to dissolve the company. Using the new "rule of reason" theory, Alcoa was found guilty and aluminum facilities sold to Kaiser and Reynolds. The Antitrust Division of the Justice Department is still active and the Sherman Act paramount for evaluating prospective mergers and charges of price fixing.

See also Antitrust; Morgan, John Pierpont; Northern Pacific War; Regulation of Business; Roosevelt, Theodore; Standard Oil Company

References

Atkins, Albert. "Sherman Anti-Trust Act (1890)." In *The American Economy: A Historical Encyclopedia*. Rev. ed. Edited by Cynthia Clark. Santa Barbara, CA: ABC-CLIO, 2011.

Josephson, Matthew. *The Robber Barons*. New York: Harcourt, 1962.

Mitchell, Lawrence. *The Speculation Economy: How Finance Triumphed over Industry.* San Francisco: Berrett-Koehler, 2007.

Viscusi, W., J. Vernon, and J. Harrington. *Economics of Regulation and Antitrust.* 2nd ed. Cambridge, MA: MIT Press, 1995.

Sinclair, Harry F.

Harry Sinclair (1876–1956) was an oil tycoon, willing to use political muscle and payoffs to enhance his growing empire, and became a major villain in the Teapot Dome scandal of the 1920s. He was one of the few business executives to go to prison for illicit acts. Sinclair was born in Benwood, West Virginia, on July 6, 1876, initially working as a pharmacist. He became a lease broker in the oil industry and rose to create a business empire. He merged 11 small petroleum companies in the Midwest to form Sinclair Oil in 1916, expanding refining capacity and developing oil pipelines.

Willing to play dirty to promote his own interests, Sinclair expressed considerable interest in the Teapot Dome oil reserve in Wyoming when the corrupt Harding administration came to power. In addition, he used his political connections to get drilling rights in Russia (the Russians wanted diplomatic recognition by the United States) and Iran, at the time under British oil interests. Sinclair gave $1 million to the Republican National Committee as a sweetener for expected future political favors and paid off the debt of the Republican National Committee after the 1920 election.

Sinclair signed a lease with Interior Secretary Albert Fall to take out Teapot Dome oil (the reserve estimated to contain some 135 million barrels) on a royalty basis. Fall signed the contract for Teapot in April 1922, keeping the contract confidential until the *Wall Street Journal* broke the story a week later. The Interior Department claimed the process (confidential, no bidding) a normal procedure; expressing skepticism, the Senate passed a resolution to investigate the leases by the end of the month.

Reporters for the *Denver Post* uncovered much of the Sinclair-Fall scam. The journalists then demanded a $1 million bribe from Sinclair, which he refused to pay. Negative Teapot stories continued until the million dollars got paid, at which point the paper became a supporter for Sinclair and the rest of the conspirators.

Sinclair made substantial payments to Fall, mainly in Liberty bonds (Treasury bonds issued to support World War I), rather than cash. Unlike cash, these had serial numbers, which were later verified by federal investigators. The first payment totaled $198,000, with another $71,000 added after Fall objected to the original payment as too small. When investigated, Fall claimed Sinclair acquired a part interest in Fall's ranch, although no paperwork existed.

Fall resigned from the cabinet early in 1923, shortly after giving Sinclair a new five-year contract on Teapot Dome, probably not because of political pressure, but to return to his ranch and act as a "paid political consultant" for oil man Edward Doheny and Sinclair. Fall went to Russia to promote Sinclair's interests, for which he was handsomely rewarded. He later admitted he went, but claimed to be unpaid.

After the death of President Warren G. Harding, new president Calvin Coolidge appointed a special prosecutor for the Teapot Dome scandal, which worked closely with the ongoing congressional committee. A Secret Service investigation uncovered incriminating evidence. Suits were filed for an injunction to stop the drilling of the naval reserves and cancel the leases. It took a Supreme Court ruling to void the leases, which finally came in 1927.

Criminal indictments for fraud were filed against Sinclair, Fall, and others. Sinclair had eight court cases against him. Never convicted on any charges related to bribery or Teapot Dome, he served a three-month sentence for contempt of Congress for lying. In addition, during one of the criminal trials he had all the jurors tailed by the Burns Detective Agency and offered one or more of them a bribe to vote acquittal. That led to another trial for jury tampering. While in prison for contempt of Congress, the Supreme Court upheld the guilty verdict on jury tampering. He ended up spending a total of seven months in prison.

Sinclair's reputation was ruined, but he returned to his business and remained a wealthy man. He died on November 10, 1956, in Pasadena, California.

See also Daugherty, Harry M.; Doheny, Edward; Fall, Albert B.; Roaring Twenties; Teapot Dome

References

Bates, J. Leonard. *The Origins of Teapot Dome*. Urbana: University of Illinois Press, 1963.

Dobson, John. "Sinclair, Harry Ford." In *Bulls, Bears, Boom, and Bust: A Historical Encyclopedia of American Business Concepts*. Santa Barbara, CA: ABC-CLIO, 2006.

Gentzkow, Matthew, Edward Glaeser, and Claudia Goldin. "The Rise of the Fourth Estate: How Newspapers Became Informative and Why It Mattered." In *Corruption and Reform: Lessons from America's Economic History*. Edited by Edward Glaeser and Claudia Goldin, 187–230. Washington, DC: National Bureau of Economic Research, 2006.

McCartney, L. *The Teapot Dome Scandal: How Big Oil Bought the Harding White House and Tried to Steal the Country*. New York: Random House, 2008.

Skilling, Jeffrey K.

Jeffrey Skilling ("Jeff," 1953–) was the president and chief executive officer (CEO) of Enron, convicted of securities fraud and other charges related to the accounting scandal after the failure of Enron in 2001. Skilling was born on November 25, 1953, in Pittsburg. After receiving a BS in science from Southern Methodist University and an MBA from Harvard in 1979, he worked as a consultant at McKinsey & Co., rising to partner. Skilling worked as a McKinsey consultant for

Enron beginning in 1987 to create a market in natural gas and was hired by CEO Kenneth Lay in 1990, becoming the head of Enron Gas Services. He was promoted to president and chief operating officer in 1997.

When the gas market was deregulated in the 1980s, natural gas prices proved extremely volatile. Given the lack of stability, banks were reluctant to loan money to oil and gas drillers. Enron needed the supply to match producing gas wells with utilities and other users. Skilling formed the Gas Bank to replace bank loans. Drillers were given cash up front, with the stipulation that the drillers pay back the loans in gas produced rather than cash. With long-term commitments from both buyers and sellers, the price and supply of gas remained stable and Enron became the largest gas trader. Skilling focused on trading these contracts, his "asset-light" strategy. The fact that Enron owned substantial pipelines and carried massive debt to fund these expensive assets was downplayed.

At Enron, Skilling used mark-to-market accounting (fair value, where gains and losses are recognized immediately) for long-term gas delivery and other trading contracts rather than historical cost. Mark-to-market accounting spread to other Enron operations, becoming a major accounting gimmick to promote desired earnings. Earnings volatility was common; however, Enron used long-term contracts, which increased stability. However, reliable market prices really did not exist on gas prices up to 10 years out. Pricing became an exercise in "mark-to-model," with mathematical models predicting values. Such models could be conveniently manipulated to provide gains or losses as needed.

Enron's debt load limited potential growth. Special-purpose entities (SPEs) were used to hide much of this debt, and Skilling hired Andrew Fastow as an SPE specialist. The first SPE, Cactus, was used to fund Skilling's Gas Bank. Once Enron contracted with drillers for loans for future gas, these contracts were aggregated and sold to investors to cover the cash paid to the drillers. The cash was now available to fund other Enron schemes, while the debt remained in the SPE.

Skilling's job when he became chief operating officer in 1997 was to meet analysts' quarterly earnings targets. His compensation package was based on earnings and stock price performance. Accounting manipulation became increasingly necessary to meet forecasts, with the use of mark-to-market and SPE gimmicks increasingly common methods.

Enron's price peaked at $90 in August 2000, then fell as did the entire stock market at this time. Skilling was promoted to CEO in February 2001 and resigned August 14 after serving only six months, citing personal reasons and selling $60 million of his Enron stock. Then Enron collapsed. After Skilling left, Enron reported a third-quarter 2001 loss plus a write-down in equity of over a billion dollars. The auditor required Enron to restate earnings from 1997 to 2000, a cumulative loss of an additional $1.2 billion. After being downgraded to junk, Enron was not able to borrow money and declared bankruptcy on December 2, 2001. Regulatory investigations began, followed by congressional hearings.

Skilling was indicted and charged with 35 counts of fraud, insider trading. and other wrongdoings. He was convicted of 19 counts and sentenced to 24 years in prison. He appealed the decision, but was unsuccessful and started serving his time in Colorado.

See also Accounting Fraud; Enron; Fastow, Andrew S.; Lay, Kenneth L.; Sarbanes-Oxley Act of 2002; Special-Purpose Entities at Enron

References

Eichenwald, Kurt. *Conspiracy of Fools*. New York: Broadway Books, 2005.

Giroux, Gary. "What Went Wrong? Accounting Fraud and Lessons from the Recent Scandals." *Social Research: An International Quarterly of the Social Sciences*, Winter 2008, 1205–38.

McLean, Bethany, and Peter Elkind. *The Smartest Guys in the Room*. New York: Penguin Books, 2003.

Swartz, Mimi, and Sherron Watkins. *Power Failure: The Inside Story of the Collapse of Enron*. New York: Doubleday, 2003.

Smith, Adam

Adam Smith (1723–90) was a social philosopher and economist; his masterpiece *Wealth of Nations* established classical economics. Smith was born on June 5, 1723, in Kirkcaldy, Scotland. He studied moral philosophy at the University of Glasgow and Balliol College, Oxford. Smith was appointed professor of logic at Glasgow in 1751. His *The Theory of Moral Sentiments* described the components of the "natural order" of society. Smith published *An Inquiry into the Nature and Causes of the Wealth of Nations* in 1776 as a theory of economic growth. Smith's definition of wealth is similar to the modern concept of gross domestic product. He viewed labor as the source of wealth, especially ingenuity and skills to produce useful goods. The division of labor into simple tasks increases output. Smith identified the "invisible hand," which channels self-interested humans into harmonious economic activity.

In 1759, *The Theory of Moral Sentiments* was published and Smith revised the book throughout his life. He considered it superior to the *Wealth of Nations*. He divides moral philosophy into four categories: (1) ethics and virtue, (2) liberty and privacy rights, (3) economics (called familial rights), and (4) politics (government versus individual rights). Smith starts with sympathy, associated with pity or compassion, as "the emotion which we feel for the misery of others." He describes passions, which include "bodily passions" (pain, sex, and hunger), "unsocial passions" of hatred and resentment, and love. He describes in several parts the rationale for the relatively poor attempting to become rich: "the poor man is ashamed of his poverty," "the man of rank and distinction is observed by all the world," "we desire to be respectable and to be respected . . . by the study of wisdom . . . and by the acquisition of wealth and greatness." A "sense of duty" follows from the "general rules of conduct." Prudence is "the care of the health, of the fortune, of the rank and reputation of the individual." Prudence is associated with justice, benevolence, the virtuous life, and concern for other people.

Smith's masterwork, *An Inquiry into the Nature and Causes of the Wealth of Nations*, established the classical school of economics. Central to Smith's economic perspective is his concept of the "invisible hand," described in Book IV:

> As every individual, therefore, endeavours as much as he can both to employ his capital in the support of domestic industry, and so to direct that industry that its produce may be of the greatest value; every individual necessarily labours to render the annual revenue of the society as great as he can. He generally, indeed, neither intends to promote the public interest, nor knows how much he is promoting it. By preferring the support of domestic to that of foreign industry, he intends only his own security; and by directing that industry in such a manner as its produce may be of the greatest value, he intends only his own gain, and he is in this, as in many other eases, led by an invisible hand to promote an end which was no part of his intention. Nor is it always the worse for the society that it was no part of it. By pursuing his own interest he frequently promotes that of the society more effectually than when he really intends to promote it. I have never known much good done by those who affected to trade for the public good.

Smith favored laissez-faire, the nonintervention of government because it was corrupt and inefficient, and granted monopolies and other special privileges. The role of government was limited to providing defense, public works, and related public goods, and protecting contract rights and the rule of law. Government services should be funded through customs duties, tolls, and use fees and taxes. Smith's four maxims of revenue are: they should be (1) proportional to their respective abilities (income), (2) certain and not arbitrary, (3) levied conveniently from the payer, and (4) collected at minimum cost.

Smith develops a labor theory of value. He distinguishes between value in use based on utility and value in exchange based on purchasing power. In the *Wealth of Nations*, Smith identified the "paradox of water and diamonds" (generalized as the paradox of value). Water for example is essential but has little value in exchange because of its abundance. Diamonds have a high value because of scarcity. Labor, according to Smith, is the measure of valuing all commodities. The natural price of a good (the long-run price) generates the revenue to pay wages, profit, and rent (the price paid for the use of land). Smith's labor theory of value for a commodity includes the embedded labor in production plus profits and rent.

Written before the Industrial Revolution had really taken hold, Smith's theory downplayed the role of capital. However, he did note the division of labor and introduction of machinery to increase productivity and wealth. He viewed the production of goods as productive labor, but services as unproductive.

Particularly important is Smith's analysis of competition in a free market with limited government involvement. Rather than chaos resulting from government-free markets (the government role limited to rule of law and providing basic public works), the market is self-regulating as entrepreneurs provide the goods demanded by consumers. Self-interested merchants produce the goods that are in greatest demand and therefore provide higher short-run profits. Excess profits drive competitors to produce the goods demanded, driving prices down to "natural prices." Supply and demand are matched by the "invisible hand," creating a cohesive and stable system. Economic growth is promoted by both the drive of entrepreneurs to accumulate wealth and the division of labor to expand productivity.

A large industrial base with monopoly power and substantial externalities such as pollution and poor working conditions are beyond the scope of Smith, but his analysis of competitive markets is a powerful theoretical model. Laissez-faire has been promoted by many economists, corporations, and politicians ever since.

In 1778, Smith was appointed commissioner of customs in Scotland and became a member of the Philosophical Society of Edinburgh. He died on July 17, 1790, in Edinburgh, Scotland.

Smith is considered the father of classical economics, which developed and expanded especially throughout the nineteenth century. Much of his approach is considered roughly correct. However, critics see limits to Smith. For example, John Cassidy (2009) viewed Smith as the first "utopian economist," while Cassidy thought the focus should be based on "reality-based economics" relying on real-world behavior.

See also Austrian School of Economics; Classical Economics; Keynes, John Maynard; Mercantilism

References

Cassidy, John. *How Markets Fail: The Logic of Economic Calamities*. New York: Farrar, Straus and Giroux, 2009.

Heilbroner, Robert. *The Essential Adam Smith*. New York: Norton, 1986.

Oser, Jacob. *The Evolution of Economic Thought*. New York: Harcourt, Brace & World, 1963.

Rider, Christine. "Smith, Adam." In *Encyclopedia of the Age of the Industrial Revolution, 1700–1920*. Santa Barbara, CA: Greenwood, 2007.

Social (Corporate) Responsibility

Social responsibility is an ethical approach to behavior relative to society at large. Corporate responsibility suggests acting in the best interests of all stakeholders (stock and bond investors, employees, customers, suppliers) and the public at large, including the ecosystem. Corporate responsibility is part of corporate governance role of stewardship by the board of directors.

Adam Smith focused on laissez-faire and individuals' selfishness to make markets work. Profit maximization has been the typical goal of business, and libertarians (such as economist Milton Friedman) would say that corporate responsibility means businesses maximize profits. Friedman stated that corporate responsibility is "to conduct the business in accordance with [owners'] desires, which generally will be to make as much money as possible while conforming to the basic rules of society, both those embodied in law and those embodied in ethical custom" (reported in Barton 2003, 647). This view emphasizes economic efficiency, but most social responsibility perspectives include a broader viewpoint.

Nineteenth-century industrialists focused on the interests of owners and treated employees as another cost of doing business. In 1883, railroad tycoon William Vanderbilt famously said to a reporter, "The public be damned. I am working for my stockholders." Customers often were mistreated, being sold tainted and dangerous products, as well as inferior materials. Stock and bond investors were often given little if any financial information and accounts were seldom audited. Managers typically had to face unethical government officials that had to be bought off through cash bribes or given stock. Almost no consideration was given to the environment, so that forests were clear-cut resulting in erosion and a devastated landscape, mines decimated the landscape, exotic animals were slaughtered, while toxic petroleum and chemical products dumped in the local rivers or lakes. Managers claimed that competition forced them to reduce costs to stay in business and these actions were needed to employ local people and grow the economy.

Federal and state laws started the conservation movement by setting aside lands in the nineteenth century as national and state parks, forests, and monuments to protect the most valued sites. State and then federal regulations followed slowly, eventually requiring limitations to the most devastating practices. The most widespread regulations started as part of the progressive movement of the early twentieth century and President Franklin D. Roosevelt's New Deal of the 1930s, including securities regulations, labor, welfare, and retirement benefits. National pollution regulations became effective only in the 1970s, including the establishment of the Environmental Protection Agency.

The Business Roundtable, made up of chief executive officers (CEOs) of major corporations focused on public issues, included a "Statement on Corporate Responsibilities" in 1981 that stated that business is to "serve the public interest as well as private profit" (reported in Barton 2003, 650). The Business Roundtable identified seven groups: customers, employees, financiers, suppliers, communities, society at large, and shareholders. An important part of this consideration is contract rights and responsibilities. Motivations for maintaining social responsibility include enhancing long-term profitability, reducing potential nonmarket threats such as environmental activists, and ethical considerations. Some corporations attempt to measure social responsibility using social accountability and social audits.

Corporate boards of directors have stewardship responsibility as part of corporate governance including social considerations. The board has specific legal and regulatory requirements under federal law, such as the Sarbanes-Oxley Act of 2002, but is generally free to choose whatever level of social responsibility the firm should follow. In part due to stock market short-term considerations (specifically, quarterly earnings announcements), long-term goals and ethical considerations often fall by the wayside in the search for a penny or two of quarterly earnings per share—not to mention big loss events. Consequently, most business scandals seem to include the complete lack of ethical considerations for substantial periods (or even unethical behavior as part of the overall but unstated mission of the firm). For example, Enron and many of the banks in the subprime scandal of 2008 displayed little if any regard for even minimal ethical standards.

See also Antitrust; Corporate Governance; Environmental Movement; Environmental Regulations; Ethics; Food and Drug Regulations; Justice; Pollution Externalities; Roosevelt, Franklin Delano; Roosevelt, Theodore

References

Barton, David. *Business and Its Environment*. 4th ed. Upper Saddle River, NJ: Prentice Hall, 2003.

Glaeser, Edward. *Triumph of the City: How Our Greatest Invention Makes Us Richer, Smarter, Greener, Healthier, and Happier*. New York: Penguin Group, 2011.

Soros, George

George Soros (1930–) is a hedge fund manager of Quantum Fund best known for betting against the British pound in 1992. He was born on August 12, 1930, in Budapest, Hungary, immigrated to England after World War II, and graduated from the London School of Economics. Soros worked as an arbitrage trader, analyst, and hedge fund manager. Soros created his private investment firm, Quantum Fund, in 1973.

On Black Wednesday, September 16, 1992, Quantum sold short $10 billion worth of British pounds, when the Bank of England was defending an overvalued currency. The United Kingdom gave in, withdrew from the European Exchange Rate Mechanism, and devalued the pound. The profit on the short position was estimated at $1.1 billion and Soros became "the man who broke the Bank of England." According to Schweizer (2011, 126), Soros discovered that the German and French central banks would no longer support the pound and then placed the massive bet. This and other hedge fund successes brought in billions of investor dollars.

Soros was accused of causing the Asian financial crisis of 1997 and, in fact, did short the Thai baht and Malaysian ringgit. As stated by economist Paul Krugman (1999, 160), "There really are investors who not only move money in anticipation of a currency crisis, but actually do their best to trigger that crisis for fun and profit. These new actors on the scene do not yet have a standard name; my proposed term is 'Soroi'."

Soros has been increasingly active in philanthropy and a supporter of Democratic groups and candidates. According to *Forbes*, Soros's wealth was estimated at $22 billion in 2011.

See also Derivatives; Hedge Funds; Jones, Alfred W.; Long-Term Capital Management; Speculation

References

Krugman, Paul. *The Accidental Theorist and Other Dispatches from the Dismal Science.* New York: Norton 1999.

Schweizer, Peter. *Throw Them All Out: How Politicians and Their Friends Get Rich Off Insider Stock Tips, Land Deals, and Cronyism That Would Send the Rest of Us to Prison.* New York: Houghton Mifflin Harcourt, 2011.

South Sea Bubble

The South Sea Company was a British joint stock company (an early form of corporation) given a royal warrant in 1711 to trade with South American colonies in exchange for acquiring much of the national debt of Great Britain. Speculation in the company's stock resulted in an economic bubble, which crashed in 1720 and caused considerable economic chaos. Later investigations by Parliament found massive fraud and rampant insider activities.

The South Sea Company was founded in 1711 by Robert Harley, Lord Treasurer of Britain, and John Blunt, who made a small fortune as director of the Sword Blade Company. The company received a charter for monopoly rights to trade with the American colonies of Spain, under the assumption that the War of the Spanish Succession would end on favorable terms for British trade. Harley viewed the company, in part, as a way to fund the massive government debt. Harley wanted a bank, but the charter of the Bank of England banned the chartering of any other bank as a joint stock company. Instead, the government granted a perpetual annual annuity of almost £600,000 (6% on £10 million). Cash bribes and payment of company stock persuaded aristocrats and politicians to the plan's benefits. The annuity would be paid from a projected tariff on imports from South America. The company (with government backing) persuaded holders of about £10 million in short-term government debt to exchange the debt for stock in the South Sea Company. Investors expected returns from both the government annuity and the profits from the South American trade.

Peace with Spain happened with the Treaty of Utrecht in 1713, but with only modest concessions for trade. The potential for massive trading was dashed and

Robert Harley, 1st Earl of Oxford. Harley was the Lord Treasurer of Britain, and founded the South Sea Company in 1711. (Library of Congress)

the promoters focused on what essentially became a massive Ponzi scheme. The company took on new government debt for annuity payments and traded additional government debt from private investors in exchange for stock in the company. To expand the potential for new investors, they were allowed to pay for only a small fraction of the stock price up front under a subscription plan. By 1719, the South Sea Company owned about £12 million in government debt and the equivalent of £15 million in long-term annuities. The price of the stock continued up in massive speculation, creating a stock bubble, with ripple effects on real estate and other stocks.

Other joint-stock companies were formed during this bubble period, until massive bribery resulted in the "Bubble Act" of 1720, which required all new joint-stock companies to be incorporated by an act of Parliament or royal charter (the act was not repealed until 1825). This helped protect South Sea stock prices. However, as prices reached over £1,000 a share, investors started cashing out. Company agents were forced to buy up shares to prop up the stock price. As new subscription payments came due, many investors were forced to sell shares to make the subscription payments. By September 1720, the stock price was plummeting—the bubble had collapsed.

In 1721, the House of Commons (much of the bribery and favorable sales of stock involved the House of Lords) established the "Committee on Secrecy" (selected by secret ballot) to investigate the company. The cashier of the South Sea Company, Robert Knight, fled to France with much of the incriminating evidence. (Knight was captured near Brussels, but allowed to escape in a bargain between the corrupt Robert Walpole with the backing of King George I and the Austrian emperor.)

John Blunt, a major conspirator, confessed and told about the records kept by Knight and how more than £1 million had been spent on bribes. The 33 directors were stripped of their public offices and several were jailed. Other government officials were accused of corruption and impeached. The estates of the directors were confiscated to benefit the victims and the stock of the company divided between the Bank of England and the East India Company. The company had a £14 million deficit and investors received about 50¢ on the dollar (based on par value, not the inflated stock price). The company continued until the 1850s, maintaining both a modest trade with Latin America and other ventures such as whale fishing in Greenland. Robert Walpole, who manipulated the investigations and prosecutions to save several of the major players, kept the Whig Party in power and became de facto prime minister (later earl of Oxford).

See also Bubbles and Euphoria; Law, John; Mississippi Bubble; Panics and Depressions; Ponzi, Charles; Tulip Mania

References

Balen, Malcolm. *The Secret History of the South Sea Bubble*. London: Fourth Estate, 2002.

Beckman, Robert. *Crashes: Why They Happen—What to Do*. Glasgow: Grafton Books, 1988.

Means, Howard. *Money and Power: The History of Business*. New York: Wiley, 2001.

Special-Purpose Entities (SPEs)

Structured financing and special-purpose entities (SPEs; also called special-purpose vehicles or SPVs) became increasingly common financial arrangements used predominantly by banks, beginning with First Boston repackaging auto loans for

GMAC in 1985. SPEs became something of a household word after Enron collapsed, after blatant misuse of SPEs to camouflage debt and hide losses. According to Financial Executives International:

> A special purpose entity is a separate legal entity established by asset transfer to carry out some specific purpose. This entity could be a partnership, trust or corporation. SPEs are a form of structured financing, to achieve a specific purpose based on some set of financing or operating needs. These can be used to access capital or manage risk. Examples include leasing, sales and transfer of assets to the entity which then issues debt obligations or equity for these assets, financing arrangements with third-party financial institutions, or various project development activities. (reported in Giroux 2006, 162)

To be reported as a separate entity (that is, not in the financial statements of the parent, called "off-balance-sheet") technical details must be met (including an independent investor with the equity investment at risk) or the SPE must be consolidated into the financial statements of the parent.

SPEs started in the mid-1980s, mainly by banks to achieve specific goals. Banks moved auto loans, credit card debt, and mortgages into SPEs to get them off the books (that is, to avoid reporting them as liabilities) and then securitized them for resale as debt instruments similar to bonds but with "diversified debtors." Companies could use synthetic leases primarily for tax purposes and still get off-balance-sheet treatment (getting the tax advantages of a capital lease without recording the liabilities of a capital lease). American Express used an SPE to move high-interest-cost debt into an SPE, resulting in a $150 million gains and removal of the liabilities from the balance sheet. General Motors created SPEs to redevelop closed factories with environmental problems. Airlines created SPEs to hold airplane leases to reduce massive reported liabilities.

SPE accounting can be difficult and confusing because of the underlying contracts and legal requirements and use for complex transactions. A key component of SPE accounting is determining when SPEs have to be consolidated in the financial statements of the parent company or can remain off-balance-sheet. Generally, a third party has to maintain a 10 percent equity interest (increased from 3% in January 2003, after the Enron debacle) at market value for the SPE to be off-balance-sheet. The rules for the interrelated variable interest entities (VIEs) involve relative risks and rewards rather than ownership percentages.

The SPE is subject to specific legal requirements including at least one equity investor, a trustee, and a servicer. The SPE must have an outside equity investor contributing assets (usually cash) of at least 10 percent of the fair value of assets. This is required for the originator (that is, the corporation being evaluated) to avoid consolidation (that is, to keep it off the books). The trustee is an independent third party paid a fee to advocate the interests of the SPE. The servicer provides the basic accounting and other administrative requirements, for a fee. The servicer often is the originator, such as a bank servicing the loans or mortgages that have been secured.

SPE supporters claim that there are obvious advantages to SPEs. Kahn (2002), for example, argues that:

> Like many complex instruments, SPEs were created to perform a straightforward, necessary task—isolating and containing financial risk. Businesses that wanted to perform a specialized task—an airline buying a fleet of airplanes; a company building a big construction project—would set up an SPE and off-load the financing to the new entity.

In theory, SPEs protected both sides of the transaction if something went awry. If the project went bust, the company was responsible only for what it had put into the SPE; conversely, if the company went bankrupt, its creditors could not go after the SPE's assets.

Over time, SPEs became essential components of modern finance. Their uses expanded wildly—and legitimately. For example, virtually every bank uses SPEs to issue debt secured by pools of mortgages. And companies as diverse as Target and Xerox use SPEs for factoring—the centuries-old practice of generating cash by selling off receivables.

SPEs are also a good way to keep money away from Uncle Sam. Most tax-avoidance techniques using SPEs cleverly exploit discrepancies between accounting rules and tax laws. Synthetic leases are a good example.

The potential for abuse was demonstrated by Enron's failure and the legal convictions of SPE specialist Andrew Fastow and other Enron executives for fraud. The subprime meltdown also showed many banks holding substantial assets and liabilities in SPEs to avoid violating capital requirements. Substantial Treasury Department bailouts were based, in part, on this SPE deception. The same basic rules are still in place so potential abuse can be expected to continue.

See also Accounting Fraud; Derivatives; Enron; Fastow, Andrew S.; Fraud; Securities and Exchange Commission (SEC); Special-Purpose Entities at Enron; Structured Finance

References

Eichenwald, Kurt. *Conspiracy of Fools*. New York: Broadway Books, 2005.

Giroux, Gary. *Earnings Magic and the Unbalance Sheet: The Search for Financial Reality*. Hoboken, NJ: Wiley, 2006.

Giroux, Gary. "What Went Wrong? Accounting Fraud and Lessons from the Recent Scandals." *Social Research: An International Quarterly of the Social Sciences*, Winter 2008, 1205–38.

Kahn, J. "Off-Balance Sheet—and Out of Control: SPEs Are Ripe for Abuse, but Few Went as Far as Enron's Fastow." *Fortune*, February 18, 2002.

McLean, Bethany, and Peter Elkind. *The Smartest Guys in the Room.* New York: Penguin Books, 2003.

Special-Purpose Entities at Enron

Much of Enron's illicit activities centered on its use of special-purpose entities (SPEs). SPEs became common financial arrangements by the late-1980s, especially by banks attempting to remove liabilities from their books. The SPE places assets and corresponding liabilities in a separate legal structure, a partnership, corporation, or trust, specifically to move them off the parent's financial statements.

Enron had substantial debt, common for a gas pipeline company, but chief executive officer (CEO) Kenneth Lay wanted to grow into gas trading and other activities literally around the world. Excessive debt and a low bond rating made borrowing the cash to fund growth difficult. Andrew Fastow was hired in 1990 as an SPE specialist. Fastow created Enron's first SPE in 1991 called Cactus (Enron would continue the unusual practice of giving SPEs names rather than numbers). The Gas Bank was created to loan cash to drillers to be paid back from successful wells on long-term contracts. These contracts were bundled by the SPE and sold to investors. Enron received the cash, equivalent to what was paid to the drillers, and the liabilities moved to the SPE. The purpose of Enron's use of SPEs was, according to McLean and Elkind (2003, 155) to "keep fresh debt off the books, camouflage existing debt, book earnings, or create operating cash flow."

Possibly the first Enron SPE incorporating illegal acts was Chewco. Enron created JEDI in 1993 as a joint venture with California Public Employees' Retirement System (CalPERS) to fund natural gas projects, including the purchase of several production companies. CalPERS's share of JEDI was bought out by Enron in 1997, which created Chewco to take its place. Fastow wanted to be the "independent investor" for Chewco, which was rejected as a clear violation of independence. The probable intent was to create side deals to directly benefit Fastow. Michael Kopper, an Enron employee under Fastow, became the investor, and was accepted by a very pliable board or directors and auditor, Arthur Andersen. The rationale was that Fastow was an executive but Kopper was not. Kopper borrowed most of the money for his 3 percent share, another clear violation of the rules. Chewco was later viewed as improper by the Powers Report when investigating Enron's illicit behavior.

Another well-known fraudulent act was the sham sale of power plants floating on barges off the coast of Nigeria. Enron was unable to find a buyer in 1999 when the company needed the cash. Enron made a loan with Merrill Lynch that was treated as a sale (Enron "informally" agreed to buy back the barges the next accounting period). Enron recorded a gain of $12 million and operating cash flow of $28 million—the purpose of which was to meet analysts' forecasts of $1.17 a share for the period. Another SPE, Fastow's LJM2, "bought" back the barges including a sham profit of $775,000 for Merrill Lynch.

Blatantly illegal were SPEs LJM and LJM2, with Fastow as general partner. Once again the board of directors waived the conflict-of-interest requirements. The concept was a mechanism to provide cash and/or financial benefits as needed, but mainly to meet analysts' forecasts and limit reported liabilities. Unknown to the board, Fastow also used them for side deals to enrichment himself, family members, and employees in on his schemes.

In 1998, Enron made a $10 million investment in a small Internet company called Rhythms NetConnections. Rhythms Net went public through an IPO in 1999 and that day the stock rose to $69 a share. Despite the relatively small magnitude of this investment for Enron, Fastow established an LJM entity called Swap Sub to lock in the gain using a hedge (a put option) on shares of Enron—complex but basically a sham transaction. It involved bankers from Nat West, who became the first individuals indicted (for wire fraud) in the later Enron mess.

Four new SPEs were created with LJM2, called Raptors, and used Enron stock to hedge against possible losses on Enron asset values, as well as recording illicit gains and moving liabilities off-balance-sheet. To make matters worse, Fastow became the "independent investor," self-dealing between himself and Enron. LJM2 made 20 complex, deceptive deals to benefit Enron, reportedly adding $230 million to Enron earnings. As creator and "independent investor," Fastow paid himself $59 million (Swartz and Watkins 2003, 310).

Enron stock fell along with other tech stocks late in 2000. Unfortunately, the Raptor SPEs were funded with Enron stock and could not be kept off the balance sheet once they were "underwater" (that is, the value of Enron stock, the asset, fell some $700 million and could no longer support the liabilities). The SPEs were terminated and the loss taken. Losses occurred in several other Enron businesses from Enron Broadband to the Dabhol power plant. Losses for Enron's third quarter 2001 were large and an additional write-down to equity of $1.2 billion related to the Raptors was recorded. Enron's earnings release tried to minimize the damage by stating, "Recurring third quarter earnings of $0.43 per diluted share; reports nonrecurring charges of $1.01 billion after tax; reaffirms recurring earnings estimate of $1.80 for 2001 and $2.15 for 2002." Investors were not fooled and became irate over the misinformation.

The degree of Fastow's deception was unraveled and he was fired. Auditor Arthur Andersen required an additional restatement of earnings of $1.2 billion for the period 1997–2000 primarily based on the mismanagement of Chewco. Bond rating agencies downgraded Enron's bonds to junk and the company was forced into bankruptcy at the end of 2001. Fastow was indicted on 78 criminal counts for defrauding Enron and sent to jail. Congressional hearings ultimately led to financial reform in the Sarbanes-Oxley Act of 2002. The accounting for SPE was modernized, although this does not eliminate the potential for manipulating SPEs.

See also Accounting Fraud; Derivatives; Enron; Fastow, Andrew S.; Fraud; Lay, Kenneth L.; Skilling, Jeffrey K.; Special-Purpose Entities

References

Eichenwald, Kurt. *Conspiracy of Fools*. New York: Broadway Books, 2005.

Giroux, Gary. "What Went Wrong? Accounting Fraud and Lessons from the Recent Scandals." *Social Research: An International Quarterly of the Social Sciences*, Winter 2008, 1205–38.

McLean, Bethany, and Peter Elkind. *The Smartest Guys in the Room*. New York: Penguin Books, 2003.

Swartz, Mimi, and Sherron Watkins. *Power Failure: The Inside Story of the Collapse of Enron*. New York: Doubleday, 2003.

Speculation

Speculation is an investment in uncertainty, usually buying risky assets using borrowed money. Speculators make money only when their investments increase in value. They create markets and take risks others avoid. During the post-Revolutionary period (1780s), speculators bought up depreciated currency and notes, ultimately enriching themselves at the expense of farmers, laborers, and veterans, who had to sell Continental currencies and notes at pennies on the dollar to survive. Rich merchants and bankers were major players and often privy to inside information on the potential for repayment. As secretary of the Treasury, Alexander Hamilton made good on his promise to pay off the paper and securities at par.

From the start, real estate was the favorite pastime of speculators, usually in "western land"; initially, "western" might have meant Kentucky. George Washington surveyed and speculated in raw land, as did Robert Morris (superintendent of finance during the latter part of the Revolution), and other founding fathers. Morris would end up in debtors' prison over bad investments. Some of the shadier founding fathers included Manasseh Cutler from Connecticut and William Blount of North Carolina, both of whom speculated in land using insider information, connections, and strategic bribes to acquire massive land grants. In addition to being a land speculator, Revolutionary War general James Wilkinson became a spy for Spain, paid in Spanish silver dollars.

Speculation helps create markets, and supporters insist they increase market liquidity and efficiency. Speculation in western land in the late eighteenth century was considered a "can't lose" bet until panic and market collapse sent many speculators to debtors' prison. Speculators never go away no matter at what point in the business cycle, but booms and the concomitant excess leverage expand their reach (especially to acquire more debt) and the desire to take even more risk. Even in a crash, speculators can make money—in fact, many bet heavily on expected crashes.

Hyman Minsky (1919–96) described the business cycle based on the relative supply of credit and investor confidence—an important theory related to speculation. Minsky broke lending practices into three categories based on the quality of debt: hedge finance (safe), speculative finance (moderate), and Ponzi finance (risky). Minsky's model starts with standard banking practice where loans plus interest will be paid back as they come due from operating income. When lending becomes speculative, borrowers anticipate paying back interest from operating earnings but not return of principal. The borrowers have to refinance the principal when the loan matures. In a period of market euphoria, Ponzi finance loans will not generate enough cash to pay back either interest or principal. Ponzi finance will continue if asset values rise to cover finance payments. When asset prices fall, the system collapses as loan defaults expand and companies are forced into bankruptcy. Investor euphoria caused by rapidly rising assets prices (especially in real estate and stock) drive speculative and Ponzi finance. The point when asset prices collapse is the "Minsky moment" (see chapter 2 of Kindleberger and Aliber 2005).

Derivatives such as futures and options can be used to hedge (reduce risk) or speculate. Derivatives, which can be bought on substantial margin, allow considerable speculative opportunities. George Soros bet big by selling short against the British pound in 1992 and probably made a billion dollars. With the help of derivatives, a single trader at a bank could lose a billion dollars quickly, as Nick Leeson did at Barings Bank. Long-Term Capital Management (LTCM) was a hedge fund founded in the 1990s to trade derivative instruments based on sophisticated computer models using massive leverage. The firm was extremely profitable until 1998, when a series of wrong bets led to disaster and required a Federal Reserve-sponsored bailout.

The key point is derivatives transfer risk; in a complex instrument, a sophisticated analysis is needed to determine if risks are actually reduced or compounded. As William Donaldson (chairman of the New York Stock Exchange [NYSE] and later the Securities and Exchange Commission [SEC] chairman) put it, "No matter how much hedging is done, somebody winds up holding the hot potato when the music stops."

An important modern area of speculator is in oil and gas. As energy expert Daniel Yergin (2011, 168) put it:

> The "speculator" is a "non-commercial player"—a market maker, a serious investor, or a trader acting on technical analysis. The speculator plays a crucial role. If there is no speculator, there is no liquidity, no futures market, no one on the other side of the trade, no way for a hedger . . . to buy some insurance in the form of futures against the vagaries of price and fortune.

Derivatives trading in oil futures and options exploded in the twenty-first century. In the United States, much of this activity has been on the New York Mercantile Exchange (NYMEX). A significant part of this futures market is investors such as pension funds or insurance companies using a commodities trade, in part as a bet against possible conflicts in the Middle East and other oil-rich area that could disrupt supply and cause oil prices to spike. Experts claim an "energy premium" exists, caused by these "speculators," beyond normal changes in supply and demand.

See also Bubbles and Busts; Business Cycles; Derivatives; Great Depression; Panic of 1819; Panic of 1837; Panic of 1857; Panic of 1873; Panic of 1893; Panic of 1907; Panics and Depressions

References

Kindleberger, Charles, and R. Alibe. *Manias, Panics, and Crashes: A History of Financial Crises.* 5th ed. Hoboken, NJ: Wiley, 2005.

Knoop, Todd. *Recessions and Depressions: Understanding Business Cycles.* 2nd ed. Santa Barbara, CA: Greenwood, 2010.

Reinhart, Carmen, and Kenneth Rogoff. *This Time Is Different: Eight Centuries of Financial Folly.* Princeton, NJ: Princeton University Press, 2009.

Roubini, Nouriel, and Stephen Mihm. *Crisis Economics: A Crash Course in the Future of Finance.* New York: Penguin Press, 2010.

Yergin, Daniel. *The Quest: Energy, Security, and the Remaking of the Modern World.* New York: Penguin Press, 2011.

Spoils System

The spoils system—patronage—is the practice of a winning political party giving government jobs to reward loyal members and ousting those employed by the departing losing party. New York senator William Marcy (a leader of the Albany Regency and later secretary of state) coined the phrase in 1828 with the victory of Andrew Jackson and his Democratic allies: "To the victor belong the spoils of the enemy."

Political corruption developed at all levels of government, but was particularly entrenched at state and local levels. Political machines developed by party, especially in the major cities by the late nineteenth century with the spoils system the primary driver of power and loyalty. Tammany Hall, the Democratic political machine of New York City, was the earliest, longest, and most infamous. It developed early in the nineteenth century and reached its pinnacle of infamy under Boss Tweed after the Civil War.

As national politics grew increasingly bitter—the 1800 election between sitting President John Adams against sitting Vice President Jefferson proved particularly contentious—and the two-party system emerged dominant, political partisanship and the related mud-slinging filtered down to state and local levels where nastiness and corruption ebbed and flowed ever since. The government impact on business and business corruption moved mainly to the local and state levels in this early period, primarily because most business remained a local affair under the jurisdiction of states.

The "Regency Code" of New York State developed by Martin Van Buren required statewide organization from county committees down to ward committees, with Tammany Hall representing New York City. Patronage provided the primary rewards for the faithful. Van Buren's rise to power in Washington solidified the machine by making both state and federal jobs available. In this political setting, winning was everything and Tammany Hall used every political trick to maintain political dominance. Van Buren, backed by Tammany tactics, was a major force in getting Andrew Jackson elected president in 1828.

The first six presidents, Washington to Adams, made few changes in personnel when they took office. Thomas Jefferson, a Democrat-Republican replacing Federalist John Adams, replaced the most—39. Jackson made major patronage changes, replacing 919, about 10 percent of government employees. He wanted a political culture in agreement with his philosophy. As stated by Meacham (2008, 82), "Jackson saw it as the nation's salvation." A vastly expanded spoils system on continued after the 1828 election. State and local Democrats got the jobs; political opponents were removed.

Under the spoils system, in addition to massive federal patronage, was the common practice of "salary rebates" back to the political party in power. Those wanting patronage jobs would pay on a sliding scale based on job importance and the likelihood for corruption. The Post Office was the largest employer and the sources of massive patronage. Postmaster general became a plum position for machine politicians with many postmaster and other patronage jobs in the offing. The collector of the Port of New York was considered the most lucrative position and therefore the most meaningful presidential appointment. When Democrats were in power, Tammany Hall was particularly involved in the selection.

The worst federal abuses occurred during and after the Civil War. Simon Cameron was senator and the political boss of Pennsylvania; President Lincoln named him secretary of war, one of many of his Republican rivals for president appointed to his cabinet. Corruption in the War Department was rampant under Cameron, criminal misconduct with the Union engaged in a war for its very survival. When the 1862 Revenue Act instituted an income tax, the new Office of Internal Revenue hired 4,000 employees by January 1863. These were patronage jobs, based in part on political payoffs: "Party leaders would hand out jobs from their own states: thus [Treasury Secretary Salmon] Chase approved jobs in Ohio, Lincoln in Illinois, and political boss Thurlow Weed in New York" (Giroux 2012, 92).

Calls for reform intensified after the assassination of President James Garfield by a disgruntled office seeker. The result was the Pendleton Act of 1883 (named for Ohio Democratic senator George Pendleton), which created a Civil Service Commission to evaluate job candidates based on expertise rather than politics. Civil Service at that time covered only about 10 percent of federal positions, with the remainder still based on patronage. However, by 1900 most federal jobs were handled by Civil Service, limiting patronage to senior positions. Of course, the spoils system remained for many state and local governments.

See also Burr, Aaron; Jackson, Andrew; Political Machines; Tammany Hall; Tweed, William ("Boss"); Van Buren, Martin

References

Allen, O. *The Tiger: The Rise and Fall of Tammany Hall*. New York: Addison-Wesley, 1993.

Brands, H. W. *American Colossus: The Triumph of Capitalism, 1865–1900*. New York: Doubleday, 2010.

Giroux, Gary. "Financing the American Civil War: Developing New Tax Sources." *Accounting History* 17, no. 1 (February 2012): 83–104.

Meacham, Jon. *American Lion: Andrew Jackson in the White House*. New York: Random House, 2008.

Stagflation

Two of the major problems of macroeconomics are inflation and unemployment. Stagflation occurs when both are high at the same time. Neo-Keynesian economists believed a trade-off existed between the two, since excess demand results in increased hiring but drives up prices; thus economic policies to reduce unemployment would likely cause inflation rates to rise. When stagflation hit, it was a blow to Keynesian economists.

Beginning in the late 1960s, and particularly in the late 1970s, both inflation and unemployment rose simultaneously. British politician Iain Macleod coined the term "stagflation" in 1964, indicting periods when the economy was floundering while prices were rising sharply. Economist Arthur Okun came up with the misery index (adding the inflation rate to the unemployment rate) as a measure of stagflation. Reasons suggested for the stagflation in the 1970s and 80s included the shock of the oil embargo and resulting increase in energy prices, the end of Bretton Woods Agreement in 1971 and the resulting floating currency rates (that is, no longer tied to gold), an unjustified expansionist monetary policy, and excessive government regulations.

Stagflation proved a major problem throughout most of the 1970s through the mid-1980s. The misery index remained in double digits over the 13-year period 1973–85. The maximum misery (based on annual data) was 22.6 percent in 1979, with both inflation and unemployment over 11 percent. Incumbent president Jimmy Carter lost in 1980 to Ronald Reagan starting his "Reagan Revolution." However, the solution to the inflation problem remained in the hands of Federal Reserve chairman Paul Volcker. Volcker cut the money supply and pushed interest rates to extremely high levels beginning in 1979, a painful solution (that included a "double-dip recession") that ultimately worked. Inflation and interest rates eventually came down, followed by unemployment. The inflation rate, which was 13.5 percent in 1980, fell to 3.2 percent by 1983. The unemployment rate fell from

9.6 percent in 1983 to 5.5 percent in 1988. The misery index eventually fell below 10 percent in 1986 (to 8.9%) and a sustained recovery was under way. The 1980s and1990s proved to be a boom period.

With the subprime meltdown of 2008, the unemployment rate again topped 10 percent and stagflation returned as a concern; this time it was unemployment rather than inflation that was critical. In October 2009, unemployment was 10.1 percent, but inflation was actually a negative 0.2 percent. By October of 2011, unemployment dropped somewhat to 9.0 percent, but the inflation rate was up to 3.9 percent and the misery index was 12.9 percent, reminiscent of the 1970s and 1980s.

See also Bretton Woods Agreement; Federal Reserve System; Gold Standard; Misery Index; Panics and Depressions; Volcker, Paul A., Jr.

References

Dobson, John. "Stagflation." In *Bulls, Bears, Boom, and Bust: A Historical Encyclopedia of American Business Concepts*. Santa Barbara, ABC-CLIO, 2006.

Skidelsky, Robert. *Keynes: The Return of the Master; Why, Sixty Years after His Death, John Maynard Keynes Is the Most Important Economic Thinker for America*. New York: Public Affairs, 2009.

Standard Oil Company

Standard Oil Company (SO) was the integrated oil giant controlling up to 90 percent of American oil (this was achieved about 1880) until its antitrust breakup in 1911. John D. Rockefeller was founder, chairman, and major stockholder when it was founded in 1870 as an Ohio company. The 1911 breakup created many of the largest oil companies that exist today, including ExxonMobil and Chevron.

The Civil War was a boom period for the oil industry, but after the war too many oil wells and refineries existed. Rockefeller, a major owner of refineries, believed that only cooperation across firms (called "conspiracy in restraint of trade" by critics) or consolidation could solve the problem of "ruinous competition." He dissolved his partnership in 1870 and created SO in Ohio. SO bought out many competing refiners, primarily in Cleveland, beginning in 1872. Once SO bought out major rival Clark, Payne and Company, SO became the largest refiner in the world.

SO formed a cartel with the Pennsylvania Railroad in 1871, creating a shell company called South Improvement Company (SIC), believing this a partial solution to too much competition for both refiners and railroads. The Erie and New York Central Railroads joined this conspiracy, along with many refiners. The railroads increased freight rates, but gave secret rebates to the SIC refiners. Each railroad got a specific percentage of traffic from the conspiring refineries. After the existence of SIC was discovered, the Pennsylvania legislature canceled the agreement and

This political cartoon, which appeared in *Puck* magazine in September 1904, depicts the Standard Oil monopoly as an octopus with many tentacles wrapped around the steel, copper, and shipping industries, as well as a state house, and the U.S. Capitol, and one tentacle reaching for the White House. (Library of Congress)

forced SIC to shut down. After that, political bribery became a necessary step to solve legal and political problems. "A tremendous amount of money changed hands as businessmen and legislators trafficked in mutual manipulation" (Chernow 1998, 209).

The oil industry was hit hard by the Panic of 1873, but SO was well positioned because of economies of scale, lower production costs, and plenty of cash. Many refiners sold out to SO, largely out of desperation. Most holdouts were driven out of business by SO. As a result, SO controlled all major refining centers by 1877. Lawsuits against SO and Rockefeller became commonplace. Clarion County, Pennsylvania, indicted Rockefeller and other SO executives in 1879 on conspiracy to monopolize and manipulate prices. SO executives in Pennsylvania were arrested and had to post bond. SO settled many disputes with drillers and refiners over buyouts and rebates out of court.

SO accumulated subsidiaries across the country. Because of limiting state laws, running this empire proved difficult. Regulatory investigations and other legal problems further hindered operations. SO was the parent company, but outlawed from owning corporations of other states; SO did have many out-of-state companies, but kept the information hidden. Legal solutions emerged, beginning with the trust, created by SO lawyer Samuel Dodd. The Standard trust agreement, signed at the start of 1882, created a board of trustees of nine members for the parent. The board received the stock of the 14 wholly-owned subsidiaries and shares in partially owned companies. The stockholders (not the corporations) received trust certificates in lieu of shares of the subsidiaries. Each subsidiary operated as a semi-independent corporation with a separate board of directors.

The trust worked because the subsidiaries followed orders. The board of trustees ran a complex system of committees specializing in the various aspects of manufacturing, transportation, and marketing. This use of a top-down structure under professional managers became the basic model for most big businesses during much of the twentieth century.

SO sought efficient operations. Smaller, inefficient plants were closed and refining centered on huge, modern plants in Cleveland, Philadelphia, and Bayonne, New Jersey. Cost accounting measures of performance from individual plants encouraged competition. Tracking unit costs by plant would determine relative efficiency. Oil moved increasingly by cheaper pipelines rather than by railroad. A vertical structure included a well-developed marketing plan. Middlemen were eliminated to increase revenue, product quality, and service. Cheap kerosene lamps and other products were produced to increase demand. As production and transportation costs declined, Rockefeller lowered retail prices. After he retired from active management in the mid-1890s, his successors were less willing to pass on cost savings.

SO and the railroads came under investigation by several states, providing public information on oil practices available to crusading journalists, regulators, and attorneys eager to sue. David Watson, attorney general of Ohio, discovered the illegality of SO's trust and he filed a petition against SO with the state supreme court in 1890 seeking to dissolve the giant. The state supreme court renounced the trust agreement in 1892. With New York's attorney general ready to follow suit, SO dissolved the trust.

In place of the trust, SO took advantage of New Jersey's new incorporation laws allowing holding shares in out-of-state companies. The reconstituted Standard Oil of New Jersey became the new parent, acquiring all the shares of the affiliates. The old executive committee dissolved and "elected" directors of Standard Oil of New Jersey. When New Jersey amended the incorporation laws, SO became a holding company with Standard Oil of New Jersey controlling all the affiliates in 1899.

Regulators continued to issue lawsuits. Rockefeller considered these lawsuits invalid and "fell back on his all-purpose explanation that the suits filed against him were just extortion rackets posing as public service" (Chernow, 1998, 426). SO spent large sums on political payoffs, to stop further regulations and lawsuits. Ohio Republican senator Mark ("Dollar Mark") Hanna, a Rockefeller friend and a onetime oil refiner, unsuccessfully lobbied Attorney General Watson to drop the 1890 suit against SO. Politicians on the SO payroll included Ohio senator Joseph Foraker, Senator Matthew Quay, and Representative Joseph Sibley, both from Pennsylvania.

After Rockefeller retired from full-time management in the mid-1890s, retaining the title of president, SO vice president John Archbold became the real chief executive officer. Archbold proved to be more ruthless than Rockefeller in terms of both pricing products and illegal acts such as railroad rebates (specifically outlawed by the Elkins Act of 1903 and the Hepburn Act of 1906). Archbold paid "fees" to various politicians to limit political damage, and William Randolph Hearst broke the story of Archbold's bribery in the *New York American*. Muckraking journalists Henry Demarest Lloyd and Ida Tarbell wrote popular books about Rockefeller and SO. Lloyd's was an antibusiness populist rant, while Tarbell proved more balanced and better researched; she considered Rockefeller and SO executives competent, but corrupt. Less balanced were the rants she described from all those hating Rockefeller, usually from early events around eliminating competitors and railroad rebates.

The Justice Department sued SO in 1906 under the Sherman Act, charging the company with conspiracy in restraint of trade and monopolizing the oil industry. Evidence included railroad rebates, predatory pricing, buying out or ruining competitors, and secret ownership of companies assumed to be independent. Several state suits followed the federal lead. The federal circuit court ruled against SO in 1909. The Supreme Court in 1911 upheld the circuit court's ruling—SO would be broken up, creating 33 independent SO subsidiaries.

Rockefeller was on the golf course when he heard the news of the Supreme Court decision. Turning to his playing partner, he said, "Buy Standard Oil." The SO shares were replaced by an equivalent amount in each of the new independent corporations. Most of the new companies traded on the New York Stock Exchange. Since they usually issued annual reports (unlike the original SO), investors saw the actual holdings. High dividends were paid, and within a year, the stock prices of most of the new oil companies double and continued up.

Standard Oil of New Jersey (later Exxon) remained the world's biggest oil company. The new Standard Oil of New York (later Mobil) continued to share offices with Standard Oil of New Jersey at 26 Broad. At the end of the twentieth century, Exxon merged with Mobil, still the biggest oil company and, for a time, the largest corporation in the world. In 2012, ExxonMobil has a market capitalization of almost $400 billion, second to Apple in market cap. Among the other 30 new companies were Standard Oil of California (Chevron), Continental Oil (Conoco), Atlantic Refining (ARCO and then Sun), SOHIO, and Marathon. Eventually, these separate companies became real competitors. Most merged to form even larger oil giants: ExxonMobil, ChevronTexaco, Continental now part of ConocoPhillips, and Atlantic Richfield and SO of Ohio now part of British Petroleum.

See also Antitrust; Corporations; Panic of 1873; Railroads, Nineteenth Century; Rockefeller, John Davison; Sherman Antitrust Act of 1890

References

Chernow, Ron. *Titan: The Life of John D. Rockefeller, Sr.* New York: Random House, 1998.

Dobson, John. "John Davison Rockefeller." In *Bulls, Bears, Booms, and Busts: A Historical Encyclopedia of American Business Concepts*. Santa Barbara, CA: ABC-CLIO, 2006.

State Banks, Early

Nineteenth-century banks were experiments in commercial banking, from extremely conservative to wildcat banking. Each state had its own banking rules and chartering requirements. Many served as models for future banking laws, while others allowed despicable practices with incentives that encouraged widespread fraud. Each bank issued its own paper money (usually convertible into gold or silver coins), which allowed considerable abuse including counterfeiting.

Only a few banks were chartered in the eighteenth century and all were well capitalized with substantial reserve requirements and conservative lending practices. They played a significant role during the early years of the country by creating a stable banking system, even though banks were not used by most people. By 1805 there were 75 banks, increasing to 90 by 1811. Conservative banking continued through the War of 1812.

Bank of America in New York City was the largest bank in 1815 with capital of $4 million. The bank charter caused a scandal when several Federalist politicians were accused of bribery. The commercial centers of the country had the largest banks, and bigger banks often monitored the other city and regional banks to limit corruption. New York had seven banks with $11.8 million in capital, followed by Boston with six banks and $8.6 million in capital, Philadelphia with eight banks and total capital of $7.7 million, and Baltimore, with eight banks and capital of $6.8 million (Perkins 1994, 274).

State banks were chartered at an expansive rate after the War of 1812, a period of financial innovation. Each state ran its own banking experiment, which included sound banking in some states, but bad ideas and banking collapses in others. Some states had substantial government regulation and bank supervision; other states, virtually none. There were periods of paper-currency explosions, with thousands of issues of different bank currencies, and bank failures on a wide scale. Some states outlawed banking.

Partly because of the "experimental" banking system, the period saw rapid economic growth, including cycles of boom and bust. With increased competition, banks expanded their services to farmers, retailers, and manufacturers with the accompanying greater risks. Many of the builders of canals and later railroads got initial financing from some of these new state banks.

Initially, new banks required specific state legislation for each charter, making the process a game of politics and power. Charters typically went to "Federalist banks" when they were in control, then "Democratic banks" (or Whig banks) when they were elected. Democrat governor Martin Van Buren of New York and his "Albany Regency" proved the most infamous, chartering 64 new banks (and rechartering 29) between 1829 and 1836 and concomitant allegations of bribery. Both equity shares in the proposed bank and cash bribes proved effective (Bodenhorn 2006). Eventually formal procedures for chartering corporations on a nonpartisan basis were established, with New York starting the process in 1838 with the Free Banking Act.

Generally, urban banks faced more competition and tended to operate conservatively. Rural banks, more common in the South and West, took greater risks and many got the reputation as "wildcat" and "frontier" banks. Lower reserves, greater loan volume using banknotes, and devious techniques to reduce gold redemptions meant promoters could borrow more money (and more likely go bankrupt).

Each bank had its own notes engraved, with paper printed in convenient denominations. These would be issued as loans, while customers could also deposit the money and write checks. Banks usually backed their notes by holding 20 percent or more in reserves in gold and silver. Early on, states often left the amount of reserves up to the bank, but later regulations usually required specific minimum percentages.

By the early 1850s, 1,000 state banks operated, a bonanza for engravers and printers. When presented for payment to merchants or other banks, the notes were usually discounted based on such criteria as bank reputation (usually lower discounts for urban banks) and distance away from the issuing bank. Note brokers existed in most cities, specializing in "correct" discount rates and bank reference manuals called "banknote reporters" listed the various paper in circulation and necessary discounts.

Counterfeiting added to the abuse. Thousands of banknotes circulated; multiple counterfeiting schemes emerged. The counterfeiters could modify existing notes to look like higher-denomination bills or pass on real notes of failed banks. Engraving counterfeiters could imitate specific notes of banks or print notes of banks that existed only in the con artist's creative imagination. "Utterers" passed these bills; the banks hired "snaggers" to catch them. Counterfeit notes were also listed in banknote reporters, which included reproductions and counterfeit detecting suggestions.

Various reform techniques were attempted by states, including bank associations and new state regulations. The Suffolk Bank of Boston around 1819 would not redeem notes of "country banks" unless they kept deposits at Suffolk; otherwise, Suffolk demanded specie (gold). When other Boston banks affiliated with Suffolk, Suffolk became a "clearing bank" for local notes, establishing a sense of uniformity across New England paper currency.

A Safety Fund was established in New York in 1829, including a type of deposit insurance. Member banks (those chartered by the state) paid an annual premium. The Safety Fund paid any remaining debts after liquidation when banks failed. During the Panic of 1837, total losses exceeded the amount available in the Safety Fund and the state bailed out the fund. Similar insurance plans were used in other states. Other states required detailed periodic bank examinations, but not insurance. Some states established bank commissions to supervise and examine the books of state banks. Despite these efforts, banking involved many hazards. Generally, the farther from the coast, the greater the potential hazards.

National banks were created during the Civil War and, beginning at that time, federal regulations and monitoring became more common. The Federal Reserve System as a central bank was not established until 1914.

See also Bank of North America; Bank of the United States, First; Bank of the United States, Second; Counterfeiting; Federal Reserve System; Gold Standard; Paper Money

References

Allen, Larry. "Counterfeit Money." In *The Encyclopedia of Money*. 2nd ed. Santa Barbara, CA: ABC-CLIO, 2009.

Bodenhorn, Howard. "Bank Chartering and Political Corruption in Antebellum New York: Free Banking as Reform." In *Corruption and Reform: Lessons from America's Economic History*. Edited by Edward Glaeser and Claudia Goldin, 231–258. Washington: National Bureau of Economic Research, 2006.

Goodwin, Jason. *Greenback: The Almighty Dollar and the Invention of America*. New York: Holt, 2003.

Perkins, Edwin. *American Public Finance and Financial Services, 1700–1815*. Columbus: Ohio State University Press, 1994.

Stock Crash of 1987

The crash happened on October 19, 1987—Black Monday. After a half-decade bull market, the largest stock price collapse occurred as the Dow Jones Industrial Average (Dow) dropped 508 points, almost 23 percent, to 1,739. Experts blame portfolio insurance, a derivative play designed to limit losses when stock prices fall.

Beginning in 1982 (the Dow closed at 777 on August 13, 1982, the decade low) the stock market boomed, thanks to low inflation and interest rates, plus reduced taxes. The Dow started 1987 at 1,927, up 21 percent from the previous year. The Dow continued up, hitting a high of 2,722 on August 25. September prices dropped to the 2,500 to 2,600 range. Friday, October 16, was a bad day, down 4.6 percent for the day and 9.1 percent for the week on high volume. The Dow had dropped 17.5 percent since the August 25 high.

On Monday morning, October 19, stock markets around the world dropped before the New York financial markets opened. Tokyo had a record-breaking loss, as did London—prices off 10 percent on massive selling. U.S. futures trading began at the Chicago Mercantile Exchange (Merc) a half hour before the New York Stock Exchange (NYSE) opened, with the key indicator being the Standard & Poor's (S&P) 500 stock index futures. The futures were new derivative instruments started in the early 1980s. Within minutes, the S&P 500 futures dropped 18 percent. Every trader seemingly had sell orders and pandemonium reigned. The chaos spread to New York.

When the NYSE opened a half hour after the Merc, specialists were swamped with sell orders, delaying the opening of trades on individual stocks. Pension, mutual funds, and other institutional investors led the selling, mainly in block trades of hundreds of thousands of shares. Without buyers, the main tool of the stock specialist is to lower price until buyers are found; that meant prices kept dropping. Small investors, once they heard the news, were equally panicked and started selling, mainly in the afternoon.

Portfolio insurance (PI) was a major product in the 1980s, with large, conservative investors using it to limit stock losses. The techniques called for selling the S&P 500 futures index short to offset stock losses. PI is called dynamic hedging because it requires continuous changes in the hedge as conditions change. Since the market dropped on Friday the 16th, substantial futures selling was calculated over the weekend according to the PI models, to be implemented at the start of trading on Monday. There were too many sellers having the same strategy clamoring for identical trades. As summarized by Bookstaber (2007, 18–19):

> Portfolio insurance firms sold nearly half a billion dollars of S&P futures, amounting to about 30% of the public volume. The futures prices dropped precipitously and the stock market had

Headlines about the stock market plunge of Monday, October 19, 1987. Wall Street was devastated by the 508-point plunge, the largest percentage drop in history (down 23%). (AP/ Wide World Photos)

not even opened. About 15 minutes into the futures market decline, we started to see activity from an unexpected quarter, cash-futures arbitrageurs. Their attempts to capitalize on the apparent chasm between the cash and futures prices would be the red flag that triggered the stampede in the NYSE.

Arbitrageurs, not a worldwide panic, made matters worse, with their sell orders based on the Friday closing prices. The strategy was to sell short, assuming the sell order would be at the Friday close (the hedge play to simultaneously buy the futures long at the lower prices). Since many stocks were late to open and prices collapsed, the arbitrageurs recorded substantial losses and made the collapse worse. As prices kept dropping, the PI paradigm called for more selling. According to Bookstaber, PI programs sold over a billion dollars in futures that afternoon. The S&P 500 futures performed even worse than stocks, down 29 percent for the day.

Some experts predicted a depression and the stock collapse continued. Others thought Black Monday an anomoly with no lasting effects. They, in fact, were correct. October 19 was the worst of four down trading days in a row. New Federal Reserve (Fed) chairman Alan Greenspan flooded the market with cash after Black Monday, the first "Greenspan put." Beginning on Tuesday the market went up and on October 21 was up over 10 percent. The Dow closed at 1939, up slightly from the start of the year but down 40 percent from the August 25 high. The economy kept booming, with gross domestic product up 3.4 percent for the year.

In addition to program trading, especially PI, other factors were involved in the crash. The market fell the previous week. Market chaos existed in Asia and Europe before opening in the United States Monday morning. A correction was not unexpected, with the Dow tripling over the decade and up 40 percent for the year in September. Reported bad news included rising interest rates to support a declining dollar. Interest rates on long-term Treasuries were still high, making bonds an attractive alternative to stocks.

Several investigations were started including the Brady Commission, named for future Treasury Secretary Nicholas Brady. Prior to October 19, the worst day for the market had been Black Tuesday, October 29, 1929. That day the Dow was down 13.5 percent. That market collapse led to the Great Depression. By comparison, the Dow dropped almost 23 percent on Black Monday. The market had different regulators: the stock markets came under Securities and Exchange Commission (SEC) scrutiny, while the Commodity Futures Trading Commission regulated the futures market. Brady wanted a single regulatory agency such as the Fed to coordinate all markets, as well as "circuit breakers" to shut down markets after some level of market collapse. SEC chairman David Ruder called for higher margin requirements on stock-index futures and SEC regulation of this market. Greenspan favored PI and other computer-trading techniques and generally thought markets should not be regulated.

American markets survived this crisis and no major regulatory changes made. Financial innovations were increasingly quantitative and little understood by financial leaders. The new derivatives and other methods were adopted when short-term profits could be made with no understanding of the long-term risks. Throughout the rest of the 1980s and well into the twenty-first century, as volatility and risks increased, financial markets became less regulated. Unfortunately, future financial crises would be related to specific new derivative instruments and other complex financial innovations.

See also Commercial Banks after the Federal Reserve; Crash of 1929; Derivatives; Federal Reserve System; Greenspan, Alan; New York Stock Exchange; Panics and Depressions; Portfolio Insurance

References

Bookstaber, Richard. *A Demon of Our Own Design: Markets, Hedge Funds, and the Perils of Financial Innovation*. Hoboken, NJ: Wiley. 2007.

Hafer, Rik. "Crash of 1987." In *The Federal Reserve System: An Encyclopedia*. Santa Barbara, CA: ABC-CLIO, 2005.

McMurray, Scott, and Robert Rose, "The Crash of '87: Chicago's 'Shadow Markets' Led Free Fall in a Plunge That Began Right at Opening." In *Panic: The Story of Modern Financial Insanity*. Edited by Michael Lewis, 20–24. New York: Norton, 2009.

Stock Option Manipulation

Corporations often grant managers and employees stock options. Options permit the holder to purchase stock at a set price (called the exercise price) over some fixed time period. The most common price is the closing market price of the stock at the issue date of the options. The use of stock options is a form of employee compensation, widely used especially in high-tech companies. The advantage of the options is the holder participates in the success with no risk if the stock price collapses. As the stock rises, the value of the options increases. If the stock price plummets, the holder does not exercise the option (and therefore does not experience a loss).

The major advantage of options to the corporations was the idea of "free compensation." Prior to 2006, as long as the exercise price was the market price or higher at issue date, no compensation expense had to be recorded in the financial statements. In terms of the income statement, it was a zero cost form of management compensation. The Financial Accounting Standards Board (FASB) eliminated this advantage with State of Financial Accounting Standards (SFAS) No. 123R, which became effective in 2006. Options are now recognized as a compensation expense. In theory, holding options should make the incentives of the managers identical to the owners of the company. Since the benefit of options is future ownership and managers increase options value by increasing the value of the company, management incentives should parallel owner incentives. Firms can recruit successful, high-priced executives and retain existing managers and employees by issuing stock options liberally. It is a relatively long-term focus, because options vest only after some period of time (typically three to five years).

Stock options as a form of employee compensation have been used for decades, but were not common until the 1990s, especially desirable when income tax rates were lowered with the Tax Reform Act of 1986. The Revenue Act of 1950 made options for employees both legal and practical. As stock prices started rising in the 1990s, options became more lucrative—and the compensation of choice for executives. Options were also a deduction for tax purposes to the corporation when exercised by the holder. Start-ups became big option issuers (in lieu of larger salaries), while corporations large and small added options to executive pay packages. Before the stock bubble of 2000, some 65 companies each had over a billion shares of options outstanding. With the stock market crash beginning in early 2000, the price of stocks and therefore the value of options dropped precipitously and often became worthless (the term "underwater" was widely used).

Economics theory indicated that options give employees a greater incentive to promote the interests of shareholders. Harvard professor Michael Jensen was an early proponent and coauthored an influential *Harvard Business Review* article in 1990. The school of hard knocks proved that options made meeting quarterly earnings targets an executive obsession—and the prime motive for extreme earnings manipulation. Jensen later recanted on options somewhat, but insisted that executives still should hold considerable equity interests in various forms.

The FASB decided to require the expensing of options in the early 1990s and a political fight was on. As former Securities and Exchange Commission (SEC) chairman Arthur Levitt put it, "Whenever the FASB tried to crack down by tightening accounting standards, it ran into a phalanx of corporate, Congressional, and auditor opposition" (Levitt 2002, 107). High-tech and other corporate lobbyists bombarded the SEC and Congress. Lobbyists claimed the FASB was "anti-business"; earnings per share would drop; American firms would not be competitive; innovation would stop. Connecticut senator Joe Lieberman led the charge, with bipartisan help from other politicians. Lieberman's legislation would have crippled the FASB, requiring the SEC to ratify every FASB pronouncement and specifically barring the SEC from enforcing FASB's option expensing requirement. Levitt advised the FASB to back off, which the board did.

The result was SFAS No. 123 in 1995, which allows companies to either (1) expense the options based on Black-Scholes or other options pricing models, or (2) provide *pro forma* disclosures in the notes, that is, show the calculate net income as if options were expensed. Most companies used note disclosure rather than expensing options, although some companies including Dow 30 giants General Electric and Microsoft switched to expensing options.

When employees exercise stock options, the employee pays cash to the company equal to the exercise (or strike) price determined at the date of grant. The company records this transaction as an increase in paid-in capital. In addition, the difference between the market price and exercise price (essentially the "profit" from holding the options) is a tax-deductible item.

Lowenstein (2004) cited Disney chief executive officer (CEO) Michael Eisner as the option king for poor performance. During the 1990s and early 2000s, Eisner collected some $800 million in options and other compensation while Disney's stock price fell. As Lowenstein (2004, 51) put it, "Never has a CEO reaped such a fortune from such prolonged mediocrity." Eisner had competition. Oracle CEO Larry Ellison made $706 million in 2001, while Oracle's stock return was a negative 57 percent. Enron executives cashed out before the company's bankruptcy in 2001, with similar stories at other failing companies. The scandals at Enron and the rest were linked directly to the fixation on stock price. The evidence suggests that corporate executives insisted on always meeting analyst forecasts, because stock prices could get pummeled when targets were missed by as little as a penny a share, a disastrous short-term focus.

Giroux (2006, 93) analyzed the four tech companies from the Dow Jones Industrial Average (Dow 30), all expected to be large issuers of options. These are summarized for fiscal year 2004.

Table 21. Stock Option Manipulation

Company	Stock Options Outstanding (millions)	Shares Outstanding (millions)	Options to Shares Outstanding
Microsoft	949	10,771	8.8%
Hewlett-Packard	550	2,911	18.9
Intel	884	6,253	14.1
IBM	252	1,646	15.3

Potential dilution (of shares) is estimated using the ratio of options to shares outstanding. Microsoft has the lowest percentage at 8.8 percent, because outstanding options are down from 1,796 million options in 2001. Beginning in 2004, Microsoft shifted to restricted stock in place of options and allowed employees to transfer options to J. P. Morgan. The other three tech firms have hundreds of millions of options outstanding. Across the Dow 30 outstanding options averaged 9.0 percent of shares outstanding.

Several stock ownership alternatives to options exist, including restricted stock, phantom stock, and stock appreciation rights (SARs). They tend to be more flexible than stock options, and the benefits (usually increases in fair value) are usually treated as compensation expenses by the corporations. Restricted stock gives an employee the futures right to shares of stock (the shares eventually vest and no longer subject to the restrictions). Vesting usually involves working for a certain number of years or until specific performance goals have been met. Restricted stock makes holders closer to normal shareholders because restricted stock retains value even if the stock price goes down.

Phantom stock and SARs are promises to pay a bonus (usually cash), usually based on value of the stock. Earnings management concerns exists with all of these. Of most concern are the relative level of compensation to senior executives and the specific terms of compensation agreements. The actual and potential rewards should be based on real performance. These are summarized in Table 21 (for fiscal-year 2004).

See also Accounting Standards; Financial Accounting Standards Board (FASB); Revenue Recognition and Manipulation; Securities and Exchange Commission (SEC); Stock Options Scandals

References

Dobson, John. "Stock Options." In *Bulls, Bears, Boom, and Bust: A Historical Encyclopedia of American Business Concepts*. Santa Barbara, CA: ABC-CLIO, 2006.

Giroux, Gary. *Earnings Magic and the Unbalance Sheet: The Search for Financial Reality*. Hoboken, NJ: Wiley, 2006.

Levitt, Arthur, and Patricia Dwyer. *Take on the Street: What Wall Street and Corporate America Don't Want You to Know*. New York: Pantheon Books, 2002.

Lowenstein, Roger. *Origins of the Crash: The Great Bubble and Its Undoing*. New York: Penguin Press, 2004.

"Perfect Payday: Options Scorecard." *Wall Street Journal*, September 4, 2007. http://online.wsj.com.

Stock Option Scandals

Corporate stock options are employee benefits allowing employees to acquire shares in the firm's stock at a set price, which can be exercised at a later date. Executives at Enron, WorldCom, and other high-fraud companies had large options stakes, which influenced their behavior and were in part responsible for earnings manipulation and ultimate collapse. The incentives were clear: Meeting quarterly earnings targets was essential to ensure the massive option payoffs. If earnings forecasts were not met, the stock price could collapse, costing the executives millions.

Beginning in 2006, companies had to expense options, making them less of an earnings manipulation issue because of the reduced incentives to issue options. Incentives associated with options did not disappear, only the amount of options issued. Especially during 2005, speed vesting became the trend. Since companies had to expense options beginning in 2006, speed vesting allows early vesting (and exercising of options); the options vested in 2005 required no expensing.

Mid-decade option scandals included backdating and spring-loading—how companies gave options to executives for additional illicit gains. In backdating, the grant date is set to an earlier date when the stock price was lower. When the holders exercise the options, this increases their gain. Spring-loading occurs when companies give options just before good news, expected to boost stock price. The *Wall Street Journal* reported some 186 companies handing out millions of options to executives and other employees shortly after September 11, 2001, when stock prices dropped. The Securities and Exchange Commission (SEC) investigated 130 companies by 2006 for option manipulation, including Apple and Dell Computer.

Exercise backdating became a new wrinkle: executives would fraudulently claim to have exercised options when the stock price was lower, giving them lower taxes on capital gains. Given the tax angle, the Internal Revenue Service and the Justice Department investigated many of these tax frauds.

See also Accounting Fraud; Enron; Financial Accounting Standards Board (FASB); Securities and Exchange Commission (SEC); Stock Option Manipulation; WorldCom

References

Dobson, John. "Stock Options." In *Bulls, Bears, Boom, and Bust: A Historical Encyclopedia of American Business Concepts*. Santa Barbara, CA: ABC-CLIO, 2006.

Forella, Charles, and James Bandler. "The Perfect Payday." *Wall Street Journal*, March 18, 2006. http://online.wsj.com.

Giroux, Gary. *Earnings Magic and the Unbalance Sheet: The Search for Financial Reality.* Hoboken, NJ: Wiley, 2006.

"Perfect Payday: Options Scorecard." *Wall Street Journal*, September 4, 2007. http://online.wsj.com.

Structured Finance

Structured finance is the financial practice of bundling financial assets (such as mortgages or automobile loans) to create financial asset pools to resell to credit investors. The process is called securitization. Typically a bank either originates or buys outstanding loans or mortgages, which are assets (receivables) to the bank. The bank will seek bond ratings on these packages by credit risk tranches, with the tranches least likely to have defaults rated AAA. Principal and interest collected from debtors are paid to investors periodically. Securities backed by mortgages are mortgage-backed securities (MBSs); other categories of receivables are called asset-backed securities (ABSs). The use of structured finance mushroomed in the twenty-first century and became a major factor in the subprime meltdown of 2008.

The Department of Housing and Urban Development (HUD) developed the first version of MBSs sold by the Government National Mortgage Association (Ginnie Mae) in 1970. First Boston, the first bank to use structured finance, began by repackaging auto loans for GMAC in 1985. Following First Boston, banks increasingly used securitization for standardized consumer products including auto loans and credit card receivables. The Community Reinvestment Act of 1977 encouraged banks to offer mortgages to low income families. These were soon securitized, becoming the precursors of the subprime loan debacle. Securitization approached $2 trillion by the end of 2004, roughly 8 percent of total bond market debt.

The purpose of securitization is to pool assets to create credit risk slices (called tranches). Assuming widely disbursed assets, risk is diversifiable and can be transferred to investors with varying degrees of risk tolerance. Banks used these to sell off standardized loans, including credit card receivables, mortgages, auto loans, student loans, and, to a lesser extent, corporate debt. The marketers stressed the many benefits: flexible products to create specific risk-return characteristics, specific maturities and asset types, diversification. As described by Jobst (2007, 3), "Structured finance contributes to a more complete capital market by offering any mean-variance trade-off along the efficient frontier of optimal diversification at lower transactions cost." Unfortunately, structured finance created complexity and downside, typically little understood by investors.

Forty percent of Moody's 2006 profits of $750 million came from rating structured finance instruments. There were few banks issuing these MBSs and other securitized portfolios, so a continuing relationship between the banks and Moody's suggested considerable accommodation; otherwise the banks would move all the business to S&P or Fitch. In other words, a considerable conflict of interests existed. As put by McLean and Nocera (2010, 111), "Moody's and the other rating agencies turned their backs on their own integrity." Moody's used statistical models and simulation to evaluate the expected payouts, delinquencies, and so on for the portfolio. The model, developed in 2002, used only recent history; for example, no equation existed incorporating the possibility housing prices could actually go down (even Moody's knew falling prices would torpedo the MBS market).

Lowenstein (2010) described a single MBS instrument as "Subprime XYZ." He captured the dismal history of the rating process by Moody's, which included some 13 percent delinquencies by spring 2007, with the default rate rising. Losses were estimated to be three times original projections. Because Subprime XYZ was typical, Moody's downgraded massive amounts of previously high-rated MBSs. Many of the AAA tranches made their way to junk status. Moody's improved the model in 2007, just in time for it to be useless. This market had collapsed.

Unsold MBSs and other ABSs could be repackaged as collateralized debt obligation (CDO). The CDO market started in 1987 when Drexel Burnham issued the first one for a soon-to-be-bankrupt savings and loan (S&L). Bankers packaging MBSs found low-rated tranches hard to sell. The unsold tranches of dozens or hundreds of MBSs (and other junk) were combined into new CDOs and these securities received separate bond ratings. Although these represented the riskiest of the subprime market, the majority still received AAA ratings. The perceived advantage of the CDO to investors was the high interest yield, initially about 3 percent higher than a comparably rated corporate bond. Investors looking only at yield and high ratings bought massive amounts of these, actually driving down the relative yields. Given the predatory practices used to originate these securities and the CDO processes used, these were virtually guaranteed to fail.

The government encouraged home ownership beginning in the 1970s, especially for low-income families. Lending restrictions were relaxed especially in the 1990s and early twenty-first century to encourage alternatives to standard mortgage terms. Interest rates were especially low over this period, promoting low mortgage rates and lower borrowing costs to banks and other intermediaries. The investment banks had figured out the most profitable ways to securitize mortgages. No limit seemed to exist on the amount of mortgages a bank could package and resell, given the accommodating rating agencies. In 2004, the Securities and Exchange Commission (SEC) eliminated rules on the relative leverage of investment banks; they soon increased their own portfolios of MBSs and other risky investments (often the securities they could not sell, especially the high-risk mortgage tranches), funded by cheap, short-term borrowing. Mortgage finance companies had ready customers, and investors were willing to buy anything mortgage related and AAA with few questions asked.

Citigroup had securitized transactions recorded as special-purpose entities (SPEs—that is, off-balance-sheet) of $2,154 billion in 2006—almost $2.2 trillion! More than half were in MBSs and CDOs ($1.3 trillion), but also in credit cards, auto loans, student loans, and corporate debt. Citi had total assets at the time of $1.9 trillion and total equity of only $120 billion—in other words, substantial leverage (over $30 of assets including SPEs for every dollar of equity) with vast amounts of high-risk assets. According to Citi's 10-K, securitized financial assets purchased from clients created "new financing opportunities."

See also Bond Ratings on Structured Finance; Bubbles and Euphoria; Collateralized Debt Obligation (CDO); Credit Risk; Federal Reserve System; Panics and Depressions; Risk and Risk Management; Special-Purpose Entities; Subprime Meltdown

References

Allen, Larry. "Credit Ratings." In *The Encyclopedia of Money*. 2nd ed. Santa Barbara, CA: ABC-CLIO, 2009.

Coval, Joshua, Jakub Jurek, and Erik Stafford. "The Economics of Structured Finance." Harvard Business School Working Paper 09-060. 2008.

Hafer, Rik. "Bond Rating." In *The Federal Reserve System: An Encyclopedia*. Santa Barbara, CA: ABC-CLIO, 2005.

Jobst, Andreas. "A Primer on Structured Finance." *Journal of Derivatives and Hedge Funds* 13, no. 3 (2007): 199–213.

Lowenstein, Roger. *The End of Wall Street*. New York: Penguin Press, 2010.

McLean, Bethany, and Joe Nocera. *All the Devils Are Here: The Hidden History of the Financial Crisis*. New York: Portfolio/Penguin, 2010.

Subprime Meltdown

The subprime meltdown was an early indicator of the financial crisis that reached its peak in 2008–9, based on rising mortgage delinquencies especially for subprime loans. Housing prices peaked in 2006 after a steep (and unprecedented) rise early in the century. The collapse of housing prices, rising delinquencies, and foreclosures led to a crisis of large financial firms. The result was a severe recession, the failure of large banks, the freezing up of credit markets, and a multitrillion-dollar bailout of the financial industry.

Concerns with subprime lending started by 2005, especially the lack of appropriate documentation and review by mortgage companies. By the end of 2005, housing prices started peaking in certain markets and began to slowly decline, ensuring the collapse of the subprime market given the abusive practices being used. The subprime crisis became apparent in 2006 as construction and sales fell. The percentage of subprime loans actually increased in 2006 (as prime mortgages declined), over $600 billion for the year, despite the negative housing news. Mortgage companies started failing as revenues did not cover overhead, while the subprime meltdown began in late 2006. Defaults and foreclosures rose precipitously in 2007 and dozens of mortgage companies went bankrupt. Two Bear

Stearns hedge funds collapsed in July. By mid-year the global nature of the sub-prime crisis became apparent, as major banks from France to China had large sub-prime portfolios disrupting their standard operations. Early in 2008, the National Association of Realtors announced that 2007 had the largest decline in existing house sales in a quarter century, plus a nationwide decline in home prices.

The biggest mortgage finance company, Countrywide Financial, originated 20 percent of all mortgages in the United States by 2006, with a major focus on the subprime market. The company increased leveraged (assets were 14.5 times equity) and most of the liabilities were short term, relying on overnight money. When this market dried up in the middle of 2007, the company avoided bankruptcy when Bank of America (B of A) acquired Countrywide early in 2008 for $4 billion. Several states sued Countrywide for deceptive practices, and former Countrywide chairman and chief executive officer (CEO) Angelo Mozilo faced charges of insider trading and securities fraud in mid-2009. Mozilo sold some $129 million in stock while Countrywide bought its own shares (treasury stock, which props up the stock price). In addition, the "friends of Angelo" program gave special mortgage rates to politicians, including powerful senators Chris Dodd and Kent Conrad.

Fraud dominated the mortgage story. According to the Financial Crimes Enforcement Network (FinCen) of the Treasury Department (2006), mortgage fraud increased 1,400 percent from 1997 to 2005 based on suspicious activity reports (SARs), with almost 26,000 SARs filed in 2005. Much of the increased activity related to greater levels of subprime loans and predatory practices including false statements, material misrepresentations, appraisal fraud, forged documents, and "straw buyers" (used to conceal identity).

The subprime crisis became obvious with the collapse of Bear Stearns early in 2008. Bear Stearns became one of the most successful investment banks, based on a relatively simple strategy of focusing on mortgages. Net income for 2006 at $2 billion rose over 40 percent from the previous year. According to William Cohan (2009), Bear became a "House of Cards." After a great year in 2006, 2007 turned down with income of only $212 million. Total assets for 2007 were $395 billion (not counting off-balance-sheet investments), with stockholders' equity only $12 billion—a leverage ratio of 33.5. A later J. P. Morgan analysis suggested that some $220 billion of Bear's assets were "toxic" (Cohan 2009, 94).

The Federal National Mortgage Association (Fannie Mae) and Federal Home Loan Mortgage Corp. (Freddie Mac) were government-sponsored enterprises (GSEs) established to guarantee and buy mortgages. By 2008, they held or guaranteed over $5 trillion worth of mortgages, about half the total in the United States. Many of these were subprime and large amounts were in default and subject to foreclosure. Well into the subprime crisis, Fannie increased its holdings of subprime loans and mortgages with less than 10 percent down, with the mortgages often poorly documented. The majority of the losses Fannie took in 2008 related to loans bought in 2006–7.

When the housing and mortgage markets fell, the GSEs took big losses. Fannie's 2007 10-K showed total assets of $883 billion and equity of $44 billion (leverage of

20 to 1) and a net loss of $21.6 billion for the year. Most of the mortgage securities were off-balance-sheet (plus additional loan guarantees), not directly visible to investors but still available for big losses. The 2008 annual report proved even worse. Assets increased to $912 billion and equity a negative $15 billion (negative equity is a reasonable definition of a bankrupt company) following a net loss of $60 billion for the year. Freddie was about the same size and in about the same shape. Total assets for 2008 were $851 billion, with negative equity of $31 billion following a 2008 net loss of $51 billion. The red ink continued in 2009 and beyond.

In July 2008, Treasury Secretary Paulson asked Congress for GSE reforms and authority to pump money to Fannie and Freddie, which they granted with the Housing and Economic Recovery Act (HERA) in July 2008. With the continuing collapse, consultants from Morgan Stanley suggested three alternatives about the GSE (Lowenstein 2010, 160): "(1) let the GSEs raise money on their own, which would essentially preserve the status quo; (2) 'conservatorship,' under which the twins would operate under federal stewardship; and (3) 'receivership,' close to a controlled liquidation." With foreign countries owning much of the debt, especially China and Japan, federal action was needed.

After continued Fannie/Freddie floundering, the Fed and Treasury got new GSE regulator Federal Housing Finance Agency (FHFA) to put the companies into "conservatorship" on September 7, 2008. The CEOs were fired and Treasury promised $100 billion of cash. Treasury acquired $1 billion in preferred stock in each company convertible to a 79.9 percent ownership of common stock.

Although all the big banks participated in the mortgage game using leverage, Bear received the most skepticism. On March 10, 2008, Moody's downgraded much of Bear's mortgaged-backed debt and rumors started about Bear's liquidity. Bear had $18 billion in cash, but Bear's trading partners became more and more unwilling to continue overnight funding. Mutual fund giant Fidelity Investments pulled its $6 billion a day repurchase loans. The cash was gone by the end of the week and Bear did not have enough cash to survive the weekend; the needed cash came from the Federal Reserve (Fed), some $12.9 billion. Since the Fed had no legal authority over investment banks, their lawyers used a Great Depression-era law allowing "unusual and exigent circumstances" and funneled the funds through Morgan. J. P. Morgan's CEO Jaime Dimon accepted a merger when the Fed eventually agreed to assume some $30 billion in mortgage-backed "toxic assets" and Morgan agreed to buy Bear at $2 a share (later raised to $10 a share, paying a total of a billion and a half dollars).

During 2006, Lehman was the largest securitizer of mortgage-backed securities (MBSs) at $50 billion, which became harder to sell with the growing evidence of the subprime bubble. Until sold, more and more were parked in off-shore special-purpose entities (SPEs). Senior executives at Lehman also moved more into commercial MBSs based on giant building projects being built at the top of the real estate bubble. On September 10, 2008, Lehman announced a loss of $6.7 billion over six months and a bank run similar to Bear Stearns started. Lehman needed a merger or federal bailout. Treasury Secretary Hank Paulson and New York Federal

Reserve president Tim Geithner needed a plan to save Lehman. According the Wessel (2009, 17), the options were a "liquidation consortium" to buy the various Lehman assets, including the commercial real estate; a "white knight" to buy Lehman; or bankruptcy. Simultaneously, Merrill Lynch and American Insurance Group (AIG) were failing and in need of government action. B of A, a potential Lehman buyer, agreed to acquire Merrill Lynch in another government-approved deal. With B of A out of the picture, only Barclays was left as a potential buyer, but they did not want the toxic assets, estimated at $50 billion, nor the gigantic commercial-property portfolio.

Paulson and Geithner found a consortium of banks to finance the acquisition of toxic assets and Barclays agreed on the acquisition. However, Barclays' British regulator Financial Services Authority (FSA) did not and rejected the deal without Treasury support. Paulson continued to reject government involvement. Lehman filed for Chapter 11 bankruptcy on Monday morning, September 15, the first bankruptcy of an investment bank since Drexel Burnham in 1990 and the largest bankruptcy in American history. After Lehman, credit markets collapsed and the government did not say no to further bailouts.

Insurance giant AIG became a major seller of credit default swaps (CDSs), holding over $560 billion in notional value at the end of 2007. Because defaults were historically a rare event, the logic was an immense revenue source with little likelihood of payouts. AIG sold CDSs but because they were not considered insurance, and therefore not regulated, did not hedge or establish reserves in case of defaults. After the fall of Lehman Brothers in September 2008, the rating agencies downgraded AIG's debt from AAA to A, driving down the stock price and requiring AIG to raise more collateral to support outstanding debt; finding short-term lenders became close to impossible. Federal Reserve chairman Ben Bernanke stepped in and announced a "secured credit facility" for AIG up to $85 billion on September 17. For 2008 the company lost almost $100 billion. Further bailouts of AIG continued, a total of over $180 billion.

After Lehman Brothers declared bankruptcy in September 2008, credit essentially stopped across the country and much of the world. In late October, the Fed set up the Commercial Paper Funding Facility to purchase unsecured and collateralized commercial paper to keep that market in business and provide protection to money market funds. In late November, the Term Asset-Backed Securities Loan Facility (TALF) was established to loan short-term funds to banks using asset-backed securities as collateral. Through these and other programs, the Fed restored to credit markets.

Unlike the Fed, the Treasury Department has little ability to dole out funds without legislative approval. A congressional act was necessary to provide banking capital to end the financial chaos. The Paulson/Bernanke plan essentially resulted in the Troubled Asset Relief Program (TARP), giving some $700 billion to Treasury with considerable flexibility to spend it. Paulson called the chief executive officers (CEOs) of the nine largest banks. For TARP cash equal to 3 percent of risk-weighted assets up to $25 billion, the banks would issue 5 percent preferred stock to the government plus warrants for common stock. Under pressure, all of the bank CEOs agreed. Paulson announced the plan on October 14. At the end of October, Treasury allocated $25 billion each to Citigroup and B of A, with lesser amounts to the less-troubled big banks (a total $125 billion). Complete chaos and depression were averted; however, a severe recession and slow recovery still occurred.

See also American Insurance Group (AIG); Bear Stearns; Bernanke, Ben S.; Bond Ratings on Structured Finance; Debt and Leverage; Federal Reserve System; Lehman Brothers; Paulson, Hank; Structured Finance; Troubled Asset Relief Program (TARP)

References

Cohan, William. *House of Cards: A Tale of Hubris and Wretched Excess on Wall Street.* New York: Doubleday, 2009.

Lowenstein, Roger. *The End of Wall Street.* New York: Penguin Press, 2010.

Paulson, Henry. *On the Brink: Inside the Race to Stop the Collapse of the Global Financial System.* New York: Business Plus, 2010.

Wessel, David. *In Fed We Trust: Ben Bernanke's War on the Great Panic.* New York: Crown Business, 2009.

Sunbeam

Sunbeam is a consumer products company founded in 1897 and now a subsidiary of Jarden Corp. Massive accounting fraud under Albert Dunlap in the 1990s led to bankruptcy. It was one of the many accounting scandals of the 1990s. The company was founded by John Stewart and Thomas Clark in 1897 as the Chicago Flexible Shaft Company, producing animal shears. The first Sunbeam-branded household appliances appeared in 1910, but the name of the company was not changed to Sunbeam until 1946. After financial difficulties, Sunbeam was acquired by Allegheny International in 1981, which went bankrupt in 1987.

Sunbeam emerged as a consumer products company in 1989 out of the bankruptcy of Allegheny. Sunbeam manufactured consumer products under its own name as well as Mr. Coffee, Oster, Coleman, and others. After performance declined in the mid-1990s, the board of directors hired turnaround specialist and corporate executive at Scott Paper Albert Dunlap to take over the company around in 1996. Dunlap had a reputation for restructuring companies profitably, partly through cutting expenditures and slashing employment—earning his nickname "Chainsaw Al." Almost immediately, half of the Sunbeam employees were fired and a massive restructuring loss was recorded as a special charge of some $340 million. This "big bath write-off" was blamed as the problems of the old management; however, the result was the buildup of "cookie jar reserves" that improved future earnings.

The restructuring charges including front-loading expenses into 1996 (recognizing them in the earlier period so that later periods would seem more profitable), part of the pattern of massive earnings manipulation across the company. Revenue recognition issues included bill and hold sales (billing and recording revenues before the actual sales), channel stuffing (advanced sales promising big discounts), and misstating sales guarantees. Cost manipulations misstated or did not record costs and accruals, including sales returns, advertising, warranty expenses, and product liability reserves. Some operating costs were charged to restructuring or asset impairment (part of the reserves established in 1996). Running out of schemes to meet analysts' earnings forecasts, Sunbeam booked sales that did not exist for products remaining in the warehouses in order to show rising revenues—generally moving from aggressive manipulation to fraud.

Arthur Andersen was the auditor and called for changes to the books because of the massive manipulation. When Sunbeam rejected the changes, Andersen still signed off with a clean opinion for 1997. Despite the massive fraud, 1997 earnings still fell short of analysts' expectations. With too much manipulation still on the books, desperation set in for 1998 and the board fired Dunlap. Securities and Exchange Commission (SEC)-mandated restatements wiped out much of the 1997 profit, followed by extensive legal actions by regulators and investors. Sunbeam restated earnings for fiscal years 1996–97, resulting in a stock price drop from a high of $52 to under $10 by mid-1998. Class action lawsuits and SEC investigations followed, which included auditor Arthur Andersen as a defendant. Sunbeam filed for bankruptcy in 2001, to reemerge as American Household at the end of 2002. It was acquired by Jarden Corporation in 2004.

See also Accounting Fraud; Arthur Andersen; Cendant; Earnings Manipulation; Fraud; Securities and Exchange Commission (SEC); Waste Management

References

General Accounting Office. *Financial Statement Restatements: Trends, Market Impacts, Regulatory Responses, and Remaining Challenges.* Washington, DC: GAO, October 2002.

Giroux, Gary. *Detecting Earnings Management.* New York: Wiley, 2003.

Mulford, Charles, and Eugene Comisky. *The Financial Numbers Game: Detecting Creative Accounting Practices.* New York: Wiley, 2002.

Schilit, Howard. *Financial Shenanigans: How to Detect Accounting Gimmicks & Fraud in Financial Reports.* 2nd ed. New York: McGraw-Hill, 2002.

T

Tammany Hall

Tammany Hall, the Democratic political machine of New York City, was the earliest, longest, and likely the most corrupt machine in the United States. It developed its political influence early in the nineteenth century and reached its corruption pinnacle under Boss Tweed shortly after the Civil War. Political influence, patronage, and corruption continued well into the twentieth century.

The Tammany Society was founded in 1789 as "a benevolent and charitable organization for the purpose of affording relief to the indigent and distressed member of said associated, their widows and orphans and others who may be proper objects of their charity" (Allen 1993, 19).

William Mooney, an upholsterer, was the first Grand Sachem. Under Mooney, Tammany became Democratic and increasingly political—Federalists were kicked out in a political dispute. Aaron Burr showed up for the 1800 election making a presidential run, with a genius for political organization. Burr allied with Tammany members, who learned Burr's strategy for corrupt mastery of machine politics.

Lying to newspaper reporters was a Burr specialty, using partisan newspapers and bribing reporters. On election day, Burr's cronies got out the vote. As Allen (1993, 22) summed it up, "Tammany Hall absorbed the key political techniques of Burrism—the ability of a few men to control the ward committees, the nomination process, and the means to turn out the voters—and by so doing laid the groundwork for the organization's amazing victories in the future."

Corruption by Tammany members expanded. Benjamin Romaine lost his job in the city controller office in 1806 after acquiring "free land" in the middle of Manhattan. William Mooney (the original Grand Sachem) paid himself much more than the allotted $1,500 a year and pilfered goods (his "trifles for Mrs. Mooney" defense became the standard excuse for political pilfering). John Ferguson became mayor of New York in 1815, handing out patronage jobs wholesale to Tammany cronies. With rising political clout, patronage became a tradition for Tammany cronies. Tammany faithful met immigrants at the dock, finding them living quarters, jobs, and thus faithful followers and voters. Voter fraud increased, including voting by underage males and herding new immigrants—not yet citizens—to the polls. With voting done in the open, party workers ensured that new adherents voted the party line. Tammany thugs could beat voters who voted for rival candidates.

New Tammany-controlled banks distributed thousands of shares of stock to Tammany elites. Contractors could disappear after being paid, but before paying workers. Major scandals erupted. Burr ally Samuel Swartwout got appointed by

THE "BRAINS"

THAT ACHIEVED THE TAMMANY VICTORY AT THE ROCHESTER DEMOCRATIC CONVENTION.

Political cartoon, "The Brains That Achieved Victory at the Rochester Democratic Convention," by Thomas Nast, published in *Harper's Weekly* on October 21, 1871. The engraving satirizes Boss Tweed (with a moneybag for a face) and the powerful interests of Tammany Hall. (Library of Congress)

President Andrew Jackson as collector of the Port of New York, the most lucrative tariff generator in the country. Swartwout had shady real estate holdings in New Jersey and Texas. He joined Burr's attempted coup out west, manipulated bank stocks, and attempted to corner Harlem Railroad stock. Swartwout fled the country when an investigation exposed the embezzlement of $1.2 million of customs funds. His successor as collector, Tammany boss Jesse Hoyt, defaulted to Wall Street brokers, apparently caught before embezzling vast sums.

The master of political corruption was William ("Boss") Tweed; he and his ring stole perhaps $200 million; he used tried-and-true pilfering tactics for bilking taxpayers and companies, but on an immense scale. Much of the pilfering was financed by bond issues rather than revenues, resulting in substantial debt for future generations. His crimes proved too vast to avoid prosecution. Arrested and convicted in 1871, he died in jail in 1878.

With the downfall of Boss Tweed, the entire ring was expelled from Tammany Hall. "Honest John Kelly" ("Honest" being a relative term) became the new Grand Sachem and attempted to rescue Tammany from impotence. Structural changes improved discipline and Tammany's public image. The level of graft declined, but relative corruption increased with rising political clout. As always, election success and potential patronage determined the level of political power and corruption possibilities.

Among the most interesting players in this new era was George Washington Plunkitt, who worked up the Tammany ladder to become a successful politician in both New York City and as state senator in Albany. His later memoir described long-term machine politics success: patronage, election fraud, and honest graft, limited in scope with no blatant criminal acts.

Power and corruption increased when Richard Croker became Grand Sachem after the death of Kelly in 1886; he ruled Tammany for the rest of the century. Kickbacks and bribery returned but more modestly than under Tweed. Croker's real estate business benefited from insider information and city-controlled property. He also took large security holdings from companies wanting to do business in the city. The police department was blatantly set up for plunder and allied with Tammany.

New Republican mayor William Strong started a reform movement in the 1890s, including a merit system introduced for city workers and reorganizing the Police Department. Theodore Roosevelt became a police commissioner, crusading against corruption and abuse. Corruption in the Police Department was particularly onerous under Police Chief Thomas Byrnes. Organized crime gangs had regular beats; Wall Street and other financial areas paid for additional protection. Each precinct was controlled by a captain receiving systematic bribes. Honest merchants paid protection money, while illegal businesses paid considerably more. Police jobs had to be bought; the going rate for a captain apparently was $10,000, down to $300 for a patrolman. An investigation committee estimated the annual take at $15 million. Chief Byrnes soon retired and Roosevelt was able to institute a number of reforms. However, he faced stiff opposition, which reduced his effectiveness.

At that time New York City consisted of Manhattan and the Bronx. When the city annexed Brooklyn, Queens, and Staten Island in 1898 under Republican boss Thomas Platt, Tammany's relative influence declined. Election reform requiring voter sign-in and secret ballots made election fraud more difficult. Croker and Tammany managed to returned to power, but corruption potential proved more limited.

Tammany maintained considerable influence during the early twentieth century. New York City mayor Jimmy ("Beau James") Walker, elected in 1926 and reelected in 1929, was the most colorful. The tough times with the Depression resulted in investigations of corruption that forced him to testify before the Seabury Commission. He resigned shortly thereafter and headed for Europe until the danger of criminal prosecution passed. Tammany never regained its former political power (although corruption continued, partly through organized crime) after Walker resigned in 1932. Longtime governor of New York and presidential candidate Al Smith had Tammany connections but was never accused of corruption. Political machines across the nation followed in Tammany's footsteps.

See also Bribery; Burr, Aaron; Fraud; Political Machines; Plunkitt, George Washington; Roosevelt, Theodore; Tweed, William M. ("Boss")

References

Allen, Oliver. *The Tiger: The Rise and Fall of Tammany Hall*. New York: Addison-Wesley, 1993.

Brands, H.W. *American Colossus: The Triumph of Capitalism, 1865–1900*. New York: Doubleday, 2010.

Tax Evasion and Tax Scams

Tax evasions are illegal practices to avoid paying taxes. Tax avoidance, on the other hand, is minimizing tax payments through legal means. Tax scams are any schemes to avoid taxes, either illegal practices or those skirting the line between legal and illegal. Avoiding taxes has been practiced in various forms since the first taxes were attempted in the ancient world.

Avoiding taxes has been an ongoing American practice from the beginning, with smuggling to avoid customs duties and bribing tax officials the most common forms for American colonialists. (Smuggling and bribery remain major sources of evasion around the world.) New taxes imposed by Britain were protested by the colonies, with the Boston Tea Party the one in the history books. During the first term of George Washington as president, a new excise tax on spirits led to the Whiskey Rebellion in western Pennsylvania in 1792.

Federal taxes were raised substantially to fund the American Civil War, including the introduction of the first federal income tax in the United States. Tax assessment and collection was an administrative nightmare, in part because of undereducated, low-paid bureaucrats with substantial power to set taxes. In addition to substantial errors and turnover, the assessors and collectors could often be bribed. As revenue collections increased (peaking in 1866 at $309 million), so did tax evasion and fraud. An 1868 *New York Times* article stated that the Office of Internal Revenue (OIR) had "almost become the synonym of corruption" (Giroux 2012, 13). In addition to income tax evasion, corrupt Whiskey Rings (associated with an excise tax on spirits) proved a major scandal, with OIR bureaucrats part of the rings. Detectives, predecessors of Internal Revenue Service (IRS) Special Agents, were hired to find tax fraud. The OIR seized 24 distilleries and 37 other businesses in 1875; over 50 federal officials were prosecuted and over 100 people in total convicted (Giroux 2012, 13). The income tax was abolished in 1872, although the OIR become the Internal Revenue Service in 1953.

With the reintroduction of income taxes with the Sixteenth Amendment in 1913 and high income tax rates beginning with the United States' entry into World War I, tax evasion and scams became bigger and more widespread. Lawyers and accountants fought for the right to give tax advice and prepare tax returns; both groups mastered the intricacies of tax laws to reduce taxes to little or nothing if at all possible, including techniques to just skirt the law.

Stockholders legitimately hope corporations avoid taxes, resulting in more income and cash to pay dividends and expand operations. Investors may prefer companies with aggressive tax avoidance practices, although convictions for tax evasion typically involve huge fines and possible jail time for the perpetrators. Justice and fairness could be an issue, but are difficult to evaluate since investors may ignore fairness or ethics as legitimate business practices (laissez-faire concepts consider neither). Similar to avoiding political contribution limits, tax lawyers and accountants prowl for loopholes. Hedge fund operators, such as John Paulson, pay tax at the capital gains rate of 15 percent rather than the ordinary income rate of 35 percent, even though Paulson and other hedge funds make billions.

Important to corporate tax scams are tax havens and tax shelters. A tax shelter allows the reduction of taxes, such as limited partnerships. In years past, oil partnerships were common for high-income executives. Drilling took years to produce and dry holes were common. This was not a problem, because the partnership produced large tax breaks. After the Enron bankruptcy and the fall of Arthur Andersen, two of the remaining Big Four accounting firms were charged with tax shelter fraud. KPMG paid a $456 million fine to avoid indictment (like Andersen, an indictment would have destroyed the company). Soon after that the IRS charged Ernst & Young with a tax fraud conspiracy for marketing illegal tax shelters and cheating the IRS out of more than $2 billion. In this case, federal prosecutors went after tax partners rather than the firm. After the fall of Andersen, fewer than four major accounting firms would be unacceptable (essentially, "too big to indict").

An important category of shelters is the use of offshore companies, benefiting by the differences in tax rates—particularly if the offshore subsidiary is residing in a country with a zero tax rate. The higher the tax rates in the home country, the greater the incentives to use these tax havens. A number of countries beginning with Switzerland are recognized tax havens and great places to store undocumented loot and pay considerably lower taxes. Each of 50 or so countries has some unique set of attributes for concealing money or avoiding taxes.

Major global companies headquartered in the United States have substantial earnings overseas and keep the money abroad to avoid American taxes. Part of the scheme is to move the profits of U.S.-based operations overseas. Google, for example, reached an agreement with the IRS in 2006 allowing foreign subsidiaries to keep revenues and profits abroad and ignore obvious transfer payments for intellectual property rights (such as U.S.-based patents) and licensing.

A substantial portion of tax evasion involves the underground economy, where cash transactions are made under the table and not reported as income. Small businesses are likely the largest sources of unreported income. Beginning in the 1970s, the IRS attempted to measure unreported income (the "tax gap"), estimated at $2 trillion in 2008 and resulting in lost taxes of $450 to $500 billion.

Beginning in the 1980s, derivative experts at major investment banks developed increasingly complex derivative instruments specifically to avoid taxes. Frank Partnoy (1997, 2003) described a number of these complex derivative ploys. A wealthy person could use an equity swap, effectively selling an appreciated stock without recognizing the capital gain to the IRS. According to Partnoy (1996, 182), "in recent years the capital gains taxes collected from wealthy individuals in the U.S. have been close to zero, in large part because of Equity Swaps. . . . The Equity Swaps were a pure, unadulterated tax scam." Another set of complex derivatives involved preferred stock, which has characteristics of both equity and debt (generally treated as equity and paying a set dividend). The plan created derivative instruments effectively allowing corporations to treat the preferred stock as equity on the financial statements and debt (allowing the dividends to be treated as interest and thus be tax deductible) for tax purposes. Partnoy also described the use of sham trades beginning in the 1990s at Salomon Brothers giving the appearance of losses, specifically to reduce taxes (2003, 96).

The most infamous case of tax evasion was the conviction of Mafia chief Al Capone, serving seven years in jail (1932–39). Other famous tax cases include musician Willie Nelson (1990), Associate Attorney General Webster Hubbell (1995), Congressman James Traficant (2002), Congressman Duke Cunningham (2005), Congressman Charles Rangel (2008), and actor Wesley Snipes (2008).

See also Paulson, John; Regulation of Business; Regulations and Regulatory Failures; Treasury Department

References

Giroux, Gary. "Financing the American Civil War: Developing New Tax Sources." *Accounting History* 17, no. 1 (February 2012): 83–104.

Partnoy, Frank. *FIASCO: Blood in the Water on Wall Street*. New York: Norton, 1997.

Partnoy, Frank. *Infectious Greed: How Deceit and Risk Corrupted the Financial Markets*. New York: Holt, 2003.

Teamsters and Corruption

The Teamsters union, especially under Dave Beck and Jimmy Hoffa in the post–World War II period, experienced substantial embezzlement, extortion, and fraud. The Teamsters were involved with organized crime, which led to fraud indictments against both Beck and Hoffa. Congressional hearings demonstrated fraudulent accounting and financial statements and embezzled funds by union leaders. Hoffa used union pension funds for organized crime projects, including Las Vegas casinos. Hoffa was sent to prison in 1967, pardoned by Richard Nixon, and famously disappeared in 1975. The Teamsters instituted reforms and now represent a diverse group of blue-collar workers and professionals with 1.4 million members (down from 2 million in 1976).

As heads of large organizations with substantial resources, union leaders had incentives to cheat and game the system for their own benefit. Union leaders beginning at least with Samuel Gompers, president of the American Federation of Labor (AFL), often had substantial salaries and perquisites as well as power. It was quite common for union dues to be used for personal expenses of the leaders. With few unions requiring audits or filing of audited financial statements, corruption could be easily perpetrated. According to Doron (2009, 230), "there remains today no requirement that unions undergo outside audits. As of 2000, only 63 percent of active unions with annual receipts in excess of US$200,000 received audits by outside auditors."

Teamsters were drivers of teams of horses or mules used for hauling, later truck drivers. Several local teamster unions were formed in the nineteenth century, often with the help of the American Federation of Labor (AFL). Various locals formed the International Brotherhood of Teamsters in 1903, which joined the AFL. After losing a bloody strike (21 people were killed) at Montgomery Ward in 1905, the Teamsters picked Dan Tobin as general president and he would serve for 45 years. Tobin was succeeded by Dave Beck in 1952.

Certain unions came in contact with organized crime and other shady groups, such as the Teamsters and Longshoremen. The 1920s was the period of prohibition when mob gangs gained substantial power trafficking in liquor. The term "racketeering" was coined in 1927 in a statement about the Mafia dealing with the Teamsters union.

Jimmy Hoffa attempted to unseat Dave Beck as Teamster president and called on mobster Johnny Dio in 1955 to create fake unions to boost Hoffa's delegate count. Media attention led to Senate hearings and a Justice Department investigation. The McClellan Committee (named for Arkansas senator John McClellan) held public hearings beginning in 1957 to study criminal activities and labor racketeering of unions and management, plus the need to change the law. Over 1,500 witnesses testified (343 of which took the Fifth, most famously Dave Beck). Beck admitted to receiving a $300,000 interest-free loan, which he never paid back. Hoffa and Dio were wiretaped talking of additional fake unions, which was played for the committee.

Dubofsky and Dulles (2004, 359) summed up the McClellan results:

> The evidence spread upon the public record revealed a larger degree of dictatorial union leadership, which violated every democratic principle, and more corruption, racketeering, and gangsterism on the part of union officials than even labor's severest critics had suspected. Witness after witness testified to rigged elections, the misuse of union funds, embezzlement, and theft.

The AFL-CIO expelled the Teamsters in 1957. The legislative result of the hearings was the Landrum-Griffin Act of 1959, which required stricter financial reporting, more democratic procedures in union organizations, and various restrictions on union activities.

The McClellan Committee effectively brought down Beck, but amazingly not Hoffa, who was tried but acquitted of bribery. Beck was prosecuted for embezzlement and labor racketeering in 1959, was convicted of income-tax evasion, and served 30 months in prison. Hoffa became general president in 1958. He was convicted of fraud, attempted bribery, and jury tampering in 1964 and jailed in 1967. He was pardoned by President Richard Nixon in 1971 after he resigned the Teamsters' presidency. Hoffa tried to regain power, but disappeared in July 1975, presumably after meeting with two Mafia leaders.

After the Racketeering-Influenced and Corrupt Organizations Act (RICO) passed in 1970, the Justice Department pursued unions with organized crime connections. RICO was passed to expand criminal penalties for activities of criminal organizations ("racketeering"), mainly organized crime. The 1986 President's Commission on Organized Crime identified four unions "substantially influenced and/or controlled by organized crime." In addition to the Teamsters were the International Longshoremen's Association, Laborers International Union of North America, and the Hotel Employees and Restaurant Employees International Union. In 1988, the Justice Department filed a RICO suit against the Teamsters, which was settled in 1989, placing the union under government supervision. Ron Carey became general president in 1991, but after a scheme to pilfer $885,000 in union dues was discovered, Carey was forced out of office and expelled from the union (several underlings were convicted of various crimes). Carey was replaced by James Hoffa (son of Jimmy), who had his own but less serious corruption problems.

See also American Federation of Labor/Congress of Industrial Organizations (AFL-CIO); Haymarket Affair (1886); Homestead Strike (1892); Labor Movement, U.S.; Triangle Shirtwaist Fire (1911); Wagner Act

References

Atkins, Albert. "Labor." In *The American Economy: A Historical Encyclopedia*. Rev. ed. Edited by Cynthia Clark. Santa Barbara, CA: ABC-CLIO, 2011.

Doron, Michael. "The End of the Disinterested Profession: The American Institute of Certified Public Accountants and the Union Corruption Scandals, 1957–62." *Accounting History* 14, no. 3 (2009): 221–34.

Dubofsky, Melvyn, and Foster Dulles. *Labor in America: A History*. 7th ed. Wheeling, IL: Harlan Davidson, 2004.

Zinn, Howard. *A People's History of the United States*. New York: Harper Perennial Modern Classics, 2003.

Teapot Dome

Teapot Dome was a major political-business scandal with the buying of the 1920 Republican presidential nomination, big-oil payoffs for political influence, murder, sex, suspicious suicides, blackmail, a cabinet member sent to jail for bribery, intimidation, payoffs to journalists, and even an oil-financed army in Mexico. Despite all the progressive reforms from the previous two decades, high-level corruption continued in the United States in the twentieth century.

Naval oil reserves (so that the navy could maintain a domestic supply of fuel oil) started in the early 1900s by executive order. Three major reserves included Teapot Dome (named for a sandstone outcropping called Teapot Rock) in Wyoming and Elk Hills and Buena Vista, both in California. These were off limits to public drilling. The scandal involved moving the reserves away from the navy, and then leasing the fields to oil companies for large kickbacks.

The Teapot Dome scandal started with oilman Jake Hamon hatching a plot to buy the 1920 presidential election, literally for a million dollars. The payoff to Hamon would be secretary of the interior, with plans to sell oil rights to the three naval reserves for substantial payoffs. Ohio senator Warren Harding, described as a lazy political hack, was a newspaper publisher becoming a senator of limited skill and less ambition. Harding, well down the list of viable candidates, had Harry Daugherty as campaign manager and Ohio political party boss. Daugherty agreed to Hamon's plan. When the Republican convention deadlocked, Hamon used his money and influence to swing the nomination to Harding. Hamon would be interior secretary, the position to lease Teapot Dome and other oil reserves to oil executives for substantial payoffs. In November, Harding won the presidency.

Harding's wife, Florence, however, insisted Hamon give up his mistress, Clara, and return to his wife if he wanted the Washington post. Hamon did and told Clara after the election. Not taking the news at all well, she shot and killed Hamon. Hamon and his plan died, but Hamon's conspirators Harry Sinclair, Edward Doheny, and Robert Stewart, three of the most successful oil tycoons of the day, were still around. Sinclair gave $1 million to the Republican National Committee for expected future political favors and paid off the debt of the Republican National Committee after the election.

Doheny produced the first successful oil well in Los Angeles. He created the western oil business and established a massive oil empire around Tampico, Mexico. To ensure that the Mexican government would not nationalize his site, he maintained a Mexican army of 6,000. Two naval reserve sites existed in California, Elk Hills and Buena Vista, which Doheny wanted to add to his West Coast empire. Sinclair organized Sinclair Oil as a combination of several smaller companies in the Midwest. Robert Stewart, president of Standard Oil of Indiana, the largest oil producer in Wyoming, wanted access to Salt Creek (on federal land), near Teapot Dome. The plan required Standard Oil to build a pipeline from both Teapot Dome and Salt Creek to Standard's refineries.

Albert Fall, senator from New Mexico, advised Harding during the campaign and wanted to become secretary of state. Instead, Fall got interior (Hamon's expected job). Being close to broke because of a drought on his ranch, Fall was encouraged to join the conspiracy for cash payoffs. Fall wanted to buy a neighbor's ranch, which had available water. The ranch came up for sale at the end of 1920 for $91,500. Doheny gave Fall $100,000 cash to buy the ranch, and Fall reciprocated by giving Doheny the drilling rights to the Elk Hill and Buena Vista Reserves.

Sinclair signed a lease with Fall to take out Teapot oil on a royalty basis. The Salt Creek field, going to Stewart's Standard Oil of Indiana, was part of the deal. Fall signed the contract for Teapot in April 1922, keeping the contract confidential until the *Wall Street Journal* broke the story a week later. The Interior Department claimed the process (confidential, no bidding) was a normal procedure; expressing skepticism, the Senate passed a resolution to investigate the leases by the end of the month.

Reporters for the *Denver Post* uncovered much of the Sinclair-Fall scam. They demanded a $1 million bribe from Sinclair, which he refused to pay. Negative stories about the Teapot conspiracy continued until the million dollars was paid, at which point the paper became a supporter of Sinclair and the other scoundrels.

Sinclair made substantial payments to Fall in Liberty bonds (Treasury bonds issued to support World War I). Unlike cash, these had serial numbers, which were later verified by federal investigators. The first payment totaled $198,000, with another $71,000 added after Fall insisted on a bigger payday. When investigated, Fall claimed Sinclair acquired a part interest in Fall's ranch, although no evidence supported that.

Fall resigned from the cabinet early in 1923, shortly after giving Sinclair a new five-year contract on Teapot, probably to return to his ranch and act as a "paid political consultant" for Doheny and Sinclair rather than because of political pressure. He went to Mexico to promote Doheny's interests and to Russia for Sinclair. He later admitted he went, but claimed to be unpaid.

Soon after the original announcement of the Teapot leases appeared in the press, Wisconsin senator Robert La Follette called for hearings by the Senate Committee on Public Lands to investigate these shady dealings, which started under Montana senator Thomas Walsh in October 1922. Walsh spent years sorting out the truth, while Fall was busy covering up his tracks, partly by destroying incriminating documents and defending his own actions as legal and business as usual. Walsh discovered most of the corruption beginning with Hamon and other political slush funds, but was unable to put much of it in the public record (documents were destroyed, various players fled to Europe, and so on). Walsh did get Doheny to describe the $100,000 "loan" to Fall, a major incriminating piece of the puzzle. In addition, Doheny disclosed under oath the names of former government officials on Doheny's payroll, including several former cabinet members.

Montana senator Burton Wheeler (a protégé of Walsh) introduced a resolution to investigate Attorney General Harry Daugherty on the grounds that the Justice Department did nothing to "arrest and prosecute" Fall and the oil gang. Enough evidence existed to convince new president Calvin Coolidge to fire Daugherty, which he did in March 1924. Lawsuits were filed against Daugherty, but he was never convicted. Coolidge also appointed a special prosecutor for the Teapot Dome scandal, who worked closely with the Walsh Committee. A Secret Service investigation uncovered additional incriminating evidence. Suits were filed for an injunction to stop the drilling of the naval reserves and cancel the leases. It took a Supreme Court ruling to void the leases in 1927.

Criminal indictments for fraud were filed against Fall, Sinclair, Doheny, and Stewart. Stewart became a major player by establishing a dummy corporation called Continental Trading. Continental Trading buying Teapot Dome/Sand Creek oil for $1.50 a barrel and selling the oil to Standard Oil for $1.75. The 25¢-a-barrel profit went to Stewart and other conspirators. Stewart defrauded his own company, but was acquitted in the later criminal trial. It took a bitter proxy fight (a vote by shareholders) led by John D. Rockefeller Jr. to oust Stewart as president.

Doheny paid for Albert Fall's bribery case defense, with Fall portrayed as a sick old man railroaded by the government. The Doheny cash became only a loan to a friend. The $300,000 plus in Liberty bonds and cash from Sinclair became payments to buy an interest in Fall's Three Rivers Ranch. The verdict was still guilty, making Fall the first cabinet member in American history to go to jail for a felony. He served nine months in prison, paid a $100,000 fine, and lost his ranch. Doheny won acquittal on the same charges.

Harry Sinclair had eight court cases against him. Never convicted on any crime directly related to bribery or Teapot, he served a three-month sentence for contempt of Congress for lying. In addition, during one of the criminal trials he had all the jurors tailed by Burns Detective Agency and offered one or more of them a bribe to vote for acquittal. That led to another trial for jury tampering. While in prison for contempt of Congress, the Supreme Court upheld the guilty verdict on jury tampering. He ended up spending a total of seven months in prison.

Teapot Dome was a major scandal in American history and one of only a few involving corporations bribing senior federal officials. The key players were successful politicians and businessmen—and crooks. Apparently, the culprits thought they could get away with blatant illegality at the highest levels of government. Ultimately, only a few of the major players were convicted and sent to jail.

See also Daugherty, Harry M.; Doheny, Edward; Fall, Albert B.; Fraud; Political Machines; Sinclair, Harry F.

References

Bates, J. Leonard. *The Origins of Teapot Dome*. Urbana: University of Illinois Press, 1963.

Gentzkow, M., E. Glaeser, and C. Goldin. "The Rise of the Fourth Estate: How Newspapers Became Informative and Why It Mattered." In *Corruption and Reform: Lessons from America's Economic History*. Edited by E. Glaeser and C. Goldin, 187–230. Washington, DC: National Bureau of Economic Research, 2006.

McCartney, Laton. *The Teapot Dome Scandal: How Big Oil Bought the Harding White House and Tried to Steal the Country*. New York: Random House, 2008.

Tech Bubble

The tech bubble (also called dot-com bubble) was a speculative stock price boom in Internet and other high-tech companies from the mid-1990s until 2000, when the bubble burst and stock price collapsed. NASDAQ (where many of these companies were listed) peaked over 5,000 on March 10, 2000. NASDAQ stocks collapsed, generating a recession, huge price drops, and the failure of many of the high-flyers.

At the start of the 1990s, U.S. firms appeared uncompetitive relative to Japanese and other foreign giants, especially in "rust belt" manufacturing like automobiles. Despite its vast bureaucracy, IBM set the standard for personal computers (PCs) in the early 1980s, only to be beat by small, dynamic companies like Microsoft, Apple, Compaq, and Dell. IBM almost collapsed in the early 1990s, in part because it was unable to develop a competitive PC.

During the 1980s big, centralized companies with huge bureaucracies still ruled, if poorly. Revenues and profits declined as foreign competition increased. Restructuring happened virtually nationwide, thanks in part to improved productivity related to the Information Revolution. The Dow Jones Industrial Average (Dow) almost doubled from the start of 1988 (2015) to close at 3,834 at the end of 1994. By the mid-1990s, almost half the population bought stocks or mutual funds.

Michael Lewis (2000) claimed the tech bubble started the day of Netscape's 1995 initial public offering (IPO), an unusual event since Netscape was not profitable. "The price rose from $12 to $48. Three months later it stood at $140. It was the most successful share offering in history and possibly the most famous. If Netscape had not forced the issue on the Internet, it would have just burbled in the background. In the frenzy that followed, a lot of the old rules of capitalism were suspended" (Lewis 2000, 85). Investors piled into new loss-making ventures.

The Internet excited investors. New measures of performance, from revenues to number of clicks, replaced traditional measures such as price-earnings ratios. Part of the attraction was the "small float" of new Internet and other tech IPOs, because relatively few shares were available. The tech innovators and venture capitalists took most of the shares, typically leaving only 10 percent available to the public during the IPO, including Amazon.com and Yahoo. With few shares available and insatiable demand, stock prices went straight up. Internet analysts like Henry Blodget of Merrill Lynch and Mary Meeker at Morgan Stanley were enthusiastic supporters for almost all of them.

Starting at 2,810 in 1990, the Dow hit 5,000 by the end of 1995 and stood at 11,497 by the start of the new millennium. The tech market mainly meant NASDAQ; the NASDAQ composite index started 1990 at 455, hit 5,000 in March of 2000, and reached its all-time high of 5049 on March 10, the peak of the tech bubble.

Information and communications exploded with the Internet and other new technologies. Investors wanted in. Unfortunately, "innovation and high tech" are not necessarily money makers. The airline industry, promoting an earlier stock craze, proved to be a poor long-term investment. In addition to airlines, the auto industry and computer industry saw competitors by the hundreds fail. Only a few proved successful long term: the Big Three in autos and IBM in mainframe computers (with later business strategy changes).

The tech companies had similar histories. Thousands were started in garages and dorm rooms. Amazon.com had an extraordinary business model and eventually became profitable—but it took years. Michael Dell started assembling computers in his dorm room and eventually his firm became a big, low-cost producer of PCs. Most failed, partly because of poor business models and little chance of profitability. Journalist Jack Willoughby in "Burning Up" (*Barron's*, March 20, 2000) calculated that a large percentage of the tech stocks were quickly running out of cash. On the list were Egghead.com, drkoop.com, Cybercash, and eToys. Amazon.com, also on the list, managed to survive.

After peaking on March 10, the NASDAQ composite collapsed. By October 2002, the index dropped to 1,114, down almost 80 percent. At the end of 2010, NASDAQ returned to only 2,653, 53 percent of its high—a painful lesson in euphoria. The other stock markets saw price declines, but less severe than NASDAQ. The Dow dropped from 10,941 at the start of 2000 to 8,054 at the end of 2001, down 26 percent. The broader S&P 500 Index fell 19 percent over the same period.

Tech exhibited a typical bubble/crash cycle. There were many bears by 1999 (or even earlier); even Alan Greenspan spoke of "irrational exuberance" earlier, although he did little to stop the boom (believing productivity would keep inflation down). Tech stocks, even without earnings, were money machines. As summed up by Michael Lewis (2009, 159), "In retrospect, it seems obvious that money-losing companies created by twenty-six-year-olds should never have been worth billions. But at the time, these companies appeared to have at least a shot at playing extremely important roles in wildly compelling versions of the future."

Institutional insiders started pulling out in big block trades. As Maggie Mahar (2003, 318) summed it up:

> How did they know? Some high-ranking executives knew that their own companies' earnings were fictitious. They also realized that they were running out of road: one can only restate earnings so many times. Others were in a position to know that many of the companies that they did business with were not nearly as profitable as they appeared: orders were down, and inventories were building, along with corporate debt.

The Federal Reserve raised interest rates from mid-1999 to mid-2000. In March of 2001, well after the market crash, the economy went into recession. This was a mild contraction, given the crash, September 11, and continuing business scandals that started popping up. The recession was officially over by the end of 2001. Greenspan reversed course and pumped money into the market, another "Greenspan put."

See also Blodget, Henry; Bubbles and Euphoria; Dow Jones Industrial Average; Federal Reserve System; Fraud; Greenspan, Alan; Grubman, Jack; NASDAQ; Panics and Depressions

References

Gasparino, Charles. *Blood on the Street: The Sensational Inside Story of How Wall Street Analysts Duped a Generation of Investors*. New York: Free Press, 2005.

Lewis, Michael. *Panic: The Story of Modern Financial Insanity*. New York: Norton, 2009.

Lewis, Michael. *The New New Thing: A Silicon Valley Story*. New York: Norton, 2000.

Mahar, Maggie. *Bull: A History of the Boom and Bust, 1982–2003*. New York: Harper Business, 2004.

Willoughby, Jack. "Burning Up." *Barron's*, March 20, 2000. Reprinted in Lewis, M. *Panic: The Story of Modern Financial Insanity*. New York: Norton, 2009.

Tequila Crisis

Mexico's peso collapse of 1995 was a result of rising interest rates and the misuse of credit instruments, which was one of many Latin American financial debacles. After a period of reform, the Mexican peso collapsed in late 1994, creating a financial crisis. The U.S. Treasury Department came to the rescue with a $50 billion line of credit and the Mexican economy recovered. Latin American debt crises happened repeatedly since their independence in the nineteenth century.

Latin American countries achieved independence from Spain and Portugal during the nineteenth century, often followed by unstable governments defaulting on foreign debt and nationalizing foreign companies. All the Latin American countries except Argentina defaulted on their foreign debt during the Great Depression. The countries again borrowed heavily during the 1970s and 1980s and, beginning with Mexico, defaulted on debt in the 1980s. Because much of this debt was held by American banks, Treasury Secretary Nicolas Brady devised a rescue plan, called the Brady Plan, and using World Bank guaranteed Brady Bonds.

The 1990s were no different in attracting foreign investors. Latin American governments cut deficits, reduced inflation, promoted free trade, and privatized many government companies. The "Mexican Miracle" led the list. Mexico started an era of reform in the 1980s, including the North American Free Trade Agreement (NAFTA). After controlling and stabilizing the peso, a substantial trade deficit developed when oil prices fell and the peso became overvalued. American and other foreign investors poured money into Mexico and the booming economy. Long-term problems of corruption and rural poverty were not addressed. The immediate economic problems in the early 1990s were slowing growth and a decline in foreign exchange reserves. The policy alternatives were to raise interest rates or devalue the peso. Mexico chose the latter option, but reduced the peso's value by only 15 percent. In late December 1994, the peso crashed. Mexican financiers and other leaders moved their money out of the country and domestic interest rates spiked. The value of the peso fell to half its previous value.

Much of Mexico's short-term debt was indexed to dollars (called *tesobonos*), greatly expanding the interest obligations resulting in financial crisis and a severe recession—called the "Tequila Crisis" of 1995. Once the peso was devalued, the debt was denominated in very expensive dollars. Capital flight made the problem worse. For political reasons, including the bitterness by many constituents over NAFTA, Congress refused to take action. Clinton's Treasury Department came to the rescue, using its Exchange Stabilization Fund (a cash pool not subject to congressional approval) and other sources to provide a $50 billion credit line to Mexico. Exchange rates stabilized and the crisis subsided. Economic recovery returned, and as the peso regained its value, Mexico repaid the Treasury loan. Unfortunately, the Mexican banking sector and other key industries were not restructured. The Mexico crisis, attributed in part to policy errors, had repercussions to other Latin American countries, and to economies as far away as Nigeria and Poland. Little thought was given to the potential for similar problems around the world. Within a few years, the Asian debt crisis would suffer from similar policy shortcomings and comparable results.

See also Asian Debt Crisis; Brady Plan; Derivatives; Hedge Funds; Latin American Banking Crises; Long-Term Capital Management; Treasury Department

References

Lewis, Michael. *Panic: The Story of Modern Financial Insanity*. New York: Norton, 2009.

Partnoy, Frank. *FIASCO: Blood in the Water on Wall Street*. New York: Norton, 1997.

Partnoy, Frank. *Infectious Greed: How Deceit and Risk Corrupted the Financial Markets*. New York: Holt, 2003.

Too Big to Fail

The concept of "too big to fail" started in the 1980s for U.S. banks. Continental Illinois Bank and Trust became the first big bank (it was the seventh largest at the time) to crash trying to manage the "new banking" of the 1980s; summed up by Ron Chernow (1990, 657) as "the roulette world of liability management." Rather than just deposits, bank operations were financed by money market instruments like commercial paper, Federal Reserve (Fed) funds, and jumbo certificates of deposit. These risky short-term instruments were called "hot money" (rising interest rates result in large losses), a risk often ignored by bankers. Continental made high-risk loans using hot money.

Penn Square Bank of Oklahoma repackaged some $1 billion of bad energy loans to Continental before going bankrupt in 1982. (It turned out that Penn Square gave

A protester holds a sign reading "Too Big to Fail is too Big to Allow" in front of Bank of America on Day 40 of Occupy Wall Street in New York in October 2011. (David Shankbone/CC-by-3.0)

Continental executive John Lytle some $600,000 in kickbacks to approve the loan. Lytle was sentenced to three-and-a-half years in jail.) Continental struggled on, but had its own bank run in 1984. Because other big banks had their share of bad loans (especially in real estate) and relied on hot money, the entire banking system could have collapsed after a Continental failure. The Fed pumped in billions of dollars, a consortium of banks made a huge line of credit available, and the Federal Deposit Insurance Corporation (FDIC) took an 80 percent stake. Bank of America acquired its remaining operations. In summary, Continental was the first bank "too big to fail." Smaller banks in this period using similar hot money and making bad bets were not so lucky, being gobbled up in the usual FDIC takeover.

Some authorities consider the Panic of 1825 as the first example of too big to fail. At that time London banks speculated on textiles and shipping, although warned by Parliament about overspeculation. As the panic spread credit froze up, halting commerce. The Chancellor of the Exchequer ordered the Bank of England to bail out the London banks and the panic was soon over.

The "too big to fail" doctrine became significant in the 2008 subprime meltdown as major investment banks did not have the cash to survive. The Fed and Treasury first negotiated a merger of failing Bear Stearns to J. P. Morgan Chase, Fannie

Mae and Freddie Mac were placed into conservatorship, then Lehman Brothers was allowed to fail. Credit markets collapsed and nonbank American Insurance Group was bailed out by the government. Congress passed the Troubled Asset Relief Program (TARP), used to bail out the largest banks and other big corporations including General Motors and Chrysler.

Many economics and public policy experts want to eliminate the potential of "too big to fail" as a moral hazard encouraging risky behavior: gains are private, while losses are public, that is, paid by taxpayers. That could be achieved by breaking up banks into smaller entities, such as separating commercial from investment bank operations.

See also Continental Illinois Bank; Fannie Mae and Freddie Mac; Federal Reserve System; Leverage; Subprime Meltdown; Treasury Department; Troubled Asset Relief Program (TARP)

References

Hafer, Rik. "Too-Big-to-Fail Doctrine." In *The Federal Reserve System: An Encyclopedia.* Santa Barbara, CA: ABC-CLIO, 2005.

Sorkin, Andrew. *Too Big to Fail: The Inside Story of How Wall Street and Washington Fought to Save the Financial System from Crisis—and Themselves.* New York: Viking, 2009.

Transcontinental Railroad and the Credit Mobilier Scandal

The transcontinental railroad connected Nebraska to California, linking the United States from coast to coast. Authorizing legislation passed during the Civil War, perhaps the greatest building project of the nineteenth century—the two railroad companies were the biggest corporations at the time. The lines were completed and connected at Promontory Point, Utah, in 1869. Construction corruption produced the biggest nineteenth-century business scandal, Credit Mobilier. The underlying fraud was similar to other railroads, but corrupt government officials getting caught and documented in the congressional record was unique.

The discovery of gold in California made the idea of a transcontinental railroad inevitable, favored by Abraham Lincoln and other important politicians. A government giveaway of millions of acres of federal land and cash was necessary to entice promoters, a price visionaries were willing to pay. Massachusetts senator Henry Wilson declared, "I give no grudging vote in giving away either money or land, I would sink $100 million to build the road and do it most cheerfully, and think I had done a great thing for my country" (Josephson 1934, 78).

Engineer Theodore Judah was an enthusiastic supporter of building a railroad east from Sacramento and proposed a railroad he called the Central Pacific (CP). Four California merchants backed the project: Leland Stanford, Collis Huntington,

Charles Crocker, and Mark Hopkins—"the Big Four," also called "the Associates." All four were members of the Republican Party and Stanford became California governor. The Big Four were interested in money and power, but focused on long-term success, rather than immediate pilfering, based on the potential from transportation dominance. Judah, the creator of the CP and surveyor of the initial route, died of yellow fever in 1863.

The CP was chartered by California in 1861 and the Associates attempted to raise money from skeptical investors. Acquiring enough cash proved to be a continuing problem. Judah surveyed the route from Sacramento east; Huntington went to Washington, DC, and New York with the blueprints for the CP route to find federal funding—virtually all the cash of the company went with him, some $200,000, for strategic bribes.

The Pacific Railroad bill passed in 1862, providing loans and land. The loans served as payments based on track completion at the rate of $16,000 per mile on the plains to $48,000 a mile in the mountains (these amounts were later raised as a result of intense lobbying and continued cash payments), with the land allocated in alternating sections (the "checkerboard pattern") along the right-of-way. Much of the land was sold through land companies owned by the promoters with the proceeds (after the promoters' cut) going to the railroads. Over the construction period, Congress granted 12 million acres of land and $27 million in long-term bonds to the Union Pacific (UP) and 9 million acres and $24 million in bonds to the CP.

Corruption extended beyond Washington. After the CP spent most of their capital on "lobbying," little money remained to start construction. San Francisco voters in 1863 approved a $3 million bond issue for the CP, based in part on Stanford's influence as governor. CP promoters suggested a "subsidy" from cities on the potential route. Sacramento, San Francisco, and Stockton raised the cash plus rights-of-way, land, and benefits. Journalists were paid for good publicity: the *Sacramento Union* editor received $3,600 worth of CP stock and reporters at the paper smaller amounts. Cities refusing to pay were bypassed.

The UP was created as a federal corporation by the Pacific Railroad bill with General Samuel Curtiss as temporary chairman. Two thousand shares of stock were issued and quickly subscribed at $1,000 each. A board of directors was elected and General John Dix appointed nominal UP president. However, Thomas Durant, a Wall Street speculator appointed as vice president, became the real leader.

Substantial corruption took place at the two railroads, but the big public scandal centered on the separate construction companies used to build the railroads: Credit and Finance Corporation used by the CP and Credit Mobilier (CM) at the UP. The promoters of the railroads secretly ran the construction companies and, along with influential politicians and other insiders, owned the stock.

Hired by Durant to sell UP securities, George Francis Train suggested Credit Mobilier (named after a French company) as a construction company and other devious purposes. Train found an existing "shell company," the Pennsylvania Fiscal Agency, whose charter allowed it to "become an agency for the purchase and sale of railway bonds and other securities" and authorizing the company to "borrow and loan money without limit on the resources or without the resources of the company," with "no end to the avenues open to the Agency for operation." It soon became "Credit Mobilier of America." Train sold it to Durant, claiming to have created the first "trust" in the United States (Ambrose 2000, 92–93). Under Durant and Massachusetts congressman Oakes Ames, Credit Mobilier would make the owners money whether the UP was successful or not—Durant thought the UP would never make money and diverted as much money as possible to CM.

The construction companies bought the building supplies and did the construction either directly or through subcontractors. CM made money by charging about twice the actual construction costs. Under chief engineer General Grenville Dodge, the CM profits were massive. To pay CM the UP accumulated substantial debt and drove the company close to bankruptcy. CM paid gigantic dividends; in 1868 CM paid out dividends in cash, UP stock, and bonds equaling 280 percent of CM par value. With the cash going to pay dividends first, the corrupt CM did a poor job actually paying workers, subcontractors, and suppliers.

CP Big Four member Charles Crocker supervised construction, creating the Contract and Finance Company (which was later used to build other railroads throughout California). Crocker was president and the Associates owned all the stock— phony investors were used to hide their complete control. The CP construction company made substantial profits. However, when Congress investigated, the books of the company mysteriously disappeared.

Despite the corruption, both railroads got built and their lines met at Promontory Point, Utah, on May 10, 1869. The UP was acquired by Jay Gould in 1873, becoming another looted railroad. The Big Four maintained ownership of the CP, which formed the basis of their land and railroad empire. They dominated California for the rest of the century.

Then the scandal erupted. Congressman Ames sold stock of both UP and CM to important politicians at below market prices, including Vice President Schuyler Colfax; James Blaine, Speaker of the House of Representatives and later senator, presidential candidate, and secretary of state; and James Garfield, Speaker of the House and later president. Charles Francis Adams Jr. (descendant of presidents John and John Quincy Adams) broke the story in a magazine article in 1872 entitled "The Pacific Railroad Ring," focusing on the conflict of interest and inferred massive corruption: "The members of it are in Congress; they are trustees for the bondholders; they are directors; they are stockholders; they are contractors; in Washington they vote the subsidies, in New York they receive them, upon the plains they expend them, and in the 'Credit Mobilier' they divide them" (Ambrose 2000, 320).

The *New York Sun* investigated CM in 1872 and called it "The King of Frauds: How the Credit Mobilier Bought Its Way through Congress," inferring bribery and influence peddling. The House of Representatives held hearings under the Credit Mobilier Committee. All the major players testified (UP chief engineer Grenville Dodge was an exception, because he went into hiding in Texas).

Oakes Ames became "Hoax Ames" in the press. Congress accused Ames of stock payoffs, lying to Congress, and pursuing massive overcharging and dividends payments by CM. Ames was censured by Congress in 1873 and died soon after. Ames had acquired enough shares to push Durant out of CM leadership in 1869 and Durant escaped largely untouched by the scandal; however, he was wiped out by the Panic of 1873.

CM was sued by the federal government for fraud and expropriation of funds. The Supreme Court viewed CM's conduct as legal and ruled in favor of the company. None of the perpetrators faced prosecution. UP repaid the federal debt when it became due at the end of the century, but reluctantly. The railroads fought repayment in court but eventually paid some $168 million in principal and interest.

The railroad bubble collapsed about the time the hearings concluded in 1873, too much debt for the available traffic. Jay Cooke and Son became overextended in Northern Pacific Railroad securities and shut its doors in September of 1873, followed by dozens of banks and brokerage houses. Jay Gould used this opportunity to buy enough stock to control the UP, pillaging it once again.

The Big Four built almost all of California's railroads plus other transportation systems, which they consolidated into the Southern Pacific Railroad, charging monopoly rates for transportation. They all died wealthy. Collis Huntington (the last of them) died in 1900, worth an estimated $100 million. Huntington's heirs sold out to UP. The UP still exists as the largest railroad network in the United States. Despite the corruption, California was linked to the rest of the country and the vast wilderness became settled and productive. Also on the positive side, Stanford's and Huntington's illicit wealth endowed the Huntington Library and Stanford University.

See also: Ames, Oakes; Central Pacific Railroad; Durant, Thomas; Gould, Jason ("Jay"); Railroads, Nineteenth Century; Union Pacific Railroad

References

Ambrose, Stephen. *Nothing Like It in the World: The Men Who Built the Transcontinental Railroad 1863–1869*. New York: Touchstone, 2000.

Brands, H. W. *American Colossus: The Triumph of Capitalism, 1865–1900*. New York: Doubleday, 2010.

Josephson, Matthew. *The Robber Barons*. New York: Harcourt, 1962.

Rayner, Richard. *The Associates: Four Capitalists Who Created California*. New York: Norton, 2008.

Transparency

Transparency means that all financial information of a public company is observable and fully reported based on existing accounting standards. Implied in this definition is disclosure based on financial reality. Financial information is disclosed primarily in annual and quarterly reports that present summarized information based on existing standards and available with a lag of up to 60 days for a 10-K. The basic concept of transparency is captured by Friedman (2000), using the metaphor of the African plain:

When a wildebeest on the edge of the herd sees something move in the tall, thick brush ... that wildebeest starts a stampede. They stampede to the next country and crush everything in their path. So how does one protect your country from this? Answer: You cut the grass, and clear away the bush, so that the next time the wildebeest sees something rustle in the grass it thinks, "no problem, I see what it is" (172).

Opaque reporting in good times can lead to optimistic illusion that can bid up stock prices (Enron, for example). When the bad news hits, nothing can be believed and prices collapse. "You go from believing everything to believing nothing" (Friedman 2000, 173).

Several areas of disclosure are potentially opaque, including the results of acquisitions more than a year after the merger. Another area of concern is derivatives (such as futures and options). Derivatives are usually reported in the financial statements based on fair value. However, it can be difficult to determine if a company is, in fact, hedging or speculating or how much risk exists.

Segment reporting can provide significant information on operating and geographic segments, or very little. Only limited segment reporting is required by accounting standards, while global corporations are complex and have worldwide operations. Consequently, industry and geographic segments are widespread and usually complicated. The first problem is the extreme flexibility in defining a segment. There is no obvious standardization. Disney, for example, has extensive information on the four operating segments it reports; however, if you want to evaluate the Mighty Ducks or the Anaheim Angels (which Disney owns), it cannot be done—they are part of Parks and Resorts and not reported separately.

Financial reality assumes conservative accounting, such as recognizing revenues late in the earnings process, after they have been earned and cash has been realized or realizable. If income is manipulated to meet earnings targets, financial reality and therefore transparency has been violated.

Timeliness also is important, presenting financial reports as quickly as possible so investors can act on the information. The Securities and Exchange Commission (SEC) required that the annual report (10-K) of public companies must be submitted within 60 days of the end of the fiscal year and the quarterly report (10-Q) within 45 days. Consequently, timeliness generally is less of a transparency issue.

See also Accounting Fraud; Accounting Standards; Annual Report (10-K); Earnings Manipulation; Fraud; Securities and Exchange Commission (SEC)

References

Friedman, Thomas. *The Lexus and the Olive Tree*. New York: Anchor Books, 2000.

Giroux, Gary. *Detecting Earnings Management*. Hoboken, NJ: Wiley, 2004.

Schilit, Howard. *Financial Shenanigans: How to Detect Accounting Gimmicks & Fraud in Financial Reports*. New York: McGraw-Hill, 2002.

Treasury Department

The Department of the Treasury is an executive department of the U.S. federal government, originally established by an act of Congress. Treasury prints all paper money (through the Bureau of Engraving and Printing) and mints all coins (through the U.S. Mint). All federal taxes are collected by Treasury through the Internal Revenue Service (IRS) and the federal debt also is managed by Treasury.

According to the Treasury website, the mission of the department is to:

maintain a strong economy and create economic and job opportunities by promoting the conditions that enable economic growth and stability at home and abroad, strengthen national security by combating threats and protecting the integrity of the financial system, and manage the U.S. Government's finances and resources effectively.

The basic functions of the Department of the Treasury as listed on the Treasury website include:

- Managing Federal finances
- Collecting taxes, duties, and monies paid to and due to the U.S. and paying all bills of the U.S.;
- Currency and coinage;
- Managing Government accounts and the public debt;
- Supervising national banks and thrift institutions;
- Advising on domestic and international financial, monetary, economic, trade. and tax policy;
- Enforcing Federal finance and tax laws;
- Investigating and prosecuting tax evaders, counterfeiters, and forgers.

George Washington won unanimously election as the first president in 1788. There was no mention of a cabinet in the Constitution, so Congress had to establish the Treasury Department (plus state, war, and attorney general), which it did in September 1789. Washington named Alexander Hamilton the first secretary of the Treasury. Hamilton, a lawyer and Washington's aide during the American Revolution, proved to be a financial genius.

Hamilton's job at Treasury proved difficult. As Chernow summarized Hamilton's dilemma (2004, 287):

In debating the Constitution, Hamilton knew that the issue of federal taxation and tax collectors had provoked the biggest brouhaha. As chief tax collector, he would be the lightning rod for inevitable discontent. In fact, everything that Hamilton planned to create to transform America into a powerful, modern nation-state—a central bank, a funded debt, a mint, a customs service, manufacturing subsidies, and so on—was to strike critics as a slavish imitation of the British model.

Hamilton called for a central bank, sending Congress his *Report on the Bank of the United States* in December 1790, arguing that a central bank was necessary to fund the debts of the United States. The Bank of the United States was created by Congress as a national corporation (the first), effectively the central bank of the United States from 1791 to 1811. The bank was used by Hamilton for short-term loans to cover Treasury's cash needs, with revenue sources seasonal. Beyond the commitment for government functions, the bank had authority to make commercial loans, mainly short-term loans to successful merchants.

Hamilton created a Customs Service after custom duties (tariffs) became the primary source of federal revenue. In addition to gold, he allowed payment of duties in notes from the Bank of New York (his bank) and the Bank of North America (Robert Morris's bank). The early days at Treasury were precarious, mainly because of limited revenue collections against substantial expenditure needs, including servicing the new national debt. As revenues increased and the Bank of the United States served some of the functions of a central bank, financing became less of an issue; Hamilton resigned in 1795.

Thomas Jefferson and his Democratic-Republicans took control of the federal government at the start of the nineteenth century and dominated federal politics for decades. Many of Hamilton's innovative policies including taking direct action to stop a panic were not repeated until the twentieth century. The Bank of the United States would be gone when the charter expired. Hamilton's bookkeeping and administrative system continued under Jefferson, as did the reliance on customs duties.

During the Civil War, Treasury Secretary Salmon Chase substantially raised taxes for the war effort, including the first income tax in 1862. The Office of Internal Revenue was created to collect the taxes. The major revenue source continued to be customs duties, although income and other internal taxes increased the war years. The Union created national banks subject to federal oversight. Under the National Banking Acts of 1863 and 1864, the banks could issue national banknotes printed by the federal government and backed by Treasury securities (a major rationale for the acts was the requirement that national banks hold Treasury bonds, which provided the major funding source for the Union military). The creation of national banks did not end panics and depressions but changed the role of banks when they occurred. Since the creation of a true and permanent national banking system under a central bank had to wait until the Federal Reserve Act of 1913, the on-again-off-again nature of the federal banking role contributed to the uncertainties that in turn repeatedly ignited and sustained financial crises for the next 50 years.

The United States returned to the gold standard in 1879 and the Treasury Department maintained $100 million in gold. The economy generated trade surpluses and the government operated with budget surpluses, keeping gold coming to

The United States and into the Treasury coffers. Speculation and business over-capacity cause a panic in 1893. The Panic resulted in business failures, including many railroads and banks. Foreign sales of U.S. securities dropped the supply of American gold. When the Treasury's gold hit only $9 million, President Grover Cleveland and Treasury turned to J. P. Morgan. Morgan and other banks raised $100 million in gold reserves from Europe. Federal gold bonds were issued on Wall Street and London, backed by these reserves, that sold quickly at a premium. Morgan's syndicate acquired the bonds at 104 and offered them to investors at 112. Pierpont used all his global banking experience to fill the Treasury's gold coffers, and by the middle of 1895 Treasury reserves rose to $107.5 million to avoid financial catastrophe.

The Panic of 1907 involved a stock market crash, tight money, speculation and manipulation, a failed corner and broker insolvency, bank runs, and the near insolvency of New York City. Speculation, high interest rates, and a jittery stock market preceded the panic. J. P. Morgan saved several trust companies (at the time banks could not handle estates and related trust activity) and a major brokerage house, bailed out New York City, and supported the New York Stock Exchange. Congress did not want to see a repeat of events that left the federal government as a secondary player, beholden to the Money Trust. The Aldrich-Vreeland Act established the National Monetary Commission in 1908 to reform and regulate banking. The commission and congressional Hearings—the Pujo Hearings being the most famous—resulted in the creation of the Federal Reserve (Fed) as a central bank in 1914; this was viewed as either the necessary institution to protect the banking system or a bailout mechanism for big banks financed by taxpayers. The Fed would provide the liquidity and relieve pressure from Treasury.

There were 12 years of Republican presidents (1921–33) who expressed little interest in business regulation and taxes, and government spending fell. Treasury Secretary Andrew Mellon, who made a fortune through ALCOA and banking, established government policies favoring business and Wall Street—with little regulation to speculation and predatory business practices. When the 1929 market crash and downturn hit, Mellon's response was to do nothing, famously stating, "liquidate labor, liquidate stocks, liquidate the farmers, liquidate real estate . . . purge the rottenness out of the system." Mellon wanted higher interest rates to stop the flow of gold to Europe and stabilize the value of the dollar; the United States would maintain the gold standard. This poor government response made matters worse, turning a recession into the Great Depression.

On March 4, 1933, Franklin Roosevelt was sworn in as president and took immediate action for an inherited banking crisis, announcing a national bank holiday—all banks were closed for a week and inspected by federal officials. Roosevelt submitted an emergency banking act bill to Congress on March 9 (passed and signed into law the same day) to allow healthy banks to reopen under Treasury Department supervision. Every year of the 1930s under Roosevelt, Treasury ran a deficit (stated in millions), often greater than total revenue. The public debt increased every year, although the debt as a percent of gross domestic product (GDP) increased from 40 percent to only 44 percent by the end of the decade.

World War II changed Washington from a small community to a bureaucrat-infested world center of government action, a position never relinquished. Spending, revenues, budget deficits, and the national debt all zoomed upward. Thanks to rising income taxes, federal revenues increased, but not enough to cover massive defense spending. Withholding made higher tax rates somewhat more palatable to the public. The Treasury focused on domestic sales of debt including war-bond drives, while new corporate debt was close to zero.

In the post–World War II period, the United States dominated the world economy. As the role of the country expanded in foreign wars and an expanding welfare rose, budget deficits rose, increasing the role of Treasury to finance the growing national debt. Salomon Brothers, the longtime leader in the Treasury market in the 1980s, served as a primary dealer. The Treasury system was an auction market where a select few primary dealers bid on Treasuries as they were issued. The Treasury Department had a 35 percent cap for any purchase of Treasuries issues, instituted because Salomon had routinely placed bids for far more than the amount of securities issued. Salomon trader Paul Mozer submitted false bids to increase the share for Salomon. The scandal erupted when Treasury discovered Mozer's fraud for the February 1991 five-year note. After winning all the bids (about 90% of the total auction amount) Mozer wrote up a sell ticket back to Salomon for the acquisitions of the customers, but without the usual confirmations. Salomon handled the incident poorly and Mozer continued to make false bids. When the story broke later that year, Mozer, Mozer's boss John Meriwether, and CEO John Gutfreund were fired. Salomon paid $290 million in fines and later sold to Travelers Group, now Citigroup. Mozer received a four-month sentenced and was fined over $1 million. Government investigations uncovered frauds similar to Mozer's in other government bond markets such as federal home mortgages. "Cease and desist" orders and fines went out to several Wall Street firms.

Mexican debt indexed to dollars (called *tesobonos*), greatly expanding the interest obligations, resulted in a financial crisis and a severe recession—called the "Tequila Crisis" of 1995. Given the capital flight, Mexico badly needed American dollars. For political reasons, Congress refused to act. President Bill Clinton's Treasury Department came to the rescue, using its Exchange Stabilization Fund (basically cash not subject to congressional approval) and other sources to provide a $50 billion line of credit to Mexico. Exchange rates stabilized and the crisis subsided. Economic recovery returned and Mexico repaid the Treasury loan.

Henry ("Hank") Paulson was selected by President George W. Bush as Treasury secretary in mid-2006. Along with Ben Bernanke, chairman of the Federal Reserve, and Tim Geithner, president of the New York Federal Reserve, Paulson engineered the bailout of the financial sector during the subprime crisis of 2008. Like most experts, Paulson was aware of the subprime problems and rising housing prices, but did not view it as a potential catastrophe—until it happened. After the bankruptcy of investment bank Lehman Brothers, the credit markets failed and Paulson requested what became the Troubled Asset Relief Program (TARP), a multibillion-dollar bailout of large banks. After the election of Barack Obama, Tim Geithner became Treasury secretary and continued the basic policies of Paulson.

See also Bank of North America; Bank of the United States, First; Constitution, U.S.; Duer, William; Great Depression; Hamilton, Alexander; Morgan, John Pierpont; Panics and Depressions; Paulson, Hank; Troubled Asset Relief Program (TARP); Washington, George

References

Chernow, Ron. *Alexander Hamilton*. New York: Penguin Press, 2004.

Paulson, Henry. *On the Brink: Insider the Race to Stop the Collapse of the Global Financial System*. New York: Business Plus, 2010.

Stockwell, Mary. "Hamilton, Alexander." In *The American Economy: A Historical Encyclopedia*. Rev. ed. Edited by Cynthia Clark. Santa Barbara, CA: ABC-CLIO, 2011.

U.S. Department of the Treasury. "Duties & Functions of the U.S. Department of the Treasury." http://www.treasury.gov/about/role-of-treasury/Pages/default.aspx.

Vile, John. "Hamilton, Alexander." In *The Constitutional Convention of 1787: A Comprehensive Encyclopedia of America's Founding*. Santa Barbara, CA: ABC-CLIO, 2005.

Treasury Stock

Treasury stock is the company's outstanding shares that are repurchased in the market and usually treated as a separate line item on the balance sheet as "negative equity." Equity represents the ownership interests of the corporation. Profitable companies can buy outstanding shares rather than pay dividends (or do both), often using treasury stock to pay future stock options outstanding.

A major advantage of treasury stock is it reduces the number of shares outstanding; that is, it is antidilutive. With fewer shares, earnings per share (EPS) increase relative to net income. For example, if net income is $5 million and 1 million shares are outstanding, EPS is $5. If the firm buys back 100,000 shares, the calculation is $5 million/900,000 or $5.56. EPS increased over 10 percent although net income remained the same. Buying back shares is common for companies issuing stock options or restricted stock. Stock options and other equity compensation are dilutive—they increase the number of shares outstanding and thus decrease relative EPS. By buying back a roughly equivalent number of shares, there is no net dilutive effect.

The other stated advantage of treasury stock is to increase stock price. Buying large blocks of shares will increase the price, at least temporarily. Financial analysts often claim to favor companies that "support" their own share price. Many companies actually have policies to buy back some number shares (or a certain dollar amount) over some period of time—specifically to support stock price.

Treasury stock should be analyzed in the context of the overall equity strategy of the firm. Many successful companies in the 1990s bought Treasury securities at inflated prices, presumably for future options payouts. The joint impact was a further increase of share prices and zero or reduced dividend payment. Then stock prices collapsed. The result was expensive treasury stock reducing the equity of non-dividend-paying companies, with reduced operating prospects.

A potential relationship exists among options, treasury stock, and dividends. Historically, companies have paid out substantial dividends. As companies switched to stock options, they issued fewer dividends (which are not paid to option holders) and used more cash to buy back outstanding shares. The typical rationale was to use the accumulated treasury stock to limit the dilution effect of options. Consequently, these should be evaluated together. In terms of cash flows, the use of stock options can be considered to have "inverse incentives," that is, the focus on option incentives, which leads to purchasing treasury stock and limiting or avoiding the payment of dividends. This is a beneficial strategy for executive compensation (especially for those that do not own much stock), but detrimental to investors preferring dividends.

The practice of buying back outstanding stock has a number of earnings management problems and can have a dramatic effect on the financial position of corporations. Acquiring treasury stock is problematic because:

1. Acquisition reduces both cash and stockholders' equity. If substantial, this can have a sizable effect on standard quantitative financial analysis.
2. Stock repurchasing can be used as a rationale for not paying dividends. The argument is that this is the best use of available cash and investors can "cash in" their shares if they disagree.
3. Large purchases can be used to prop up share prices (possibly when executives are exercising and cashing out their options). The buy backs may make sense if the stock price is low, but is it the best use of cash for investment?

An extreme case was Maytag, a major appliance company founded by Frederick Maytag in 1893. At the end of 2001, options outstanding were 1.4 million or 1.9 percent of outstanding shares. Accumulated treasury stock was 40.3 million shares, at a total cost of $1.5 billion. This was the major item that resulted in stockholders' equity of only $23.5 million. When compared to total liabilities of $3.1 billion, Maytag had almost no equity (less than 1% of total assets). On top of that, Maytag paid out $55.1 million in dividends, more than net income for the year. Treasury stock was rising at a good clip over the previous three years, and it was difficult to explain why, except Maytag's actions to maintain stock price. Maytag recorded a net loss for 2004 and had negative equity of $75 million. Maytag was acquired by rival Whirlpool in 2006 for less than $2 billion.

According to Giroux (2006) the 30 members of the Dow Jones Industrial Average (Dow 30) buy back their own shares and all use stock options—presumably the rationale for treasury stock. Treasury stock is normally reported on the balance sheet as a separate line item under stockholders' equity, giving the amount and number of shares repurchased. Twenty-three Dow 30 firms reported amounts ranging from $142 million for Verizon to $36 billion for Pfizer. Half the Dow firms (15) recorded treasury stock greater than 10 percent of total equity. IBM, Coca-Cola, and Merck had treasury stock greater than total stockholders' equity. Since acquiring treasury stock reduces equity, it increases the relative leverage. IBM had equity of $23.2 billion at the end of 2010 and treasury stock $96.2 billion, 415 percent of equity.

Seven Dow 30 companies did not report treasury stock on their 2004 balance sheet: American Express, GM, H-P, Intel, Microsoft, Procter & Gamble, and Wal-Mart. Companies must show annual treasury stock acquisitions on both the statement of stockholders' equity and statement of cash flows. During the six year period of 2000–2005, Wal-Mart bought back 266 million shares for $14,486 million. That represents the equivalent of 32 percent of net income over the period. Wal-Mart also exercised 41 million options over this period as well for $1.6 billion, a fraction of treasury stock purchased. The net increase of treasury stock was 225 million shares at $12.9 billion. This is not the total amount of treasury stock, but still represented 26.1 percent of total equity. All seven purchased treasury stock, which averaged 63.1 percent of net income over the six-year period 1999–2004. Not recording treasury stock on the balance sheet is a transparency issue, missing information of interest to many analysts and investors.

See also Annual Report (10-K); Debt and Leverage; Dow Jones Industrial Average (Dow); Stock Option Manipulation

Reference

Giroux, Gary. *Earnings Magic and the Unbalance Sheet: The Search for Financial Reality.* New York: Wiley, 2006.

Triangle Shirtwaist Fire (1911)

The factory fire of the Triangle Shirtwaist Company in New York City was one of the biggest industrial disasters in U.S. history. The fire resulted in 146 deaths from smoke, fire, and jumping to avoid the flames, mainly young female immigrants (the youngest was 14). Clothing manufacturing was a major industry in turn-of-the-twentieth-century New York City, home of the garment district. Triangle occupied the 8th to 10th floors of the Asch Building, producing women's blouses (called "shirtwaists"). The factory employed about 500 women willing to work for $7 to $12 a week, with a nine-hour day plus seven hours on Saturday.

As summarized by Howard Zinn (2003, 326):

> On the afternoon of March 25, 1911, a fire at the Triangle Shirtwaist Company that began in a rag bin swept through the eighth, ninth and tenth floors, too high for fire ladders to reach. The fire chief of New York had said that his ladders could reach only to the seventh floor. But half of New York's

500,000 workers spend all day, perhaps twelve hours, above the seventh floor. The laws said factory doors had to open outward. But at the Triangle Company the doors opened in. The law said the doors could not be locked during working hours, but the Triangle Company doors were usually locked so the company could keep track of the employees. And so, trapped, the young women were burned to death at their work-tables, or jammed against the locked exit doors, or leaped to their deaths down the elevator shafts.

Elevator operators saved many lives until the elevator rails buckled because of the heat. Bystanders witnessed 62 people jumping to their death, many on fire. The owners, Max Blanch and Isaac Harris, who fled the building on the roof, were indicted on charges of manslaughter but were acquitted. They lost a civil suit resulting in the payment of compensation of $75 per victim.

An investigation of the fire was conducted under Robert Wagner as chairman of the State Factory Investigating Committee. (Later, as New York senator, Wagner sponsored the Wagner Act of 1935, which provided federal protection for workers and labor unions.) New York City's fire chief identified 200 factories with conditions making fires similar to Triangle likely. Committee findings resulted in 60 new state laws regulating labor and working conditions. A New York City Committee on Public Safety was formed to identify problems and lobby for safety legislation. The American Society of Safety Engineers was founded in New York City in October 1911.

Despite new regulations, fires and accidents continued. In 1904, 27,000 workers were killed on the job in the United States and 50,000 accidents happened in New York. In 1914, 35,000 people were killed and 700,000 injured. During the 1920s, on-the-job deaths averaged 25,000 a year and 100,000 people permanently disabled (Zinn 2003, 327, 382).

See also American Federation of Labor/Congress of Industrial Organizations (AFL-CIO); Carnegie, Andrew; Homestead Strike (1892); Labor Movement, U.S.; Wagner Act

References

Atkins, Albert. "Labor." In *The American Economy: A Historical Encyclopedia*. Rev. ed. Edited by Cynthia Clark. Santa Barbara, CA: ABC-CLIO, 2011.

Livesay, Harold. *Samuel Gompers and Organized Labor in America*. Boston: Little, Brown, 1978.

Zinn, Howard. *A People's History of the United States*. New York: Harper Perennial Modern Classics, 2003.

Troubled Asset Relief Program (TARP)

TARP was the U.S. government bailout to address the financial crisis of 2008, based on the Emergency Economic Stabilization Act passed in October 2008.

Treasury Secretary Henry ("Hank") Paulson later said, "The financial system essentially seized up and we had a system-wide crisis" (reported in Cohan 2009, 446).

In March 2008 Paulson, Treasury, and the Federal Reserve (Fed) under Chairman Ben Bernanke and New York Federal Reserve President Timothy Geithner engineered a takeover of failed investment bank Bear Stearns by J. P. Morgan Chase, including a $30 billion government "buyout" of $30 billion in Bear's toxic assets. Later in the year, the federal government seized government-sponsored enterprises Fannie Mae and Freddie Mac and placed them in conservatorship. After a failed attempted federal bailout, investment bank Lehman Brothers declared bankruptcy in September 2008 and credit essentially stopped across the country and much of the world. TARP was an attempt to provide capital to the banking system as part of the effort to restore confidence in the financial system in the United States.

Unlike the Fed, the Treasury Department has little ability to dole out funds without legislative approval. A congressional act was necessary to provide banking capital to end the financial chaos. The Paulson/Bernanke plan essentially resulted in the Troubled Asset Relief Program (TARP), giving some $700 billion to Treasury with considerable flexibility to spend it. The initial idea was to ask for $500 billion, and Bernanke, Paulson, and Securities and Exchange Commission (SEC) chairman Christopher Cox met with the congressional leaders, presenting a stark picture that inaction meant complete meltdown of the financial system. Paulson wanted to buy the toxic assets from the banks; the alternative plan (which Bernanke preferred) was to inject funds directly into the banks (which paralleled the Reconstruction Finance Corporation used during the Great Depression and the bailout response in other countries), requesting $700 billion. The congressional leaders asked for a written plan, resulting in a three-page Treasury draft written up over the weekend.

A sticking point of TARP was pricing the toxic assets to be bought. Too high meant taxpayers lost money; too low meant bigger losses for the banks reducing capital even further. Congress rejected the plan on September 29, in part based on voter protests. The Dow proceeded to drop about 780 points, some 7 percent. The TARP bill passed on the second try, October 1. In the meantime it became clear that action was needed quickly and buying toxic assets would be a slow process. Paulson agreed to Bernanke's plan of injecting cash directly to the banks, which was allowed in the legislation. The Fed could provide liquidity to the system, but not capital—which the TARP money could do.

On October 12 Paulson called the chief executive officers (CEOs) of the nine largest banks (Citigroup, JP Morgan, Wells Fargo, Bank of America, Goldman Sachs, Morgan Stanley, Merrill Lynch, State Street Corporation, and Bank of New York Mellon) and invited them to Treasury. Bernanke described the Fed's plans to buy commercial paper; Federal Deposit Insurance Corporation (FDIC) head Sheila Bair outlined new guarantees of bank debt, then Geithner described the new direct investment in bank capital called the capital purchase program (CPP). For TARP cash equal to 3 percent of risk-weighted assets up to $25 billion, the banks would issue 5 percent preferred stock to the government plus warrants for common stock. After a bit of arm twisting, all of the bank CEOs agreed. Paulson announced the plan on October 14. At the end of October, Treasury allocated $25 billion each to Citigroup and Bank of America (B of A), with lesser amounts to the less-troubled big banks (a total of $125 billion). Citi and B of A, badly in need of the funds, received further TARP cash plus asset guarantees for additional hundreds of billions. Other banks applied for similar funding.

Many critics of TARP focused on the moral hazard of bailing out the failing banks effectively causing the crisis, privatizing gains and socializing losses. Economist Joseph Stiglitz (2010, 80) stated, "Nine lenders that combined had nearly $100 billion in losses received $175 billion in bailout money through TARP and paid out nearly $33 billion in bonuses, including more than $1 million apiece to nearly five thousand employees."

Funds also were distributed to many banks as well as nonbank financials such as American Express and American Insurance Group (AIG), plus auto giants General Motors and Chrysler. Only in March 2009 did Treasury announce the Public-Private Investment Program to buy toxic assets, a program similar to the original purpose of TARP. It did not prove very effective, in part because of the difficulty of actually valuing toxic assets. In April 2009, the FASB issued a Final Staff Position (FSP FAS 157-4) providing guidance when asset prices are based on "disorderly sales" (such as forced liquidation), "not indicative of fair value." Guidance suggested using a "cash-flow derived value," effectively eliminating the need to mark down the distressed mortgages to market value. This new FASB rule proved effective in eliminating the stress caused by writing down the financial assets to market value. Banks were much less willing to sell the toxic assets at a big loss when they could keep it on their books at a higher value.

Congress held hearings criticizing Treasury and others for misusing funds; the hyperbolic rage spread to media pundits attacking TARP. It did not help that banks were not loaning much money even after the cash injections, while some financial institutions seemed to be using the funds to buy other banks; for example, PNC Financial Services acquired National City Corp for almost $6 billion within hours of an $8 billion TARP grant. In addition, according to Reuters, banks receiving hundreds of billions in bailout funds spent over $100 million on campaign contributions and lobbying, while paying large salaries and bonuses to executives and key employees (people were particularly outraged by bonuses to executives of bailed out AIG, Merrill Lynch, Freddie Mac, and Fannie Mae). Much of this played out during the period after the election of a new president and the "lame duck" session of Congress, adding to the confusion. With a new administration in place in mid-January 2009, Geithner replaced Paulson at Treasury, while Bernanke stayed in place, maintaining policy continuity. Ex-Goldman executive William Dudley replaced Geithner at the New York Fed, maintaining that Goldman-government connection.

Simultaneously with TARP, the Fed and others went into action to protect the short-term credit markets. The FDIC established the Temporary Liquidity

Guarantee Program to guaranty new unsecured debt of banks and other financials. In late October, the Fed set up the Commercial Paper Funding Facility to purchase unsecured and collateralized commercial paper to keep that market in business and provide protection to money market funds. In late November, the Term Asset-Backed Securities Loan Facility (TALF) was established to loan short-term funds to banks using asset-backed securities as collateral, again financed through a special-purpose entity (SPE). Much of this market was made to nonbanks like General Electric (GE) Credit, where funding had almost disappeared. The lending ceiling had to be raised to $1 trillion to support this market. Between open-market operations (the Fed funds rate dropped to 1% at the end of October) pumping hundreds of billions of cash into the economy and these various programs, the government claimed to prevent a complete meltdown of the credit markets, at a cost of several trillion dollars.

In December 2008, the National Bureau of Economic Research announced that the country had entered recession in December 2007—the housing mess indeed pushed the economy over the edge. Unemployment continued up, stock prices down, and the average American was up in arms against the financial-regulatory complex. In mid-December, Fed action brought the Fed funds rate down to zero, the zero interest rate policy (ZIRP). Even under Greenspan, the interest rate policy never dropped below 1 percent. By the December meeting, the Fed increased its total lending to $2.3 trillion, from $940 billion before the Lehman bankruptcy (Wessel 2009, 251).

During this time, Treasury and the Fed provided pragmatic but seemingly ad hoc decisions. Although they used extraordinary powers, little obvious planning and few long-term economic goals existed. The Fed and Treasury continued to provide huge sums to sustain the financial system, maintain liquidity, and keep interest rates low. Multiple regulatory failures contributed to the crisis, and the financial institutions central to the mess seemed to return to normal with little obvious contrition. New regulations, perhaps a complete overhaul, were needed. Congress held numerous hearings, various regulatory agencies studied the issues and issued proposals, and the White House announced new regulatory efforts. Different views on the fix plus political infighting delayed real change, made more difficult by financial industry lobbying.

Congress and the regulators made a number of changes within existing laws. The Home Ownership and Equity Protection Act (HOEPA) went into effect in 1995, but Alan Greenspan's Fed did little with the new powers for regulating mortgages. Bernanke announced changes in 2008, including standardizing prime lending practices, banning deceptive practices, requiring ability-to-pay standards and income verification of borrowers, escrow account rules for taxes and insurance, and so on. Congress passed the Fraud Enforcement and Recovery Act, signed into law May 20, 2009, to enhance criminal enforcement of federal fraud laws, including greater funding. Section 5 of the act created the Financial Crisis Inquiry Commission to examine the causes of the current crisis, which issued its final report in January 2011. The Dodd-Frank Financial Reform bill "to promote financial stability" and present a regulatory overhaul plan passed in 2010.

See also Bernanke, Ben S.; Bond Ratings on Structured Finance; Debt and Leverage; Federal Reserve System; Financial Accounting Standards Board (FASB); National Bureau of Economic Research; Paulson, Hank; Structured Finance; Subprime Meltdown; Treasury Department

References

Allen, Larry. "Troubled Asset Relief Program." In *The Encyclopedia of Money*. 2nd ed. Santa Barbara, CA: ABC-CLIO, 2009.

Cohan, William. *House of Cards: A Tale of Hubris and Wretched Excess on Wall Street.* New York: Doubleday, 2009.

Paulson, Henry. *On the Brink: Insider the Race to Stop the Collapse of the Global Financial System.* New York: Business Plus, 2010.

Stiglitz, Joseph. *Freefall: America, Free Markets, and the Sinking of the World Economy.* New York: Norton, 2010.

Wessel, David. *In Fed We Trust: Ben Bernanke's War on the Great Panic.* New York: Crown Business, 2009.

Trust Movement

Trusts are business combinations with a board of trustees created to eliminate competition in an industry. This legal entity operates under a trust agreement wherein a single board of trustees controls the operations of the members, generally to fix prices and allocate market share. The first trust was created by Standard Oil lawyer Samuel Dodd in 1872 to allow Standard to operate legally across state lines using a multitude of corporations chartered in different states. The trust was attacked by reforming journalists and regulators, and federal antitrust legislation, beginning with the Sherman Antitrust Act of 1890, was passed in an attempt to limit the damage caused by price fixing and monopoly power.

Manufacturing firms expanded production and markets after the Civil War, but faced antiquated state laws and cutthroat competition limited potential growth. Too many small competitors existed in most industries, many with limited expertise producing shoddy products. John D. Rockefeller's Standard Oil was one of the first industrialists that tried to solve this set of problems. Various types of pools and cartels were attempted to rein in competitive pressures (called "conspiracies in restraint of trade" by regulators), with only modest success since conspirators had incentives to break agreements (which were nonenforceable) for their own benefit. Business combinations in various legal forms became the strategy of choice. Rockefeller's Standard Oil was a leader in both movements. After the success of Standard, investment bankers moved into the consolidation movement. J. P. Morgan's experience with reorganizing and consolidating failed railroads was used to consolidate industries.

Standard Oil's trust went into effect in 1882. Under Dodd's scheme, stockholders received trust certificates in exchange for their shares in the individual companies (subsidiaries). The nine trustees became the directors of all the companies under the trust agreement and centrally controlled operations, including product pricing, quantities produced, and dividends paid by the subsidiaries to the trust. Although Ohio declared Standard's trust illegal, the trust moved operations until better legal combinations became available. Hundreds of companies combined under various trust agreements across many industries.

Revised state incorporation laws provided a better monopoly-creating option to the trust agreement, with New Jersey leading the way by solving the problem of owning corporations across states. Holding companies made owning virtually entire industries possible. As Mitchell (2007, 31) states: "New Jersey presided over the degradation of corporate integrity from 1889 to 1913 . . . It is how New Jersey changed the face of American corporate capitalism." Forming a large consolidated near-monopoly became legal and relatively efficient with a top-down management structure using the holding company.

Facing severe financial problems, New Jersey joined other states by becoming accommodating to big business. New Jersey created not only favorable legislation but a separate corporate agency (the Corporation Trust Company of New Jersey) specifically to provide all the necessary assistance to incorporate in New Jersey, beginning in 1889. Incorporation rates in New Jersey increased to about 2,000 by 1900. The state paid off its massive debt. When John Moody, founder of Moody's Investors Service, studied trusts in 1904 he discovered that 170 out of 318 analyzed (53.5%) were chartered as New Jersey corporations.

The holding company became the primary mechanism for monopoly power around the turn of the twentieth century. The holding company corporation held the stock of the subsidiaries rather than a board of trustees. The 1889 holding company act allowed New Jersey corporations to own stock and bonds in other New Jersey corporations, and changes in the law became increasingly accommodating. By 1899, corporations could acquire the stock of other companies whether the acquisition was a New Jersey corporation or not, the acquirer could buy these subsidiaries using their own shares rather than cash (it also allowed the acquisition of stock for property), and holding companies could exist solely as a finance company strictly to own shares of other corporations. With these benefits, Standard Oil reorganized as a New Jersey holding company in 1899.

Morgan created the Edison Electric Illuminating Company; his mansion became the first private residence in New York with electricity, supplied by Edison in 1878, and his office the first on Wall Street. The consolidation of Edison Electric and competitor Thomson-Houston produced General Electric in 1892. Morgan also organized American Telephone and Telegraph, International Harvester, Western Union, Westinghouse, and, the biggest of all, United States Steel.

When Republican William McKinley was elected president in 1896, Wall Street expected federal antitrust action to stop and mergers exploded. Combination increased from fewer than 70 in 1897 to over 1,200 in 1899. Consolidated industries included whiskey, lead, matches, nails, coal, sugar, and even bananas, and industrial giants became fixture on the New York Stock Exchange. The assassination of McKinley in 1901 brought Theodore Roosevelt to the presidency. "Teddy the Trustbuster" increased antitrust prosecutions, including a suit against Morgan's Northern Securities Company in 1902 under the Sherman Antitrust Act. Later legislation in 1914 passed the Clayton Antitrust Act and established the Federal Trade Commission. Antitrust prosecutions were sometimes successful and limited monopoly power, but big business was well established in the United States.

See also Antitrust; Carnegie, Andrew; Morgan, John Pierpont; Rockefeller, John Davison; Roosevelt, Theodore; Sherman Antitrust Act of 1890; Standard Oil Co.; United States Steel

References

Clark, Cynthia. "Trusts." In *The American Economy: A Historical Encyclopedia*. Rev. ed. Santa Barbara, CA: ABC-CLIO, 2011.

Josephson, Matthew. *The Robber Barons*. New York: Harcourt, 1962.

Mitchell, Lawrence. *The Speculative Economy: How Finance Triumphed Over Industry*. San Francisco: Berrett-Koehler, 2007.

Tulip Mania

Tulip Mania was an "asset bubble" created in Holland by interest in rare tulips, followed by a quick and steep collapse. The Golden Age of Dutch commerce, the early seventeenth century, was interrupted by the first speculative bubble—for tulips. Tulips were introduced from the Ottoman Empire into the Netherlands (then called the United Provinces) in the mid-sixteenth century. They became a coveted luxury good, and prices rose and continued to rise through 1836, at wildly inflated prices. Then the market collapsed in February 1637.

When the tulip arrived in Europe in the mid-sixteenth century, the wealthy of Germany and the Netherlands became major buyers. The Netherlands was starting its "golden age" around a large Dutch merchant fleet, the development of the corporation, and the stock exchange in Amsterdam. The tulip grew extremely well in the country; bankers made investments in tulip farming as well as in tulips. Tulips became a speculative vehicle and separate tulip markets developed. The Dutch also appreciated other flowers; the price of hyacinths, for example, also rose in price.

The *Semper Augustus* was a tulip of beauty, with midnight-blue petals topped by a band of pure white and accented with crimson flares. In 1624, the Amsterdam man who owned the only a dozen specimens was offered the exceptionally large sum of 3,000 guilders for one bulb, but turned it down. At the time ordinary tulips were sold by the pound. Around 1630, professional tulip traders made markets for rare tulips for connoisseurs and increased demand from speculators. Since it took seven years to grow a tulip from seed, supply did not keep up. By 1636, all tulips increased in price, especially the rare ones, and a futures market for bulbs started. Bulbs auctions typically took place at taverns rather than a formal exchange.

Although price data from the period are limited, the crash apparently started as a mundane event. In Haarlem at a routine bulb auction, there were few buyers, in part became of an outbreak of bubonic plague in early 1637. Soon the traders and speculators realized the market had turned and panic spread across the Netherlands. Despite the efforts of traders, the market collapsed.

Later books exaggerated the damage to the economy, especially an 1841 book by the Scottish journalist Charles Mackay, *Extraordinary Popular Delusions and the Madness of Crowds*. Robert Beckman reports: "The Netherlands was plunged into a depression" (1988, 28). According to later scholars, the impact on the Dutch economy probably was small. Most traders were able settle their debts for a fraction of their liability. The tulip trade never interfered with the Amsterdam stock market, which continued on with little impact.

See also Bubbles and Euphoria; Law, John; Market Manipulation; Mississippi Bubble; Panics and Depressions; South Sea Bubble

References

Balen, Malcolm. *The Secret History of the South Sea Bubble*. London: Fourth Estate, 2002.

Beckman, Robert. *Crashes: Why They Happen—What to Do*. Glasgow: Grafton Books, 1988.

Dash, Mike. *Tulip Mania: The Story of the World's Most Coveted Flower and the Extraordinary Passions It Aroused*. New York: Three River Press, 1999.

Means, H. *Money and Power: The History of Business*. New York: Wiley, 2001.

Tweed, William M. ("Boss")

William Tweed ("Boss," 1823–78) was the head of New York City's Tammany Hall machine and perhaps the most corrupt politician in American history. Tweed was born April 3, 1823, in New York City and joined the family chair-making business as a young man. He started in politics as a Democratic city alderman in 1851. As the Democrats gained control from the Whigs, the level of corruption increased substantially and the Board of Aldermen became known as the "Forty Thieves." Corruption tricks included a land deal, where Tweed helped arrange the purchase of land for the city; the land was purchased for about $30,000, but sold to the city for over $100,000. The Forty Thieves pocketed much of the difference, with Tweed's share about $3,000. As Tweed rose in prominence, so did his share of the loot.

After an undistinguished term in the House of Representatives, Tweed came back to New York, avoiding public office but building his behind-the-scenes power base. He was appointed to the Board of Education of the city, then named to the important Board of Supervisors. Tweed's greed knew no bounds. According to Horace Greeley: "Here is a man of decided talent, untiring industry, and considerable executive ability, who might have been anything he chose if Providence had blessed him with a reasonable share of honesty" (quoted in Allen 1993, 67).

Tweed placed himself in positions of power and developed allies to carry out his schemes through city and county governments, plus Tammany's influence in the New York State government in Albany. Tweed's "Ring" included "Slippery Dick" Connolly, the money man; corrupt judge George Barnard (who later certified Tweed as a lawyer, providing another useful sideline); Peter ("Brains") Sweeny (Spider Sweeny, also known as Peter the Paragon); plus members of the Board of Supervisors John Briggs and Walter Roche. Patronage was always central to the power of Tammany, and Tweed expanded the Tammany reach, with thousands of people beholden to Tweed and the Ring. On the plus side, the Tammany machine provided valuable social services to constituents.

Tweed was named Tammany Hall Grand Sachem (leader) in 1863, after Grand Sachem Isaac Fowler fled to Mexico when he was discovered to have stolen $150,000 in post office cash. Now "the Boss," Tweed had Tammany allies as ward leaders in all 22 city wards—achieving total control over elections and patronage. With his power base assured, Tweed became chairman of the New York County Democratic General Committee and state senator. The 1868 election proved so corrupt that congressional hearings followed, but reform legislation passed by the legislature was vetoed by Governor John Hoffman, a Tammany crony.

A particularly corrupt episode for the Tweed Ring was the construction of a new county courthouse, authorized in 1858. The initial budget of $250,000 included a hefty share for rebates and payoffs. Tweed's greed continued unabated. A further $800,000 was appropriated in 1864, later expanded beyond 1 million dollars. Investigations followed, but the investigators found no corruption—they also were paid off.

The level of Tweed's graft was beyond the level of available taxes; consequently, vast sums of cash were borrowed. Bonded debt in 1868 was $36 million, increasing by $70 million by 1871. The Boss had a thorough process for corruption. He had the city appropriate $1.5 million as its share to construct the Brooklyn Bridge, for example, but only after a cash-laden valise arrived full of cash, plus his personal cut of Brooklyn Bridge stock, some 560 shares. "Gifts" of stocks and bonds became standard procedure for companies doing business in New York City. According to Rebecca Menes (2006, 75), "apparently, corrupt politicians found it easiest and safest to steal from projects that the voters and bond buyers thought were worth building."

Tweed acquired New York Printing Company and Manufacturing Stationers' Company, soon handling all the city's printing and business supplies at exorbitant rates. Companies doing business in New York were instructed to deal with if they wanted city business. To better bilk the government out of more construction money, Tweed bought a marble quarry. As a licensed lawyer, Tweed charged high fees for political influence—his legal knowledge being limited; one of his biggest clients was the Erie Railroad, the "scarlet woman of Wall Street." The Ring bought its own bank, the Tenth National Bank, keeping the city's funds and promoting other financial shenanigans.

By 1870, Tweed achieved almost complete political power with Tammany allies throughout local and state government. "Elegant Oakey" Hall was mayor of New York City and Tammany crony John Hoffman governor of New York. With multiple sitting judges in tow, Tweed controlled the executive, legislative, and judicial branches locally and had substantial power statewide.

Most newspapers provided favorable reporting, aided by bribed journalists and a big-city advertising budget. But not all. The Republican (at the time) *New York Times* was the major opponent. The *Harpers Weekly's* political cartoonist Thomas Nast showed caricatures of Tweed as a fat, corrupt buffoon, which did real damage. As Tweed apparently put it: "Stop them damned pictures. I don't care so much what the papers say about me. My constituents don't know how to read, but they can't help seeing them damned pictures!" Tweed offered Nast a $500,000 "fellowship" to travel abroad, which Nast turned down.

Former city sheriff and Tammany member James O'Brien sought revenge after Tweed reneged on a $300,000 payment O'Brien thought he deserved. He found another Tammany turncoat in Matthew O'Rourke, a city bookkeeper. O'Rourke transcribed incriminating bookkeeping records showing overcharging and kickbacks, which he gave to O'Brien. O'Brien forwarded the records to the *New York Times*. After refusing a $5 million bribe, the *Times* began publishing the corruption evidence in 1871 as a "Gigantic Frauds in the Rental of America." Later stories exposed the courthouse project ("The Secret Accounts") and others.

Mayor Oakey Hall turned on Tweed, and an investigation committee was started by the Board of Aldermen, providing additional damaging evidence. Tweed's Ring blamed controller "Slippery Dick" Connolly for all the corruption and he was fired.

The investigation and prosecution were led by lawyer and Democratic politician Samuel Tilden. Tilden turned Connolly into a prosecution informant, allowing him to remain controller. Andrew Green became Connolly's deputy, who forwarded incriminating evidence to Tilden. The Ring accounts at National Broadway Bank were accessed by Green, which exposed the laundering of kickback money to Tweed and his Ring. The Booth Committee at about the same time validated the *New York Times'* published accusations.

Tweed's candidates were defeated by Tilden's (running as independents) in the 1871 election, breaking the political power of the Ring; the culmination of Tammany's fall was the arrest of Tweed. Of all the criminals discovered, only Tweed and Hall came to trial. Fleeing the country or prosecution deals for immunity (or both) became the alternatives. Connelly, for example, was arrested despite his cooperation, but fled to Europe after making bail. Sweeny fled to Canada. Judge Barnard was impeached but not prosecuted. Amazingly, Hall was acquitted. Tweed, on the other hand, was found guilty. Although sentenced to 12 years in jail, Tweed was released after only 1 year. When arrested again on civil charges, he fled to Spain. The Spanish extradited Tweed back to New York where he spent the rest of his life behind bars. Others paid only nominal fines, representing a small fraction of the ill-gotten gains. The successful prosecution of Tweed catapulted Tilden to the New York governor in 1874. His run for president two years later became another episode of political corruption (Tilden won the popular vote, but lost in the House of Representatives against Rutherford B. Hayes—called "Rutherfraud" by the Democrats). Tweed returned to prison and died in Ludlow Street Jail on April 12, 1878.

See also Burr, Aaron; Fraud; Political Machines; Robber Barons; Tammany Hall

References

Allen, Oliver. *The Tiger: The Rise and Fall of Tammany Hall*. New York: Addison-Wesley, 1993.

Josephson, Matthew. *The Robber Barons*, New York: Harcourt, 1962.

Menes, Rebecca. "Limiting the Reach of the Grabbing Hand: Graft and Growth in American Cities, 1880–1930." In *Corruption and Reform: Lessons from America's Economic History*. Edited by Edward Glaeser and Claudia Goldin, 63–94. Washington, DC: National Bureau of Economic Research, 2006.

Tyco International

Tyco is a large American conglomerate involved in a 2002 financial scandal sending chief executive officer (CEO) Dennis Kozlowski to jail. Tyco Laboratories was founded by Arthur Gandus in 1960 as a holding company focused primarily on high-tech science, going public in 1962 and transforming into a conglomerate through acquisitions. Kozlowski joined Tyco in 1975, became president and chief operating officer in 1989, then CEO in 1992. He became "Deal-a-Day Dennis" after some 1,000 acquisitions. The name was changed to Tyco International in 1993 to better reflect its new status as a global leader, and in 1996 it became part of the Standard and Poor's 500. Aggressive acquisition accounting provided substantial growth and rising earnings. Revenue increases averaged almost 50 percent a year from 1997 to 2001. The acquisition of ADT Security Services (with a $6 billion price tag) was structured as a reverse takeover allowing Tyco to use ADT's Bermuda registration to shelter foreign earnings. The Securities and Exchange Commission (SEC) investigated Tyco's acquisition accounting in 1999, but did not charge Tyco.

Tyco's most egregious accounting was associated with its merger with the CIT group. Tyco's acquisition of CIT Group, the biggest independent commercial financial company in the United States, for $9.2 billion in 2001 proved to be a disaster. Deceptive techniques used by Tyco became public with this acquisition. CIT continued to issue financial statements after the merger to maintain a high credit rating. Tyco used "spring loading," requiring CIT to modify accounting policies before the acquisition and make various write-offs and adjustments, with the intent of

Tyco International chairman and chief executive officer Dennis Kozlowski in 2002. He was convicted of corruption and other crimes in 2005. (AP Photo/Shawn Baldwin)

improving the perceived performance of the parent immediately after the acquisition. Before the merger date, CIT disposed of $5 billion in poorly performing loans, made downward adjustments of $221.6 million, increased the credit-loss provisions, and took a $54 million charge to acquisition costs. Revenues for CIT were extremely low just before the deal and dramatically increased after the deal. CIT reported a net loss just before the acquisition date.

After the merger, CIT reported net income of $71.2 million. That increased Tyco's earnings for the September 2001 quarter. CIT's name was changed to Tyco Capital but suffered problems with credit, since it was now tied to Tyco. Ultimately, this new business segment was sold. Tyco recorded an after-tax loss of $6.3 billion. For the year ended September 30, 2002, Tyco had a net loss of $9.4 billion.

Kozlowski was initially indicted in 2002 for evading $1 million in New York sales tax on paintings he bought with money borrowed from Tyco. He resigned in June. Later, he and Mark Swartz, former chief financial officer (CFO), were charged with over three dozen felonies from "enterprise corruption and grand larceny" for raiding Tyco of some $600 million (Huffington 2003, 35).

Unlike most of the scandal-plagued companies, like Enron and WorldCom, Tyco did not go bankrupt. However, its bond rating was downgrading and it suffered a large stock price drop. Tyco paid $50 million to the SEC in 2006 to settle accounting fraud charges and paid $3 billion to settle a class action lawsuit by shareholders

(Tyco's auditor, PricewaterhouseCoopers, paid an additional $225 million). The company split into three separate companies in 2007: Convidien, Tyco Electronics, and Tyco International.

See also Accounting Fraud; Acquisition Accounting; Enron; Kozlowski, L. Dennis; Securities and Exchange Commission; WorldCom

References

Giroux, Gary, "What Went Wrong? Accounting Fraud and Lessons from the Recent Scandals." *Social Research: An International Quarterly of the Social Sciences*, Winter 2008, 1205–38.

Huffington, Arianna. *Pigs at the Trough: How Corporate Greed and Political Corruption Are Undermining America*. New York: Crown, 2003.

Varchaver, Nicholas. "The Big Kozlowski." In *SCANDAL!: Amazing Tales of Scandals that Shocked the World and Shaped Modern Business*, 47–52. New York: Time Inc. Home Entertainment, 2009.

U

Union Pacific Railroad

The Union Pacific (UP) is the largest railroad in the United States, covering much of the central and western parts of the country (from Chicago and New Orleans to the Pacific coast). The Pacific Railroad Act of 1862 created the UP to construct a railroad west from Omaha, Nebraska, to meet the Central Pacific line to be built from California east. The two met in 1869 at Promontory Point, Utah, completing perhaps the greatest construction project of the nineteenth century. Substantial corruption took place at the two railroads, but the big public scandal centered on the separate construction companies used to build the railroads: Credit and Finance Corporation used by the Central Pacific and Credit Mobilier (CM) by the Union Pacific. The promoters of the railroads secretly ran the construction companies and, along with influential politicians and other insiders, owned the stock.

The Pacific Railroad bill, passed by Congress in 1862 and signed by President Abraham Lincoln, created the Union Pacific Railroad and provided loans and land to both the UP and Central Pacific. General Samuel Curtiss served as temporary chairman of UP. Two thousand shares of stock were issued and quickly subscribed at $1,000 each. A board of directors was elected and General John Dix was appointed UP president. However, Thomas Durant, a Wall Street speculator appointed as vice president, became the real leader.

The federal loans were made as the track was completed: $16,000 per mile on flat land to $48,000 a mile in the mountains (later raised as a result of intense lobbying), with the land allocated in alternating sections (the "checkerboard pattern") along the right-of-way. Much of the land was sold through land companies owned by the promoters with the proceeds (after the promoters skimmed off their cut) going to the railroads. Over the construction period, Congress granted 12 million acres of land and $27 million in long-term bonds to the UP.

One of the requirements of the Pacific Railroad bill was no concentration of ownership. Durant managed to gain control of about half the stock of UP by buying shares in other people's names. Hired by Durant to sell UP shares, George Francis Train suggested CM (named after a French company) as a construction company. Train found an existing "shell company," the Pennsylvania Fiscal Agency," bought by Train and transformed as "Credit Mobilier of America," and sold it to Durant. Under Durant and Massachusetts congressman Oakes Ames, CM would make the owners money long before UP was operational. Durant thought the UP would never make money and diverted as much money to CM as possible. Under UP chief engineer General Grenville Dodge, the CM profits were massive. UP payments to CM nearly drove UP to bankruptcy. CM paid gigantic dividends, but struggled to pay workers, subcontractors, and suppliers. Despite the corruption, the transcontinental railroads got built and the lines of UP and Central Pacific met at Promontory Point, Utah, on May 10, 1869.

Then the CM scandal erupted. Congressman Ames sold stock of both UP and CM to important politicians at low prices. Historian Charles Francis Adams Jr. (he would serve as UP president for a time) broke the story in 1872, claiming conflicts of interest and inferring massive corruption: "The members of it are in Congress; they are trustees for the bondholders; they are directors; they are stockholders; they are contractors; in Washington they vote the subsidies, in New York they receive them, upon the plains they expend them, and in the 'Credit Mobilier' they divide them" (Ambrose 2000, 320). The *New York Sun* called it "The King of Frauds: How the Credit Mobilier Bought it Way Through Congress," inferring bribery and influence peddling. The House of Representatives held hearings and the major players testified.

Congress accused Ames of stock payoffs, lying to Congress, and pursuing CM massive overcharging and dividends payments. Ames was censured by Congress in 1873 and died soon after. Durant escaped largely untouched by the scandal; however, he was wiped out by the Panic of 1873. CM was sued by the federal government for fraud and expropriation of funds. The Supreme Court ruled CM's conduct as legal and none of the perpetrators faced prosecution. UP repaid the federal debt of $168 million after it became due at the end of the century, but only after losing in court.

UP went bankrupt for the first time during the Panic of 1873, four years after completing the line to Promontory Point. The railroad was reorganized by speculator Jay Gould and failed during the Panic of 1893—to emerge from bankruptcy in 1897. Charles Francis Adams, who broke the story of the CM scandal, served as president of the UP from 1884 to 1890. Despite mismanagement but aided by mergers, the UP became the country's biggest railroad. Acquisitions included the Missouri Pacific, Western Pacific, Chicago and North Western, and the Southern Pacific.

The UP now operates a network over 32,000 miles of track, covering 23 states over most of the central and western United States west from Chicago, one of four major railroads (the others are Burlington Northern, CSX, and Norfolk Southern) that control 90 percent of the United States' freight. After the failure of Penn Central in 1970, in part due to overregulation of the industry, deregulation and a weak regulator in the Surface Transportation Board (STB) granted increased economic power to the remaining railroads. A major problem became the potential for monopoly power of captive ("single-served") shippers and the potential for price conspiracies. Lawsuits accuse the railroads of exactly that, specifically charging them of conspiring to set surcharge fees.

See also Ames, Oakes; Durant, Thomas; Fraud; Interstate Commerce Commission; Railroads, Nineteenth Century; Transcontinental Railroad and the Credit Mobilier Scandal

References

Ambrose, Stephan. *Nothing Like It in the World: The Men Who Built the Transcontinental Railroad 1863–1869*. New York: Touchstone, 2000.

Brands, H. W. *American Colossus: The Triumph of Capitalism, 1865–1900*. New York: Doubleday, 2010.

Josephson, Matthew. *The Robber Barons*. New York: Harcourt, 1962.

Kimes, Mina. "Showdown on the Railroad." *Fortune*, September 26, 2011, 160–72.

Rayner, Richard. *The Associates: Four Capitalists Who Created California*. New York: Norton, 2008.

United States Steel

J. P. Morgan created United States (U.S.) Steel in 1901 as the first billion-dollar corporation (as measured by market value)—creating both the largest steel company and largest corporation in the world. It was the pinnacle of the trust movement, with mergers and combinations of major companies in dozens of industry. The result was industry dominance and near-monopoly power. The company was built primarily on the acquisitions of Carnegie Steel, Federal Steel, and National Steel, with a combined output of about two-thirds of all American production. It is still the largest steel maker in the United States, producing about 10 percent of domestic steel (about the same amount it produced in 1901), but only the 10th largest in the world.

Steel is an alloy of iron with a specific carbon content (which varies by grade). Steel was created in the ancient world, but large-scale production started with the Industrial Revolution. Modern steel production began with the Bessemer process introduced in 1858, which improved steel quality and allowed large mass production.

Andrew Carnegie entered into iron and steel in 1872, forming a company to manufacture Bessemer steel, and this became his sole interest, selling off his other companies primarily after the Panic of 1873. The demand for steel rails by railroads was a major reason. At the time, the American iron industry was primitive, and most high-quality steel was purchased from Britain. He invested in iron manufacturing earlier and used that knowledge as a springboard to dominate steel. Carnegie inspected Bessemer plants in England before organizing a partnership, which ultimately dominated the industry. Borrowing heavily in Europe and purchasing the patent rights to the Bessemer process, he built various steel plants, including the Edgar Thomson Works in 1875, at the time considered the most modern plant in the world. Using modern equipment, economies of scale, a sophisticated accounting system, and close control over productivity, he became the low-cost producer. As one of the world's largest freight customers, Carnegie also received secret rebates from the railroads. He was able to lower his selling prices below competitors' and still make substantial profits.

Carnegie believed in competition and generally stayed away from price conspiracies. The exception was to join them to discover competitors' costs. He would stay in a pool only when it allowed him to run at full capacity. His focus on full production, low cost, and using the newest high equipment and procedures resulting in Carnegie Steel being the largest producer of coke, pig iron, and steel rail by the late 1880s. To further his competitive advantage, he built integrated steel complexes with a diversified product line and used vertical integration to increase his advantage, buying operations from ore and coal mines to producing finished products. A chemist was on staff to further exploit raw materials and by-products. He adopted new technology as soon as it was available, such as the Thomas process, an improvement on Bessemer. He plowed most of the profits back in the business, rather than paying higher dividends. In 1900, Carnegie Steel produced about 3 million tons of steel, while Federated produced 1.2 million and National 1.4 million. Carnegie was the low-cost producer, earning about $13.50 per ton compared to over $8 for Federated and $5.70 for National.

J. P. Morgan famously bought out 66-year-old Carnegie's empire for $480 million, the biggest payoff until well into the twentieth century. Morgan stated: "Mr. Carnegie, I want to congratulate you on being the richest man in the world." With Carnegie Steel and over 200 other related companies, Morgan created U.S. Steel. Morgan capitalized the firm for $1.4 billion—considerably more than the book value of the combined firms or what he paid to acquire them. Elbert Gary of Federated Steel was named executive committee chairman and Charles Schwab became the first president. The company had over 200 manufacturing plants, 41 mines, and a thousand miles of railroad track. Thanks to the investment banking practice of "watering the stock," U.S. Steel was considered greatly overcapitalized—that is, net assets were overstated relative to actual values. The Bureau of Corporations estimated that the real property of the company was actually $682 million rather than $1.4 billion (Warren 2001, 22).

Without much competition, U.S. Steel became less innovative and less efficient. The company avoided price cutting and encouraged new competitors to maintain high prices, even when demand fell during downturns. Despite bans by the Interstate Commerce Commission, the company continued to receive substantial railroad rebates. Other steel companies, notably Bethlehem Steel (run by Charles Schwab after ending his stint at U.S. Steel in 1903), competed successfully and increased market share. U.S. Steel's market share dropped to 50 percent by 1911. Production came under substantial cost pressure as demand remained down until World War I. Production was devastated during the Great Depression, but output roughly doubled during World War II from 1905 levels, reaching record production levels.

As new products were introduced (such as line pipes for oilfields and thin-flat-rolled products), U.S. Steel's failure to innovate led to a lower market share and lower relative profitability. During the 1930s, the company had multiple loss years including losing over $587 million from 1933 to 1935. Although Carnegie had a superb accounting system, U.S. Steel did not have a comprehensive system covering all subsidiaries, meaning that costs could not be effectively analyzed—another factor in the company's reduced efficiency. Demand zoomed during World War II, and employment levels peaked at over 340,000 (dropping to just over 50,000 by the turn of the century). Total American output was 80 million tons in 1945, about two-thirds of the global total. U.S. Steel production peaked at 35 million tons in 1953 and dropped as world production expanded and the American share fell, in large part because of rising labor and materials costs relative to global competitors.

U.S. Steel had a poor record of labor relations during its long history and also on environmental issues. The company was forced to recognize the United Steelworkers Union in the 1930s and suffered long strikes in 1946, 1959, and 1986. The company was one of the largest producers of air pollution (plus water pollution and toxic wastes), releasing millions of tons of ammonia, hydrochloric acid, and other toxic compounds. The company was sued by the Environmental Protection Agency and various states and paid millions of dollars in penalties.

In an attempt to diversify, U.S. Steel acquired Marathon Oil in 1982 and changed the name to USX in 1991. The steel unit was spun off in 2001, again taking the name U.S. Steel. The Edgar Thomas Works is still producing steel near Pittsburgh, Pennsylvania, although the Gary Works in Gary, Indiana, is the largest domestic facility.

See also Carnegie, Andrew; Labor Movement, U.S.; Monopolies and Other Combinations; Morgan, John Pierpont; Pollution Externalities; Railroads, Nineteenth Century

References

Ennis, Lisa. "Carnegie, Andrew." In *The American Economy: A Historical Encyclopedia.* Rev. ed. Edited by Cynthia Clark. Santa Barbara, CA: ABC-CLIO, 2011.

Josephson, Matthew. *The Robber Barons.* New York: Harcourt, 1962.

Livesay, Harold. *Andrew Carnegie and the Rise of Big Business.* New York: Longman, 2000.

Morris, Charles. *Money, Greed, and Risk: Why Financial Crises and Crashes Happen.* New York: Times Business, 1999.

Warren, Kenneth. *Big Steel: The First Century of the United States Steel Corporation, 1901–2001.* Pittsburgh: University of Pittsburgh Press, 2001.

Utilitarianism

Utilitarianism is a philosophical and economic perspective on behavior to maximize happiness (utility) or welfare, assuming that morality is the calculus of costs and benefits. British philosopher Jeremy Bentham (1748–1832) developed this ethical theory. The highest principle of morality according to Bentham is the overall balance of pleasure over pain. Maximizing utility applies to individuals, communities, and governments. As he stated in *A Fragment of Government* (1776), "It is the greatest happiness of the greatest number that is the measure of right and wrong." He also viewed utility as a measure of usefulness—greater usefulness means greater value and a higher price for a product.

Bentham's approach was criticized as failing to respect individual rights in the sum of overall "satisfaction." Utility preferences are not judged—that is, they do not consider independent moral considerations; overall utility is based on aggregate preferences using "a single currency of value" (Sandel 2009, 41), essentially computing all costs and benefits into the equivalent of dollars.

John Stuart Mill (1806–73), son of Bentham collaborator James Mill, defined utilitarianism as "the greatest happiness principle," the process of producing the largest aggregate happiness among people. He considered utilitarianism as "the ultimate appeal on all ethical questions." He was a proponent of free markets, but viewed intervention on markets such as a tax on alcohol as potentially appropriate on utilitarian grounds. *On Liberty* (1859) described the nature and limits of legitimate power exercised by society over individuals. Each individual, according to Mill, can act as he or she wants as long as the actions do not harm others (the "harm principle"). Individuals also are precluded from doing harm to themselves or their property under the harm principle. Acts of omission such as failure to pay taxes also are "harms." Rather than Bentham's single scale of happiness, Mill distinguishes "higher pleasures" from lower ones, evaluating relative quality and creating "two-level utilitarianism." Critics such as John Rawls argue that attempting to aggregate individuals' "happiness" is futile.

See also Austrian School of Economics; Behavioral Economics; Classical Economics; Ethics; Justice; Keynes, John Maynard; Mercantilism; Professional Ethics; Smith, Adam

References

Bentham, Jeremy. *A Fragment on Government*. 1776. London: Nabu Press, 2010 (reprint).

Heilbroner, Robert. *The Essential Adam Smith*. New York: Norton, 1986.

Oser, Jacob. *The Evolution of Economic Thought*. New York: Harcourt, Brace & World, 1963.

Rider, Christine. "Smith, Adam." In *Encyclopedia of the Age of the Industrial Revolution, 1700–1920*. Santa Barbara, CA: Greenwood, 2007.

Sandel, Michael. *Justice: What's the Right Thing to Do?* New York: Farrar, Straus and Giroux, 2009.

Weintraub, E. Roy. "Neoclassical Economics." In *The Concise Encyclopedia of Economics*. 2007. http://www.econlib.org.

V

Value at Risk (VaR)

Value at risk (VaR) is a risk measure analyzing the potential loss on a portfolio of financial assets for some period, usually one day. Quants at J. P. Morgan developed the first VaR model in 1994 to measure relative risk on a day-to-day basis and convert into a dollar amount the maximum potential loss (typically based on a 95% probability and assuming normality—the famous Gaussian distribution or bell curve). This was after chief executive officer (CEO) Dennis Weatherstone asked for a "4:15 report" (15 minutes after the market closed) on all firm risks. VaR proved to be a useful tool for comparing relative risk and could suggest how to allocate new funds. VaR expanded to most banks as a risk method and a technique to determine the amount of capital needed. However, the limitations of the method seemed to be ignored and encouraged overconfidence in high-risk behavior and low levels of capital.

Problems with VaR were demonstrated early, including the failure of large hedge fund Long-Term Capital Management's (LTCM). The hedge fund sustained a $550 million loss in one day, August 21, 1998. The VaR models of LTCM implied that losses sustained were virtually impossible—perhaps once during the life of the universe. Managers at the fund did not react to minimize their losses, counting on the markets to reverse themselves as predicted by the model. The VaR models suffered two major problems. First, only five years' worth of data was used. Second, the models were based on "normal data" (the bell-shaped curve that works when analyzing probabilities of card games), but seldom worked as well with long-term financial data—subject to "fat tails." As summarized by Niall Ferguson (2008, 328): "To put bluntly, the Nobel prize winners had known plenty of mathematics, but not enough history. . . . And that, put very simply, was why Long-Term Capital Management ended up being Short-Term Capital Mismanagement."

Large companies are required by the Securities and Exchange Commission (SEC) to analyze their risk management procedures. Virtually all large banks use VaR to analyze risk. According to Jorion (2009), risk management systems construct the distributions of risk factors, collect portfolio positions and analyze according to risk factors, construct the distribution of profit and losses over the day (or other period), and summarize by a VaR number, which represents the worst loss within the confidence interval selection. VaR captures expected risks including regular dispersion, such as within the 95 percent confidence level. However, risk models are backward looking (based on historical information), and unexpected volatility and changing risk distributions may not be captured by VaR (such as when housing prices collapsed in the mid-2000s; the resulting liquidity risk to major banks also was not picked up by VaR). "Immeasurable risk" as described by Nassim Taleb as "Black Swans" (also called Knightian uncertainty) cannot be predicted by any model.

See also Black Swans; Commercial Banks after the Federal Reserve; Debt and Leverage; Investment Banks; J. P. Morgan Chase; Long-Term Capital Management; Risk and Risk Management; Speculation

References

Ferguson, Niall. *The Ascent of Money: A Financial History of the World.* New York: Penguin Press, 2008.

Jorion, Philippe. "Risk Management Lessons from the Credit Crisis." *European Financial Management* 15, no. 5 (2009): 923–33.

McLean, Bethany, and Joe Nocera. *All the Devils Are Here: The Hidden History of the Financial Crisis.* New York: Portfolio/Penguin, 2010.

Taleb, Nassim. *The Black Swan: The Impact of the Highly Improbable.* New York: Random House, 2007.

Van Buren, Martin

Martin Van Buren (1782–1862) was the eighth president of the United States (1837–41), serving during the Panic of 1837, and secretary of state under Andrew Jackson. Van Buren was a dominant figure in organizing the Democratic Party and a major creator of machine politics at the state level. He was born in Kinderhook, New York, on December 5, 1782, studied law, and entered politics as a supporter of Aaron Burr. Learning from New York City's Tammany Hall, Van Buren was active in machine politics at the state level in what became known as the "Albany Regency." He served in state offices until elected U.S. senator in 1821, where he continued his control of New York State politics from Washington.

Van Buren's rise to power in Washington solidified his machine by making both state and federal jobs available. In this political setting, winning was everything, and Democrats used every trick to maintain political dominance. Van Buren, backed by Tammany tactics, was a major force behind getting Andrew Jackson elected president in 1828. Van Buren became Jackson's secretary of state in 1829. The Regency continued but with little guidance from him. Van Buren became Jackson's vice president in the 1832 election. During his second term, Jackson refused to recharter the Second Bank of the United States. Van Buren succeeded Jackson as president in 1836—the first machine politician holding the presidency.

During Jackson's presidency, the elimination of the Second Bank as agent for federal funds reduced discipline in the banking system and set the stage for rampant speculation, fueled by torrents of paper money. Late in his second term, Jackson demanded gold for federal land sales to dampen land fever and withdrew funds from various banks to send cash to the states. Banks began to fail as a result and the Panic of 1837 ensued. Because the Second Bank's charter expired, there was no central bank to dampen the blow. By the time the panic hit, Van Buren was president and he took the blame. The panic was followed by a five-year depression, and Whigs called the president "Martin Van Ruin." He was renominated by the Democrats, but lost to Whig candidate William Henry Harrison. After running on the Free-Soil ticket in 1848, he retired to Kinderhook. He died on his estate on July 24, 1862.

See also Bank of the United States, Second; Burr, Aaron; Jackson, Andrew; Panic of 1837; Political Machines; Tammany Hall

References

"About the White House: Martin Van Buren." http://www.whitehouse.gov.

Clark, Cynthia. "Jackson, Andrew." In *The American Economy: A Historical Encyclopedia*. Rev. ed. Edited by Cynthia Clark. Santa Barbara, CA: ABC-CLIO, 2011.

Vanderbilt, Cornelius ("Commodore")

Cornelius Vanderbilt ("Commodore," 1794–1877) was an American tycoon in steamships and railroads. He was the country's richest man when he died, worth an estimated $100 million. Biographer T. J. Stiles's summary: "Vanderbilt was an empire builder, the first great corporate tycoon in American history. Even before the United States became a truly industrial country, he learned to use the tools of corporate capitalism to amass wealth and power" (2009, 4–5). Vanderbilt was born on Staten Island, New York, on May 27, 1794, and worked on his father's Staten Island farm and small sailing ship used to ferry produce to Manhattan; then he established his own ferry service.

The Commodore made his fortune with steamboats, earning him the honorary title "Commodore." Robert Fulton and partner Robert Livingstone had a government monopoly on steamboat traffic in New York, which Vanderbilt's employer, Thomas Gibbons, fought; piloting Gibbons's steamship to New York, Livingstone obtained an injunction against Gibbons's ships and had Vanderbilt arrested. Gibbons filed lawsuits to break the monopoly and also received a similar monopoly agreement from New Jersey. The "celebrated steamboat controversy" lawsuit was finally settled by the Supreme Court in 1824 (*Gibbons v. Ogden*) in a landmark decision on the Commerce Clause. Daniel Webster represented Gibbons, and Chief Justice John Marshall wrote the opinion that ended the monopoly. As stated in the New York *Evening Post*, "The Steam Boat grant is at an end." Of course, Gibbons and Vanderbilt had to face the increased competition as well.

Gibbons and Vanderbilt provided competition and were joined by many more competitors. John Stevens and his family would replace the Livingstones as major competitors. Many routes, such as New York City to Philadelphia, included both boats and stagecoaches along the way. Stevens intended to make the stagecoach obsolete with the recently created railroad. The family received a corporate charter for the Camden and Amboy Railroad from the New Jersey legislature, giving them virtually complete control of railroading in the state. Vanderbilt painfully learned the lesson that success meant focusing on transportation rather than exclusively on steamships. Unlike a fleet of steamboats, railroads required a corporate structure to raise the necessary funds, and all the early railroads built short routes due to limited capital available, the focus being on land routes connecting to existing water routes and regional commerce.

Vanderbilt launched his own steamboat, the "Citizen," in 1828, beginning his career as a transportation entrepreneur (Gibbons died in 1826). He stretched his own resources to create a growing fleet. He faced considerable competition around New York City, changed routes based on demand and competition, started rate wars to eliminate competitors, and blackmailed other competitors to leave certain routes. As he bought more steamships, Vanderbilt pioneered new routes.

Vanderbilt saw the railroads as the next great transportation technology. He acquired railroad shares in the 1840s, eventually buying the Harlem Railroad and the Hudson River Railroad and turning them from decrepit money-losing railroads to efficient, profitable lines. He would link up the short rail lines with his own steamboats. His primary plan was to systematically seize power of the transportation companies around New York City.

During the California gold rush beginning in 1849, Vanderbilt developed ocean-going steamship lines using a route through Nicaragua to California, then started transatlantic lines from New York City to Europe. His shipping empire also included a shipyard and manufacturing of marine steam engines.

The Commodore moved to more grandiose plans, beginning with the acquisition of the New York & Harlem Railroad (Harlem) in the early 1860s and ending up controlling the giant trunk line, New York Central. The New York Central was an 1853 consolidation of about a dozen less-successful lines, creating a line paralleling the Erie Canal from Albany to Buffalo. Vanderbilt expanded the Harlem and moved on to Harlem competitor Hudson River Railroad. Both railroads connected to the New York Central and provided railroad access to New York City. He sold out his steamship interest about the same time to concentrate on railroads. To protect his growing interests in New York, Vanderbilt ended up controlling the New York Central by 1867 and gradually consolidated his holdings, creating a railroad empire across the state and the best route to the West, "the Water Level Route," paralleling the Erie Canal and Hudson River.

Vanderbilt's plan called for a productive railroad empire (Josephson, 1962, 69):

1. Buy your railroad;
2. Stop the stealing that went on under the other man;
3. Improve it in every practicable way within a reasonable expenditure;

4. Consolidate it with any other road that can be run with it economically;
5. Water the stock;
6. Make it pay a large dividend.

Vanderbilt would effectively have monopoly power over New York State with the acquisition of the Erie Railroad. This was the view of most early analysts, including Charles Francis Adams and Matthew Josephson. (However, later biographer T. J. Stiles concluded that the moves against the Erie were revenge against Daniel Drew—and later Jay Gould and Jim Fisk—rather than control.) Before the annual stockholders' meeting, Vanderbilt acquired enough stock and proxy votes to have majority control and buying continued. Drew was treasurer of the Erie and immediately plotted a counterstrategy to enrich himself. Using Erie convertible bonds, Drew and allies Gould and Fisk quietly converted the bonds to stock and started selling.

The Commodore bought the new stock, unaware these were brand-new securities. Once alerted, he had Judge George Barnard of the New York State Supreme Court (and member of the Tammany Ring) issue contempt proceedings against the Erie directors. The Drew gang caught wind that arrest loomed and fled across the Hudson to New Jersey with all the loot, including some $7 million in cash. Drew, Gould, Fisk, and the other directors, now called the Erie Ring, moved the Erie headquarters to Jersey City. Neither they nor the Commodore were done conniving.

The Erie Ring had their Albany forces convince the New York legislature to introduce a bill legalizing the convertible bond-to-stock issue and forbid consolidation of the Erie with Vanderbilt's New York Central. The Commodore's forces and big purse convinced the legislators to defeat the bill. Jay Gould arrived in Albany carrying cases of cash. A new bill, looking like the one just defeated, soon surfaced in the Senate. Gould won this round and the bill passed.

The next stage was the House version. But the Commodore had had enough and sent this note: "Drew. I'm sick of the whole damned business. Come and see me. Van Derbilt" (Josephson 1934, 133). They settled up. The Commodore sold his stock back to the Erie Ring for around $5 million, a million or two dollars short of what he paid for it, and stayed away from the Erie from then on.

Vanderbilt lost the Erie war, but he continued his railroad empire. In 1869, he consolidated the Hudson River Railroad into the New York Central and later leased the Harlem Railroad to the New York Central. The Commodore died on January 4, 1877 in New York City, leaving an estate estimated at $100 million, mostly to his son William. The Vanderbilt railroad empire continued, including the acquisition of lines west from Buffalo. William later sold much of his railroad holdings to European investors using J. P. Morgan as broker.

See also Corporations; Drew, Daniel; Erie Railroad; Fisk, James ("Jubilee Jim"); Gould, Jason ("Jay"); Morgan, John Pierpont; Raiding the Erie Railroad, 1868; Railroads, Nineteenth Century; Watering Stock

References

Adams, Charles Francis, and Henry Adams. *Chapters of Erie and Other Essays*. Boston: James A. Osgood, 1871.

Brands, H. W. *American Colossus: The Triumph of Capitalism, 1865–1900*. New York: Doubleday, 2010.

Dobson, John. "Vanderbilt, Cornelius." In *Bulls, Bears, Boom, and Bust: A Historical Encyclopedia of American Business Concepts*. Santa Barbara, CA: ABC-CLIO, 2006.

Josephson, Matthew. *The Robber Barons*. New York: Harcourt, 1962.

Stiles, T. J. *The First Tycoon: The Epic Life of Cornelius Vanderbilt*. New York: Vintage Books, 2009.

Vesco, Robert L.

Robert Vesco (1935–2007) was an American businessman, known prominently as "the undisputed king of the fugitive financiers" (Noah 2001) for fleeing after pilfering Investors Overseas Services (IOS). Vesco was born in Detroit, Michigan, on December 4, 1935. After dropping out of high school, he bought and sold aluminum and bought an aluminum plant. Vesco acquired International Control Corporation (ICC) in 1965 and turned it into a successful conglomerate, relying on borrowing and accounting manipulation gimmicks for its success. When the market turned down in the late 1960s, he looked to another acquisition to save himself.

Vesco flew to Geneva in 1970 promising to save a floundering IOS, the Swiss mutual fund company founded by Bernard Cornfeld. Vesco launched a successful takeover using borrowed money. He proceeded to pilfer what remained of the company, in similar fashion to a nineteenth-century robber baron, accused of parking some $235 million of IOS money in dummy corporations. With Securities and Exchange Commission (SEC) embezzlement charges against him imminent, Vesco took the corporate jet to Costa Rica, allegedly with $200 million in IOS securities. He spent the rest of his life in Costa Rica, Cuba, and other countries with no extradition laws to the United States.

Vesco contributed to the Watergate scandal when he gave $200,000 to Richard Nixon's 1972 presidential campaign, which came out in the Watergate hearings. Three Nixon aids were indicted but not convicted, and Nixon was forced to resign from the presidency. Vesco remained a fugitive. He was arrested in Cuba and died in Havana on November 23, 2007.

See also Accounting Fraud; Acquisition Accounting; Cornfeld, Bernard; Fraud; Investors Overseas Services (IOS)

References

Hutchinson, Robert. "The Looting of IOS." In *SCANDAL!: Amazing Tales of Scandals That Shocked the World and Shaped Modern Business*, 86–103. New York: Time Inc. Home Entertainment. 2009.

Noah, Timothy. "Know Your Fugitive Financiers!" *Slate*, February 20, 2001. http://www
.slate.com.

Volcker, Paul A., Jr.

Paul Volcker (1927–) is an American economist, was chairman of the Federal
Reserve (Fed) from 1979 to 1987, and was chairman of the Economic Recovery
Advisory Board from 2009 to 2011. Volcker headed the Fed during the period of
double-digit inflation from the late 1970s to the early 1980s and is generally credited with reducing inflation using extremely tight money (reducing the money supply and increasing interest rates).

Volcker was born on September 5, 1927, in Cape May, New Jersey. He graduated from Harvard with an MA in economics and joined the Federal Reserve Bank
of New York. He later worked at Chase Manhattan Bank and the U.S. Treasury.
Volcker became president of the New York Fed in 1975 and served until becoming
chairman of the Fed in 1979.

At the Fed, Volcker inherited severe inflation (the consumer price index or CPI
averaged 11.3% in 1979) and pursued a tight-money policy (reducing the money supply and increasing interest rates). With the economy in recession, inflation increasing,
and the misery index topping 20 percent, President Jimmy Carter lost to Ronald Reagan in 1980. Volcker remained at the Fed and increased the federal funds rate to
20 percent by June 1981, while the prime rate hit 21.5 percent. The "Volcker Recession" led to calls for his resignation. The high interest rates had severe economic reper-
cussions, especially in agriculture and construction. However, the tight monetary
policy worked; interest rates dropped, the CPI fell to 3.2 percent by 1983, the
economy recovered, and the misery index dropped below double digits by 1986.
Volcker retired from the Fed in 1987, replaced by Alan Greenspan.

After his service at the Fed, Volcker served in investment banking, researched
corruption in the Iraq Oil for Food program for the United Nations, and served on
various commissions. In 2009, he was appointed by President Barack Obama to
chair to new Economic Recovery Advisory Board. Volcker proposed a number of
new bank regulations including banning investment banks from proprietary trading
(basically, prohibiting the banks from speculating in the financial markets), known
as the "Volcker Rule." He retired in 2011.

See also Debt and Leverage; Federal Reserve System; Gold Standard; Greenspan, Alan;
Misery Index; Stagflation; Treasury Department

References

Cassidy, John. "The Volcker Rule." *The New Yorker*, July 26, 2010. jttp://www.newyorker
.com.

Hafer, Rik. "Volcker, Paul." In *The Federal Reserve System: An Encyclopedia*. Santa
Barbara, CA: Greenwood, 2005.

W

Wagner Act

The National Labor Relations Act (Wagner Act) of 1935 was a New Deal law providing federal protections for labor to form unions, engage in collective bargaining, strike, and use other activities to promote their demands. The act was upheld by the Supreme Court in 1937, creating what labor called its "Magna Carta." The act was named for its sponsor, New York Democratic senator Robert Wagner (1877–1953), a member of President Franklin Roosevelt's "Brain Trust" and a leader in developing New Deal legislation.

The act established the role of the federal governments as the regulator and arbiter of labor issues. A three-member National Labor Relations Board (NLRB) was established to protect the rights of labor to organize unions and bargain collectively. Section 7 of the act states: "Employees shall have the right of self-organization, to form, join, or assist labor organizations, to bargain collectively through representatives of their own choosing, and to engage in concerted activities, for the purpose of collective bargaining or other mutual aid or protection."

Employers were banned from firing workers or joining unions or engaging in various "unfair labor practices." Section 8 of the act states:

> It shall be an unfair labor practice for an employer- (1) To interfere with, restrain, or coerce employees in the exercise of the rights guaranteed in section 7. (2) To dominate or interfere with the formation or administration of any labor organization or contribute financial or other support to it: *Provided*, That ... an employer shall not be prohibited from permitting employees to confer with him during working hours without loss of time or pay. (3) By discrimination in regard to hire or tenure of employment or any term or condition of employment to encourage or discourage membership in any labor organization: *Provided*, That nothing in this Act or in any other statute of the United States, shall preclude an employer from making an agreement with a labor organization (not established, maintained, or assisted by any action defined in this Act as an unfair labor practice) to require as a condition of employment membership therein, if such labor organization is the representative of the employees in the appropriate collective bargaining unit covered by such agreement when made. (4) To discharge or otherwise discriminate against an employee because he has filed charges or given testimony under this Act. (5) To refuse to bargain collectively with the representatives of his employees.

Various critics attempted to limit or repeal the act. After World War II, Republicans gained control of Congress in 1947 and had the votes to limit the act. The Taft-Hartley Act was passed over President Harry Truman's veto. Taft-Hartley prohibited various "unfair labor practices" including wildcat strikes, secondary boycotts, closed shops, and union donations to federal political campaigns. Union shops were restricted and states were allowed to pass right-to-work laws (which banned closed union shops), making unionization difficult in the 23 states that passed right-to-work laws.

See also American Federation of Labor/Congress of Industrial Organizations (AFL-CIO); Labor Movement, U.S.; New Deal; Roosevelt, Franklin Delano; Teamsters and Corruption

References

Atkins, Albert. "Labor." In *The American Economy: A Historical Encyclopedia*. Rev. ed. Edited by Cynthia Clark. Santa Barbara, CA: ABC-CLIO, 2011.

Dubofsky, Melvyn, and Foster Dulles. *Labor in America, A History*. 7th ed. Wheeling, IL: Harlan Davidson, 2004.

National Labor Relations Board. National Labor Relations Act. http://www.nlrb.gov/national-labor-relations-act.

Robertson, Ross. *History of the American Economy*. 3rd ed. New York: Harcourt, Brace, Jovanovich, 1973.

Washington, George

George Washington (1732–99) was the commander-in-chief of the Continental Army during the American Revolution, chairman of the Constitutional Convention, and first president of the United States. More than any other person, Washington was responsible for the creation and success of the United States. He was born on February 22, 1832, in Westmoreland County, Virginia. His father, Augustine, was a relatively successful tobacco planter but died when George was only 11. Rather than going to college, he became a surveyor. Washington trained for a military career and fought in the French and Indian War (1754–63), rising to the rank of colonel.

Washington focused on property as the basic measure of wealth and began land speculation in 1750, buying 1,500 acres in the Shenandoah Valley. His interest in accumulating land never stopped. He was involved in syndicates in 1763 for draining Dismal Swamp in southeast Virginia for farmland (the group used bogus names to claim a larger grant) and the Mississippi Land Company in the Ohio Valley. He surveyed "bounty lands" for French and Indian War veterans and claimed the best land for himself. Later speculation included buying land around the future Washington, DC.

Washington entered politics early, running for the Virginia House of Burgesses in 1758. Rather than promises, his campaign featured liquor (his expense account showed 34 gallons of wine, three pints of brandy, 13 gallons of beer, eight quarts of cider, and four gallons of rum punch) to entice voters. He won in a landslide and served in the House for the next 16 years. Washington was elected as a Virginia delegate to the First Continental Congress in 1774.

After the skirmishes at Lexington and Concord in 1775, the Second Continental Congress took over the troops around Boston and appointed Washington general and commander-in-chief of the Continental Army. For the remainder of the war, the general would have difficulty with both the professional British Army supported by the biggest navy in the world and getting the necessary resources to maintain an army in the field. He would suffer a massive defeat attempting to defend New York City in 1776, before victories at Trenton and Princeton in late 1776 and early 1777. He would have few battles after that, but maintained an army in the field for the rest of the war. The defeat of Cornwallis at Yorktown in 1781 essentially ended the conflict, although the Treaty of Paris actually ending the war was not finalized until the next year and signed in 1783. He stopped a potential revolt of his officers in Newburgh, New York, over lack of pay literally with a speech. Putting on his new spectacles, he stated: "Gentlemen, you must pardon me. I have grown gray in your service and now find myself growing blind." Washington resigned his commission and returned to his plantation, Mount Vernon in Virginia, after the war, attempting to get his finances back in order.

The economy was in depression, the Continental currency was worthless, and the central government under the Articles of Confederation was weak and unable to raise revenues. The Shays Rebellion (1786–87) was a revolt against high taxes in western Massachusetts, considered by many the last straw of the existing government. James Madison, Alexander Hamilton, and others used the poor economy and the Shays Rebellion to promote a Constitutional Convention to convene in Philadelphia in May of 1787. Virginia delegates included George Washington and James Madison. All states except Rhode Island eventually sent delegates, including such other luminaries as Alexander Hamilton, John Adams, Thomas Jefferson, Benjamin Franklin, John Jay, and Patrick Henry.

The Constitutional Convention opened in May 1787. Although originally convened to revise the Articles of Confederation, the agenda shifted to the creation of a new government. With George Washington elected president of the Convention, a strong executive would emerge. Solving this and many other issues took most of the summer, finishing on September 17. The slavery question was not solved. Despite the efforts of the many antifederalists, 11 of the 13 state conventions ratified it by the following July.

The Constitution of 1787 established a republic, the rule of law, and a reasonably powerful federal government. It starts with the preamble, written by George Mason: "We the People of the United States, in Order to form a more perfect Union, establish Justice, insure domestic Tranquility, provide for the common defense, promote the general Welfare, and secure the Blessings of Liberty to ourselves and our Posterity, do ordain and establish this Constitution for the United States of America." It is followed by seven articles. The first three identify the functions of the three branches of government.

The Electoral College unanimously chose George Washington as the first president in March 1789. He was inaugurated on April 30, 1789. The Constitution made no mention of a cabinet, but Congress approved four departments for the new government (inherited from the Continental Congress): Foreign Affairs (renamed State), War, Post Office, and Board of Treasury (Treasury Department). Considerable conflict developed between Alexander Hamilton at Treasury and Thomas Jefferson at State. The realist Hamilton, relying on the "necessary and proper clause," established a working revenue system through customs duties and other sources, called for a central bank (soon to be the First Bank of the United States), and assumed the debts of the Continental Congress and states.

Soon after Washington was inaugurated in 1789, James Madison drafted a dozen amendments to the Constitution. These were reduced to 10, becoming the Bill of Rights. Congress approved the amendments in September 1789; the process was completed through state approval and the Bill of Rights was formally adopted in December 1791. The Constitution did not address political parties. Washington did not believe in parties, thinking all citizens should be concerned with the best public policy available. However, the supporters of a strong federal government (and particularly a strong president) became Federalists, and the supporters of a weak federal government became Anti-Federalists. Washington and second president John Adams did not claim to belong to any party but were labeled Federalists. Anti-Federalist Jefferson soon became leader of the Democratic-Republicans. Political parties have been around as central to government and public policy ever since.

The United States industrialized throughout the nineteenth century, becoming the major industrial power before 1900. The interconnected roles of business, finance, and government have been debated and changing ever since Washington. The change included new interpretations of the Constitution, including what the founders thought. The major ideological split was between those of the Hamilton ilk favoring the implied powers of the "necessary and proper" clause versus the Jeffersonian "strict constructionism" perspective.

Washington was aware that his actions would set precedents and remained careful when making decisions. He initially dealt with Congress in person over treaties and other matters, but became so enraged over the bickering involved that he stopped this practice. He also initially consulted with the Supreme Court. Chief Justice John Jay would not give an opinion if there was a chance the court might later have a court decision on the issue. In case after case, later presidents looked to the actions taken by Washington. He planned to resign after getting the process in order, perhaps after two years. Aides convinced him to stay because of impending issues (especially war between France and Great Britain), and he ran for a second term (again elected unanimously). Washington became increasingly enraged at the actions of Jefferson's Democratic-Republicans, especially the personal attacks in their partisan newspapers, and became increasingly a Federalist partisan himself. The Democratic-Republicans gained control of the House of Representative in 1792 and increased their influence after that. Jefferson became president in 1800 and his party dominated over the next 60 years.

Ron Chernow summarized his accomplishments (2010, 770):

Washington's catalog of accomplishments was simply breathtaking. He had restored American credit and assumed state debt; created a bank, a mint, a coast guard, a customs service, and a diplomatic corps; introduced the first accounting, tax and budgetary procedures; maintained peace at home and abroad; inaugurated a navy, bolstered the army, and shored up coastal defenses and infrastructure; proved that the country could regulate commerce and negotiate binding treaties; protected frontier settlers, subdued Indian uprisings, and established law and order amid rebellion, scrupulously adhering all the while to the letter of the Constitution. During his successful presidency, exports had soared, shipping had boomed, and state taxes had declined dramatically. Washington had also opened the Mississippi to commerce, negotiated treaties with the Barbary states, and forced Britain to evacuate their northwestern forts. Most of all he had shown a disbelieving world that republican government could prosper without being spineless or disorderly or reverting to authoritarian rule. In surrendering the presidency after two terms and overseeing a smooth transition of power, Washington had demonstrated that the presidency was merely the servant of the people.

Slavery was a major issue for Washington and the country. By the end of the Revolution, the North was in the process of eliminating slavery, but slavery remained on a massive scale in the South. Washington was a major slaveholder, with slaves that he owned, those of his wife, Martha, and "dower slaves" kept for the benefit of Martha's children and grandchildren and various relatives. He thought the system inefficient, but did not release his slaves while alive (freedom came in his will). He also made no attempt to end slavery as public policy. Part of the problem was that slaves represented a substantial part of his wealth, the majority of the slaves he controlled were not owned by him, and there was little sympathy in the South for releasing slaves. Most plantation owners favored the limited government of Jefferson and his party, and many considered Washington a turncoat to the South.

After serving eight years as president, Washington retired to Mount Vernon in 1797, focusing on farming and various business interests. He died at Mount Vernon on December 17, 1799.

See also Bank of the United States, First; Constitution, U.S.; Hamilton, Alexander; Morris, Robert.

References

Chernow, Ron. *Washington, A Life*. New York: Penguin Press, 2010.

Perkins, Edwin. *American Public Finance and Financial Services, 1700–1815*. Columbus: Ohio State University Press, 1994.

Waste Management

Waste Management (WM) provided landfill and other waste management services, the result of several business combinations. WM was involved in one of the major accounting scandals of the 1990s, primarily related to fraudulent recording of expenses from 1992 to 1997.

Dean Buntrock and Wayne Huizenga merged their two small garbage collection businesses in 1968, calling the new company Waste Management. WM went public in 1971 and acquired over 100 landfill and garbage collection firms. Huizenga stepped down in the 1980s to found Blockbuster and other businesses, leaving Buntrock in control. Business expanded as local governments left the garbage business and WM moved in—political contributions, lobbying, and outright bribes aided this transition. WM developed a reputation for violating antitrust and environmental regulations, leading to millions of dollars in fines.

WM had a long history of earnings manipulation beginning by the early 1990s specifically to meet earnings targets as garbage became less profitable. Blatant expense misstatement included acquisition manipulation and manipulating depreciation expense and other accounts associated with property, plant, and equipment. The main techniques were: (1) to lengthen the useful lives and overstate the salvage value of vehicles, containers, and equipment, and (2) incorrectly calculate interest capitalization on landfill construction projects. In 1995, WM recorded a large gain on a sham transaction. Auditor Arthur Andersen was complicit in this, possibly because of the huge consulting fees (almost three times the $7.5 million audit fees). Andersen, aware of the understatement of expenses, still gave the company a clear opinion year after year, usually claiming "immateriality."

Securities and Exchange Commission (SEC) charges stated: Defendants' improper accounting practices were centralized at corporate headquarters. . . . They monitored the company's actual operating results and compared them to the quarterly targets set in the budget" (General Accounting Office 2002, 221). WM restated earnings in 1998 (for fiscal years 1992–97), a total of $1.3 billion in undeserved earnings, the largest earnings restatement up to that time. The company settled a stockholder lawsuit in 2001, and the SEC fined WM and auditor Arthur Andersen. USA Waste Services acquired WM in 1998 but kept the Waste Management name. New accounting fraud issues emerged, resulting in an additional $1.2 billion write-off. The company cleaned up its accounting in the twenty-first century and has a market capitalization over $17 billion.

See also Accounting Fraud; Acquisition Accounting; Arthur Andersen; Cendant; Fraud; Rite Aid; Securities and Exchange Commission (SEC); Sunbeam

References

Davidson, Sidney, and G. Anderson. "The Development of Accounting and Auditing Standards." *Journal of Accountancy*, May 1987, 110–27.

Dobson, John. "Crash." In *Bulls, Bears, Boom, and Bust: A Historical Encyclopedia of American Business Concepts*. Santa Barbara, CA: ABC-CLIO, 2006.

Giroux, Gary. *Detecting Earnings Management.* New York: Wiley, 2003.

General Accounting Office. *Financial Statement Restatements: Trends, Market Impacts, Regulatory Responses, and Remaining Challenges.* Washington, DC: General Accounting Office, October 2002.

Mulford, Charles, and Eugene Comisky. *The Financial Numbers Game: Detecting Creative Accounting Practices.* New York: Wiley, 2002.

Schilit, Howard. *Financial Shenanigans: How to Detect Accounting Gimmicks & Fraud in Financial Reports.* 2nd ed. New York: McGraw-Hill, 2002.

Watering Stock

Stock watering meant artificially inflating asset values and was considered a form of securities fraud in the late nineteenth and early twentieth centuries. Daniel Drew is credited with inventing the term. Drew started as a cattle drover in New York. Cattle were kept from water until just before being weighed for sale. Then the cattle were led to the water troughs and became bloated. Drew used a variety of methods to manipulate stock prices, using the same "watering the stock" jargon.

Antitrust advocates considered the practice of "watering the stock" illicit, especially for business combination. Watering stock took various forms during the nineteenth and into the twentieth century. Both bonds and stock were expected to trade around par value, often set at $100 a share. Investors expected a security with a $100 par to be backed by $100 of tangible net assets, plus a dividend yield based on par. Because equity was considered riskier than bonds, dividend yields were expected to be higher than bond interest rates. If a company's corporate bonds paid 5 percent, the expected dividend on preferred stock might be 6 percent of par value. Common stock was the riskiest and a higher dividend was expected, say 7 percent. The price of common stock usually stayed around $100 if the dividend was sustained. Stock prices could drop precipitously if dividends fell, but there was unlimited upside for those willing to take the risk—investment favorites could trade considerably above $100. Financial statements were seldom issued, and reported earnings (this was a period before accounting standards) were viewed skeptically even if disclosed.

When investment banks began combining companies into industrial giants late in the nineteenth century, "overcapitalization" was viewed as a significant problem. When an investment bank bought out a competitor in an industry of interest, the seller expected a "buyer's premium"—cash or securities worth more than the book value of the company. This could be based on assets more valuable than recorded on the books, future earnings potential, or just a willingness to pay a high negotiated price. When packaging the new industry-dominating combination, the banker would include the prices paid for all acquisitions plus a substantial banker's commission and other fees. The assets could be stated at a higher "market" value. Thus the total selling price exceeded the original net assets (assets less liabilities, equal to equity) of the consolidated business. This overcapitalization represented one definition of "watered stock."

The concept of overcapitalization became an issue of concern to politicians, crusading journalists, and regulators. A study by the United States Industrial Commission looked at almost 200 industrial combinations, discovering that the combined issues of stocks and bonds sold at over $3 billion, but the net tangible assets were valued at only $1.5 billion. The interpretation was watering the stock (overcapitalization) by over 100 percent, one definition of massive fraud. One interpretation at the time was that bonds and preferred stock became investment likely supported by assets, while common stock was backed only by "water." The difference between "fair value" (based on earnings power) and book value is now well known, but sophisticated valuation techniques as well as appropriate accounting standards had to be developed over the twentieth century.

Although the primary investment focus for turn-of-the-twentieth-century investors remained dividends, more executives recognized the importance of future earnings to determine valuations: virtually unlimited upside for common stock. In practice, preferred stock usually traded close to par value, while common stock could fluctuate wildly, based on dividends, earnings, or rumors.

Another form of stock watering was the use of stock dividends. The board of directors might declare a stock dividend of 5 percent and expect the stock price to remain unchanged (in part because reporting of these stock dividends was not widespread), although equity would now be 5 percent higher. Maintaining the same dividend yield would be more difficult.

See also Annual Report (10-K); Corporations; Drew, Daniel; Morgan, John Pierpont; Railroads, Nineteenth Century

References

Dobson, John. "Monopoly." In *Bulls, Bears, Boom, and Bust: A Historical Encyclopedia of American Business Concepts.* Santa Barbara, CA: ABC-CLIO, 2006.

Josephson, Matthew. *The Robber Barons.* New York: Harcourt, 1962.

Mitchell, Lawrence. *The Speculative Economy: How Finance Triumphed over Industry.* San Francisco: Berrett-Koehler, 2007.

Whitney, Richard

Richard ("Dick") Whitney (1888–1974) was an American investment banker, president of the New York Stock Exchange (NYSE), and a felon—convicted of embezzlement. Whitney played a part in Black Thursday, October 24, 1929, and preached the significance of the NYSE. Politicians and journalists attending the Pecora Hearings saw an arrogant banker unwilling to admit that the NYSE was subject to even the smallest error. Ultimately, Whitney proved to be a crook and embarrassed Wall Street.

Whitney was born in Boston on August 1, 1888, into a wealthy family. Whitney joined his brother George in New York City in 1910 and established his own brokerage firm, Richard Whitney and Company. He purchased a seat on the NYSE and relied on George's Goldman Sachs connection (George was a Goldman partner) for most of his brokerage business. He lived the life of a very rich man on borrowed money, spending more than he could afford. Whitney speculated on Wall Street using his insider information and gambled. He invested in bootleg liquor and a Florida fertilizer company before that state's economy collapsed.

Whitney's big day in Wall Street history came on Thursday, October 24, 1924, known as Black Thursday. This was the start of the stock market crash of 1929. The major bankers ("Money Trust") formed a stock pool to support the market. Whitney, then NYSE vice president and acting president, entered the NYSE trading floor on behalf of the bankers at the start of the afternoon, going to the United States Steel specialist and bidding the market price of 205 for 10,000 shares. He circled the floor, placing orders on about 20 major stocks. That ended the panic and the market recovered. Unfortunately, the market started dropping the next week. The bankers did not attempt another pool. The crash continued, and by 1932 the stock market lost 90 percent of its value.

Whitney was effectively ruined by the crash. Instead of declaring bankruptcy, he used the remaining stock in his company as collateral for loans based on asking price (when, in fact, the stock had little or no value). In addition to big bank loans and borrowed funds from anyone willing to loan it, he started embezzling.

Whitney was a trustee of the NYSE Gratuity Fund, which made cash payments to the estates of deceased members. Whitney, as broker to the fund, sold bonds, kept the cash, and continued to loot the fund for over $1 million. He did the same from the New York Yacht Club where he was treasurer. When caught, he "replaced" the embezzled funds. Whitney confessed his crimes to his brother George and asked for a $1 million emergency loan. George arranged the loan but did not report the crime.

Whitney's total indebtedness came to $27 million, and the story finally emerged in 1938. Whitney's firm was suspended for insolvency and the NYSE voted misconduct charges against him. District Attorney Thomas Dewey indicted Whitney for grand larceny, and President Roosevelt, when informed, famously exclaimed: "Not Dick Whitney!" Whitney pleaded guilty to the charges and was sentenced to 5 to 10 years in prison. His brother George and other Morgan partners involved were censured by the Securities and Exchange Commission.

After parole in 1941, Whitney managed a dairy farm and then served as president of a textile company. He died on December 5, 1974, in Far Hill, New Jersey.

See also Crash of 1929; Fraud; Goldman Sachs; Great Depression; New York Stock Exchange; Pecora Commission; Securities and Exchange Commission (SEC)

References

Dobson, John. "Crash." In *Bulls, Bears, Boom, and Bust: A Historical Encyclopedia of American Business Concepts*. Santa Barbara, CA: ABC-CLIO, 2006.

Galbraith, Kenneth. *The Great Crash 1929*. Boston: Houghton Mifflin, 1988.

Wiggin, Albert

Albert Wiggin (1868–1951) was an American banker, president and chairman of Chase National Bank. He established Chase Securities Corporation as an investment bank in the early 1920s and speculated on his own, sometimes to the detriment of his bank.

Wiggin was born in Medfield, Massachusetts, on February 21, 1868. He went to work for a Boston bank in 1892 and by 1904 became a vice president of Chase National Bank in New York City. He became president in 1911 and chairman in 1917. Under Wiggin, Chase grew rapidly, largely by acquisitions and the creation of Chase Securities Corp. He took Chase international with its first overseas office in London, opened in 1923.

Secretly, Wiggin set up a number of family-run corporations for speculation, relying on his insider information from Chase Securities. One of these corporations, Shermar, joined Harry Sinclair's (jailed for his involvement in the Teapot Dome scandal) pool to manipulate Sinclair Oil stock. Beginning in the summer of 1929 as the economy was heading for recession, Wiggin sold short some 42,000 shares of Chase National, his own bank. Simultaneously, he authorized Chase Securities to prop up the bank's stock to increase his illicit profits. All this was done on bank credit, not his own money, netting him some $4 million in profit. To complete his nefarious scheme, he cheated on his income tax by setting up a Canadian securities company and buying and selling stocks with his wife to show artificial losses. He retired from the bank in 1932 as a banking icon. As a parting gift, the board gave him a $100,000-a-year pension. His scams came out in the Pecora Hearings. Asked by Pecora for his rationale for selling his own stock short, he stated: "I think it is highly desirable that the officers of the bank should be interested in the stock of the bank."

Wiggin died on May 21, 1951, at 83.

See also Commercial Banking after the Federal Reserve; Crash of 1929; Great Depression; Pecora Commission; Tax Evasion and Tax Scams

References

Dobson, John. "Crash." In *Bulls, Bears, Boom, and Bust: A Historical Encyclopedia of American Business Concepts*. Santa Barbara, CA: ABC-CLIO, 2006.

Galbraith, Kenneth. *The Great Crash 1929*. Boston: Houghton Mifflin, 1988.

Wilkinson, James

James Wilkinson (1757–1825) was a Continental Army officer, governor of Louisiana Territory, general during the War of 1812, and spy for Spain. He was often forced to resign high positions due to corruption charges, incompetence, or accusations of conspiracy but was never convicted of a crime. He managed to maintain the trust of George Washington and other leaders and was reappointed to high positions. Wilkinson was born on a farm near Benedict, Maryland, and studied at the University of Pennsylvania. Commissioned as a captain in 1775, he served in a number of battles including the victory at Saratoga. When sent with official dispatches to Congress, he embellished his own role at the battle and was promoted to brigadier general, causing considerable consternation among army officers. He served as clothier general late in the Revolution but was forced to resign over accounting "irregularities."

After the war he became a politician and land speculator in Kentucky. Opposing the U.S. Constitution, he attempted to get Kentucky to separate from Virginia and join Spanish America. Wilkinson met with the Spanish governor in New Orleans, Esteban Miró, and swore allegiance to Spain. He provided intelligence to Spanish authorities for cash payments in Spanish silver dollars, including the mission of the Lewis and Clark expedition.

In 1804–5, he seems to have been a conspirator with Aaron Burr to establish a separate nation in the West (he would later accuse Burr of treason and testify against him). Since the only evidence of Burr's treachery was a letter in Wilkinson's handwriting, Burr was acquitted. Despite accusations of abuse, President Thomas Jefferson appointed Wilkinson governor of northern Louisiana after the Louisiana Purchase of 1803, a position he lost due to abuse of power.

Wilkinson became senior officer in the army during the periods 1796–98 and 1800–1812. Serving as major general in the War of 1812, Wilkinson was relieved of command after two failed campaigns. Going to Mexico for a Texas land grant, he died in Mexico City on December 28, 1825. Long after his death, Wilkinson's spying activities were discovered, based on published correspondence with the Spanish governor of Louisiana, Miró.

See also Burr, Aaron; Constitution, U.S.; Profiteering during the American Revolution; Washington, George

Reference

Chernow, Ron. *Washington, A Life*. New York: Penguin Press, 2010.

WorldCom

WorldCom was a large telecommunications company, becoming the second largest long-distance company in the United States behind AT&T, seemingly a success from the deregulation of the telecom industry in the 1980s. The tech bubble collapsed in 2000, and Enron became a major accounting scandal when it failed in late 2001. By the middle of 2002, Congress and the financial press paid little attention to accounting scandals, and business as usual was likely. WorldCom declared bankruptcy in July 2002, becoming the new largest bankruptcy in American history,

Former Worldcom CEO Bernard Ebbers exits Manhattan federal court with his wife, Kristie, by his side following his sentencing on July 13, 2005, in New York. Ebbers was sentenced to 25 years for orchestrating an accounting scandal that bankrupted the once giant telecommunications company. (AP Photo/Louis Lanzano)

replacing Enron. WorldCom had a peak market value of $115 billion, almost double Enron's $63 billion. With that, Congress passed the Sarbanes-Oxley Act to reform the financial system within days. Five WorldCom executives pled guilty or were convicted of securities fraud and other illegal acts, including former chief financial officer (CFO) Scott Sullivan and former controller David Myers. Chief executive officer (CEO) Bernard Ebbers was convicted of securities fraud and conspiracy and sentenced to 25 years in prison.

Bernard Ebbers cofounded Long Distance Discount Service in 1983 and he became CEO in 1985. The company grew big after 70 mergers and the name was changed to WorldCom in 1995. MCI Communications was acquired in 1998 for $42 billion—a company much larger than WorldCom at the time

WorldCom looked solid, based on the 2001 10-K, with total assets of $104 billion and stockholders' equity $58 billion (resulting in a reasonable debt to equity ratio of 79.3%). However, almost $51 billion of the assets were goodwill and other intangibles, while cash totaled less than $1.5 billion, indicating the substantial premium prices paid for acquisitions (in bankruptcy goodwill is worthless). According to the

10-K, earnings were off for 2001, with net income of $1.5 billion compared to $4.1 billion the previous year. Revenues were down and operating expenses up. Net income for the first quarter of 2002 was $172 million, down from $610 for the same quarter in 2001. But even this poor performance was incorrect (Giroux 2006, 25).

WorldCom internal auditor Cynthia Cooper found operating expenses charged as capital expenditures in 2002, double counting of revenues, and debt not recorded. CFO Scott Sullivan was fired; auditor Arthur Andersen resigned; Ebbers resigned in April. On June 25, 2002, WorldCom announced $3.8 billion in accounting errors ($3.1 billion for 2001 and $800 million for first quarter 2002), mainly by capitalizing "line costs," fees to other telecom companies for network access rights, which are operating expenses. With the required restatements, net losses were now reported for both 2001 and first quarter 2002. Further review found that the total amount of operating expenses that were erroneously capitalized were $11 billion. WorldCom filed for bankruptcy in July 2002, the largest accounting scandal until the failure of Lehman Brothers in 2008. The company emerged from bankruptcy in 2004 as MCI. The Sarbanes-Oxley was passed within a few days of the World-Com failure.

See also Accounting Fraud; Earnings Manipulation; Ebbers, Bernard K.; Enron; Fraud; Sarbanes-Oxley Act of 2002; Securities and Exchange Commission (SEC)

References

Eichenwald, Kurt. *Conspiracy of Fools*. New York: Broadway Books, 2005.

Giroux, Gary. *Earnings Magic and the Unbalance Sheet: The Search for Financial Reality*. Hoboken, NJ: Wiley, 2006.

Giroux, Gary. "What Went Wrong? Accounting Fraud and Lessons from the Recent Scandals." *Social Research: An International Quarterly of the Social Sciences*, Winter 2008, 1205–38.

Y

Yazoo Land Scandal

The first real estate scandal in the United States involving four firms dealing in fraudulent claims on western lands (now in the state of Mississippi) in the 1790s. The companies were organized to buy land from the state of Georgia, including the Virginia Yazoo Company headed by Patrick Henry (later joined by other companies). Various Georgia politicians became stockholders as political payoffs. Georgia's governor George Matthews signed the Yazoo Act in 1795 to sell some 40 million acres around the Yazoo River (near Natchez, Mississippi) to benefit land speculators. When details were made public, public outrage caused the next Georgia governor to nullify the act. The state refunded the money, but some of the speculators refused and took Georgia to court. Their land purchases were upheld by the Supreme Court in *Fletcher v. Peck* in 1810, one of the earliest rulings overturning a state law. The Supreme Court ruled the land sales as binding contracts that could be invalidated by a later law. Congress awarded various Yazoo claimants over $4 million.

The first attempt at Georgia land speculation was in 1785, when Governor George Mathews signed the Bourbon County Act, which established Bourbon County, Georgia, around the Yazoo River (near what is now Natchez, Mississippi), pushed by land speculators with political connections. Under pressure from the federal government, Georgia dissolved Bourbon County in 1788 (some of the land was claimed by Spain and Native American tribes). In 1789 three companies, the South Carolina Yazoo Company, the Virginia Yazoo Company, and the Tennessee Company were established to buy land from Georgia. The governor agreed to sell 20 million acres of land for $207,000 (about 1¢ an acre). The deal collapsed when the companies attempted to pay with worthless currency.

The major scandal happened in 1794 when, once again, four new companies (Georgia Company, Georgia-Mississippi Company, Upper Mississippi Company, and Tennessee Company) persuaded the Georgia legislature to sell 40 million acres for $500,000, with many Georgia legislators as stockholders. Governor Mathews signed the Yazoo Act in 1795. The act was nullified a year later by the new governor, Jared Irwin. The speculators holding on to the land would be vindicated by the Supreme Court decision in 1810. However, in 1814 the federal government took control of the lands and paid off the various Yazoo claims. Land speculation, often with considerable political support, would continue throughout much of the nineteenth century and, at least occasionally, in the twentieth century.

See also Constitution, U.S.; Cutler, Manasseh; Fraud; Washington, George

References

Genovese, Peter. "Yazoo Land Companies." In *The American Economy: A Historical Encyclopedia*. Rev. ed. Edited by Cynthia Clark. Santa Barbara, CA: ABC-CLIO, 2011.

Land in Georgia: The Pine Barrens Speculation and Yazoo Land Fraud. http://www.ngeorgia.com/history/land.html.

Z

ZZZZ Best

ZZZZ Best (pronounced Zee Best) was a small insurance restoration company in the 1980s, successful only because of major fraud. Founder Barry Minkow (1967–) was convicted on many counts and given a 25-year jail sentence.

Minkow was still in high school when he started a carpet-cleaning business in his parents' garage in 1982. Not successful, he kept the business going through stealing, fraudulent credit card charges, and check kiting. He then claimed to start an insurance restoration business and created a fake company, Interstate Appraisal Services, to verify his business. Minkow was able to get substantial bank loans based on false information. A Ponzi scheme was concocted with fake billings and revenues for insurance restoration, apparently including organized crime connections. The company's chief financial officer, Charles Arrington, was in on the fraud, while the auditor did not adequately verify the insurance restoration records—relying on fake documents and a fake restoration job he was shown.

Minkow took ZZZZ Best public in 1986 with a $15 million initial public offering and a listing on NASDAQ. ZZZZ Best reached a stock price high of $18 early in 1987, making Minkow worth $100 million on paper. He negotiated to acquire the larger KeyServe (the carpet cleaner for Sears) for $25 million financed with junk bonds through Michael Milken at Drexel Burnham. Unfortunately for Minkow, the *Los Angeles Times* printed a story about Minkow's earlier fraudulent credit card uses, and Drexel Burnham backed out of the merger. Instead, bankers called their loans to ZZZZ Best and auditor Ernst & Whinney (now Ernst & Young) discovered the fraud and resigned from the audit.

Minkow resigned from the firm and an internal investigation accused Minkow of embezzling $23 million from ZZZZ Best. Minkow was indicted in Los Angeles, convicted of 57 federal charges of racketeering, securities fraud, embezzlement, and other crimes, sentenced to 25 years in jail in 1989, and ordered to pay $26 million in restitution. After serving over seven years in prison, he was paroled in 1995. In 2001 he founded Fraud Discovery Institute, which assisted the Federal Bureau of Investigation (FBI) and other regulators in shutting down various Ponzi schemes. Unfortunately, he attempted to extort money from home builder Lennar Corp. through false claims and hints that the executives at Lennar were committing fraud. He pleaded guilty to conspiring to manipulate Lennar stock in 2010 and was sentenced to five years in jail and payment of $583 million in restitution.

See also Accounting Fraud; Auditing since SEC Regulation; Fraud; Insider Trading; Junk Bonds; Milken, Michael R.; Ponzi Scheme

References

"Insurance Scams, Credit Card Fraud, Money-Laundering—ZZZZ Best Tried the Lot." *The Motley Fool*, November 2, 2009. http://www.fool.co.uk.

Parloff, Roger. "The All-American Con Man." *Fortune*, January 16, 2012, 79–91.

Previts, Gary, and Barbara Merino. *A History of Accountancy in the United States.* Columbus: Ohio State University Press, 1998.

Timeline

Scandal	Period	Description
Present at the American Revolution	1770s–1780s	Smuggling and bribery were standard business practices; paper currency and note speculation were common; land speculation (note that Robert Morris, the first superintendent of finance, landed in debtors' prison for land speculation) was a continuing problem. Considerable profiteering, especially dealing with the quartermasters, took place throughout the American Revolution.
Counterfeiting	From the 1770s	Counterfeiting paper money first became a big problem when Britain counterfeited Continental currency during the American Revolution, attempting to destroy the value of American money. Counterfeiting was particularly prevalent in the first half of the nineteenth century when state banks issued their own currency. With thousands of legitimate issues on the market, counterfeiting became a major criminal industry.
Early banking	Started in 1784	There were no banks in the United States under the British and not much in the way of money. Alexander Hamilton founded the Bank of New York in 1784, shortly after the end of the Revolution. The new federal government, again under Hamilton as secretary of the Treasury, founded the Bank of the United States in 1791, which acted much like a central bank until de-chartered in 1811. State banks would mushroom early in the nineteenth century, the primary source of paper money, which encouraged speculation,

(continued)

Scandal	Period	Description
		inflation, and early bubbles. Western banks would fuel land speculation (paid for with borrowed bank cash), a major cause of the Panic of 1837.
The birth of Tammany Hall as a political machine	Started in 1789	William Mooney was the first Grand Sachem. Aaron Burr turned Tammany into a political machine for the 1800 election. Tammany would later emerge as New York City's corrupt political machine for the Democratic Party, relying on "ward bosses" to bring in the vote, especially from the influx of immigrants, and provide patronage.
Brokers and speculators in action	1792	New York brokers initially bought and sold securities (federal and state bonds, state banks, and later canals) and also ran lotteries, insured ship cargoes, and so on. The first real Wall Street crook, William Duer, a former Treasury official under Hamilton, speculated on bank stocks based on illicit inside information. He would ultimately go bankrupt and spend the rest of his life in debtors' prison. Stocks were, in part, sold at auction. The Buttonwood Agreement formalized the process of what eventually became the NYSE, after the Duer debacle. The securities business expanded along with the economy.
Yazoo land scandal	1790s	Real estate scandal orchestrated by Georgia politicians selling raw land in Mississippi.
The stock market	Mid-nineteenth century	Daniel Drew, Jay Gould, and Jim Fisk are the original Robber Barons. They manipulated stocks, caused "bear runs" to collapse stock prices, and cornered markets. They gained control of companies, pilfered them internally, and sold out at inflated prices. They spent no time in jail, partly from bribing judges and politicians, but mainly because there were few laws dealing with corporations and markets that could be broken.
Munitions manufacturers	1861	Northern munitions manufacturers sold vast quantities of munitions to the Confederacy before war was declared. In addition to lack of patriotism, this proved shortsighted, because the Confederacy paid on credit—which went uncollected.

Scandal	Period	Description
		The manufacturers fleeced the Union military after that, the usual war profiteering.
Tax cheating	1860s and beyond	A multitude of tax evasion schemes sprang up as new taxes were instituted to pay for the Civil War, from income tax (relatively easy to avoid), to stamp taxes (counterfeit stamps were issued), to various excise taxes (there were schemes large and small to evade liquor and tobacco taxes).
John D. Rockefeller and the rise of big business	1860s and beyond	Rockefeller obtained secret rebates from competing railroads to transport his refined oil to markets from Cleveland. With the lowest production and transportation costs, Rockefeller forced competitors to combine with his (for cash or stock) at his rates or face ruin through cutthroat competition. Standard Oil became a trust and eventually had a virtual monopoly on the oil industry. Other industries followed Rockefeller's lead. He is viewed today either as one of the great entrepreneurs in the United States or as a ruthless robber baron (or both). In any case, he became the richest man in the United States. There were many successful entrepreneurs both before and after Rockefeller including Cornelius Vanderbilt and Andrew Carnegie.
Credit Mobilier	1862–72	The Central Pacific and the Union Pacific were awarded lucrative contracts to build railroad lines connecting all the way to California. Credit Mobilier, contracted to build the line for the Union Pacific, was actually a front for the Union Pacific promoters, and they enormously overcharged the railroad for construction costs. Congressional investigations in 1872 demonstrated that huge payments in cash and stock to politicians led to federal legislation generous in land grants and government loans.
Raiding the Erie	1868	Commodore Vanderbilt, after an illustrious career in shipping, decided late in life to go into railroading and acquired the New York Central. He went after the Erie Railroad, a close competitor in the state then controlled by Daniel Drew

(*continued*)

Scandal	Period	Description
		(plus fellow conspirators Jay Gould and Jim Fisk). Vanderbilt wanted monopoly power. When Vanderbilt tried to corner the market in Erie stock, Drew printed and issued massive amounts of new securities (possibly illegally). Vanderbilt ultimately "surrendered" and reached an accommodation with Drew. They looted the railroad once again, which collapsed in 1873.
Cornering Gold	1869	Jay Gould and Jim Fisk attempted to corner the gold market; Treasury Secretary George Boutwell released gold from the federal stock, foiling their plans. After that, Gould and Fisk bribed judges to void contracts they broke.
Boss Tweed	Post–Civil War	William ("Boss") Tweed headed Tammany Hall, the corrupt Democratic machine that ran much of New York City. Corruption and bribery existed on such a vast scale that Tweed was eventually tried and convicted of bribery and became one of the few crooked politicians who actually died in jail. Thomas Nast's cartoons made him particularly infamous.
Failure of Jay Cooke	1873	The investment house of Jay Cooke facilitated much of the financing for the Civil War. Cooke got caught up in railroad speculations and construction of the Northern Pacific. Overextended, the company folded, causing the Panic of 1873.
Northern Pacific	1890s	The two most powerful financial groups in the nation fought for the Northern Pacific Railroad (and thus domination of transportation in the middle of the United States): J. P. Morgan and James Hill versus Edward Harriman and Standard Oil money. It ended in a draw and they colluded to dominate railroad rates across the nation. By 1900, virtually all railroads were organized into six trust systems controlled by Morgan and other New York bankers. Teddy Roosevelt established his trust-busting credentials by breaking up the Northern Pacific Trust, which was upheld by the

Scandal	Period	Description
Great corporate merger movement	1897–1903	Supreme Court—a small victory for the government regulation of monopolies. Promoted by J. P. Morgan and others, giant corporations were created by acquisitions of major competitors in dozens of industries. U.S. Steel, established with the acquisition of Carnegie Steel and most competitors, became the first billion-dollar corporation in 1902. Considered a scandal at the time for creating monopolies and "stock watering" (with the stock "valued" at greater than book value); the promoters (and the acquired companies) pocketed the difference—considered robber barons or smart bankers.

Twentieth-Century Scandals

Company	Year	Description
The stock market	1900	State law attempts to regulate the New York Stock Exchange and other markets were not particularly effective; market manipulation, lack of disclosure, and general corruption continued to be rampant.
Food and drugs	1906	The filth and labor conditions were intolerable (as described in Upton Sinclair's *The Jungle*). Congress passed the Meat Inspection Act in 1906. Drugs also were unregulated and often contained opium and other addictive drugs. Congress passed the Pure Food and Drug Act in the same year.
Panic of 1907	1907	Speculators tried to corner United Copper and failed, leading to brokerage bankruptcy and a stock collapse. Morgan rescued most of the New York trust companies, New York City, and other companies. J. P. Morgan's "bailout" led to congressional hearings and reform legislation.
Standard Oil	1911	Rockefeller's Standard Oil became one of the first giant industrial firms and held a monopoly position. It was sued for antitrust violations and convicted by the Supreme Court—then broken up into separate oil companies primarily

(continued)

Company	Year	Description
		geographically, most of which were highly successful and are still around.
Charles Ponzi	1920	Ponzi used International Reply Coupons to entice investors, promising a 50 percent gain in 45 days. By paying off early investors, he collected millions of dollars from unsuspecting Bostonians. The Massachusetts bank commissioner shut him down and he spend a few years in prison.
Teapot Dome	1920s	Oilman Jake Hamon essentially "bought" the nomination of Warren G. Harding for the presidency with a million dollars. The payoff was supposed to be secretary of the interior where he would lease oil properties at Teapot Dome and similar sites in California for large bribes. He was killed by his mistress before Harding took office, but the plan went forward, involving additional corrupt oilmen and politicians. The fall guy proved to be Albert Fall as secretary of the interior, who actually carried out the leases (and accepted bribes). Oilman Harry Sinclair and others involved generally got away.
NYSE	Before 1930	Insider trading was common and legal. "Preferred list" sales of new securities at discount prices before the public issues were the norm. Stock pools existed, syndicates established by investment bankers and brokers to manipulate stock price. Before the Great Depression, prices of at least 100 stocks were openly rigged. Information was considered a private matter, which allowed companies to manipulate, misrepresent, and conceal information.
The Crash	1929	By the summer of 1929, the economy was in recession, with industrial production peaking in June. Stock prices continued to new highs and the Great Bull Market continued into September. The first panic occurred on October 24, Black Thursday. Prices continued down: from a peak of 386, the Dow tumbled to 41 in 1933. The market had no credibility with the public. From 1929 to 1932, 11,000 banks failed, gross national product

Company	Year	Description
		(GNP) declined 10 percent annually, steel production fell to 12 percent of capacity, and unemployment hit 25 percent.
Krueger and Toll	1920s and 1930s	Ivar Kreuger refused to disclose financial information, hiding a bankrupt company. Interest and dividend payments were paid regularly from the cash receipts of new securities issues. Kreuger's suicide followed the financial collapse of his empire in the early 1930s.
Samuel Insull and utility pyramiding	1920s	Insull's holding company acquired utilities with limited equity, only enough to maintain control. It was a pyramid, since there were several layers of acquisition, again buying just enough equity to maintain control. Ultimately, only a small amount of equity held the empire together. The debt was paid by the continued dividends from the utilities up to the holding company. When the economy collapsed in 1929, the pyramid collapsed. Insull's was the most infamous utility pyramid, and there was a similar scheme in railroads by the Van Sweringen brothers and others.
McKesson & Robbins	1937	Massive fraud by the president (Philip Musica), including bogus receivables and inventory; these were missed by the auditor, Price Waterhouse, since these were not confirmed. Audit procedures changed as a result of this case, and audit regulation is considered essential.
General Electric and Westinghouse	1940s to 1950s	GE, Westinghouse, and other manufacturers of heavy electrical equipment conspired to fix prices to boost performance. Sued by the Justice Department for Sherman Act violations, they paid big fines and several executives were sent to jail.
Penn Central	1970	1968 merger of New York Central (part of Cornelius Vanderbilt's empire in the mid-nineteenth century) and Pennsylvania Railroad (the "training ground" of Andrew Carnegie)—two of the oldest railroads, with long histories, but failing. After the merger, dividends continued and the board was well paid, but rising debt and declining cash led to bankruptcy. The bankruptcy was long

(continued)

Company	Year	Description
		and difficult, but service continued—eventually by the federal government through Amtrak.
LTV	1970s	One of the original conglomerates from the 1950s, which seemed successful because of accounting gimmicks associated with acquisitions and divestitures. The firm appeared very profitable, but the "magic" profits came from the accounting tricks associated with business combination. Ultimately, new acquisitions became impossible and the company was forced into bankruptcy.
Equity Funding	1972	Massive computer fraud of insurance company. Financial statements for 1964 were fraudulent, followed by a cover-up using false insurance policies and inserting bogus data into computer system. It was finally shut down by the SEC in 1972, based on whistle-blower information.
ZZZZ Best	1980s	ZZZZ Best went from virtually nothing to a giant in the insurance restoration business; records showed tremendous growth. However, most of the actual restoration projects did not exist. It turned out, like McKesson & Robbins, that many executives were crooks. This suggested the importance of background checks on new audit clients as well as confirmation of construction projects.
Lincoln Savings	1980s	Part of the savings and loan scandal of the 1980s; deregulation of this industry and ongoing interest rate problems led to massive fraud and other problems, requiring a federal bailout. Charles Keating was one of many S&L executives convicted and sent to jail.
Drexel and Milken	1980s	Michael Milken discovered that non-investment-grade debt (junk bonds) was not that risky and potentially quite profitable. He created a massive junk bond market that fueled leveraged buyouts and acquisitions. Overspeculation, insider trading, and other shady practices forced Drexel into bankruptcy and Milken to jail.
	1986	A CPA audit partner was convicted of accepting bribes to falsify financial statements of EMS

Company	Year	Description
EMS Governmental Securities		Governmental Securities, which defrauded Home State Bank in Ohio.
BCCI scandal	1988	Criminal corporate structure centered in Abu Dhabi, beginning in the 1970s. Acquired U.S. banks and used American politicians as front men. Criminal behavior included global drug money laundering, bribery, arms trafficking, and tax evasion, not to mention a multitude of financial crimes. Layered corporate structure including shell corporations. U.S. indictments started in 1988 and the firm collapsed in 1991.
Salomon Brothers	1991	Salomon submitted false bids to the U.S. Treasury to purchase more bonds than allowed. The company was fined $290 million, the largest up to that time. It was acquired by Travelers Group (now Citigroup) soon after.
Barings Bank	1995	Baring Brothers was one of the early British private banking companies and the oldest existing bank in the world. A single rogue trader, Nick Leeson, speculated on the Japanese Nikkei 225 stock market and lost $2.2 billion, bringing down the company. Too bad no one in charge had a clue what he was doing.
Waste Management	1997	In 1997, Waste Management had the largest earnings restatement up to that time, $1.4 billion, for the 1992–97 period, associated with understated expenses included inflated useful lives and salvage value of fixed assets. Arthur Andersen was the auditor.
Long-Term Capital Management	1998	Arbitrage kings of the 1990s, but competition forced them to take increasing risks. It was the collapse of Russian debt and ruble that caught them on the wrong side of their derivative speculation. They failed when their trading strategies went awry and could have taken down the financial markets without the intervention of the Federal Reserve.
Sunbeam	1998	Al Dunlap was hired in 1996 to turn the company around. Sunbeam was profitable by 1997, due to

(*continued*)

Company	Year	Description
		premature revenue recognition, channel stuffing, bill and hold, ignoring returned merchandise, and other gimmicks. After an internal investigation, Dunlap was fired and Sunbeam wrote off $1.2 billion in earnings. Arthur Andersen was the auditor.
Cendant	1998	Conglomerate that gobbled up many well-known firms, including Ramada, Coldwell Banker, and Avis. HFS acquired CUC International to form Cendant, but after the acquisition, fraud was discovered in sales and receivables. Cendant lost billions in market value and eventually settled a shareholder suit for $2.8 billion.
New York Stock Exchange	1998–99	Floor brokers convicted of trading for their own profit. SEC enforcement action against NYSE for failure to supervise floor brokers.
Rite Aid	1999–2000	Retail drugstore chain with a multitude of accounting issues, many related to acquisitions; auditor KPMG resigned in 1999; misstatements related to maintenance costs were capitalized; leases were recorded as sales; compensation costs were capitalized; charges for store closures were not expensed; improper inventory & cost of goods sold. The SEC investigation and class action lawsuits were filed.

Twenty-First-Century Scandals

Company	Year	Description
Enron	2001	Declared bankruptcy on December 2, 2001, after restating earnings in the third-quarter 10-Q, indicating major problems with special-purpose entities. Ongoing investigations by the SEC, Justice Department, and others; executives were convicted and class action lawsuits were filed.
Global Crossing	2002	Overstated revenue and earnings over network capacity swaps and then declared bankruptcy; were investigated by the SEC and FBI.

Company	Year	Description
WorldCom	2002	Recorded improper expenses of $3.8 billion and then declared bankruptcy; under investigation for accounting fraud and other violations; the amount of improper expenses uncovered approached $11 billion. CEO Bernie Ebbers was convicted and sent to prison.
Tyco	2002	Conglomerate with questionable practices on accounting for acquisitions and other issues. Restated 1999–2001 financials based on merger-related restructurings plus other problems with reserves. The CEO and CFO were convicted and sent to prison.
Qwest	2002	Subject to criminal investigation by the Justice Department and an accounting practice probe by the SEC, associated with "hollow swaps."
Adelphia	2002	Cable TV operation charged with overstating earnings; former CEO John Rigas was convicted of looting the company, which went bankrupt.
Imclone	2002	Insider trading charges were filed against the former CEO for selling stock after the FDA rejected a new drug; was also alleged to have tipped off Martha Stewart, other friends, and relatives.
Merrill Lynch, Salomon, Smith Barney, Credit Suisse, Goldman Sachs, J. P. Morgan, and others	2002	Major investment banks settled with the New York attorney general, SEC and other regulators on deceptive stock analysis and other brokerage-related practices. The total fine was a combined $2 billion or so, plus other sanctions and agreement to correct deceptive practices.
HealthSouth	2003	Accused of accounting fraud involving $1.4 billion in earnings and $800 million in overstated assets. The former CFO and others pleaded guilty to fraud charges; the CEO was acquitted.
The mutual funds scandal	2003	Mutual funds have only limited SEC regulation requirements and often poor corporate governance, yet have been considered highly ethical. That changed when New York Attorney General Eliot Spitzer sued them on several counts. Some pundits consider the mutual fund scandal as egregious as Enron.

(continued)

Company	Year	Description
Fannie Mae	2004	$16 billion in fraudulent accounting practices and extensive payouts to ousted executives; earnings were restated and executives were fired.
AIG	2005	Internal control weaknesses and poor corporate governance; the CEO was fired.
Stock option back dating	2006	Back dating options grant date to lower stock price; dozens of companies were investigated by SEC; plus related stock option practices of spring-loading, speed vesting, and exercise back dating.
Subprime loans	2007	Massive number of mortgage loans to subprime borrowers, often using predatory practices. Mortgages then repackaged through securitization and sold as bonds. Huge losses taken at major financial institutions and many executives were fired. Multiple SEC and FBI investigations.
Bear Stearns	2008	Rumors of impending collapse because of toxic assets and excessive short-term borrowing caused a "bank run" on short-term lending. A Treasury-Federal Reserve bailout allowed J. P. Morgan to acquire Bear after Fed agreed to "buy" $30 billion of the most toxic assets.
Fannie Mae and Freddie Mac	2008	With trillions of dollars in mortgages and mortgage guarantees (and "backstopping" the entire mortgage markets), the feds nationalized Fannie and Freddie when the Federal Housing Finance Agency put them in conservatorship.
Merrill Lynch	2008	On the verge of failing at the same time as Lehman, Bank of America bought Merrill at a high price for a bankrupt company. Later attempts to back out of the deal proved futile.
Lehman Brothers	2008	On the cusp of bankruptcy, all attempts to find a buyer or provide other types of support proved futile and Lehman filed for bankruptcy, the largest ever in the United States. The resulting panic shut down the credit markets until saved by the Federal Reserve.
Bernie Madoff	2008	Madoff, a successful NASDAQ trader, created a $50 billion Ponzi scheme claiming sophisticated market-trading techniques. Despite many allegations, the SEC never uncovered the fraud.

Company	Year	Description
		Madoff fessed up only after he ran out of money in the market meltdown of 2008.
Bank rescues to avoid a complete financial meltdown	2008–9	Various banks failed; Goldman Sachs and Morgan Stanley reorganized as bank holding companies. TARP funds used to provide capital to Citigroup, Bank of America, and other big banks nearing collapse. Fed cash and zero-interest policy plus TARP funds kept the bank system functioning. Throughout the entire period, huge bonuses to failed and near-failed banks proved a gigantic scandal: why should the government provide billions to support massive executive compensation and allow millions of ordinary Americans to suffer unemployment?
Goldman Sachs	2010	The SEC accused Goldman of fraud using CDO sales.
Raj Rajaratnam	2011	Founder of hedge fund Galleon Group charged with insider trading and convicted in 2012.
British Petroleum (BP)	2012	BP pled guilty to criminal misconduct in the Deepwater Horizon oil spill and agreed to pay a $4.5 billion criminal penalty in a plea deal with the Department of Justice. BP had a history of avoiding safety issues and other fraudulent acts.

Regulation by Government and the Private Sector

Issue	Period	Description
Constitution, new government	1787–96	Following victory and the Treaty of Paris in 1783, the country did poorly under the Articles of Confederation. The Constitution established the federal system still in place. George Washington proved to be a great leader in establishing procedures for a successful federal government. Treasury Secretary Alexander Hamilton gave us a tax, banking, and

(continued)

Issue	Period	Description
		credit system favoring merchants and industry.
First Bank of the United States	1791–1811	This was the first federal corporate charter and first attempt at creating a central bank. This conservative bank worked reasonably well, limiting the amount of speculation possible by state banks. Southern leaders opposed the bank and the bank failed to be rechartered in 1811—just in time for the War of 1812.
Taxation	1790 and beyond	Important to the new country was a set of revenue sources to fund government and pay the national debt, mainly a holdover from the Revolution. Customs duties were the primary revenue source, and this continued until the Sixteenth Amendment of 1913 allowed the income tax.
Second Bank of the United States	1816–36	After the fiasco of the War of 1812, the country learned its lesson that a government bank was essential in times of trouble. So the Second Bank was chartered. It functioned well, except its "hard money" policy and competitive position against state banks angered farmers and state bankers. Andrew Jackson apparently hated all banks and refused to renew the charter of 1836—just in time for the Panic of 1837.
State banking laws	1800–1860	Each state had unique banking laws, from stringent to lax—essentially multiple experiments in banking. Banks created paper currency, which stoked speculation and resulting panics. Some states provided significant restrictions, inspections, and various forms of "insurance" protection. Banks failed by the thousands; plus counterfeiting ran rampant.
Civil War legislation	1861–65	The Union was financially unprepared for the Civil War. New emergency legislation included issuing government paper money

Issue	Period	Description
		("greenbacks"), new tax laws that included the first federal income tax, and the creation of the national banking system, regulated by the Treasury Department.
Munn v. Illinois	1876	Munn was a grain elevator operator with monopoly power to set outrageous prices (and engaged in other corrupt practices). Illinois passed legislation to regulate and set grain-warehousing prices (part of the Granger laws trying to get farmers relief from railroads and other big business), which Munn challenged in court. The Supreme Court, based on the "public interest" argument, upheld the state law, the start of relatively successful regulation of business by both state and federal governments.
Interstate Commerce Commission	1887	The Interstate Commerce Commission Act created the ICC in an attempt to regulate railroads engaged in interstate commerce. It proved only modestly successful until the ICC was given authority to regulate railroad rates, early in the twentieth century.
Sherman Antitrust Act	1890	The Sherman Act was the first attempt to regulate price fixing and monopoly practices of big business through federal regulation. The act outlawed price-setting conspiracies, with mixed results in court. Long term, the government won several high-level cases.
CPA licensing	1896	New York became the first state to license accountants, calling them certified public accountants. Existing auditors were "grandfathered in"; others would be tested for competence. CPA licensing is now required in all states.
Pure Food and Drug Act, Meat Inspection Act	1906	Thanks to Upton Sinclair's muckraking novel *The Jungle* and corroboration by the Neill-Reynolds report, the feds began to

(*continued*)

Issue	Period	Description
		regulate food and drug products. The Meat Inspection Act required federal inspection of livestock before and after slaughter and sanitary conditions. The Food and Drug Act initially concerned product labeling, but led to the Food and Drug Administration and the outlawing of various poisonous "medicines" and adulterated foods.
Clayton Act, Sixteenth Amendment, Federal Reserve Act, Federal Trade Commission Act	1913, 1913, 1914, and 1914, respectively	Following the congressional (Pujo) hearings of 1913, the federal government passed these key acts to regulate business and banking. The Clayton Act, an antitrust law, attempted to tighten requirements beyond the Sherman Act. The Sixteenth Amendment allowed federal income taxes (essential for financing World War I), after income taxes were ruled unconstitutional in the 1890s. The Federal Reserve Act created the Federal Reserve System as a central bank regulating monetary policy and banks, as well as printing paper money. The Federal Trade Commission Act created the FTC, again primarily for antitrust purposes (e.g., price fixing).
Securities Act and Securities Exchange Commission Act	1933 and 1934	Following congressional hearings (Pecora Commission), FDR´s New Deal created the SEC. The SEC regulates the securities markets and has authority over financial reporting.
Financial Accounting Standards Board	1973–present	The FASB replaced the Committee on Accounting Procedure (1938–59) and the Accounting Principles Board (1959–73) as the accounting standard-setting body, with a much-improved structure to promote independence, a research staff, and substantial due process (the public is involved). It had continued political problems with auditors, business, and

Issue	Period	Description
		Congress, but is still in business. It will likely be superseded by the International Accounting Standards Board sometime in the distant future.
Foreign Corrupt Practices Act	1977	The act forbids payment of bribes in foreign countries to promote business activity. Most other developed countries passed comparable legislation. It also mandated minimum internal control practices.
Community Reinvestment Act	1977	Requires banks to increase lending to minority communities in an attempt to end "red-lining."
Advertising ban lifted on auditors	1979	Pressure by the Justice Department and Federal Trade Commission led to elimination of rules against advertising and direct solicitation by auditors, resulting in increased competition and the "audit as a commodity." The results included reduced audit costs, "a deterioration of professional values," and lower-quality audits. This increased the likelihood of earnings manipulation and corporate scandals.
Garn-St. Germain Act	1982	Deregulated the thrift industry after inflation and increasing interest rates pushed the industry toward collapse. Results proved catastrophic.
Basel Accords (Basel I)	1988	The Basel Committee on Banking Supervision (under the Bank of International Settlements in Basel, Switzerland) established minimum capital requirements, 8 percent of risk-weighted assets.
Public Securities Litigation Reform Act	1995	This federal law greatly reduced auditor legal culpability, seemingly leading to more aggressive audits; consulting fees rose, increasing the importance of keeping audit clients happy.

(continued)

Issue	Period	Description
Corporate governance regulations	Beginning in 1999	Minimum corporate governance requirements have expanded since Enron, based on federal laws (Sarbanes-Oxley), SEC regulations, and new stock exchange requirements.
Gramm-Leach-Bliley Act	1999	Reversed the Glass-Steagall Act, allowing commercial and investment banks to combine.
Commodity Futures Modernization Act	2000	Deregulated over-the-counter derivatives, although Fed bailouts were required after OTC derivative scandals.
Regulation FD ("Fair Disclosure")	2001	SEC regulation requiring "full disclosure" when companies talk to financial analysts and other outsiders. Companies must make earnings announcements (and other disclosures) available to the public at the same time such disclosures are made to analysts. Usually, the companies "simulcast" the announcement on the Internet.
Sarbanes-Oxley Act	2002	Federal legislation after Enron and related congressional hearings. The act establishes a new Public Company Accounting Oversight Board (PCAOB) to regulate auditors. New SEC and PCAOB rules implemented the act's provisions, including tighter corporate governance rules, greater SEC oversight, and reporting on corporate internal controls.
Basel II	2004	Recommendations on capital allocation to be more risk sensitive. Various updates from 2005 to 2009.
Fed tightens regulation	2008	After the housing collapse and subprime loan debacle, the Federal Reserve exercised its responsibility to regulate mortgage origination.
Troubled Asset Relief Program	2008	After the failure of Lehman and collapse of the credit markets, Congress passed the $700 billion TARP bill to bail out the banking system. Initial funds were given to

Issue	Period	Description
		"buy" capital in the biggest banks, increasing confidence that these "too-big-to-fail" banks would survive with government support.
March to federal regulation of banking system	2009	Congressional hearings, the Obama Financial Reform Plan issued by Treasury, and the Financial Crisis Inquiry Commission—opposed by massive from banking and the business community—to reach reform consensus. Legislation in the works.
Dodd-Frank Bill	2010	Federal attempt to reform the financial system, including increased regulation of derivatives, a consumer protection agency, increased federal agency coordination, an improved structure to liquidate troubled big financials, a limitation on private equity investments by banks, and a requirement that stockholders vote on executive compensation.
Basel III	2010	Tightens capital requirements, including increased Tier I capital to 6 percent, plus "capital conservation buffer," and a "countercyclical buffer" in emergency conditions. Rules will be phased in from 2013 to 2019.

Subprime Meltdown Timeline (2006–11)

January 23, 2006	Attorneys general (49 states) announce that Ameriquest agreed to pay $325 million for settle charges of customer abuse. Roland Arnall, former head of Ameriquest and Bush fund-raiser, shortly thereafter becomes ambassador to the Netherlands.
February 7, 2007	Subprime originator New Century announces an earnings restatement associated with repurchases (based on early payment defaults) and goes bankrupt in April.
June 20	Merrill Lynch seizes $800,000 in assets from Bear Stearns hedge funds.
July 20	Bear Stearns hedge funds closed. About the same time, Lehman closed its subprime mortgage subsidiary, BNC.

(continued)

July–August	Subprime mortgage-backed securities are found in investment portfolios around the world.
August 6–9	The August Factor, where hedge funds took huge and unexpected losses on stock positions and other investments, then the chaos stopped. The high leverage and underlying risk, plus computerized trading, seemed to be the major causes, but the problems were ignored as markets recovered.
August 9	French bank BNP Paribus closes three investment funds with large MBS portfolios, claiming liquidity dried up.
January 11, 2008	Bank of America announced the acquisition of Countrywide Financial, the nation's largest mortgage finance company, for $4 billion.
January 30	Standard & Poor's announced it would cut credit ratings on $534 billion in subprime MBSs.
March–June	Over 400 people arrested by FBI for mortgage fraud based on sting operations.
March 16	Bear Stearns acquired by J. P. Morgan, with a $30 billion "contribution" from the Federal Reserve, after a long, chaotic weekend orchestrated by Treasury and the Fed.
March 31	Treasury Department issues the *Blueprint for a Modernized Financial Regulatory System*, calling for the modernization of the system.
June 19	Bear hedge fund operators Ralph Cioffi and Matthew Tannin arrested by the FBI for fraud.
July 31	The Housing and Economic Recovery Act (HERA) is passed, which created the Federal Housing Finance Agency (FHFA) to regulate Fannie and Freddie and gave government broad authority to inject financial support into the GSEs.
September 7	Federal Housing Finance Agency places Fannie Mae and Freddie Mac into conservatorship.
September 10	Lehman announced a quarterly loss of $3.9 billion.
September 14	Bank of America announced the acquisition of Merrill Lynch; the deal was finalized on January 1, 2009.
September 15	Lehman Brothers files for bankruptcy, after another chaotic weekend by with the feds.
September 17	Federal Reserve bails out American International Group (AIG) by lending $85 billion.
September 20	Treasury Secretary Hank Paulson issues his plan to save the system, which eventually became TARP.
September 21	Goldman Sachs and Morgan Stanley convert to bank holding companies; therefore subject to regulation by the Fed.
September 25	Washington Mutual seized by FDIC and the assets sold to J. P. Morgan.

October 3	Emergency Stabilization Act creates a $700 billion Troubled Assets Relief Program (TARP) to purchase "toxic assets" of banks. It had initially been voted down by the House on September 29.
October 3	Wachovia seized by FDIC and acquired by Wells Fargo.
October 6–10	Dow drops 22 percent for the week, the worst week ever.
October 13	Fed creates Temporary Liquidity Guarantee Program to guaranty new bank debt.
October 14	Announcement of preferred stock purchases under TARP, including $25 billion each to Citigroup and Bank of America and lesser amounts to J. P. Morgan, Wells Fargo, Goldman Sachs, and other banks.
October 27	Fed creates Commercial Paper Funding Facility to purchase commercial paper.
November 25	Fed creates Term Asset-Backed Securities Facility to loan short-term funds secured by asset-backed securities.
December 1	National Bureau of Economic Research announced a recession started in December 2007.
December 16	Federal Open Market Committee drops the fed funds rate to 0–0.25 percent, the ZIRP (zero interest rate policy) plan.
February 17, 2009	American Recovery & Reinvestment Act signed into law, a $787 billion stimulus goody bag of tax cuts, unemployment benefits, and broad domestic spending.
March 3	Fed announces Term Asset-backed Securities Loan Facility (TALF) to loan against asset-backed securities.
March 23	Treasury announces Public-Private Investment Program to buy toxic assets from banks; a scaled-back program accepts private partners later in the year.
March 26	Treasury outlines framework for regulatory reform focusing on systemic risks; including higher capital reserve requirements, risk management criteria, registration of hedge funds, and oversight and disclosure of OTC derivatives.
April 9	FASB Staff Position (FSP) FAS 157-4 effectively eliminated the need to mark down securitized mortgages and other financial assets as their market values plummet.
April 30	After a TARP bailout, auto maker Chrysler declares bankruptcy; General Motors goes under on June 1.
May 7	Bank regulators release results of stress tests on 19 largest banks; all banks "pass," but 10 are required to raise additional capital. Nine of 10 (all except GMAC) raise needed capital by year-end.
May 13	Treasury proposal to increased regulation of OTC derivatives, including increased authority of the Commodities Futures Trading Commission.

(continued)

May 20	Fraud Enforcement & Recovery Act to improve enforcing violations of financial fraud. The act created the Financial Crisis Inquiry Commission to examine the causes of the crisis.
June 17	Ten banks repay the Treasury $68 billion in TARP money.
June 17	Treasury proposal to create a Financial Services Oversight Council to monitor financial markets, share information across various agencies, and make recommendations on financial regulations.
June 30	Treasury proposal to create a new Consumer Financial Protection Agency.
July 8	Legacy Securities Public-Private Investment Program (PPIP) announced for public and private investments to buy mortgage-backed and other securities issued before 2009
July 15	Congress appoints the Financial Crisis Inquiry Commission on causes of the crisis, which holds its first meeting on September 17.
October 19	Dow hits 10,000 for the first time since October 2008.
January 13–14, 2010	Financial Crisis Inquiry Commission holds its first hearing, including heavy hitting bankers Lloyd Blankfein of Goldman, Jamie Dimon of J. P. Morgan, and John Mack of Morgan Stanley.
February 1	Fed Facilities (commercial paper, asset-backed commercial paper, money market liquidity, etc.) programs expire.
February 23	FDIC announces "problem banks" increase to 702 with over $400 billion in assets by year-end 2009.
February 24	Freddie Mac announces a 2009 loss of $21.6 billion; two days later Fannie May announces a loss of $72.0 billion. Losses continued quarter after quarter.
March 11	Lehman's Repo 105 scam exposed. Lehman (and others) borrowed using repurchase agreements (using 105% of assets as collateral), but recorded them as sales.
May 6	"Flash Crash"; Dow drops almost 1,000 points, about 10 percent, in 10 minutes; apparently caused by futures selling, leading to large volume of computer stock trading.
June 16	Fannie and Freddie delisted from NYSE after Fannie's stock trades for less than a dollar for over a month.
July 15	Goldman Sachs settles with the SEC on fraud charges related to ABACUS 20078-ACI, a CDO offering; Goldman paid a $550 million fine.
July 21	President Obama signs the Finance Reform (Dodd-Franks) Bill to fix a broken finance system.
September 12	Basel III beefs up capital standards for banks in 27 countries, including the United States. Simplified, a bank's total capital must be 8 percent plus a conservation buffer of 2.5 percent, to be phased in over several years.

September 20	National Bureau of Economic Research announces that the recession ended in June 2009, becoming the longest since World War II, 18months, with the largest drop in GDP, 4.1 percent.
January 22, 2011	Financial Crisis Inquiry Commission issued its final report, roughly the size of a phone book for a large Chinese city.
March 1	SEC charged former Goldman Sachs and Procter and Gamble board member Rajat Gupta with insider trading. He was convicted in June 2012.

Glossary

10-K	An annual financial report submitted to the Securities and Exchange Commission by registered corporations.
10-Q	A quarterly financial report submitted to the Securities and Exchange Commission by registered corporations.
8-K	Form submitted to SEC for specific events; e.g., acquisitions.
Above-the-line earnings	Earnings from current operations, such as operating income or earnings before interest and taxes.
Abuse	Excessive or improper use of a resource, intentional diversion, or misuse.
ABX Index	Market index of a basket of subprime mortgage-backed securities; can be used as a benchmark of performance.
Accounting choice	A discretionary alternative for reporting various financial items, such as depreciation.
Accounting fraud	Intentional misstatement of financial information.
Accounting standards	Financial accounting rules, often drafted by regulatory agencies as a response to accounting scandals.
Acquisition	The procurement of the right to manage a company; gained through a business combination (merger) or the appropriation of voting shares sufficient to have effective management.
Acquisition accounting	Alternative accounting methods used in mergers, a major area of accounting scandals, especially since the 1950s.
Adverse selection	Poor market results caused by the disparity in information held by buyers and sellers (asymmetric information).
Agency costs	Costs incurred by agencies as a result of information asymmetries, adverse selection, and moral hazard.
Agency theory	The theory that all contracts have a principal and an agent; principals attempt to write efficient contracts to maximize wealth and minimize agency and other transaction costs.

Aggressive accounting	Accounting choices designed to show increased revenue, decreased expenses, or other beneficial results.
Altman's Z-score	A financial model used to evaluate credit risk.
Ambiguity aversion (uncertainty aversion)	Preference for known risks over unknown risks.
Analysts' forecasts	Predictions of future earnings per share (or other performance measures) by professional financial analysts.
Annual report	Financial statements and company report for the fiscal year.
Antidilutive	Actions that decrease the number of shares of common stock outstanding, especially buying back company shares (treasury stock).
Antitrust laws	Regulation of anticompetitive behavior beginning in the United States with the Sherman Act of 1890.
Arbitrage	Profiting from price difference between two or more markets by buying in the low-cost market and selling in the high-cost market.
Asian debt crisis	Financial crisis stated in July 1997 in Thailand caused by overleverage and an asset bubble.
Asset-backed securities (ABSs)	Financial securities backed by a pool of assets, including mortgages.
Assets	Items owned by a company or individual that have probable future economic benefits based on past transactions or events.
Audit	An external review performed by licensed professionals to ensure financial reporting is in conformance with generally accepted accounting principles.
Auditing	Financial accounting gatekeeping, certifying that financial statements conform to accounting principles; part of the regulatory process.
Austrian School of economics	The school of economic analysis inspired by Friedrich Hayek, Carl Menger, and others in Austria, emphasizing market forces and a libertarian perspective.
Availability cascade	A self-sustaining chain of events, often starting from a minor event and leading to panic and large-scale government action.
Backdating stock options	Corporate issuance of stock options with the "issue date" recorded at an earlier date when the stock price (and therefore exercise price) were lower, allowing the recipient to increase profits when the options were exercised.
Back-pocket sales	Fictitious sales recorded only if needed to make earnings targets.

Bailout	A rescue from financial distress, usually by a government agency; panics and other crises often require bailouts of major banks and other players.
Bait-and-switch	The practice of "baiting" customers, typically by offering something for a low price, followed by "switching" the terms of an arrangement; a form of fraud.
Balance sheet	A financial statement showing the assets, liabilities, and stockholders' equity at the financial reporting date.
Banana republic	Latin American countries in which the government is essentially controlled by American agricultural interests.
Basel Accords	Global agreement on bank capital requirements.
Bear market	A stock market downturn of at least 20 percent lasting two or more months.
Bear market rally	A stock market price increase of about 20 percent in an overall bear market, giving the mistaken signal that the market is headed up.
Bear raids	Attempts by sellers to drive down stock price to cover a short position or buy shares at a reduced price.
Bear Stearns exemption	The elimination of equity requirements for the top investment banks by the Securities and Exchange Commission in 2004.
Bear trap	A situation in which short sellers are forced to cover their positions at higher prices; a bear trap occurs when short sellers are wrongly convinced the market will shortly sink in price; can occur because of gossip reported in the financial press.
Behavioral economics	The use of psychological factors to understand economic decision-making.
Below-the-line earnings	Comprehensive earnings that include net income plus other gains and losses not reported on the income statement.
Beltway bandits	Private contractors around Washington, DC, providing consulting services.
Beta (β) analysis	Analysis of the Beta coefficient, a term that derives from the slope of a market model; can be used to analyze systematic risk for stock selection. A value of $\beta = 1$ means the stock moves directly with the market.
Big bath write-off	A large write-off recorded as a loss, often taken when new management reorganizes and blames old management for all the problems.
Big Four	Major auditing firms; the basic accounting gatekeepers of most large corporations.

Bimetallism	The use of both gold and silver as money, or minting gold and silver coins as legal tender; silver was typically valued at 16 times the price of gold during the nineteenth century.
Black horse cavalry	Corrupt New York State legislators at the end of the nineteenth century who blackmailed and bribed constituents (especially corporations) for profit. Such legislators would typically introduce bills against the constituents' interest, only to kill the bills for appropriate cash payments.
Black market	Any market for goods and services outside government power and regulation; unreported and possibly illegal activities.
Black swan	A rare market event that deviates beyond normal expectations and is difficult to predict; identified by Nassim Taleb.
Black-Scholes	A complex economic model used to price options; it made possible substantial derivatives trading.
Blue sky laws	State laws that regulate the trade of securities; such laws attempt to protect the public from "blue sky merchants" who sell speculative securities with no substance.
Bond ratings	Ratings of credit risk by ratings agencies such as Moody's and Standard & Poor's, with "investment-grade ratings" ranging from AAA (highest) to BAA.
Bona fide hedging exemption	A waiver issued by the Commodity Futures Trading Commission allowing speculation of commodities futures; first issued to Goldman Sachs subsidiary J. Aron in 1991.
Book value (carry value)	The dollar value of assets and other items presented on the balance sheet, usually based on historical cost.
Bottom line	Revenues and gains minus expenses and losses; used to measure earnings performance over an accounting period.
Bounded rationality	The theory that individuals are rational but limited in their knowledge and ability to process information.
Boycotts	Voluntarily abstention from buying from or dealing with specific people or organizations as a protest, usually for political and/or economic reasons.
Brady Plan	A restructuring plan in 1989 devised by Treasury Secretary Nicolas Brady to transform defaulted Latin American bank loans into dollar-denominated bonds.
Breaking the buck	A situation in which a money market fund loses value and drops below $1, or the benchmark at which the fund maintains its net asset value.
Bretton Woods	Post–World War II agreement on international trade that led to the creation of the World Bank and International Monetary Fund.

Bribery	The exchange of money for something of value; the most fundamental type of corruption.
BRIC	Acronym for Brazil, Russia, India, and China as large, fast-growing developing countries.
Broker	A middleman who creates a market for buyers and sellers without taking an equity position in the goods or securities being sold.
Bubble	A period when assets trade substantially above their fundamental value.
Bull market	A period when stock market prices are rising, associated with increasing investor confidence.
Bulls and bears	Optimists and pessimists, respectively, on future stock prices.
Bunkering (illegal oil bunkering)	Stealing oil from pipelines and other sources, often to support insurrections or criminal activities.
Business combinations	Mergers of companies to form bigger firms; reasons for business combinations include reduction of competition, vertical integration, and economies of scale.
Business cycle	Fluctuations in economic activity, including a boom phase and a contraction (recession or depression).
Business ethics	Moral principles related to the operations, financing, and reporting of a business.
Cadillac plans versus ghetto plans	Terms used to describe the substantial pension and health care plans that many corporations provide for executives and the poor plans provided for ordinary workers.
Call (call option)	An option (derivative) allowing the buyer the right to buy an asset at a particular price for some period.
Capital	Wealth in the form of money or property used in a business; equity of an individual or company.
Capital asset pricing model	The relationship of individual security return to the market return.
Capital markets	Markets for debt and equity securities to raise long-term funds.
Capital structure	Composition of debt and equity, measuring relative leverage.
Capitalism	Economic system with private ownership of production and prices, with production and distribution determined by market mechanisms.
Capture theory	The theory that regulatory agencies can work on behalf of the regulated industry (be "captured") rather than the public interest.

Carried interest	Share of profits of private equity and hedge fund partners taxed at the capital gains rate of 15 percent.
Cartel	A formal agreement among competing firms, usually to fix prices, production levels, and/or market share.
Cash flow statement	A financial statement showing cash inflows and outflows from operations, investments, and financing.
Central bank	A regulatory-sanctioned bank responsible for monetary policy of a country and providing liquidity to the banking system when needed.
Channel stuffing	Shipments to wholesalers or others using deep discounts to encourage acceptance.
Cheap money	Credit (loans) available at low interest rates.
Chinese Wall	Barriers to information flow, intended to separate departments that make investment decisions from those that have proprietary market information; a Chinese Wall should prevent conflicts of interest and illegal insider trading.
Circuit breaker (market)	Procedures intended to halt market trading because of a large price drop that can eliminate market liquidity.
Citizens United	Landmark 2010 Supreme Court case determining that the First Amendment prohibits the federal government from restricting political expenditures by corporations and labor unions.
Civil virtue	Habits of individuals important to the success of a community.
Class action lawsuits	Lawsuits in which a large group of people collectively bring court claims.
Classical economics	The first "modern school" of economics beginning with Adam Smith's *Wealth of Nations* in 1776, with a focus on laissez-faire policies.
Clayton Act	Antitrust act of 1914 seeking to prohibit various anticompetitive practices.
Clearinghouse, bank	Voluntary associations that cash ("clear") checks in large cities; usually managed by one of the leading member banks. Other types of clearinghouses clear and settle various derivatives and securities transactions.
Closed shop	Labor and business agreements requiring employers to hire only union members.
Collateral	Physical assets pledged by a borrower to the creditor in case of loan default.
Collateralized debt obligation (CDO)	A package of debt usually repacked from previous securitized agreements and sold by risk tranches; proven to be particularly toxic in the subprime crisis beginning in 2007.

Collective bargaining	Negotiation between employers and employee groups (unions), usually concerning wages, benefits and working conditions.
Collusion	Agreement among competing organizations to limit competition, often by deception such as price setting, kickbacks, dividing markets, or limiting production.
Commerce Clause	An enumerated power listed in Article 1, Section 8 of the U.S. Constitution giving Congress the power to regulate commerce with foreign governments and among states.
Commercial banks	Government-chartered organizations that accept deposits and make commercial loans; the first American bank was the Bank of North America chartered in 1781.
Commercial paper	Unsecured short-term (under 270 days) notes issued by corporations with low credit risk.
Commodities markets	Formal market trading of raw products such as food, metals, and oil and derivatives using standardized contracts.
Commodity Futures Trading Commission (CFTC)	Federal commission established in 1974 to regulate the trading of futures and options.
Commodity risk	The potential for price changes in commodities such as agricultural goods or oil.
Common good	The collective "good" shared by members of a community; utilitarians refer to the idea of the greatest good (utility) for the greatest number of people when making ethical decisions.
Compliance costs	Time and money spent by companies or individuals on tax and regulatory requirements.
Conflict of interest	A situation in which an individual has the potential to benefit personally from information or a from decision made in an official capacity.
Conglomerates	Large corporations made up of unrelated subsidiaries.
Consensus analyst forecast	Average forecast of earnings per share (or other definition of performance) by the major professional financial analysts tracking a specific company's stock.
Constitution, U.S.	The overall set of rules for the United States, establishing a framework for organizing the federal government and the relationships between the federal government and states.
Consumer Financial Protection Bureau	Federal bureau designed to protect American consumers from predatory financial practices; part of the Dodd-Frank Act.

Continental currency	Paper currency issued by the Continental Congress during the Revolutionary War.
Controlled markets	Markets in which prices and/or volume of goods are controlled by government regulation.
Cookbook accounting	Specific accounting rules that must be implemented without regard to professional judgment or financial reality, such as lease accounting.
Cookie jar reserves	Reserve accounts used to smooth earnings. Examples include allowances for doubtful accountings on accounts receivable, increasing reserves (reducing earnings) when performance is strong, and decreasing reserves (increasing earnings) when performance is weak.
Corner	Investors buy all available shares, possibly to foil a bear raid (when sellers sell to drive down prices).
Corporate governance	The board of directors and the structure in place to oversee the management of a corporation or other organization.
Corporate responsibility (social responsibility)	The practice of self-regulation on the part of businesses in order to comply with ethical, legal, and cultural norms and to have a positive impact on stakeholders and the environment.
Corruption	An abuse of power or resources for personal gain.
Corruption Perception Index	Ranking of countries by perceived levels of corruption, from New Zealand and Denmark (least corrupt) to Somalia (most corrupt).
Counterfeiting	Creating bogus currency or securities (or other goods); especially common in American banking in the early nineteenth century.
Counterparty risk	The probability that the other party to a finance contract will default on its obligation.
Crash (market crash)	A large drop in stock prices (or other asset prices).
Creative destruction	The tendency of capitalism, identified by Joseph Schumpeter, to foster innovation, entrepreneurship and other advances in business, followed by periods of collapse.
Credit analysis	Procedures in financial analysis used to evaluate the investment prospects of a debt instrument.
Credit default swap (CDS)	A type of derivative that pays off if a debt instrument defaults; a major part of the subprime meltdown (e.g., CDSs sold by American Insurance Group).

Credit rating	An estimate of credit worthiness made by rating agencies, with ratings from Aaa (highest) to C (lowest) by Moody's and similar ratings by Standard and Poor's.
Credit rationing	Action by lenders to limit the supply of additional credit even when borrowers are willing to pay higher interest rates.
Credit risk	The probability a firm will default on liabilities or declare bankruptcy.
Creeping takeaways	Slow reduction of benefits, especially employee pension and health benefits; a common practice of businesses.
Crony capitalism	A system in which business and government officials enjoy a close relationship, resulting in favoritism such as tax breaks, favorable regulations, or outright grants/giveaways.
Cross-market arbitrage	Buying and selling related securities on different markets at the same time, such as a stock or exchange-traded fund simultaneously with related derivatives (futures or options).
Curley effect	The effect of perverse political incentives that make government worse; named for Boston mayor James Curley (1874–1958) who provided poor people benefits (so they would vote for him) that were ultimately bad for the city.
Currency swap	An agreement to make payments in one currency in exchange for the obligations in another currency.
Cyclically adjusted P/E (CAPE or PE10) ratio	Price/earnings (PE) ratio created by Yale professor Robert Shiller using the inflation-adjusted S&P 500 Index divided by 10-year average trailing earnings per share (also inflation adjusted).
Dark pools	Financial assets and liabilities that are unregulated and generally hidden from the marketplace, such as many over-the-counter derivatives.
Dead peasant insurance	Life insurance policies that corporations taking out on employees. These provide benefits to the corporation, such as a tax-free cash return when the individuals die ("mortality dividends"). They also offset executive deferred compensation.
Debt and leverage	Borrowed money. Credit risk increases with debt; companies with high leverage are most susceptible to failure during panics and business downturns.
Default risk	The probability that a firm will not pay interest and/or principal when due.
Defined-benefit plan	Retirement plan in which an employer guarantees annuity payments to retirees; usually based on final salary and years of service.

Defined-contribution plan	Retirement plan in which an employer contributes to employee pension fund (such as a 401 (k)) and has no further obligation.
Deflation	A decrease in the general price level which increases the value of money; a negative inflation rate.
Democratic capitalism	A political and economic system that emphasizes free markets but also considers social justice issues such as unemployment insurance and aid to the poor.
Deregulation	The elimination or simplification of government regulations, especially those that limit market forces.
Derivatives	Contracts derived from existing contracts such as futures and options; derivatives have been involved in several scandals since the 1980s.
Dialectic	Use of dialogue by people holding different points of view; popularized by Plato's Socratic dialogues.
Dirty surplus	Gains and losses recorded directly to equity and not on the income statement.
Disinflation	A slow-down in the rate of inflation.
Diversification	The practice of creating an investment portfolio that holds a broad selection of stocks, bonds and other assets, attempting to maximize the risk-return trade-off.
Dividend yield	Dividends per share divided by stock price; a measure of direct cash return on investment.
Double-dip recession	A recession followed by a short recovery, then another recession.
Dow Jones Industrial Average (DOW)	Stock index of 30 major industrial firms, the most common indicator of stock market performance.
Due process	Procedures followed by regulatory agencies to allow public input during the various phases of the regulatory-setting process.
Earmarks	Congressional provision, often supported by a specific congressperson, for funds to be spent on specific projects, usually for personal or political benefits. Earmarks also take to form of preferential tax exemptions.
Earnings management	Operating and discretionary accounting methods used to adjust earnings to a desired outcome.
Earnings manipulation	Aggressive accounting techniques used to inflate earnings in a particular accounting period.
Earnings per share (EPS)	Net income converted to a per-share basis (calculated as basic EPS or diluted EPS).

Earnings quality	The extent to which earnings represent economic reality, associated with conservative accounting and full disclosure.
Earnings restatements	Revision by a corporation of public financial information that was previously reported erroneously.
Earnings surprise	A situation in which actual reported earnings are greater or less than expected, usually measured by quarterly earnings announcements relative to analysts' forecasts.
Ecology	The study of living organisms and their interrelationships with the environment.
Economic consequences	Unintended results that occur after changes in regulation or other factors.
Economic crisis	Various types of banking panics, recessions, stock price crashes, or currency collapses.
Economic forecasts	Quarterly, annual, and long-term predictions of corporate earnings per share and other factors, published by financial analysts.
Economic reality	Financial information free of distortions that hide actual results.
Economic regulation	Government restrictions on market participants related to price, quantity, product quality, and entry and exit from markets.
Economies of scale	Unit cost advantages associated with large size, especially in manufacturing; large plants should be more efficient and produce goods at a lower unit cost than small plants.
Ecosystem	Interaction between living organisms and their environment.
Edgeworth box	Economic analysis representing the distribution of resources.
Efficient contracting	Writing contracts to maximize principal's wealth and minimize transaction costs.
Efficient markets	An economic theory positing that market information is immediately reflected in capital prices in an unbiased fashion.
Egalitarian	Adjective describing the idea that people should have equal economic, social and political rights. An egalitarian agenda may also focus on removing economic inequalities among people.
Ellsberg paradox	Contradiction that results from people's aversion to uncertainty; individuals' choices violate expected utility in economic experiments and therefore appear paradoxical.
Enforcement actions	Legal actions taken by the Securities and Exchange Commission's Enforcement Division, based on regulatory violations by corporations.

Entrepreneur	An individual who organizes a business and assumes the risks related to potential profit.
Environmental movement	Various political, scientific, and conservation advocates addressing environmental, issues, including pollution, climate change, and maintaining the natural world.
Equity stripping	Mortgage refinancing gimmicks in which a lender eliminates a mortgage holders' equity through fees and service charges.
Escape clause	Contractual terms that allow a party to avoid having to perform according to the contract, common in real estate and employee pension and health agreements.
Ethics	System of moral principles, including the rules of conduct for individual, group, or cultural actions.
Euphoria	The boom phase of an economic cycle, leading first to asset bubble, then a crash.
Eurodollars	Deposits denominated in dollars outside the United States and subject to little regulation.
Eurozone	Economic and monetary union of 17 European Union member states adopting the Euro (€) as a common currency.
Event risk	Uncertainties associated with any number of potential events, such as fires, earthquakes, or hostile governments.
Exchange-traded fund (ETF)	An investment fund traded on a stock exchange like a stock.
Exchequer	Government financial manager and collector of taxes and other revenues for the United Kingdom.
Executive compensation	Compensation based on salary plus bonuses and stock participation based on job performance.
Externalities	Costs (or benefits) not included in market prices and incurred by parties not part of the transaction, such as pollution.
Extortion	Process by which a person gets or attempts to get money, property, or services from someone through coercion.
Fair-value accounting	The practice of recording assets and liabilities at their market value (or another measure of current value) at the financial statement date.
Fairness	Decisions or behavior free from bias or injustice; social justice.
FASB Staff Position (FSP) FAS 157-4	Accounting pronouncement passed in 2008 allowing firms to avoid mark-to-market for financial assets where markets "are not orderly."
Fascism	Radical government under a totalitarian single-party state; a private sector exists but is controlled by the government.

Fat-tail events	Extreme events expected to occur rarely. Experience shows that fat-tail events are quite common in financial markets.
Federal funds (fed funds) rate	Interest rate at which member banks lend money (federal funds) from Federal Reserve balances to other member banks; a primary measure of short-term interest rates and used as a target rate by the Federal Reserve.
Federal Home Loan Mortgage Corp (Freddie Mac)	Government-sponsored enterprise (GSE) chartered to buy and guarantee mortgaging, created in1970.
Federal National Mortgage Association (Fannie Mae)	New Deal program established to promote home ownership by guaranteeing and buying mortgages, privatized in 1968 as a government-sponsored enterprise (GSE).
Federal Reserve (Fed)	American central bank established in 1914, with increasing economic and banking responsibilities ever since.
Federal Trade Commission	Independent federal regulatory agency to provide consumer protection and prevent anticompetitive business practices.
Financial Accounting Standards Board (FASB)	Authoritative body establishing generally accepted accounting principles in the United States for commercial and nonprofit firms.
Financial Analysts	Specialists who use financial and other information to make forecasts and recommendations about corporate earnings, equity investments, and other measures.
Financial Crisis Inquiry Commission	Ten member commission established by Congress in 2009 to investigate the causes of the subprime crisis; report issued in 2011.
Financial engineering (computational finance)	The use of mathematical economics, programming, and other quantitative techniques to make risk management decisions through hedging, trading, and other techniques.
Fiscal policy	Strategy used by government for spending and taxes, analyzed for its economic impact.
Food and Drug Administration (FDA)	Federal agency of the Department of Health and Human Services responsible for promoting public health, food safety, pharmaceutical products, and other issues.
Foreign Corrupt Practices Act	Congressional legislation banning bribery of foreign officials and providing increased oversight over corporate financial practices.
Foreign exchange risk	Risk associated with currency fluctuations against all other currencies, creating substantial risk for global companies.

Forwards and futures	Agreements between buyers and sellers to deliver an asset in exchange for cash (or other financial instrument) at a fixed price on a specific future date; a future is a forward contract traded on an organized exchange.
Fraud	Intentional deception for personal gain, common in financial and accounting crises and often illegal.
Free markets	Markets where prices are determined by supply and demand, without government interference.
Free-rider problem	The use of goods or service by people or organizations ("free riders") who do not pay for them.
Free trade	Government policy of noninterference with respect to imports and exports.
Front loading	Recognizing revenues, expenses, or other items in advance, usually for illicit purposes.
Front running	The illegal practice of executing a personal trade or for a customer in advance of a public announcement or a client trade.
G.I. Bill	Servicemen's Readjustment Act of 1944 provided benefits to returning World War II veterans, including mortgage loans and college and other education funding.
Gambler's ruin	The theorem that a gambler playing a game with a negative expected value will eventually go broke.
General equilibrium theory	Theoretical economic principles that explain the behavior of supply, demand, and prices in interacting markets.
Generally accepted accounting principles (GAAP)	Comprehensive set of accounting standards established by the FASB and predecessor bodies.
Gilded Age	Term coined by Mark Twain for the period from the end of the Civil War in 1865 to the end of the century, an era of industrial growth and business abuse.
Gini coefficient (Gini index)	A measure of inequality of a distribution from 0 to 1, usually used as a measure of income or wealth distribution. A value of 0 would mean perfect equality; a value of 1, maximum inequality.
Gold standard	Historic system (no longer in use) in which currencies were pegged to gold by weight and currencies were redeemable in gold.
Goodwill	Acquisition price of a target company less the fair value of the net assets of the target, used with the purchase method of merger accounting.

Government corruption	The misuse of power by government officials for illicit personal gains; including embezzlement, graft on public contracts and franchises, regulatory corruption, and insider trading.
Government-sponsored enterprise (GSE)	A financial corporation created by Congress, such as Fannie Mae, to promote credit for mortgages, education or other purposes.
Granger movement	Farmer-based organizations created beginning in the 1860s to increase the economic and political power of farmers.
Great Depression	Economic catastrophe of the 1930s caused by a stock market crash in 1929 and counterproductive acts by the Federal Reserve and federal government fiscal policy.
Greater fool theory (survivor investing)	The assumption that risky investments are worthwhile because they can be sold later to "a greater fool."
Greenbacks	U.S. paper currency issued during the Civil War.
Greenspan put	Monetary policy of former Federal Reserve Chairman Alan Greenspan, designed to flood the financial markets with cash after a crash or other financial debacle.
Gross domestic product (GDP)	Market value of all final goods and services produced in a country in a year, used as a measure of overall economic activity.
Group of 20 (G-20)	Finance ministers and central bank governors from 20 major economies, usually meeting at annual summits to discuss international financial issues.
Group of Seven (G7)	International group of finance ministers from France, Germany, Italy, Japan, United States, United Kingdom, and Canada (Russia was added in 1997 to form the G8).
Hedge Funds	Investment funds with fewer than 100 investors (thus not subject to Securities and Exchange Commission regulations), usually associated with derivatives trading.
Hedging	Techniques used to protect against adverse movements in prices, interest rates, foreign currency, or other risks.
High-frequency trading	Use of sophisticated technology tools to rapidly trade securities usually for brief time periods (resulting in no investment position at the end of the trading day).
Historical cost accounting	The practice of recording assets and liabilities at their historical acquisition costs; assets and liabilities may be depreciated or amortized over time.
Holding company	A parent company that owns the outstanding stock of other companies.

Honest graft	The use of a political position and insider information for personal gain, but without committing illegal acts.
Horizontal merger	Acquisition of a direct competitor, thus increasing market share and reducing competition.
Hostile takeovers	Acquisition of another company without the approval of the board of directors of that company.
Hyperinflation	Out-of-control price levels, usually with the price level up over 100 percent for a short period of time (e.g., three years).
Illiquidity	The inability of a firm to pay its creditors when obligations come due; refers to a lack of ready cash, rather than insolvency.
Impossibility theorem	Economist Kenneth Arrow's "proof" that no voting system can reflect the preferences of individual citizens.
Income smoothing	Earnings management techniques used by businesses to smooth out erratic revenue and earnings behavior.
Income statement	Financial statement showing revenues, expenses, net income, and earnings per share for an accounting period.
Index futures	Futures contracts pegged to a specific market index, such as the S&P 500.
Index	A group of assets packaged as a market measure, with the Dow Jones Industrial Average and S&P 500 the most common stock indexes.
Industrial Revolution	Eighteenth- and nineteenth-century industrialization in agriculture, manufacturing, transportation, mining, and technology, greatly increasing productivity.
Inflation	Increase in the general price level of goods and services that decreases the value of money, measured using a price index such as the consumer price index (CPI).
Information asymmetry	Imbalance of information between two parties to a transaction; this "veil of ignorance" can lead to poor decisions by the party without proper information.
Initial public offering (IPO)	Process by which a corporation issues common stock for the first time; the first IPO was the Dutch East India Company in 1602.
Insider trading	Trade in securities by insiders; illegal if in anticipation of pending non-public information or act such as an acquisition decision.
Insolvency	Situation in which the liabilities of a firm exceed its assets, thereby creating negative equity and usually associated with bankruptcy.

Interest groups	Associations seeking influence and publicity for a specific cause, including special interest groups seeking political power in Washington.
Interest rate risk	Interest rate fluctuations, complicated by fixed versus variable rate loans and duration (maturity dates).
Interest rate swap	A contract to exchange fixed for floating interest payments on bonds and other credit instruments.
Interlocking directorship	An arrangement where executives from competing firms (also bankers) hold positions on each other's boards of directors.
Internal control	Organizational procedures used to direct, measure and monitor transactions; processes used to protect organizational resources and prevent and detect fraud.
International Monetary Fund (IMF)	International organization offering technical advice, loans and monitoring of sovereign countries, especially developing countries.
Investment banks	Financial intermediaries for securities buyers and sellers; investment banks traditionally raise money for businesses and governments using securities and have branched out into many investment-related services.
Investment-grade bond rating	The highest bond rating categories (Standard & Poor's AAA to BBB; Moody's Aaa to Baa), considered to have relatively low credit risk.
Investment trust	Collective investment fund with similarities to mutual funds and private equity investments, created in Britain and used extensively in the United States during the 1920s.
IPO allocation	Distribution of shares of stock through an investment bank at a certain price; enacted by a company going public using an initial public offering.
Iron law of wages	Economic theory of nineteenth-century economist David Ricardo that wages always tend toward subsistence levels.
Irrational exuberance	Term associated with overoptimism in the markets based on a speech given by Federal Reserve Chairman Alan Greenspan in 1996 to the American Enterprise Institute, defined by Robert Shiller as "wishful thinking on the part of investors that blinds us to the truth of our situation."
Jevons paradox	Observation that technology increases efficiency but resource use rises as consumption increases; named for nineteenth-century British economist William Jevons, who identified the paradox while analyzing coal consumption.

Joint stock company	Type of corporation started in England in 1600 with the East India Company, based on a Royal Charter.
Junk bonds	Corporate bonds with a below investment grade rating (Moody's Ba and below); Michel Milken first made a viable market out of these in the 1980s.
Just price	Philosophical concept identified by medieval theologian Thomas Aquinas who was attempting to set standards of fairness, including a ban on usury; the theory that prices should be based on relative labor.
Justice	Concept of moral rightness based on legal, ethical, rational, or religious tenants; also, acting fairly.
Kantian ethics	Moral system positing that people have a duty to act according to universal law (called a categorical imperative); named for philosopher Immanuel Kant (1724–1804).
Keynesian economics	Macroeconomic theory of John Maynard Keynes, advocating government action to stabilize the economy over the business cycle, especially during depressions.
Kickback	A negotiated bribe where a "commission" (or bribe) is paid for services performed.
Knightian uncertainty	Immeasurable risk that cannot be calculated, named for American economist Frank Knight; similar to Taleb's "Black Swan."
Labor movement	Development of unions as collective organizations agitating for better pay, benefits and working conditions for employees.
Laddering	Investment banking technique requiring customers (investors) to purchase multiple financial products, either by purchasing stocks at different maturity dates, or by receiving shares in an initial public offering and agreeing to buy more shares in the secondary market.
Laissez-faire	Market system free from state interference, including tariffs, taxes, and granting monopolies; associated with Adam Smith's *Wealth of Nations* (1776).
Land speculation	The practice of borrowing money to buy land in anticipation of price increases.
Law of one price	The economic theory that, in an efficient market, identical goods in different markets (such as New York and London) would have only a single price.
Lease	Contract agreement for the use of assets on a rental or fee basis for a set period of time.

Leverage	The relative debt to equity of a business or individual; credit risk increases with leverage and most financial collapses are associated with overleverage.
Leveraged buyout (LBO)	Acquisition of a company where most of the purchase price is financed through borrowing.
Liability	Amount owed, priced at the probable future economic sacrifices resulting from present obligations.
Liar loan	Mortgage made with no documentation of income or other relevant facts.
Libertarian	Political/economic philosophies emphasizing freedom, liberty, and limited government.
LIBOR (London Interbank Offered Rate)	Interest rate European banks charge to each other for short-term loans.
Liquidity bridge	An arrangement to provide cash to banks at times of financial crisis, a basic tool used by the Federal Reserve and other central banks.
Liquidity trap	Period of time (usually during a depression) when further injections of cash will have no effect on interest rates nor on economic activity—part of the "Keynesian revolution."
Liquidity	(1) Ability of an entity to pay obligations as they come due; (2) ability of an asset or security to be bought or sold in a market without affecting price.
Lobbying	The practice of individuals or lobbying groups influencing government decisions, usually to benefit special interests.
Lock-up	A scheme used by nineteenth-century speculators for withdrawing large sums of money from Wall Street banks to reduce the supply of money and cause stock prices to drop.
Logrolling	Vote trading by legislators or other trading favors (quid pro quo); based on an American custom of neighbors assisting one another in rolling logs to build cabins.
London Interbank Offered Rate (LIBOR)	Interest rate European banks charge to each other for short-term loans.
Lump-sum tax	Fixed amount of tax such as a poll (head) tax where everyone pays the same amount; the most efficient tax in economics (but regressive).
Macroeconomics	Branch of economics focusing on the structure and behavior of the whole economy, including gross domestic product, unemployment, and price indexes.

Making the number	Financial analysts' term, used to describe corporations that meet their quarterly earnings forecasts, usually based on earnings per share.
Management buyout (MBO)	Acquisition of a company by the executives of that company, often with substantial borrowed money.
Margin calls	Opportunities for investors to buy securities from brokers on credit (margin); if market price falls below the equity position of shares, brokers can require the investors to cover the difference.
Marginal utility	Gain (or loss) in utility from an increase in consumption of one additional unit of a good or service; in microeconomics virtually all decisions are made at the margin.
Marginalism	Economic focus on changes in quantity of goods, services and utility.
Market capitalization (market cap, also market value)	The total equity value of a corporation calculated as stock price times number of shares outstanding.
Market failure	A situation in which allocation of goods and services is not efficient (a non-Pareto optimality according to economists).
Market maker	A company or individual who quotes both a buy and a sell price for a financial instrument and will buy or sell at those stated prices.
Market manipulation	Attempts by speculators, owners, and others to move stock prices for personal gains.
Market model	Financial model used to compare individual equity return with the market return for the same period.
Market value risk	Price fluctuations for items that trade on a market, including stocks, currencies, and commodities.
Marketable securities	In accounting these are debt securities that are market traded and typically held for a short period of time as a cash equivalent; in finance, any security traded on a formal market.
Markets	A formal system for the exchange of goods and services.
Mark-to-market	The practice of restating securities to market value on a daily basis.
Mark-to-model	The practice of using financial models to price securities that do not trade in formal markets. Common in situations where there are no active market prices.
Matching principal	An accounting principle in which expenses related directly to revenues are recognized along with those revenues,

including both product and period costs. Contrasts with cash accounting, in which expenses are recognized at cash payout, regardless of when an obligation was incurred.

Material weakness   A deficiency in internal control that could lead to a material misstatement in financial statements.

Materiality   The relative importance of an item, transaction, or discrepancy; according to the Financial Accounting Standards Board, "information is material if its omission or misstatement could influence the economic decision of users."

May Day (1975)   The first day of May 1975, when the Securities and Exchange Commission banned fixed fees by brokers for buying and selling stocks.

Medicare fraud   Fraudulent use of Medicare health care reimbursements by individuals and organizations, estimated at $50 billion a year.

Mercantilism   Economic doctrine from the seventeenth and eighteenth centuries promoting trade between home countries and colonies, where the home country provided finished products and colonies raw materials.

Merger   A combination of two companies into a single corporate entity.

Microeconomics   The branch of economics that studies the behavior of individuals and firms and how they allocate resources.

Military-industrial complex   Reciprocal relationship between government and defense contractors and other businesses leading to oversupply of military hardware.

Milker bill   Legislation designed to generate income for a politician, often a form of extortion (also called a juicer bill).

Minsky moment   The point in a business cycle when markets fail after a period of speculation and a massive selloff of assets occurs; named for economist Hyman Minsky.

Misery index   Index created by economist Arthur Okun adding the unemployment rate to the inflations rate; it peaked at over 20 in the early 1980s.

Monetarism   A school of thought in economics that emphasizes the role of government in controlling the amount of money in circulation.

Monetary policy   The policy set by the central bank (the Federal Reserve in the United States) regarding interest rates and money supply, usually operationalized by trading in government securities.

Money illusion   The tendency of people to be misled by both inflation and deflation; causes delayed adjustments to real price changes.

Money laundering	The practice of moving money to hide its origins; usually associated with illegal activities.
Money market	A financial market for short-term funds, including commercial paper, repurchase agreements, and Treasury bills.
Money trust	Group of major banking houses, including J. P. Morgan and other Wall Street giants; around the turn of the twentieth century, the money trust dominated banking and industry on a national scale.
Monopoly	A corporation exercises monopoly power when it maintains control of an industry, used mainly to set prices and output levels.
Moral hazard	The relative risk taken on by a party to a financial action; usually associated with the failure to take full responsibility for consequences. Moral hazard can be increased in certain situations, for example where there is potential for government bailout.
Mortgage	A loan agreement with real property serving as collateral.
Mortgage-backed securities (MBSs)	Securitized debt instruments backed by a pool of mortgages with payments made from mortgage cash flows.
Multivariate model	An equation using several variables to explain another variable of interest.
Mutual funds	Professionally managed investment portfolios, subject to Securities and Exchange Commission regulations and widely available as investment vehicles.
Naked shorts	Short selling without first borrowing the securities, which can result in a "failure to deliver."
NASDAQ (National Association of Securities Dealers Automated Quotations)	American stock exchange with the largest number of listings and trading volume.
National Bureau of Economic Research	Private nonprofit organization for economic research, especially known for determining the start and end dates of recessions in the United States.
Neoclassical Economics	Economic school of Alfred Marshall and others with a focus on "marginalism" and analytical approaches to microeconomics.
Net assets	Total assets less total liabilities, equivalent to stockholders' equity.

Net income	Bottom line measure of an income statement, including revenues minus expenses (plus most gains and losses); used to measure earnings performance by a company.
New Deal	The set of programs initiated by Franklin Roosevelt to pull the country out of the Great Depression of the 1930s.
New York Mercantile Exchange (NYMEX)	Formal marketplace for commodities, including futures in agricultural products and oil.
New York Stock Exchange (NYSE)	World's largest stock exchange by market value of listed companies, founded in 1792.
Normalizing earnings	The practice of using additional relevant information to recalculate earnings presented in an income statement; used to better measure "financial reality."
Notional value	Total face value of a leveraged position's assets, used frequently in evaluating derivatives.
Off-balance-sheet financing	Contractual arrangement designed to ensure that assets and liabilities like operating leases and special purpose entities are not recorded on an organization's balance sheet; a likely source of earnings management.
Oligopoly	A market or industry dominated by a small number of sellers.
Opportunism	Self-interested behavior that violates ethical norms of behavior.
Options	Agreements giving a party the right to buy (call) or sell (put) a specific quantity at a specific price (exercise price) until a specified maturity date.
Other comprehensive income	Gains and losses reported directly to stockholders' equity and not on the income statement, also called "dirty surplus."
Over-the-counter derivatives	Various derivatives not traded on an exchange, providing little transparency and subject to abuse.
Panic selloff	Sudden substantial decline in securities prices based on perceived bad news; approximately a 10 percent or greater decline in market prices in one day (often called capitulation).
Panics and Depressions	Market panics (usually selloffs of securities) followed by depressions were common throughout the United States in the nineteenth century, replaced by less severe recessions after the Great Depression. A panic usually refers to a credit crisis, associated with a large-scale withdrawal of bank deposits.
Paper money	Legal tender, often produced during wars and financial stress when convertibility to gold is banned; periods of paper money are often associated with speculation and easy credit.

Par value	The stated or face value of a security.
Paradox of thrift	A central tenant of Keynesian economics; states that saving money during a recession decreases aggregate demand and decreases both consumption and economic growth.
Paradox of value (Adam Smith's paradox of water and diamonds)	Apparent contradiction in relative values; water is essential for life but has low value because of its abundance, while diamonds have high value because of their scarcity.
Pareto optimality	The most efficient point in a system of resource distribution, or the point at which no one can be better off without someone being worse off. Named for Italian economist Vilfredo Pareto (1848–1923).
Pareto principle (80–20 Rule)	Describes the tendency of a small number of causes to exert the greatest number of effects on a system; visible in economic systems where 20 percent of a population controls 80 percent of the wealth; named after economist Vilfredo Pareto.
Patent	A form of licensing designed to grant exclusive intellectual property rights for a limited period in exchange for the public disclosure of an invention.
Patent troll	An individual or company who buys or controls patents in order to sue successful companies as "patent infringers."
Patronage (spoils system)	The use of governmental resources to reward individuals for election support, usually political appointments.
Pay-as-you-go	Practice of funding expenses from current cash without regard to future commitments; for example, retirement obligations are often managed poorly in this way.
Peak oil (also called Hubbert's Peak)	The concept of a maximum production point for oil, after which production levels will drop and prices rise.
Pecora Commission	Senate investigating body that examined the market crash of 1929, named for chief counsel Ferdinand Pecora.
Pension	A long-term contract to provide retirement benefits to employees; the two major types of pensions are defined-benefit plans and defined-contribution plans.
Permanent income hypothesis	The theory put forth by Milton Friedman (1912–2006) that consumers base consumption on long-term income expectations rather than current income.
Phillips curve	Measures the expected inverse relationship of inflation and unemployment; named for economist William Phillips.

Pigovian tax	Tax levied on economic activity generating negative externalities (e.g., pollution), named for British economist Arthur Pigou (1877–1959).
PIIGS	Portugal, Italy, Ireland, Greece, and Spain—countries within the Eurozone with government overspending and uncompetitive economies with the potential to default during the European sovereign debt crisis.
Pirate bank	A virtual bank established to shelter, manage, or launder the cash of the rich—usually for tax and/or unlawful purposes.
Plausible deniability	A term first used by Central Intelligence Agency Director Allen Dulles during the Kennedy years to justify withholding information from senior officials to protect them from repercussions of illegal or unethical practices.
Poison pill	Corporate strategy adopted to discourage hostile takeovers; for example, by allowing current shareholders to buy additional shares at a discount.
Political corruption	Misuse of power by government officials for illicit purposes, including (a) excess payments to public officials; (b) actions violating laws or implicit social norms; and (c) illicit payments that generate losses for society.
Political machines	Political organizations designed to win elections through patronage and various illicit acts; political machines developed in major cities and some states throughout the nineteenth century.
Pollution externalities	Environmental costs on society from industrial production and other economic activities not transmitted through prices.
Pollution	Introduction of contaminants into the environments.
Ponzi scheme	Get rich schemes promising huge gains from nonexistent activities; named for Charles Ponzi (1882–1949).
Pooling of interests	An accounting procedure (no longer allowed) for business acquisitions meeting specific criteria; assets and liabilities of acquired firm essentially recorded at book value.
Pools	Associations of businesses in a specific industry for specific purposes, usually to fix prices and divide markets.
Populism	Political movement in defense of the rights and powers of people against the elites.
Portfolio insurance	A derivative hedge intended to limit losses on stock portfolios; selling S&P 500 futures against falling stock prices; common in the 1980s.

Portfolio theory	The concept that financial risk is reduced in a diversified portfolio of securities relative to a single security.
Predatory pricing	Setting product or service prices low to drive competitors out of the market.
Preferred list	Sale of new securities to preferred customers and others at discount prices before they are initially issued to the public; the practice still exists and is now called spinning.
Price discrimination	Charging different prices for the same good or service to different markets.
Price-earnings ratio (PE)	Stock price divided by annual earnings per share, a measure of the "market premium" for earnings; the historic average PE is about 15.
Price/earnings-to-growth (PEG) ratio	PE/long-term earnings growth rate; PE is compared to earnings growth as a measure of PE "reasonableness."
Price fixing	Conspiratorial practice of setting prices, thus eliminating competition; outlawed by the Sherman Act.
Primary markets	Capital markets where new securities are initially issued.
Prime rate	The lending rate offered by commercial banks to the most creditworthy corporate customers.
Private equity	Equity capital funds not on a public exchange and not subject to Securities and Exchange Commission mutual funds regulations, typically investing in private companies or buyouts of public companies.
Pro forma earnings	Hypothetical income based on assumptions other than those presented in the 10-K (based on generally accepted accounting principles).
Product differentiation	Efforts to distinguish goods and services from those provided by competitors using nonprice factors such as perceived quality.
Product safety	Regulation of manufacturing and sale of various consumer items and banning of dangerous products.
Professional ethics	Business standards of behavior expected of professionals, often imposed by licensing or certification.
Program trading	Trading of securities (usually baskets of stocks) executed by computer programs that track market conditions, often based on stocks relative to index futures.
Progressive movement	Political movements in the late nineteenth to early twentieth century that aimed to provide social and economic reforms in response to industrialization.

Prospect theory	Descriptive risk theory of decision making, suggesting that losses are viewed differently than gains.
Proxy statement	Annual report issued by a company in advance of annual shareholders' meeting; includes information useful to stockholders for voting.
Prudent man rule	A fiduciary duty of money managers to invest as a "prudent man" would (based on the nineteenth-century court case *Harvard College v. Armory*).
Public Company Accounting Oversight Board (PCAOB)	Nonprofit organization created by the Sarbanes-Oxley Act of 2002 to oversee audits of public companies (those trading on American stock exchanges).
Public goods	Goods that cannot be denied to others, such as fresh air or defense; the opposite of private goods; presumably, public goods should be provided by government.
Public interest	General welfare related to policy debates and the nature of government.
Public policy	Government regulations and other actions related to specific issues, in a manner consistent with laws and customs.
Pujo hearings	Congressional hearings in 1912–13 investigating Wall Street power and the Money Trust, named for subcommittee chairman Arsene Pujo.
Pump and dump	An attempt to boost stock price using false information and then sell after prices move higher.
Purchase method	Accounting procedures used for business acquisitions; acquired firm is stated at actual market price.
Put (put option)	Derivative allowing the buyer to sell an asset at a particular price for some time period; a put protects value in case of a crash.
Quant (quantitative analyst)	Sophisticated financial analyst who uses mathematical risk-based models and techniques, especially for investment strategies.
Quantitative easing	Federal Reserve program starting in late 2008 after the collapse of Lehman Brothers to inject liquidity into the banking system.
Racketeering	Extorting money illegally (e.g., by coercing individuals to purchase "protection" or insurance against recriminations) or other illegal business practices, usually related to organized crime.
Random walk hypothesis	Financial theory stating that professional analysts and portfolio managers cannot outperform a randomly selected stock portfolio.

Rational expectations	The hypothesis that economic values are correct (that is, errors are random rather than systematic).
Rawls's theory of justice	The theory put forth by political and ethical philosopher John Rawls that distributive justice (proper allocation of goods and income) can be derived from a variation of the social contract; his theory of justice as "fairness" attempts to reconcile liberty and equality.
Recession	Business cycle contraction, typically measured as declining gross domestic product for two consecutive quarters.
Reconstruction Finance Corporation (RFC)	Independent federal agency established in 1932 to aid state and local governments, banks and other organizations.
Redlining	Limiting the ownership and selling of real estate by race to specific geographic areas as a means of racial segregation.
Regulation FD (Fair Disclosure)	Securities and Exchange Commission regulation that mandates public companies to disclose material information to all investors at the same time.
Regulation Q	Federal law prohibiting banks from paying interest rates on savings accounts above the ceiling established by the Federal Reserve; now repealed.
Regulations and enforcement	Government rules designed to regulate business and other activities and limit existing abuses.
Regulatory arbitrage	The use of legal loopholes by corporations and other organizations to circumvent regulations through "financial engineering," restructuring, relocation and other techniques.
Regulatory circuit breakers	Central banking and government techniques designed to limit booms and provide liquidity during financial crises.
Related-party transactions	An exchange or transaction with an executive, board member, or other individual directly connected with the company.
Rent seeking	Attempt to get economic rents (monopoly profit) by manipulating the environment, such as lobbying.
Repo 105s	Repurchase agreements and accounting gimmicks used to record a short-term loan as a "sale."
Repurchase agreement (Repos)	Sale of a security with an agreement to buy back the same security; primarily, a short-term lending arrangement.
Reputation risk	Perception of trustworthiness; damage to reputation can cause loss of revenue and market share to a company.

Restricted stock	Stock not fully transferable, especially equity compensation in a corporation which must usually be held for some period before it vests.
Revenue recognition	Criteria for recognizing revenues when revenue is (1) realized and (2) earned; timing (deciding when to recognize revenue) a key issue.
Risk	Exposure to loss; potential that a certain action will lead to a loss (or other undesirable outcome).
Risk aversion	Aversion to accepting an uncertain payoff rather than a more certain, but lower expected payoff.
Risk management	Techniques used by corporations to reduce or control for potential adverse consequences (uncertainty), primarily related to prices, interest rates, and foreign currency.
Risk premium	Increased return expected on a risky asset relative to a risk-free asset.
Robber barons	Powerful nineteenth-century American bankers and businessmen who used questionable business practices to achieve their wealth and power.
Round-trip transactions	Business transactions with related parties for the sole purpose of meeting sales and earnings targets.
Rule of law	Protection of the rights of individuals and their property, based on English common law.
Sarbanes-Oxley Act	Federal law passed in 2002 to increase the regulations on auditors, corporate governance, and securities markets.
Savings and Loan Associations (S&Ls)	Thrifts in the United States specializing in accepting deposits and making mortgages.
Scandal	A widely publicized incident that involves allegations of wrongdoing, disgrace, or moral outrage.
Secondary markets	Capital markets where previously issued securities can be traded, such as the New York Stock Exchange.
Securities and Exchange Commission	Federal agency established by the SEC Act of 1934 to regulate U.S. securities markets, including accounting and financial reporting.
Securitization (structured finance)	Practice of packaging financial loans into bonds and other securities; misuse of this practice was a cause of the subprime meltdown.
Shadow banking	Nondepository financial entities (such as investment banks, money market funds, and hedge funds) that provide some of the services of commercial banks.

Shell corporation	A legal company without assets that serves as a vehicle for business transaction, often for illicit purposes.
Sherman Act	1890 federal act to ban monopolies and conspiracies in restraint of trade.
Short selling	Selling a security the seller does not own (shares have to be borrowed).
Short squeeze	Short sellers have problems buying shares to cover their positions because of rapidly rising prices and lack of availability of shares.
Smuggling	Transportation of goods or people prohibited by laws and regulations; the most common response to regulation and taxes since the dawn of time.
Social accountability	Measurement of a firm's commitment to employee, safety, and environmental laws and its respect for human and environmental rights and ethical standards.
Social contract	Philosophical construct used to evaluate the origin of society and the legitimacy of the state; used by Thomas Hobbes, John Locke, Immanuel Kant, John Rawls, and others. In some sense, the U.S. Constitution is a social contract.
Socialism	Economic system with social (usually governmental) ownership of production and social management of the economy.
Social justice	Efforts to create a society that respects equality and human rights, often by establishing progressive taxes, access to health care, and a sustainable ecosystem.
Social responsibility	The idea individuals and organizations have some obligation to benefit society at large.
Solvency	The excess of current assets over current liabilities, a measure of liquidity and the ability to pay obligations as they come due.
South Sea Bubble	Financial bubble created by the fraudulent South Sea Company, a British joint stock company, which crashed in 1720.
SPDR	Exchange-traded funds trademarked by Standard & Poor's, named for S&P Depository Receipts (with the ticker symbol SPY on the New York Stock Exchange) and designed to track the S&P 500 stock index.
Special-purpose entities	Separate legal entities created by corporations to keep liabilities off-balance-sheet and to accomplish other purposes.
Speculation	Investing in uncertain conditions, usually using borrowed money to acquire higher-risk assets.

Speed vesting of stock options	Advancing the vesting date of stock options before 2006 when options had to be expensed.
Spin-life policies ("death bonds")	Life insurance policies sold by policy holders to investors who then sell them to banks to package and sell as securitized debt.
Spinning	The practice of investment banks of giving shares in an initial public offering to favored clients and other selected people such as politicians.
Spoils system (patronage)	A political arrangement in which the winning party rewards cronies with government jobs as the main form of party loyalty.
Spread (bid-ask spread)	The difference in price for an immediate sale (ask) and purchase (bid); the size of the spread is a measure of relative liquidity in a securities market.
Spring loading	The practice of recording options in advance of probable market increases to manipulate accounting records.
Spring loading of stock options	Corporate issuance of stock options in advance of "good news" announced by the company, increasing the value of the options.
Stagflation	The combination of high inflation, high unemployment, and high interest rates.
Stakeholders	Any individual or group affected by the decisions of a business (stockholders, bondholders, employees, customers, suppliers); important from the perspectives of social responsibilities and corporate governance.
Standard & Poor's (S&P) 500	A stock index of 500 of the largest U.S. companies based on market value.
State capitalism	Economic system in which commercial activities are owned and operated by the government, creating wealth for political purposes.
Stock crash of 1987	Stock market crash where the Dow Jones Industrial Average dropped 23 percent on October 19, 1987, caused in part by widespread use of portfolio insurance strategies.
Stock dilution	Actions that increase the number of shares of common stock outstanding, such as issuing stock options, restricted stock, convertible bonds, or stock dividends.
Stock exchanges	Organizations established to publicly trade equity shares in the secondary market for specific companies.
Stock options	Employee benefits that allow employees to acquire a set number of shares in firm stock at a set price, which can be

exercised only after vesting, typically only if stock price is higher than the exercise price.

Stock pools   Syndicates established by investment banks and others to manipulate stock prices, especially prevalent during the 1920s.

Stop-loss orders   Investor instructions to brokers to sell the stock when a stock drops to a specific price; the purpose of which is to minimize losses.

Straddle   A technique of purchasing both call and put options on some underlying investment, bought at the same strike price and expiring at the same time, so that the holder can profit from price changes whichever direction the price moves.

Stress test   An analysis of the stability of a given organization or entity; 2009 Treasury Department analysis of the capital adequacy of 19 largest bank holding companies.

Strike   Organized political action in which employees refuse to work by either walking off the job or staying put but not working (a sit-down strike).

Strikers   Lobbyists specializing in corruption; middlemen between transactions of legislators and corporations and other individuals, common in the nineteenth century.

Structured finance (securitization)   Practice of packaging loans into bonds and other securities; misuse of this practice was a cause of the subprime meltdown.

Stub quote   a buy or sell order placed well off a security's current market price, used as a safety net or speculation on a potentially volatile market.

Subprime loans   Mortgages and other loans made to customers with less than prime credit ratings at higher interest rates

Subprime meltdown   2008 global financial crisis based in part on the collapse of the sub-prime mortgage market in the United States.

Sucker's rally   A temporary stock price rise in the absence of fundamental information that supports the price move.

Swaps   Derivative contracts in which parties exchange one series of payments for another.

Synthetic collateralized debt obligations (SCDOs)   Complex derivative instruments usually based on a portfolio of underlying credit default swaps.

Systemic corruption   Institutional or cultural processes (incentives, no transparency, low pay, culture of impunity) leading to massive illegality such as bribery, extortion, or embezzlement.

Systemic risk	Circumstances leading to the potential for the collapse of the entire financial system or market, such as banks that are "too big to fail."
Tailgating	Purchase or sale of a security, making the same transaction as a customer; similar to front-running, but not illegal.
Tammany Hall	Democratic political machine of New York City, infamous for the corruption of "Boss" Tweed after the Civil War.
Tax avoidance	Minimizing tax obligations through legal means, using available tax breaks.
Tax evasion	Illegal tax avoidance.
Tax haven	Country with lower tax rates and/or without due process.
Tax scams	Various illicit techniques used to reduce tax liabilities.
Taylor rule	Monetary policy rule on how central banks should change nominal interest rates in response to changes in inflation rates and other economic indicators; e.g., a 1 percent increase in inflation calls for an increase in interest rates greater than 1 percent; named for economist John Taylor.
Teaser loan	Adjustable-rate mortgage starting with an artificially low initial rate that increases over time.
TED Spread	The difference in interest rates on three-month Treasury bills and LIBOR (an interbank loan rate), a measure of credit risk in the overall economy.
Tequila Crisis	Mexican peso and debt collapse in 1994, in which the Mexican financial system was bailed out by the U.S. Treasury Department.
Thrifts	Savings and loan associations in the United States specializing in accepting deposits and making mortgages.
Tight money	Situation in which credit is hard to get and available at high interest rates only.
Too big to fail	The idea that companies, especially banks, can be too large to go bankrupt without disrupting the economy, necessitating a government bailout.
Tranche	A slice of a securitized portfolio of debt agreements based on relative risk (mainly related to default but also prepayments).
Transactions costs	Costs of issuing and completing contracts, including agency costs.
Transparency	Complete financial disclosure according to conservative accounting methods; the representation of economic reality.
Treasury Department	Executive department of the federal government established in 1789 to manage government revenue and debt, print paper

	currency, mint coins, and collect taxes through the Internal Revenue Service.
Troubled Asset Relief Program (TARP)	U.S. government bailout designed to address the fiscal crisis of 2008; TARP primarily provided capital to troubled large banks.
Trust	A legal entity formed to monopolize an industry; a trust usually involves a single board of trustees that fixes prices and divides market share.
Tulip Mania	A bubble created in Holland by interest in rare tulips resulting in a substantial price rise in the eighteenth century, followed by a quick and steep collapse.
Ugly-duckling loans	Risky loans provided by used car dealers selling cars to customers with questionable credit histories (a form of subprime loan).
Underground economy	Market activity hidden from official view, usually involving illicit activities or avoidance of taxes and other regulations.
Underwriter	A middleman between buyers and sellers taking an equity position in the goods or securities being sold.
Union	Worker organization established to achieve common goals, usually higher wages and better working conditions.
Utilitarianism	An economic perspective and ethical philosophy in which proper decisions are understood to be those that maximize overall "happiness."
Utility	Economic measure of satisfaction from consuming goods and services.
Value at risk (VaR)	Measure of potential risk of loss for some period (usually one day), developed for banking institutions.
Variable-interest entity (VIE)	An entity holding a controlling interest (but not based on voting rights), according to the Financial Accounting Standards Board FIN 46; similar to a special-purpose entity.
Veil of ignorance	Lack of fundamental information needed for decision making; also a concept used by philosopher John Rawls to determine just allocation of resources as part of a social contract.
Venture capitalists	Investors who provide money to startup firms and small businesses with perceived growth potential.
Vertical integration	The practice of expanding operations at different points in the production/supply/distribution of a specific product.

Vertical merger	Acquisition of an "indirect" competitor, that is, a competitor in the same basic industry but generally in a different market segment.
Virtue	Moral excellence; a pattern of behavior based on high moral standards.
VIX (Chicago Board Options Exchange Volatility Index, "fear index")	Financial index based on the volatility in large capitalization U.S. stocks based on call and put option prices, specifically designed to measure the expected movement in the Standard & Poor's 500 index over the next 30 days.
Volcker rule	Prohibition of private equity trading by banks as recommended by former Federal Reserve chairman Paul Volcker.
Vulture capitalists	Investors in failing firms who hope to turn them around at a profit; massive layoffs and bankruptcy are common techniques used.
Wall Street	The financial center of the United States, located in New York City.
War profiteering	Individuals or organizations making excess profits from selling weapons and other goods to parties at war.
Washington consensus	A set of economic and political prescriptions for fiscal discipline, market reform, and global trade in developing countries.
Waste	Excessive expenditure, consumption, or squandering of resources; unnecessary costs due to inefficient or ineffective practices.
Watering stock	The financial practice of overstating asset values, a common practice associated with business combinations around the turn of the twentieth century.
Whistle-blower	Employee of a company or other entity who comes forward with information that may be incriminating to the company.
White knight	Friendly acquirer of a target company subject to a hostile takeover.
Wildcat banking	Aggressive banking practices (including low reserves) used in various states especially in the first half of the nineteenth century.
Wildcat Strike	Strikes taken by workers without the authorization of the union.
Working capital	Current assets less current liabilities, a widely used indicator of liquidity.

Y2K (Millennium Bug)   The year 2000, when computer programs using two-digit abbreviation for calendar years were predicted to crash.

Yellow-dog contracts   Employment contracts that require employees to agree not to join any union.

Zero interest rate policy (ZIRP)   Practice used by Japanese and United States central banks to keep short-term interest rates at zero (or at least very low) to stimulate economic activity through monetary policy.

Bibliography

Adams, Charles, and Henry Adams. *Chapters of Erie and Other Essays*. Boston: James A. Osgood, 1871.

Ahamed, Liaquat. *Lords of Finance: The Bankers Who Broke the World*. New York: Penguin Books, 2009.

"A Hard Climb." *The Economist*. September 6, 2009. http://www.economist.com.

Akerlof, George, and Paul Romer. "Looting: The Economic Underworld of Bankruptcy for Profit." *Brookings Papers on Economic Activity* 1993, no. 2 (1993): 1–73.

Akerlof, George, and Robert Shiller. *Animal Spirits: How Human Psychology Drives the Economy, and Why It Matters for Global Capitalism*. Princeton, NJ: Princeton University Press, 2009.

"Allegheny Corp." *Time*, February 11, 1929. http://www.time.com.

Ambrose, Stephan. *Nothing Like It in the World: The Men Who Built the Transcontinental Railroad 1863–1869*. New York: Touchstone, 2000.

Anderson, William. *The Price of Liberty: The Public Debt of the American Revolution*. Charlottesville: University Press of Virginia, 1983.

Baker, Dean. *Plunder and Blunder: The Rise and Fall of The Bubble Economy*. Sausalito, CA: PoliPoint Press, LLC, 2009.

Bamber, Bill, and Andrew Spencer. *Bear Trap: The Fall of Bear Stearns and the Panic of 2008*. New York: Brick Tower Press, 2008.

Bandler, James, and Nicholas Varchaver. "How Bernie Did It." *Fortune*, May 11, 2009, 51–71.

Barr, Andrew, and Irving Galpeer. "McKesson & Robbins." *Journal of Accountancy*, May 1987, 159–61.

Barton, David. *Business and Its Environment*. 4th ed. Upper Saddle River, NJ: Prentice Hall, 2003.

Bentson, George, and A. Hartgraves. "Enron: What Happened and What We Can Learn From It." *Journal of Accounting and Public Policy* 21 (Summer 2002): 105–27.

Berenson, Alex. *The Number: How the Drive for Quarterly Earnings Corrupted Wall Street and Corporate American.* New York: Random House, 2003.

Bernanke, Ben. "The Financial Crisis and Community Banking." March 20, 2009. http://www.federalreserve.gov.

Bernanke, Ben. "Financial Innovation and Consumer Protection." April 17, 2009. http://www.federalreserve.gov.

Bernanke, Ben. "Money, Gold, and the Great Depression." 2004. http://www .federalreserve.gov.

Bernstein, Peter. *Wedding of the Waters: The Erie Canal and the Making of a Great Nation.* New York: Norton, 2005.

Bodenhorn, Howard. "Bank Chartering and Political Corruption in Antebellum New York: Free Banking as Reform." In *Corruption and Reform: Lessons from America's Economic History.* Edited by Edward Glaeser and Claudia Goldin, 231–58. Washington: National Bureau of Economic Research, 2006.

Bookstaber, Richard. *A Demon of Our Own Design: Markets, Hedge Funds, and the Perils of Financial Innovation.* Hoboken, NJ: Wiley, 2007.

Brands, H. W. *American Colossus: The Triumph of Capitalism, 1865–1900.* New York: Doubleday, 2010.

Bremmer, Ian, and Nouriel Roubini. "How the Fed Can Avoid the Next Bubble." *Wall Street Journal,* October 5, 2009. http://www.online.wsj.com.

Brill, Steven. "On Sale: Your Government. Why Lobbying Is Washington's Best Bargain." *Time,* July 12, 2010, 28–35.

Brunner, Robert, and Sean Carr. *The Panic of 1907: Lessons Learned from the Market's Perfect Storm.* Hoboken, NJ: Wiley, 2007.

Cassidy, John. *How Markets Fail: The Logic of Economic Calamities.* New York: Farrar, Straus and Giroux, 2009.

Cassidy, John. "Rational Irrationality: The Real Reason That Capitalism Is So Crash-Prone." *The New Yorker,* October 5, 2009. http://www.newyorker.com.

Chernow, Ron. *Alexander Hamilton.* New York: Penguin Press, 2004.

Chernow, Ron. *The House of Morgan: An American Banking Dynasty and the Rise of Modern Finance.* New York: Atlantic Monthly Press, 1990.

Chernow, Ron. "Where Is Our Ferdinand Pecora?" *New York Times,* January 5, 2009. http://www.nytimes.com.

Cohan, William. *House of Cards: A Tale of Hubris and Wretched Excess on Wall Street.* New York: Doubleday, 2009.

Colbert, David. *Eyewitness to Wall Street: Four Hundred Years of Dreamers, Schemers, Busts and Booms.* New York: Broadway Books, 2001.

Collier, Christopher, and James Collier. *Decision in Philadelphia: The Constitutional Convention of 1787.* New York: Ballantine Books, 1986.

Colvin, Geoff. "Alan Greenspan Fights Back: From Main Street to Wall Street to the Beltway, the Former Fed Chief Has Been the 'Designated Goat' for the Country's Financial Woes. Now the Maestro Takes on His Critics." *Fortune*, March 1, 2010, 82–89.

Committee of Sponsoring Organizations of the Treadway Commission (COSO). *Report of the National Commission on Fraudulent Financial Reporting*. New York: COSO, 1987.

COSO. *Fraudulent Financial Reporting: 1987–1997: An Analysis of US Public Companies*. New York: COSO, 1999.

Cramer, James. *Confessions of a Street Addict*. New York: Simon & Schuster, 2002.

Department of the Treasury. *Financial Regulatory Reform: A New Foundation: Rebuilding Financial Supervision and Regulation*. Washington, DC: Treasury Department, 2009.

Dodd-Frank Wall Street Reform and Consumer Protection Act. H.R. 4173. 2010. http://www.govtrack.us/congress.

Dos Passos, John. "Robert Morris and the 'Art Magick.' " In *Great Stories of American Businessmen, from American Heritage*, 19–25. New York: American Heritage, 1972.

Eichenwald, Kurt. *Conspiracy of Fools*. New York: Broadway Books, 2005.

Ellis, Charles. *The Partnership: The Making of Goldman Sachs*. New York: Penguin Press, 2008.

Ellis, Joseph. *American Creation: Triumphs and Tragedies at the Founding of the Republic*. New York: Knopf, 2008.

Fabozzi, Frank. *The Handbook of Mortgage-Backed Securities*. New York: McGraw-Hill Professional, 2005.

Federal Reserve Bank of St. Louis. "The Financial Crisis: A Timeline of Events and Policy Actions." http://timeline.stlouisfed.org.

Feldman, Noah. *Scorpions: The Battles and Triumphs of FDR's Great Supreme Court Justices*. New York: Twelve (Hachette Book Group), 2010.

Ferguson, E. James. *The American Revolution: A General History, 1763–1790*. Homewood, IL: Dorsey Press, 1971.

Ferguson, Niall. *The Ascent of Money: A Financial History of the World*. New York: Penguin Press, 2008.

Financial Crimes Enforcement Network. *Mortgage Loan Fraud: An Industry Assessment Based upon Suspicious Activity Report Analysis*. 2006. http://www.fincen.gov.

Financial Crisis Inquiry Commission. *The Financial Crisis Inquiry Report*. Washington, DC: U.S. Government Printing Office, 2011.

Fox, Justin. "The Bailout's Biggest Flaw." *Time*, September 2009, 44–45.

Fox, Justin. *The Myth of the Rational Market: A History of Risk, Reward, and Delusion on Wall Street*. New York: Harper Business, 2009.

Friedel, Frank. *Franklin D. Roosevelt: A Rendezvous with Destiny*. Boston: Little, Brown, 1990.

Friedman, Thomas. *The Lexus and the Olive Tree*. New York: Anchor Books, 2000.

Furth, B., L. Lessing, and H. Vind. "McKesson and Robbins: Its Fall and Rise." *Fortune*, May 1940. Reprinted in *SCANDAL!: Amazing Tales of Scandals That Shocked the World and Shaped Modern Business*, 180–94. New York: Time Inc. Home Entertainment, 2009.

Galbraith, Kenneth. *The Great Crash 1929*. Boston: Houghton Mifflin, 1988.

Gasparino, Charles. *Blood on the Street: The Sensational Inside Story of How Wall Street Analysts Duped a Generation of Investors*. New York: Free Press, 2005.

Gasparino, Charles. *The Sellout: Three Decades of Wall Street Greed and Government Mismanagement Destroyed the Global Financial System*. New York: Harper Business, 2009.

Gasparino, Charles. "Three Decades of Subsidized Risk: There's a Reason Dick Fuld Didn't Believe Lehman Would Be Allowed to Fail." *Wall Street Journal*, November 6, 2009, http://online.wsj.com.

Geisst, Charles. *Collateral Damaged: The Marketing of Consumer Debt to America*. New York: Bloomberg Press, 2009.

Geisst, Charles. *Monopolies in America: Empire Builders & Their Enemies from Jay Gould to Bill Gates*. Oxford: Oxford University Press, 2000.

General Accounting Office. *Financial Statement Restatements: Trends, Market Impacts, Regulatory Responses, and Remaining Challenges*. GAO-03-138. Washington: General Accounting Office, October 2002.

Gentzkow, Matthew, Edward Glaeser, and Claudia Goldin. "The Rise of the Fourth Estate: How Newspapers Became Informative and Why It Mattered." In *Corruption and Reform: Lessons from America's Economic History*. Edited by Edward Glaeser and Claudia Goldin, 187–30. Washington, DC: National Bureau of Economic Research, 2006.

Gibby, Darin. *Why Has America Stopped Inventing?* New York: Morgan James, 2012.

Gibson, Charles. *Financial Reporting & Analysis*. 8th ed. Cincinnati, OH: South-Western College, 2001.

Gilman, H., and D. Burke. "Wall Street 2010: A Fortune Roundtable Moderated by CNBC's Becky Quick." *Fortune*, May 3, 2010, 190–200.

Giroux, Gary. "Annual Reports of the Minehill and Schuylkill Haven Railroad Company: 1844–1864." *The Accounting Historians Notebook*, April 1998, 9–10, 30–33.

Giroux, Gary. *Detecting Earnings Management.* New York: Wiley, 2004.

Giroux, Gary. *Dollars & Scholars, Scribes & Bribes: The Story of Accounting.* Houston, TX: Dame, 1996.

Giroux, Gary. *Earnings Magic and the Unbalance Sheet: The Search for Financial Reality.* New York: Wiley, 2006.

Giroux, Gary. *Financial Analysis: A User Approach.* New York: Wiley, 2003.

Giroux, Gary. "What Went Wrong? Accounting Fraud and Lessons from Recent Scandals." *Social Research: An International Quarterly of the Social Sciences,* Winter 2008, 1205–38.

Gladwell, Malcolm. *Outliers: The Story of Success.* New York: Little, Brown, 2008.

Gladwell, Malcolm. *What the Dog Saw and Other Adventures.* New York: Little, Brown, 2009.

Glaeser, Edward, and Claudia Goldin, eds. *Corruption and Reform: Lessons from America's Economic History.* Washington, DC: National Bureau of Economic Research, 2006.

Goldberg, Richard. *The Battle for Wall Street: Behind the Lines in the Struggle That Pushed an Industry into Turmoil.* Hoboken, NJ: Wiley, 2009.

Goodwin, Jason. *Greenback: The Almighty Dollar and the Invention of America.* New York: Holt, 2003.

Gordon, John. *The Great Game: The Emergence of Wall Street as a World Power, 1653–2000.* New York: Scribner, 1999.

Gordon, John. "The Public Be Damned." *American Heritage,* September/ October 1989. http://www.americanheritage.com.

Government Accountability Office. *Information on Recent Default and Foreclosure Trends for Home Mortgages and Associated Economic and Market Developments.* GAO-08-78R. 2007. http://www.gao.gov.

Greenspan, Alan. *The Age of Turbulence, Adventures in a New World.* New York: Penguin Press, 2007.

Greenspan, Alan. Speech at America's Community Bankers annual convention. Washington, DC, October 19, 2004.

Healy, Paul, and J. Wahlen. "A Review of the Earnings Management Literature and Its Implications for Standard Setting, *Accounting Horizons,* December 1999, 365–83.

Henninger, Daniel. "Bring Back the Robber Barons." *Wall Street Journal,* March 4, 2010. http://finance.yahoo.com.

Henry, David. "Mergers: Why Most Big Deals Don't Pay Off." *Business Week,* October 14, 2002, 60–70.

Henry, David, and Matthew Goldstein. "The Bear Flu: How It Spread." *Business Week,* December 31, 2007. in Lewis, Michael, *Panic: The Story of Modern Financial Insanity.* New York: Norton, 2009.

"How SEC Regulatory Exemptions Helped Lead to Collapse." September 18, 2008. http://bigpicture.typedap.com.

Huffington, Arianna. *Pigs at the Trough: How Corporate Greed and Political Corruption Are Undermining America.* New York: Crown, 2003.

"Investment Trusts." *Time*, February 4, 1929. http://www.time.com.

Johnson, Simon. "The Quiet Coup." *The Atlantic*, May 2005. http://www.theatlantic.com.

Johnson, Simon, and James Kwak. *13 Bankers: The Wall Street Takeover and the Next Financial Meltdown.* New York: Pantheon Books, 2010.

Jones, Jennifer. "Earnings Management During Import Relief Investigations." *Journal of Accounting Research* 29 (1991): 193–228.

Josephson, Matthew. *The Robber Barons.* New York: Harcourt, 1962.

Keynes, John. "An Open Letter to President Roosevelt." *New York Times*, December 31, 1933. Reprinted at http://newdeal.feri.org.

Kindleberger, Charles, and Robert Aliber. *Manias, Panics, and Crashes: A History of Financial Crises.* 5th ed. Hoboken, NJ: Wiley, 2005.

Krugman, Paul. *The Return of Depression Economics and the Crisis of 2008.* New York: Norton, 2009.

Law, Marc, and Gary Libecap. "The Determinants of Progressive Era Reform: The Pure Food and Drugs Act of 1906." In *Corruption and Reform: Lessons from America's Economic History.* Edited by Edward Glaeser and Claudia Goldin, 319–42. Washington, DC: National Bureau of Economic Research, 2006.

Levitt, Arthur, and Paula Dwyer. *Take on the Street: What Wall Street and Corporate America Don't Want You to Know.* New York: Pantheon Books, 2002.

Levitt, Steven, and Stephan Dubner. *SuperFreakonomics.* New York: Morrow, 2009.

Lewis, Michael. *The Big Short: Inside the Doomsday Machine.* New York: Norton, 2010.

Lewis, Michael. *Liar's Poker: Rising through the Wreckage on Wall Street.* New York: Penguin Books, 1989.

Lewis, Michael. *Panic: The Story of Modern Financial Insanity.* New York: Norton, 2009.

Livesay, Harold. *Andrew Carnegie and the Rise of Big Business.* New York: Longman, 2000.

Livesay, Harold. *Samuel Gompers and Organized Labor in America.* Boston: Little, Brown, 1978.

Lowenstein, Roger. *The End of Wall Street.* New York: Penguin Press, 2010.

Lowenstein, Roger. *Origins of the Crash: The Great Bubble and Its Undoing.* New York: Penguin Press, 2004.

MacLeish, Archibald. "The Swedish Match King." *Fortune*, May–July 1933. Reprinted in *SCANDAL!: Amazing Tales of Scandals That Shocked the World and Shaped Modern Business*, 53–72. New York: Time Inc. Home Entertainment, 2009.

Mahar, Maggie. *Bull: A History of the Boom and Bust, 1982–2004*. New York: Harper Business, 2004.

McCartney, Laton. *The Teapot Dome Scandal: How Big Oil Bought the Harding White House and Tried to Steal the Country*. New York: Random House, 2008.

McCullough, David. *Mornings on Horseback*. New York: Simon & Schuster, 1981.

McDonald, Duff. *Last Man Standing: The Ascent of Jamie Dimon and JP Morgan Chase*. New York: Simon & Schuster, 2009.

McDonald, Laurence, and Patrick Robinson. *A Colossal Failure of Common Sense: The Inside Story of the Collapse of Lehman Brothers*. New York: Crown Business, 2009.

McGee, Suzanne. *Chasing Goldman Sachs: How the Masters of the Universe Melted Wall Street Down and Why They'll Take Us to the Brink Again*. New York: Crown Business, 2010.

McLean, Bethany. "The Fall of Fannie Mae." *Fortune*, January 24, 2005. Reprinted in *SCANDAL!: Amazing Tales of Scandals That Shocked the World and Shaped Modern Business*, 280–303. New York: Time Inc. Home Entertainment, 2009.

McLean, Bethany, and Joe Nocera. *All the Devils Are Here: The Hidden History of the Financial Crisis*. New York: Portfolio/Penguin, 2010.

McNichols, Maureen. "Research Design Issues in Earnings Management Studies." *Journal of Accounting and Public Policy* 19 (2000): 313–45.

Menes, Rebecca. "Limiting the Reach of the Grabbing Hand: Graft and Growth in American Cities, 1880–1930." In *Corruption and Reform: Lessons from America's Economic History*. Edited by Edward Glaeser and Claudia Goldin, 63–94. Washington, DC: National Bureau of Economic Research, 2006.

Mitchell, Lawrence. *The Speculative Economy: How Finance Triumphed Over Industry*. San Francisco: Berrett-Koehler, 2007.

Morgenson, Gretchen, and Joshua Rosner. *Reckless Endangerment: How Outsized Ambition, Greed, and Corruption Led to Economic Armageddon*. New York: Times Books, 2011.

Morris, Charles. *The Trillion Dollar Meltdown*. New York: Public Affairs, 2008.

Morris, Edmund. *The Rise of Theodore Roosevelt*. New York: Random House, 1979.

Morris, Roy. *Fraud of the Century: Rutherford B. Hayes, Samuel Tilden, and the Stolen Election of 1876*. New York: Simon & Schuster, 2003.

Mulford, Charles, and Eugene Comisky. *The Financial Numbers Game: Detecting Creative Accounting Practices.* New York: Wiley, 2002.

Mund, Vernon. *Government and Business.* 4th ed. New York: Harper and Row, 1965.

Myers, James, Linda Myers, and Thomas Omer. "Exploring the Term of the Auditor-Client Relationship and the Quality of Earnings: A Case for Mandatory Auditor Rotation?" *The Accounting Review* 78, no. 3 (2003): 779–99.

Office of the Special Inspector General for the Troubled Asset Relief Program. *Quarterly Report to Congress.* July 21, 2009. http://www.sigtarp.gov.

Partnoy, Frank. "Derivative Dangers." 2009. http://www.npr.com.

Partnoy, Frank. *FIASCO: Blood in the Water on Wall Street.* New York: Norton, 1997.

Partnoy, Frank. *Infectious Greed: How Deceit and Risk Corrupted the Financial Markets.* New York: Holt, 2003.

Partnoy, Frank. "A Revisionist View of Enron and the Sudden Death of 'May.'" *Villanova Law Review*, Vol. 48, No. 4, 2003, 1245–80.

Paton, William, and Arthur Littleton. *An Introduction to Corporate Accounting Standards.* New York: American Accounting Standards, 1940 (reprinted in 1974).

Patterson, Scott. "How the 'Flash Crash' Echoed Black Monday." *Wall Street Journal*, May 18, 2010, A-1.

Patterson, Scott. *The Quants: How a New Breed of Math Wizards Conquered Wall Street and Nearly Destroyed It.* New York: Crown Business, 2010.

Paulson, Henry. *On the Brink: Insider the Race to Stop the Collapse of the Global Financial System.* New York: Business Plus, 2010.

Penman, Stephan. *Financial Statement Analysis & Security Valuations.* Boston: McGraw-Hill Irwin, 2001.

Perkins, Edwin. *American Public Finance and Financial Services, 1700–1815.* Columbus: Ohio State University Press, 1994.

Phillips, Kevin. *Bad Money: Reckless Finance, Failed Politics, and the Global Crisis of American Capitalism.* New York: Penguin Group, 2008.

Previts, Gary, and Barbara Merino. *A History of Accountancy in the United States.* Columbus: Ohio State University Press, 1998.

Pujo Committee Report. *Money Trust Investigation: Investigation of Financial and Monetary Conditions in the United States Under House Resolutions Nos. 429 and 504.* 1913. http://fraser.stlouisfed.org.

Rayner, Richard. *The Associates: Four Capitalists Who Created California.* New York: Norton, 2008.

Reinhart, Carmen, and Kenneth Rogoff. *This Time Is Different: Eight Centuries of Financial Folly.* Princeton, NJ: Princeton University Press, 2009.

Renehan, Edward. *Dark Genius of Wall Street: The Misunderstood Life of Jay Gould, King of the Robber Barons*. New York: Basic Books, 2005.

Report of the Committee on Banking and Currency. June 6, 1934. http://www.sechorical.org.

Revsine, Lawrence, Daniel Collins, and W. Johnson. *Financial Reporting & Analysis*. 2nd ed. Upper Saddle River, NJ: Prentice Hall, 2002.

Robertson, Ross. *History of the American Economy*. 3rd ed. New York: Harcourt Brace Jovanovich, 1973.

Robinson, Eugene. *Disintegration: The Splintering of Black America*. New York: Doubleday, 2010.

Roubini, Nouriel, and Stephen Mihm. *Crisis Economics: A Crash Course in the Future of Finance*. New York: Penguin Press, 2010.

"Sachems & Sinners: An Informal History of Tammany Hall." *Time*, August 22, 1955. http://www.time.com.

Sandel, Michael. *Justice: What's The Right Thing to Do?* New York: Farrar, Straus and Giroux, 2009.

SCANDAL!: Amazing Tales of Scandals That Shocked the World and Shaped Modern Business. New York: Time Inc. Home Entertainment, 2009.

Schilit, Howard. *Financial Shenanigans: How to Detect Accounting Gimmicks & Fraud in Financial Reports*. 2nd ed. New York: McGraw-Hill, 2002.

Schipper, Katherine. "Commentary: Earnings Management." *Accounting Horizons*, December 1989, 91–102.

Schultz, Ellen. *Retirement Heist: How Companies Plunder and Profit from the Nest Eggs of American Workers*. New York: Portfolio/Penguin, 2011.

Schweizer, Peter. *Throw Them All Out: How Politicians and Their Friends Get Rich Off Insider Stock Tips, Land Deals, and Cronyism That Would Send the Rest of Us to Prison*. New York: Houghton Mifflin Harcourt, 2011.

Securities and Exchange Commission. *Report and Recommendations Pursuant to Section 401(c) of the Sarbanes-Oxley Act of 2002 on Arrangement with Off-Balance-Sheet Implications, Special Purpose Entities, and Transparency of Filings by Issuers*. Washington, DC: Securities and Exchange Commission, 2005.

Shiller, Robert. *Irrational Exuberance*. 2nd ed. Princeton, NJ: Princeton University Press, 2005.

Skidelsky, Robert. *Keynes: The Return of the Master—Why, Sixty Years after His Death, John Maynard Keynes Is the Most Important Economic Thinker for America*. New York: Public Affairs, 2009.

Sloan, Allan. "How to Really Fix Wall Street." *Fortune*, May 24, 2010, 54–60.

Sloan, Allan. "What's Still Wrong with Wall Street." *Time*, November 9, 2009, 24–29.

Smith, Richard. "The Great Electrical Conspiracy. In *SCANDAL!: Amazing Tales of Scandals That Shocked the World and Shaped Modern Business*, 104–19. New York: Time Inc. Home Entertainment, 2009.

Sobel, Robert. *Panic on Wall Street: A History of America's Financial Disasters*. Washington, DC: Beard Books, 1968.

Sobel, Robert. *The Pursuit of Wealth: The Incredible Story of Money throughout the Ages*. New York: McGraw-Hill, 2000.

Sorkin, Andrew. "Preparing for the Next Big One." *New York Times*, June 29, 2010. http://www.nyt.com.

Sorkin, Andrew. *Too Big to Fail: The Inside Story of How Wall Street and Washington Fought to Save the Financial System from Crisis—and Themselves*. New York: Viking, 2009.

Standard & Poor's. *S&P/Case-Shiller Home Price Indices*. n.d. http://www.standardandpoors.com.

Stewart, James. *Den of Thieves*. New York: Simon & Schuster, 1992.

Stiglitz, Joseph. *Freefall: America, Free Markets, and the Sinking of the World Economy*. New York: Norton, 2010.

Stiglitz, Joseph. *The Roaring Nineties: A History of the World's Most Prosperous Decade*. New York: Norton, 2003.

Stiles, T. J. *The First Tycoon: The Epic Life of Cornelius Vanderbilt*. New York: Vintage Books, 2009.

Surowiecki, James. *The Wisdom of Crowds*. New York: Doubleday, 2004.

Swartz, Mimi, and Sherron Watkins. *Power Failure: The Inside Story of the Collapse of Enron*. New York: Doubleday, 2003.

Taibbi, Matt. "The Great American Bubble Machine." *Rolling Stone*, July 2009. http://www.rollingstone.com.

Taleb, Nassim. *The Black Swan: The Impact of the Highly Improbable*. New York: Random House, 2007.

Toffler, Barbara. *Final Accounting: Ambition, Greed, and the Fall of Arthur Andersen*. New York: Broadway Books, 2003.

"Top Ten Investor Traps." *Yahoo! Finance*, April 9, 2010. http://finance.yahoo.com.

Treasury Department. *Blueprint for a Modernized Financial Regulatory Structure*. March 2008. http://www.treas.gov.

U.S. Census Bureau. *Statistical Abstract of the United States* (various years). http://www.census.gov.

Varchaver, Nicholas. "The Big Kozlowski." *Fortune*, November 18, 2002. Reprinted in *SCANDAL!: Amazing Tales of Scandals That Shocked the World and Shaped Modern Business*, 47–52. New York: Time Inc. Home Entertainment, 2009.

Wallis, John. "The Concept of Systemic Corruption in American History." In *Corruption and Reform: Lessons from America's Economic History.* Edited by Edward Glaeser and Claudia Goldin, 23–62. Washington, DC: National Bureau of Economic Research, 2006.

Watts, Ross, and Jerold Zimmerman. *Positive Accounting Theory.* Englewood Cliffs, NJ: Prentice-Hall, 1986.

Wessel, David. *In Fed We Trust: Ben Bernanke's War on the Great Panic.* New York: Crown Business, 2009.

Willoughby, Jack. "Burning Up." *Barron's*, March 20, 2000. Reprinted in Lewis, Michael. *Panic: The Story of Modern Financial Insanity.* New York: Norton, 2009.

Zeff, Stephen. "How the U.S. Accounting Profession Got Where It Is Today, Part I." *Accounting Horizons*, September 2003, 189–205.

Zeff, Stephen. "How the U.S. Accounting Profession Got Where It Is Today, Part II." *Accounting Horizons*, December 2003, 267–86.

Zuckerman, Gregory. *The Greatest Trade Ever: The Behind-the-Scenes Story of How John Paulson Defied Wall Street and Made Financial History.* New York: Crown Business, 2009.

Zuckoff, Mitchell. *Ponzi's Scheme: The True Story of a Financial Legend.* New York: Random House Trade Paperbacks, 2006.

Index

Boldface page numbers indicate main entries in the Encyclopedia.

Ponzi scheme, 381–82, 435, **465–67**, 506,
551, 655. *See also* Madoff, Bernard L.
Pooling of interests, 8–9, 372–73
Poor Company, 79–80
Porter, Horace, 246
Portfolio insurance (PI), **467–68**, 569–70
Portfolio magazine, 237
Posner, Victor, 283, 317, 343, 379–80
Post Office, 560
Potter, Orlando, 439
Powderly, Terrance, 16
Preferred list (on initial public offerings),
468–69, 508, 662
Prepaid revenue items, 502
President's Commission on Organized
Crime, 590
Preston, Andrew, 48
Price, Samuel, 70
Price discrimination, 109
Price-earnings (PE) ratio, 171–72,
179–80, 191
Price earnings growth (PEG) ratios, 179–80
Price fixing, **469–71**, 541
Price Waterhouse audit firm, 1, 6, 37, 38,
68–70, 300, 328, 367–69
PricewaterhouseCoopers (PwC),
208, 494, 623
Prince, Chuck, xxxvii
Principles of Economics (Marshall), 108
Principles of Economics (Menger), 43, 108
*Principles of Political Economy and
Taxation* (Ricardo), 107
Private Securities Litigation Reform Act.
See Litigation Reform Act of 1995
Privatization, 162
Procter, William, 471
Procter & Gamble derivatives losses,
471–72
Professional ethics, **472–73**
Profiteering during the American
Revolution, **473–75**
Profit maximization, 548
Prohibition, 349
Projected benefit obligation (PBO),
452–53, 454
"Prospect Theory" (Kahneman and
Tversky), 63

Proxy statement, **475–76**
PSE (Philadelphia Stock Exchange),
95–96, 414
Public Company Accounting Oversight
Board (PCAOB), 6, 35, 40, 42, 473,
476–77, 529, 530–32, 674
Public-Private Investment Program, 613
Public Securities Litigation
Reform Act, 673
Public Utility Holding Act
of 1935, 297, 537
Public Works Administration
(PWA), 260, 412, 519–20
Puck magazine, 510, 563
Pujo, Arsène, 477
Pujo hearings, xxxiii, 120, 215, 302,
386–87, 391, 394, 433, **477–78**, 512
Pulitzer, Joseph, 257
Pullman, George, 479
Pullman Strike, 330–31, 432, **479–80**
Purchase method, 8–9, 373
Pure Food and Drug Act. *See* Food and
Drug Act
Putin, Vladimir, 526
PWA (Public Works Administration), 260,
412, 519–20
PwC (PricewaterhouseCoopers),
208, 494, 623
Pyramiding. *See* Holding company
pyramiding
Pyramiding leveraged trusts, 448

Quantum Fund, 274, 313, 528, 549–50
Quartermasters, 473–74
Quay, Matthew, 564
Quest, 468–69
Qwest, 667

R&D (research and development),
217, 422, 440
Racketeer Influenced and Corrupt
Organizations Act (RICO), 295,
380, 590
Racketeering, 589
Radio Corporation of America
(RCA), 341, 507
Radio-Keith-Orpheum (RKO), 507

About the Author

Gary Giroux is Shelton Professor of Accounting at Texas A&M University. He received his PhD from Texas Tech University and has been at Texas A&M for more than 30 years, teaching financial analysis and other courses. Gary has published over 60 articles, including publications in *Accounting Review, Journal of Accounting Research, Accounting, Organizations and Society*, and *Journal of Accounting and Public Policy*. He is the author of five books, including *Earnings Magic and the Unbalance Sheet, Financial Analysis: A User Approach, Detecting Earnings Management*, and *Dollars & Scholars, Scribes & Bribes: The Story of Accounting*. His primary research areas are governmental accounting, business history and auditing.